Cloud Application Security Essentials with Azure

Azure application security, confidential computing, app identity, authentication, and authorization

Rouskov Y R

www.bpbonline.com

First Edition 2025

ISBN: 978-93-65894-691

LIMITS OF LIABILITY AND DISCLAIMER OF WARRANTY

The information contained in this book is true and correct to the best of author's and publisher's knowledge. The author has made every effort to ensure the accuracy of these publications, but the publisher cannot be held responsible for any loss or damage arising from any information in this book.

All trademarks referred to in the book are acknowledged as properties of their respective owners but BPB Publications cannot guarantee the accuracy of this information.

To View Complete
BPB Publications Catalogue
Scan the QR Code:

www.bpbonline.com

Dedicated to

My family in

Bulgaria and USA

About the Author

Rouskov Y R has completed his master's degree in computer science. He has about 30 years of experience in software development, primarily at Microsoft, where he served as **software development engineer** (**SDE**), SDE lead, and a software architect specializing in identity of all types – enterprise and consumer. One can find his name on many patents in digital identity.

About the Reviewers

- **John Mathew** is a Cybersecurity professional with 8 years of experience in the field; he specializes in penetration testing, ethical hacking, red teaming, and blue teaming. John holds a bachelor of technology in computer science and engineering and has earned notable accolades, including first place in capture the flag contests and certifications such as ISC Certified in Cybersecurity and EC-Council Certified Ethical Hacker.

  Outside of work, John is an avid reader and enjoys playing video games. He believes that "Security is a myth and Testing is inevitable," a philosophy that drives his commitment to excellence in Cybersecurity.

- **Mahmoud H. Neana** is an experienced technology professional with extensive hands-on expertise in Cybersecurity and cloud computing security. With a career built on practical, real-world experience across diverse environments, Mahmoud combines technical depth with a strong commitment to industry best practices. He holds multiple professional certifications that demonstrate his advanced knowledge and dedication to the field. He is known for his sharp attention to detail and ability to translate complex security concepts into clear, actionable insights. He remains a passionate advocate for robust cloud security standards and actively shares his expertise through professional engagements, writing, and mentorship.

- **Derek Botti** is a passionate security and infrastructure integration practitioner with extensive professional experience in the domains of systems integration, cloud native architectures, and hybrid cloud security. He is a holder of ITIL and TOGAF Certifications as a master architect.

  Derek specializes in Cybersecurity and loves working with customers on helping them in getting the most from migrating workloads to the cloud.

  He is currently working in security operations and engineering and part of research and development in his current role.

Acknowledgement

There are a few people I want to thank for the continued and ongoing support they have given me during the writing of this book. First and foremost, I would like to thank my wife and my mother for continuously encouraging me for writing the book. I could have never completed this book without their support.

I am grateful to Microsoft, where I spent time and effort working on identity components used in Microsoft software running on all types of devices and operating systems.

And, of course, special thanks must go to all end users. I have learned a lot from them based on the feedback, both formal and informal, provided to me.

My gratitude also goes to the team at BPB Publications for being supportive enough to provide me with enough time to finish the book. Digital security is a vast and very active area of research. It was hard, if not impossible, to explore different classes of problems in a single book, especially by not making it too voluminous.

Preface

This book addresses application security – an area of growing importance in today's digital reality.

Our understanding of security incorporates that of the general public. There are few things authors would like to point out. Details aside, it is asserted that; there is no absolute security. Anything can be broken given sufficient incentive. The cost to break a system has to be justified by the prize if successful. At the same time, the penalty on failure has to be acceptable, and security is grounded on economic principles.

It is desirable that there is no well-known and easy to execute method that leads to a compromise.

Emergence of clouds and blockchains adds some context as most applications run in one of these environments.

This book is divided into 9 chapters. Covered are security basics as well as most common techniques to strengthen application security posture in the cloud and blockchains.

Chapter 1: Introduction to Application and Cloud Security – Typical application architectures are examined. Application pieces run on consumer machines as well as clouds and blockchains.

Chapter 2: Different Clouds and Confidential Compute Promise – There are many clouds owned by different companies. An applications want to exist in more than one cloud for resiliency reasons. Then, there needs to be a platform with common security characteristics that is available in all clouds.

Chapter 3: Public and Private Clouds – A definition about what can be called private and public is provided. Historically, private entities have been associated with enhanced security. Reasons for this are described and examined in detail. And while it is understandable why private entities are required by customers, it is less clear how being private strengthens the security posture.

Chapter 4: Application Identities – This should be an interesting topic. Basically, the author presents techniques used by application vendors, clouds and devices to help consumers distinguish application X from applications pretending to be X.

Chapter 5: Compute, Storage and Networking in the Cloud - The compute infrastructure available in the cloud or elsewhere consists of these elements. From security point of view, these are valuable resources that need protection.

Chapter 6: Authentication and Authorization– The main concept is that access to resources needs to be authorized. Authentication is about establishing an identity used to perform authorization.

Chapter 7: Encryption- Explains how encryption is used to protect data in rest and in transit. There are some differences between the two which are considered important. The concept of two factor authorization is brought in.

Chapter 8: Economic Models – The gist is that there are many economic models in existence and security is fundamental to all.

Chapter 9: Summary - The main ideas presented in each chapter are summarized.

Code Bundle and Coloured Images

Please follow the link to download the
Code Bundle and the ***Coloured Images*** of the book:

https://rebrand.ly/v9tivln

The code bundle for the book is also hosted on GitHub at **https://github.com/bpbpublications/Cloud-Application-Security-Essentials-with-Azure**. In case there's an update to the code, it will be updated on the existing GitHub repository.

We have code bundles from our rich catalogue of books and videos available at https://github.com/bpbpublications. Check them out!

Errata

We take immense pride in our work at BPB Publications and follow best practices to ensure the accuracy of our content to provide with an indulging reading experience to our subscribers. Our readers are our mirrors, and we use their inputs to reflect and improve upon human errors, if any, that may have occurred during the publishing processes involved. To let us maintain the quality and help us reach out to any readers who might be having difficulties due to any unforeseen errors, please write to us at :

errata@bpbonline.com

Your support, suggestions and feedbacks are highly appreciated by the BPB Publications' Family.

Piracy

If you come across any illegal copies of our works in any form on the internet, we would be grateful if you would provide us with the location address or website name. Please contact us at business@bpbonline.com with a link to the material.

If you are interested in becoming an author

If there is a topic that you have expertise in, and you are interested in either writing or contributing to a book, please visit www.bpbonline.com. We have worked with thousands of developers and tech professionals, just like you, to help them share their insights with the global tech community. You can make a general application, apply for a specific hot topic that we are recruiting an author for, or submit your own idea.

Reviews

Please leave a review. Once you have read and used this book, why not leave a review on the site that you purchased it from? Potential readers can then see and use your unbiased opinion to make purchase decisions. We at BPB can understand what you think about our products, and our authors can see your feedback on their book. Thank you!

For more information about BPB, please visit www.bpbonline.com.

Join our Discord space

Join our Discord workspace for latest updates, offers, tech happenings around the world, new releases, and sessions with the authors:

https://discord.bpbonline.com

Table of Contents

1. Introduction to Application and Cloud Security 1
Introduction 1
Structure 2
Objectives 2
Security metrics 2
Application security 3
Code injection 3
Authorization logic bugs 3
App security summary 4
Modern app architecture 4
Cloud security 6
Cloud app administrator identity 6
App deployment identity 6
Cloud admin identity 6
Blockchain approach 8
Blockchain's approach to preventing app compromises 8
Economy of security 9
Cloud security conclusions 9
Security vs. availability ANDs and ORs 10
Azure 12
Future appears serverless 13
Azure Security Services 13
Conclusions 16
Exercises 17

2. Different Clouds and Confidential Compute Promise 19
Introduction 19
Structure 20
Objectives 20
Cloud admin compromise should not be fatal 20
Promise of confidential computing 21
Bootstrapping Enclave proofs 23

Clean room setup 24

Identity provider for users, apps, and Enclaves 25

Compute and storage 26

Compute and storage architecture security considerations 28

Blockchain architectures 29

Features of Azure 29

Types of Enclaves 30

Different philosophies 31

Achieving public blockchain confidentiality 33

Homomorphic encryption 33

Tumblers 34

Other techniques 34

Blockchain architecture summary 35

Conclusion 35

Points to remember 35

Exercises 36

References 36

3. Public and Private Clouds 37

Introduction 37

Structure 37

Objectives 38

Understanding public and private clouds 38

Definition and semantics of public cloud 38

Definition and semantics of private clouds 40

Security benefits of private cloud 43

Private cloud availability gains 43

Hybrid clouds 46

Multi-cloud setup 46

Multi-cloud deployment considerations 48

Multi-tenancy 51

Noisy neighbor 53

Blockchain principles 53

Public and private parts for Azure 54

Virtual private clouds and virtual networks 56

Protecting guests 57

Guest valuables to protect 57
Azure VMWare solution 61
Defense in depth 62
Canonical cloud architecture 62
Request anatomy 64
Cloud security features 69
Conclusion 70
Exercises 72

4. Application Identities 73
Introduction 73
Structure 74
Objectives 74
Application structure 75
Applications on devices 75
Applications in the cloud 76
Rules of thumb 80
Protocols and libraries 82
Names 84
Non-unique identifiers 85
Non-immutable identifiers 85
Cloud and device applications 87
Public and confidential applications 87
Role of certificates 88
Transport Level Security 92
Code signing 93
OAuth2 and OpenID Connect 94
Role of OpenID Connect 95
ID tokens 95
Access tokens in OAuth2 95
Applications on a blockchain dApps 96
Blockchain applications 96
dApp identity 98
Client dApp identity 98
Service dApp identity 98
Azure applications 100

Application tenancy ... *101*
First party applications ... *102*
Data partitioning patterns ... 102
Partitioning on users ... *103*
Partitioning on applications ... *103*
Partitioning within organization ... *104*
Implementing identity flows ... 104
Putting it together in code ... 107
Conclusion ... 108
Exercises ... 109

5. Compute, Storage and Networking in the Cloud ... 111
Introduction ... 111
Structure ... 112
Objectives ... 113
Greenfield and brownfield ... 113
Types of infrastructure ... 113
Security angle ... 114
Compute ... 114
Stateless compute ... *116*
Storage ... 116
Networking ... 117
Historical perspective ... 119
Blockchain architecture ... 120
Cell architectures ... 122
Serverless cloud architectures ... 124
Assets to protect within compute and storage ... 125
Compute assets to protect ... *125*
Storage assets to protect ... *126*
Azure ... 127
Azure compute ... *127*
Azure storage ... *128*
Azure storage and database security ... *130*
Azure networking services ... *132*
XYZ as a service ... *133*
Other Azure services ... *135*

Queues and asynchronous processing ... 136
Kubernetes concepts ... 138
Scaling architectures ... 139
Kubernetes Event-Driven Autoscaler ... *139*
Edge Computing ... *139*
Conclusion ... 140
Exercises ... 141

6. Authentication and Authorization ... 143
Introduction ... 143
Structure ... 144
Objectives ... 144
Concepts that support the authorization process ... 144
Tickets, tokens, assertions, and other artifacts ... *146*
Bearer ticket presentation ... *146*
Proof-of-possession ticket presentation ... *147*
Non-repudiation ... *148*
Authentication mechanics ... 150
Multi factor authentication ... *150*
MFA goals ... *150*
Knowledge ... *151*
Possession ... *152*
Bio ... *153*
Phish-resistant authentication ... *154*
Symmetrical and asymmetrical models ... *157*
Authorization process ... 158
Delegation and impersonation ... *161*
Blockchains implementations ... 162
Authentication in blockchains ... *165*
Authorization in blockchains ... *166*
Keys in blockchains ... *167*
Cloud offerings with Azure ... 168
Azure authentication ... *168*
Azure authorization ... *170*
Conclusion ... 173
Exercises ... 173

7. Encryption 175
Introduction 175
Structure 176
Objectives 177
Data encryption and decryption concepts 177
Encrypting data at rest 178
Managing keys *181*
On the Question of Trust *184*
Encryption options 185
Encryption granularity and re-encryption *186*
Encryption partitioning *186*
Re-encryption *188*
Encrypting data in transit 188
Transports featuring TLS *190*
Integrity and confidentiality of data 191
Few practical considerations *193*
Encryption in transit practical considerations *193*
Encryption at rest considerations *195*
Blockchains and encryption 197
Azure storage encryption 198
Encryption location *199*
Granularity *199*
Key management 199
Common pattern for data access 202
Conclusion 203
Exercises 206

8. Economic Models 207
Introduction 207
Structure 208
Objectives 208
Investing in security 208
Zero trust compliance initiative 209
Economic models 210
Economic anatomy of an attack *210*
Devices and hardware model 211

Device security 211
Software model 213
Security context implementation guide 215
Software security 217
Advertising model 221
Advertising security 222
Cloud 223
Cloud security 225
Blockchains 225
Security angle 226
Other models 229
Security considerations 231
Business models evolution 231
Azure Cloud example 233
Blockchain design 234
Conclusion 236
Exercises 237

9. Summary 239
Introduction 239
Structure 239
Objectives 240
Chapter 1: Introduction to Application and Cloud Security 240
Chapter 2: Different Clouds and Confidential Compute Promise 243
Chapter 3: Public and Private Clouds 244
Chapter 4: Application Identities 245
Chapter 5: Compute, Storage and Networking in the Cloud 248
Chapter 6: Authentication and Authorization 251
Chapter 7: Encryption 254
Chapter 8: Economic Models 255
Conclusion 256

Index 259-264

Chapter 1
Introduction to Application and Cloud Security

Introduction

To start, we will pose and try to answer the key question: *The chapter provides a definition for the term security.* The term is being used a lot and without a proper definition, semantics is left to the reader's imagination.

To quote a popular saying: *You cannot manage what you cannot measure*

While most of us have an intuitive notion of **security** meaning, a more formal definition would be useful to enable managing it. Asking stakeholders would result in some confusing answers. Sure, highly publicized security issues are bad for business. Also, consider that a security issue, publicized or not, is bad on its own. There are many examples. Every day, we hear that user data held by a well-known company is exposed. The ones we do not hear about could be worse. Most stakeholders care, and rightfully so, about maintaining good standing with customers, so having a **good security posture** pays off. Let us try to define the meaning of **good security posture**. To be able to claim having a good security posture, it is helpful to introduce metrics to support these claims.

One way to do it is as follows: **security** can be described by a set of assertions (some call them security invariants) of the type:

It should (not) be true that … <insert assertion that must hold true/.

For example:

It should be true that every service the app provides authorizes the requestor.

It is important to note that while the assertions improve the security posture, they do not **guarantee** absolute security. Assertions address a specific threat vector that is known to be exploited by attackers, for example, using unauthorized requests to gain access to valuable information. However, knowing all threat vectors is not possible. Consider that having the assertions enables us to measure security posture. Even though all threat vectors may not be possible, addressing the known ones is very valuable.

Structure

In this chapter, we will go through the following topics:

- Security metrics
- Application security
- Application security summary
- Azure

Objectives

This chapter is about framing the notion of security. It introduces the concepts of application security, cloud application hosting, and cloud security. An important goal is to enable application owners to refer to the security of the application and the hosting/ cloud environment using some concrete terms, versus the generic statement that **my app is secure**.

This requires having security metrics to describe security posture. The concrete statement would be that *my app measures to a security level of 9 according to some criteria*. The criteria could be derived from the security metrics section above, or customers may have their own criteria, like meeting certain certification requirements.

Security metrics

It would be great if app owners could express the security posture of the app with some simple metric, for example, one should be able to say *My app is rated at a nine security level*.

There is no widely accepted metric to suggest one, and security can be measured relative to the breach probability for some fixed time, say the next year. To formalize, we can write:

```
SecLevel = (1-BreachProbabilityInNext1yr)*10
```

To substitute some values, a SecLevel of nine would mean a 10% chance of a breach in the next year.

Given that breach probability would be hard to estimate, the total SecLevel can also be defined as a sum of SecLevels contributed by individual assertions. The rationale is that each assertion reduces the compromise probability along some known attack vector. As previously mentioned, absolute security cannot be guaranteed as all attack vectors cannot be known. That is why the computed SecLevel can never reach the max value, which would imply zero compromise probability. Another assumption is that each assertion contribution is independent of contributions made by other assertions. Formula in the following:

```
SecLevel = max(9.5, sum(1..n, seclevel(assertion_i))
```

A few words about the various certifications offered, take FedRamp as an example. Each certification consists of an assertion set where assertions and compliance criteria are defined by the certifying authority. To be able to compare certifications or estimate how valuable a certification is, a mapping function to a security level would be useful. Then, it can be inferred how a certification reduces the compromise probability.

Application security

This section defines the meaning behind application security. To start with, it should be noted that if the application has vulnerabilities, these will be carried over, no matter where the application runs. Or, to put it another way, the application platform, cloud, or other, will not mitigate existing application vulnerabilities. For example, let us consider an email app that gives any customer's mail to whoever requests it using some **magic** request parameters. This would be considered by most to be a vulnerability. It would persist no matter where the application runs.

Typical app vulnerabilities are described in the following sections.

Code injection

This is probably the most discussed issue. Buffer overruns, SQL injection, etc., fall into this category. Basically, any issue where the attacker supplied code/instructions as part of some well-crafted request executes in the deployed app context.

Giving requestors such power presents security problems.

Authorization logic bugs

One of the hard problems is defining the semantics behind **proper authorization**. This would be a subjective call. What is **proper** for some may not be so for others. One way to approach the issue is to require that all authorization rules are visible and are expressed in some language that clearly conveys the semantics behind them. In the example, there should be a rule stating that anyone can see any customer's mail. Then, it would be up to the app owners/stakeholders to determine if this is acceptable. Again, the requirement is that authorization rules are visible and reviewable. To put that down as a security assertion, we can write:

Authorization rules for accessing any app resource should be clear and regularly reviewed.

App security summary

Neither of the above issues, app-enabled code injection and authorization bugs, is mitigated by the cloud hosting environment or cloud provider. These terms would be used interchangeably going forward.

Let us point out that the cloud provider may introduce security issues independent of those in the hosted apps. These issues will be the focus of the book. Readers should not expect directions on app security, but rather directions on utilizing security controls from the cloud provider that help mitigate issues rooted in the hosting environment.

The apps need compute, storage, and networking. These are given by the cloud provider. If compute or storage is under attacker control, apps using those resources would be compromised. Compute and storage will be discussed later in the book. What should be important is that networking should not be playing a role in the security posture, see **zero trust network access (ZTNA)**. Networking is super important; that said, apps should not rely on it for security. For example, a request coming from a given network cannot be assumed to be made by a **trusted** client.

Modern app architecture

Modern apps have a service component. To illustrate, the most common app architecture looks like the following figure:

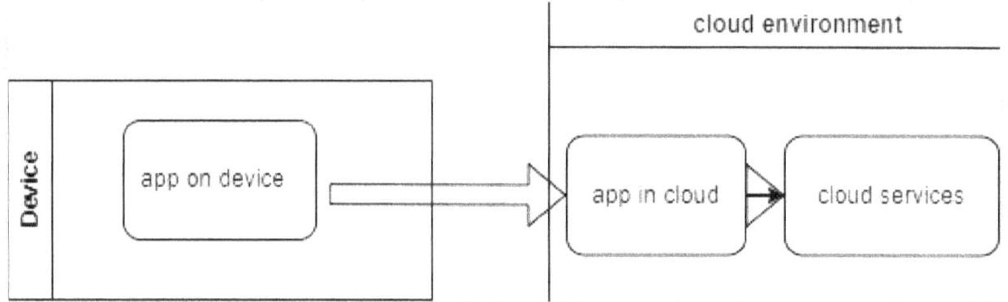

Figure 1.1: *Modern app architecture*

The architecture is that the app on the device talks to the cloud app, which can talk to various cloud services to deliver needed functionality.

An alternative, simpler but more limited, architecture is to have the app compute fully on the device and utilize storage and other services from the cloud provider. There is no cloud service in the following figure. The app on the device talks directly to a cloud service instead of a cloud app API.

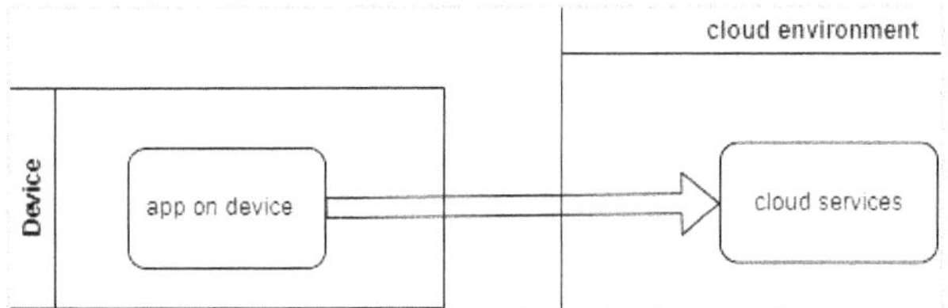

Figure 1.2: Architecture without having cloud app

Next, a few points are presented to contrast the two architectures, with and without the app cloud service.

It is asserted that having a cloud app service provides needed flexibility by decoupling the on-device app logic from the specific cloud implementation.

App on device talking to app service (as shown in *Figure 1.1)* allows for:

- Run the app service anywhere, unlocking multi-cloud as the app on the device is now independent of any cloud services.
- Allows for moving computation to the app service and, thus, simplifying the app on the device as it only needs to call the app service APIs and visualize results.

The following are the drawbacks:

- If the cloud service is not available, the app on the device can stop functioning. The reasons could be as simple as an interrupted network connection. Similar considerations exist for the simpler architecture, and cloud services may not be available for network or other reasons. It is addressed by adding a local cache on the device. If the cloud service is not available, cached results are returned.
- In general, cloud/network access is needed for the app to function properly. The caching techniques can mask short outages. It is generally not possible to completely mirror cloud service functionality in the local cache.
- Such considerations always come into view when the cloud is part of the solution.

To address the availability concern, the app service needs to have a local **cache** implementation that is always available. There are existing techniques to implement, and since this is not security-related, we will not go into more detail. It should be sufficient to state that the app cloud service can be modeled by a set of cloud-hosted APIs: API1..APIn.

Refer to the following figure:

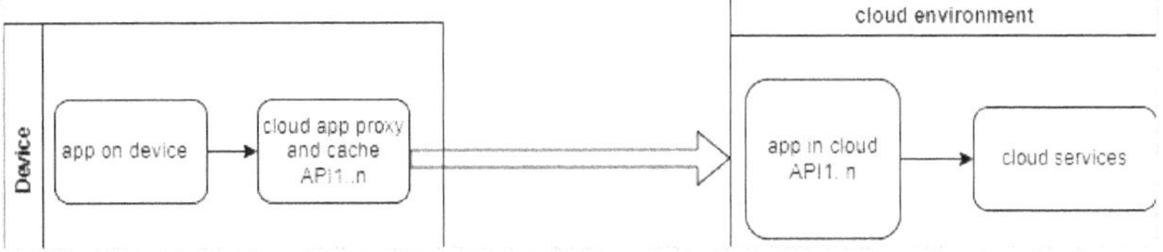

Figure 1.3: Architecture showing cloud app and local cache

The above figure is an enhanced version of *Figure 1.1*. It introduces cache and decomposes the cloud app into a set of APIs. This way, security can be expressed with requirements to call the cloud API, and these boil down to authentication and authorization concepts discussed later.

Cloud security

To start with, define the personas with respective identities involved in running the app on some cloud. It should be assumed that all identities are issued by the **identity provider (IdP)** selected by the cloud provider. More details on this will be provided in later chapters.

Cloud app administrator identity

This is the identity used to allocate cloud resources to the app. A typical model used by cloud providers is the notion of **subscription** as a grouping concept of the resources.

For example, a compute resource can be a VM or a Kubernetes cluster. The subscription owner can request that these clusters be available to run the app. There can be a storage resource used by the app deployed on the compute clusters.

App deployment identity

This is the identity authorized by the cloud app administrator to push code/executables to the cloud compute resources that are part of the subscription.

The identity logically belongs to the app owner, and the rights to deploy can be delegated to some identity available to the cloud provider. The alternative to delegation would be to provide credentials to the cloud provider, enabling app deployment identity impersonation.

Cloud admin identity

This is an identity owned by the cloud provider organization. It is authorized to access the various resources (servers in the cloud), though it is not related to any specific app.

Security assertion:

Compromising one identity should not lead to app compromise.

This may be easier said than done, but it is still worth aiming for such an outcome. Note the main idea behind this, which is to **assume compromise** and then arrive at some acceptable state security-wise. That said, the Cloud app administrator is still very sensitive since it defines what would be the identity used for app deployment, so a compromised app admin can change the app deployment ID to something they have control over. To counteract this possibility, additional controls would be needed, like having another identity-approved app deployment do the changes. Let us explore the question: Why is it important to separate deployment from admin identities?

To uphold the stated security assertion, we want it to be true that a compromised app admin identity cannot deploy code and that a compromised deployment identity can only deploy code that meets requirements set by the admin- signed code with a specific key or code hashed to a specific value, whatever is supported by the cloud provider deployment process.

Refer to the following link to see how to grant permissions in Azure: **https://learn.microsoft.com/en-us/azure/role-based-access-control/role-assignments-steps**

It is important to note that Azure uses identities issued by Entra ID IdP (former **Azure Active Directory AAD**). Since Entra issued IDs can represent users, workloads, or devices, any type of identity can be assigned any role.

The so-called **privileged** roles, which include the ability to deploy code, can trigger notifications on new assignments **https://learn.microsoft.com/en-us/azure/role-based-access-control/role-assignments-alert**.

However, what seems to be missing is the ability of the subscription owner to specify that only certain binaries can be deployed on the compute resources.

While some attempts have been made to require code signing (see **https://support.microsoft.com/en-us/topic/kb5022661-windows-support-for-the-azure-code-signing-program-4b505a31-fa1e-4ea6-85dd-6630229e8ef4**), it is about having Windows validate Azure signatures, but this work seems to be paused. It should be noted that these efforts lean on Windows server OS, while most services run on Linux OS. There needs to be some OS native support leveraged by the cloud provider. To rephrase, there needs to be a way to tell the OS to only allow the execution of binaries signed by the given authority key. The common mobile OSs, Android and iOS, have this configured by default; only apps signed by respective app store keys are allowed to execute.

The desired state is that the compute nodes part of the **secure subscription** would only execute code with pre-defined properties, which are most often signatures using some configured key or key chaining to a trusted authority (a key).

The following figure is an illustration:

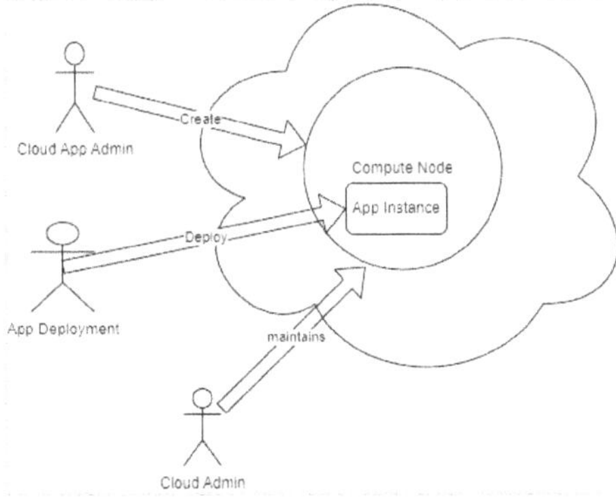

Figure 1.4: *The different personas*

This is a difficult task as the **code signature** needs to be verified by the execution environment, and these environments vary greatly depending on the language and its compile/interpret property. There are native binaries loaded by the OS, bytecode executed by some virtual machine, or script code that is interpreted. All these layers should be capable of checking signatures, which is a tall order. Blockchain job is a bit easier as dApps come in a single format and are executed by a single VM (e.g., EVM).

See the reddit Linux discussion on the subject for interesting insights - **https://www.reddit.com/r/linuxquestions/comments/8l8daj/why_doesnt_the_linux_kernel_naively_support/**

It should be stated that having partial support (no scripts) for signed binaries should be possible. Support for selected scripts can be added to respective interpreters. There is no doubt that major cloud providers will add such support to the compute resources they offer to customers, which would enable the desired behavior.

The issue of mitigating the potential compromise of the cloud admin will be discussed in subsequent chapters. There, we will go over confidential computing concepts, exploring how to mitigate cloud admin compromise. The main idea is that the cloud admin could access cloud resources, but not act as the identity that owns the subscription to which these resources belong.

Most of the confidential computing efforts are dedicated to solving the problem of protecting the customer workloads against cloud admin/cloud infra compromises.

Blockchain approach

We will look at the ETH chain, though the principles should apply to any chain implementation. To start with, the personas involved in blockchain is fewer. There is no **cloud admin** as each compute node has a separate owner (in general). The basic premise is that each node does not need to be secure, but N/2 nodes do. Compare this to a cloud environment where nodes are the same, and a cloud admin breach can affect multiple customers.

More details on this subject will be provided in later chapters. Here, it should be sufficient to note that a **cloud admin** is not present in blockchain architectures, along with related security concerns.

Blockchain's approach to preventing app compromises

Note that the app deployment persona does not exist. In the dApp ETH model, the app is represented by a fingerprint (hash). As a side effect, the app cannot change, which has security benefits, but also practical limitations, as all apps need to be updated eventually. By using the hash, we also do not need a signing certificate issued by a trusted CA.

The following figure is a blockchain model illustration:

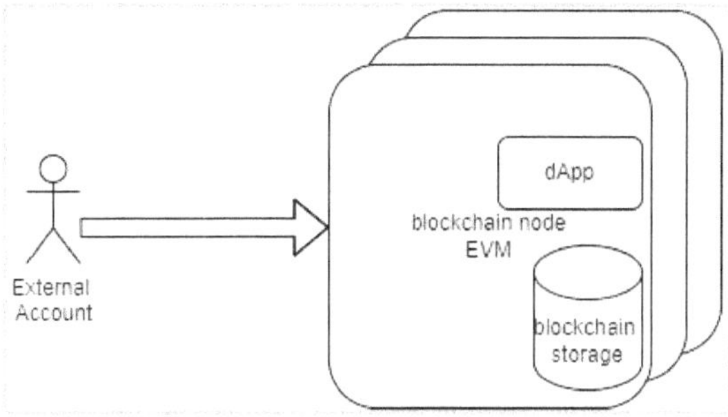

Figure 1.5: *dApp in blockchain network*

Economy of security

There is a whole chapter dedicated to the subject. Here, it should be sufficient to state the main idea, which is that the cost of executing a breach should not exceed the expected benefits for the attackers to make it worthwhile.

To express this, we can write:

```
BreachValue = BenefitsFromBreach/BreachCost
```

Resource owners could influence both values on the right, though benefits estimation is difficult, as some benefits may not be obvious. The cost is much more malleable; we want to make it as high as possible. Using 2FA, having distinct roles and identities for different operations is part of this effort. The attacker needs to breach multiple identities, and breaching each should be made as hard as possible.

Cloud security conclusions

The most important question most stakeholders have in their minds is about the security of the cloud environments:

We will try to provide some guidelines that would help answer the question.

A suggested approach would be to consider the amount of investments in the area. Arguably, the more one invests, the higher the returns will be. Big companies, what some call **hyperscalers,** lean on size to invest heavily in areas customers are sensitive to, security being a major one.

It is common to consider the cost per server. Owning/monetizing many servers, like hyperscalers do, allows for keeping the cost per server low, while the overall investment may be significant.

As a result, companies that offer many servers can afford big investments at relatively low per-server cost. To illustrate, Microsoft, Amazon, Google, etc., can afford to invest heavily in security without hurting their bottom line in a significant way.

To address the original concern about cloud security, cloud architectures strive to reduce the blast radius caused by potential cloud admin compromise.

While absolute security is hard to measure, using the investment amount heuristic, then the companies offering cloud services are investing the most, so if one is to make a choice, going to the cloud should be a no-brainer, right?

The cloud is organized so it can run existing apps that used to run on-premise, meaning servers owned by app owners.

The term **cloud native** refers to apps that are written with the cloud environment in mind and will not be run on-premises. While that is a great story, these apps could be run on-premises.

If not the cloud, then another option would be to embrace the s blockchain environments where apps are written as **smart contracts,** also known as dApps. One can try to guess when dApps will take over **regular** apps running in the cloud or on-prem. There will be many examples in the book showcasing the advantages and disadvantages of dApps from a security point of view.

Security vs. availability ANDs and ORs

Though it may not be immediately obvious, there is a tradeoff between security and availability. To use an example to illustrate, consider two nodes, Node1 and Node2, running the app (in the general model, there are N nodes). A request can be executed with the same results on either one. If one of the nodes is down for some reason, the end-to-end system is still functional as the other one picks up all the load. This provides needed availability, but it can be argued that security is lowered. An attacker could compromise Node1 OR Node2, whichever is easier, so it seems like the overall security posture is weakened by having multiple nodes. However, if the effort to compromise Node1 is the same as that for Node2, the security posture is not changed, as either node can be compromised with the same effort.

This raises the question: if Node1 and Node2 are the same from a security point of view, why are they different for availability? The answer, while it may be obvious, is still worth stating:

- Capacity increases with identical nodes. Say, we need our app to handle X requests/second, and each node can handle X/m. With n>m nodes, assuming even request>node distribution, the n nodes can handle the needed capacity load.
- Resilience to individual node failures for reasons other than software bugs, as these software bugs would be present on all nodes. We are assuming failures of individual nodes where all nodes are identical, so the only reason a node can fail while others do not should be a hardware issue specific to the node or its environment.

Since it is not always possible to have identical nodes, from a security point of view, stakeholders need to make the call on the relative value of increased capacity/resilience vs widening the security exposure. For example, adding a new datacenter provides extra compute and storage capacity and adds to the security exposure, as different datacenters have different security characteristics (the most common example is having different security guards). Even if the new datacenter is **more secure** than existing ones, it is still different and, hence, increases the compromise probability.

We need to define the rule(s) to follow so that adding capacity is considered in the context of security exposure. As well as identifying the party responsible for making the call. There is hardly a universal rule that can be followed to do this. A sensible approach to tackling this issue would be to estimate downtime probabilities with and without the extra capacity and attach dollar costs to each so there is something to compare. Say 1% probability of downtime to 100k$, 1% probability of having a security issue to 200k$.

Back to the party, making the calls. This should be the app admin persona based on business requirements set by app owners. The cloud providers will provide compute and storage resources in different datacenters. The app admin can assign resources to the app.

Refer to the following figure for visualization:

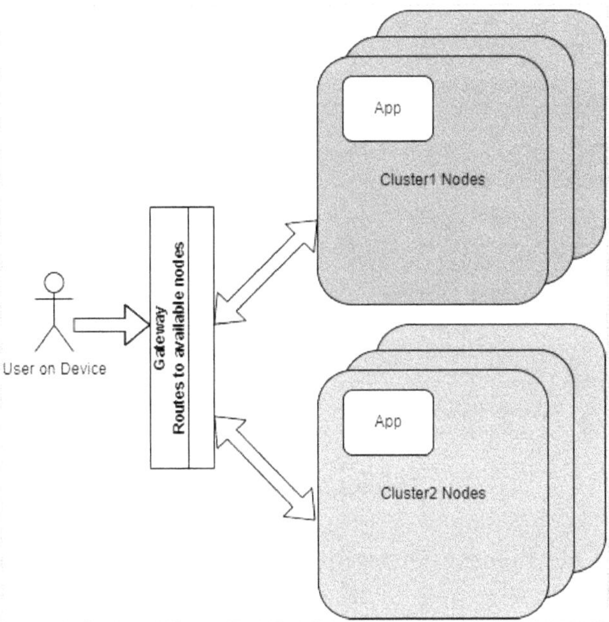

Figure 1.6: *Nodes in different clusters*

See the two clusters. Nodes within a cluster can be assumed to have the same security characteristics, but the same cannot be said for nodes in different clusters. So, while having multiple clusters could be good for capacity and availability, it does increase the security exposure, as the attacker can breach a node in either cluster to compromise the app.

Azure

This section will go over some of the processes in the Azure Cloud. A few things to note:

- To use Azure resources, one needs to have an Entra ID (formerly AAD or Microsoft ID). If the customer is already using services from Microsoft, like Office 365, they must have an Entra ID already.
- Consumer IDs (**Microsoft Account** (**MSA**)) can be used as well. An Entra directory is created automatically, and the MSA is projected there, creating a new Entra ID.
- Signup is through the Azure portal: **https://portal.azure.com**.
- Compute resources to run customer workloads. Experience when choosing a compute resource. Refer to the following figure:

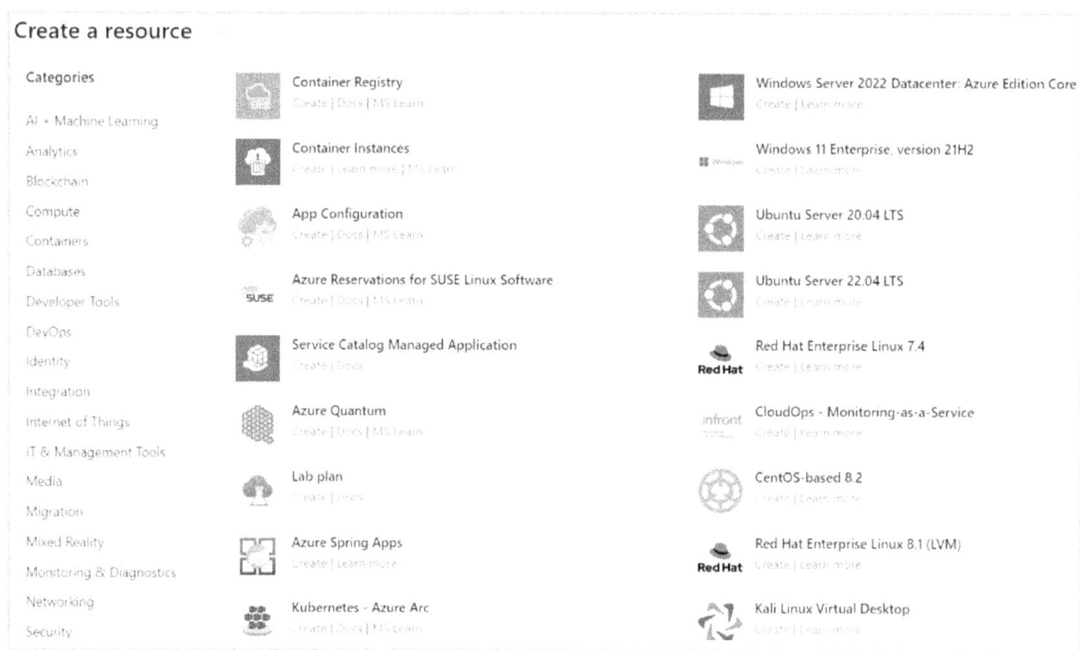

Figure 1.7: *Azure portal*

These are a handful of choices, not to mention that the list is incomplete. The choice guidelines are as follows:

If we are migrating an app to Azure, then the choice would be pre-determined. We need to match the environment expected by the app. Most often, these would be Linux VMs. Then, there is a choice to be made for new apps. Worth considering a solution that works multi-cloud, such as Kubernetes (container orchestration). Kubernetes APIs should be the same for all Kubernetes clusters.

Future appears serverless

Let us take a moment to reflect on server-full patterns. Not too long ago, apps were running on a single server. Then, someone figured out we could add more servers to increase capacity and availability. Things like **stateless** front-ends came into existence. Since the front-ends were **stateless** (this does not mean there was no data, but that the data was not per request), one could easily add more, if required. However, if this is the case, why expose individual machines at all? Enter the serverless concept. Serverless does not mean that there are no servers, but rather that these servers are not exposed to customers. Customers deal with higher-level abstractions such as an execution environment for their apps, which is provided regardless of the underlying infrastructure in the form of servers, etc. Common examples of serverless compute are **AWS Lambda** or **Azure Functions**. Serverless refers to the compute resources used to run the app code. In the **classic** model, the customer subscribes to some VMs or containers and runs their app there. These VMs (or containers) mimic the familiar app environment the app used to run in. The Customer needs to manage the compute resource type; for example, figure out how many VMs are needed to deliver the needed app performance and procure them. With serverless, customers can focus on the performance numbers, not the number and location of VMs.

Example perf characteristics: throughput measured in requests/second and latency observed by clients in various world locations. Say, clients in the East US should experience latency of less than 0.2 seconds for 99% of requests (known as p99).

Azure Security Services

Azure offers the following security services: view from the portal. Refer to the following figure:

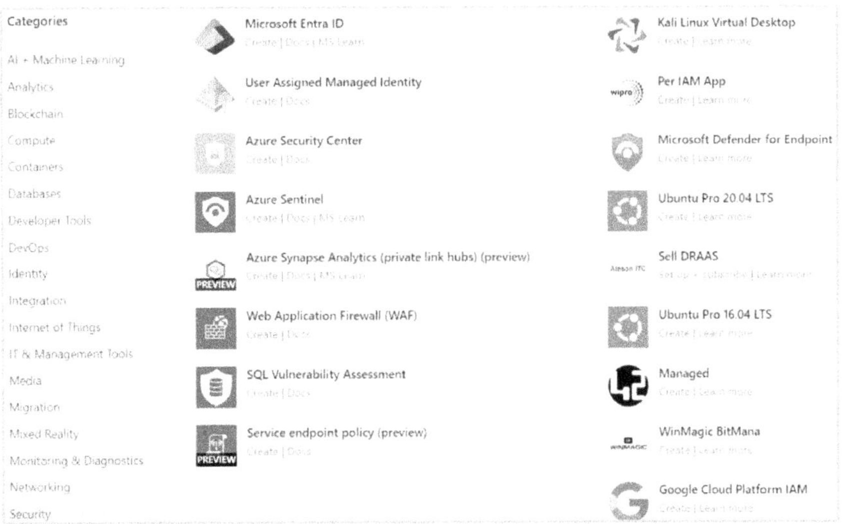

***Figure 1.8:** Selection of Azure Security Services at the Azure Portal*

It may be confusing to some that some of the services offered require that the app run in the Azure cloud, and some do not. For example, apps using Entra IDs can run anywhere, but apps using managed identities (user or system assigned) must run on an Azure compute resource that supports such assignments. To summarize, all services are available through Azure subscriptions, but some can be made available through other channels. Some services require that the consuming apps run on Azure; others do not.

In the following section, we will explain Entra IDs in detail:

- **Entra ID:** This is the IDP for Azure, as well as all Microsoft Cloud Services, including O365, etc. The tenancy model will need some more clarity. There is a requestor identity tenant and a resource app tenant. These could be the same, but not necessarily. There are cases where the requestor and resource IDs reside in different Entra tenants, and one must choose one of the options in the following:
  - o **Option 1**: Use the requestor identity tenant. The resource app is instantiated there (assuming it is a multi-tenant app). This is the default mode for Microsoft apps. The advantage is that all apps end up in the same org (requestor) tenant, which allows them to authenticate to each other easily as they exist in 1 place.
  - o **Option 2**: Use the resource app tenant. The requestor's identity is projected there (also known as the guest). This is the option used when the resource app is only available in a single tenant. Many third-party apps are architected this way. The advantage is that the requestor identity does not need to be Entra ID, as the resource app tenant could be configured to accept other IdPs. For example, the app can work with Google and Facebook IDs, in addition to Microsoft Entra.
  - o **Option 3**: Create another directory tenant, project requestor ID, and resource app in it. Azure does this when the requestor is a consumer **Microsoft Account (MSA)**.

  To illustrate these, see the following figure:

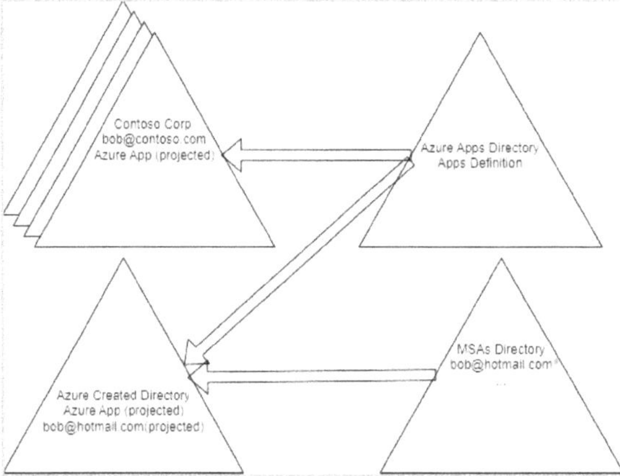

Figure 1.9: Entra IDs

Shown are options 1 and 3. For org identities (*bob@contoso.com*), the Azure app is projected into the corporate Contoso directory. If the requestor is a consumer identity, then a new directory is created, and the consumer ID (*bob@hotmail.com*) is projected there.

- **Managed identities (user-assigned):** Managed identities are a very useful Azure feature. The basic premise is that a workload/app identity can be given to an Azure resource. This creates a bit of ambiguity, and here is the reason:

  Let us define Azure compute resources as ones capable of running customer workloads. VMs, containers, functions, etc., all fit the definition of a compute resource. This is important because customer workloads can access the managed identity assigned to the compute resource they are running on, which creates the ambiguity.

  The managed identities could identify and represent the compute resource or the customer workload running on it.

  A case can be made both ways. If we are to choose, let us go with the workload. After all, workloads need to have identities, and we do not want them to have to manage secrets. A managed identity assigned to the underlying compute satisfies these requirements.

  However, what about non-compute resources that do not run customer workloads? A managed identity assigned to such a resource represents the resource itself.

  The following figure illustrates the compute scenario:

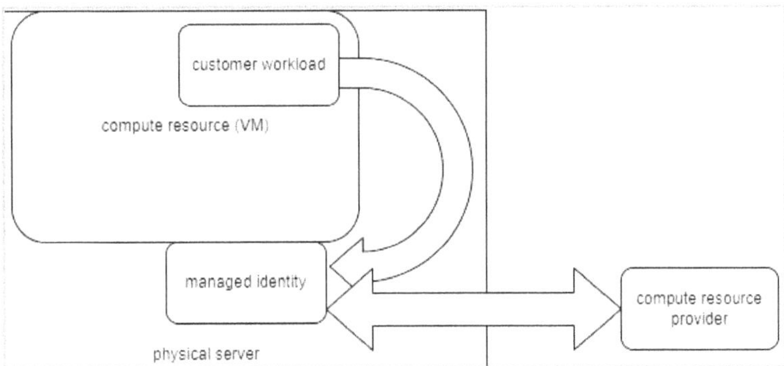

Figure 1.10: *Customer workload on Azure compute resource consumes a managed identity*

As one can see, the managed identity is on the physical server, provided by the compute provider (logically). The customer workload process runs on a virtual compute resource hosted on the physical server. It can call the managed identity interface component on the physical server. Any process on the VM can do so. Limiting this ability is possible to some extent, albeit outside the current scope. We can assume that anyone running on the VM can get managed identity services from the host.

- **Azure Security Center and Sentinel:** If put together, the functionality is close.

  It would be natural to question whether two experiences are needed to deliver the needed functionality.

  A deeper look at what is being offered allows us to make the conceptual difference between the entities analyzed by Defender (represented in Security Center) and Sentinel. The former analyzes objects like VMs and code repositories, while the latter deals with analyzing logs, which represent the activities going on. So, the object analysis gives out results pertaining to object state, like **Object X has security issue Y**.

  On the other hand, log analysis gives results describing activities, something like **activity X is flagged as a possible security breach because of Y**. Also, analyzing activities requires that logs be fed to the analytics engine.

  Note: **The difference between object state and activities. While the distinction makes logical sense, it should be possible to have a single UI for both.**

  There are other services as well, but we will stop here as the services described above are sufficiently complex.

Conclusions

In this chapter, we learned that the concept of security will benefit from having a way to measure it, so we can compare the security postures of apps and clouds.

The framework for future discussions on security features is an app model utilizing an app service running in the cloud. This would be a stepping-stone towards discussing multi-cloud architectures referenced in subsequent chapters. Most concepts have blockchain equivalents, which are presented and discussed. In security, it is common to focus on vulnerabilities and ways to mitigate them. A classification that is being offered is that security can relate to the app or the cloud app service it runs in. Device security is not discussed.

The most important concept is that there should not be a single point of failure, which in a security context is most often a single identity that attackers need to compromise in order to take over the app. In that context, we have defined various personas authorized to perform actions related to app deployment, definition, and cloud resource maintenance. The assertion is that compromising a single persona should not lead to app compromise – this is the realization of the **no single point of failure** concept.

Another important, and often controversial, topic is cloud security. The presented view is that cloud providers can invest heavily in raising the security posture of their respective clouds. While this is indeed the case, it should be noted that attackers are also heavily incentivized to breach the cloud(s). We discussed the economic models that enable the cloud providers to invest heavily in security solutions that meet customer demands. We discussed the tradeoffs between availability and security. It has been shown how methods to increase availability can lead to lowering the security standing. If a choice is to be made, the criteria need to consider perceived benefits from both increased availability and security.

An interesting topic is the concept of managed identities in Azure to distribute secrets to workloads running on Azure compute resources. There is some ambiguity related to the entity entitled to use the managed identity service. The ambiguity comes from the fact that some (compute) resources' purpose is to run customer workloads, while others do other things. The prescribed resolution is to have the managed identity belong to the workload if the resource supports running workloads.

In a similar context, serverless compute constructs have been described. The idea is that the customer focus is on the apps, not the platforms on which the apps run.

The next chapter will go into more detail about the use of confidential computing paradigms to deliver assertions about the security of compute and storage resources offered by the cloud providers. These will be compared to the blockchain philosophy about ensuring data integrity and security. Lack of confidentiality in public blockchains is also a major topic of discussion in the next chapter.

Exercises

1. Define your app architecture; identify app components.
   a. Describe the service component in terms of APIs offered to clients.
   b. Explain why authentication is needed and how it is done, and who is the IdP
   c. Call out what is being used for authorization
2. Define security assertions enforced by the app
   a. Point out what threats (aka attack vectors) are mitigated by each assertion
   b. Define the resulting SecLevel resulting from enforcing the assertions - use the provided SecLevel definition or provide your own.
3. Explain if the app needs secrets and how these are managed. Consider using managed identities or equivalent constructs.
4. Discuss what it would take to enable the app to run on a blockchain and the resulting tradeoffs.

Join our Discord space

Join our Discord workspace for latest updates, offers, tech happenings around the world, new releases, and sessions with the authors:

https://discord.bpbonline.com

CHAPTER 2

Different Clouds and Confidential Compute Promise

Introduction

This chapter is primarily about cloud providers' efforts to deliver confidential compute solutions to their customers. In the same context, blockchain architectures are also examined. There is a tradeoff between running apps on cloud compute resources and blockchain dApps. There are many similarities as well. The pros and cons of each are examined.

In *Chapter 1, Introduction to Application and Cloud Security*, it was stated that major cloud providers can invest heavily in security solutions. While this is indeed true, the flip side is that adversaries are also more incentivized to penetrate the cloud provider as the benefits multiply when considering potential access to apps and data of millions of cloud customers.

This setup is likely to result in a high-stakes arms race between cloud providers and attackers.

The developments in confidential computing, embraced by most clouds and blockchain fields, provide a major contribution to defense against cyberattacks and are a primary reason why we focus on them.

Structure

This chapter includes the following topics:

- Cloud admin compromise should not be fatal
- Bootstrapping Enclave proofs
- Compute and storage
- Features of Azure
- Types of Enclaves
- Different philosophies
- Achieving public blockchains confidentiality

Objectives

The main objective is to eliminate a malicious operator as a source of compromise. Both confidential computing and blockchain architectures are possible approaches. And, hence, both are covered in the chapter. It is highlighted that the philosophies behind these approaches are different, and these differences are explained.

This chapter focuses on confidential computing cloud products and blockchain architectures, ensuring that no single identity compromise can cause apps running in the cloud or on blockchain nodes. An attacker can compromise cloud or blockchain compute nodes, but not the applications that have been installed and running on those.

Cloud admin compromise should not be fatal

Some of the issues were discussed in *Chapter 1, Introduction to Application and Cloud Security*, specifically the case when the cloud admin compromise does not lead to the app compromise for all apps running in the cloud, where the compromise occurred.

The general principle is to eliminate single points of compromise. Specifically, the cloud admin compromise (suppose, leaked credentials) should not result in the compromise of all apps running on the cloud compute resources controlled by the admin.

Let us examine the subject in some more detail.

Cloud admins cannot impersonate apps running on compute resources under their control. The reason is the existence of *Secure Enclaves* within these resources. It is desired that this becomes true.

While the cloud admin can access the compute resource (server node), they cannot affect apps running within the Enclave(s) that exist inside the server node.

The Enclave within a server is shown in the following figure:

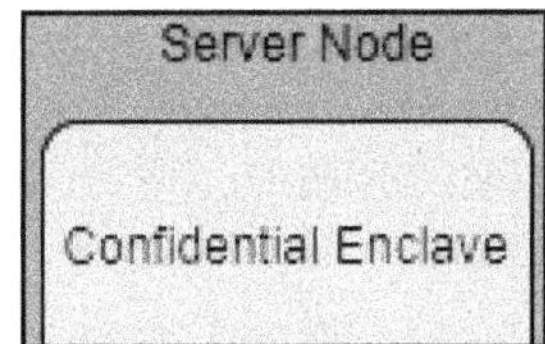

Figure 2.1: Confidential computing setup

It is implied that while the server node could be compromised and attackers can run code of their choice there, the confidential Enclave remains protected.

Let us try to reason why this is true. We want a design ensuring that physical access to a server does not translate to ownership of the apps running on the server's compute.

The explanation of design patterns unlocking this requirement is presented in the next sections.

Promise of confidential computing

Confidential computing provides real-life solutions to the problem of dealing with compromised physical security by implementing the **confidential** Enclave pattern shown in the previous section. We can start by discussing solutions for two technical problems:

- Figure out how the **Enclave** can authenticate itself to be recognized as such.
- Introduce a protocol to enable external entities to communicate with the Enclave, assuming the hosting server node is not trusted.

  The following are the solutions for the problems:

- The Enclave needs to have a key recognized as a key owned by a secure environment (Enclave). There needs to be a method to determine that the key is owned by an Enclave. Such assertion (key owned by Enclave) is provided by an attestation service in the form of a certificate attesting that the owner is an Enclave, as well as the key binding. This can be one of the cases where the level of indirection (the attestation service) is helpful in simplifying the overall architecture.

  Attestation service flow can be shown as follows:

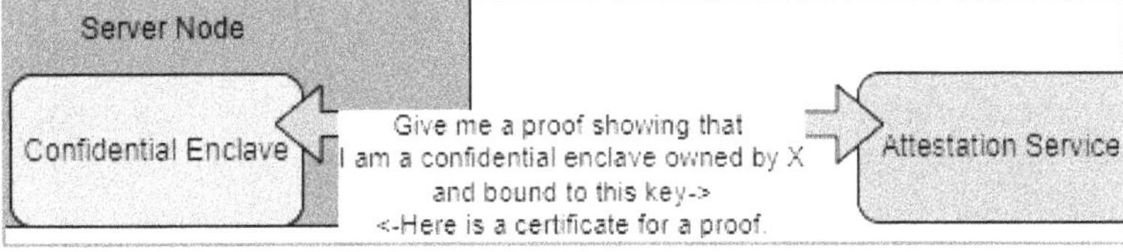

Figure 2.2: Using an attestation service to certify the Enclave

It should be noted that the exact method used to prove the requestor is, indeed, a confidential Enclave is known only to the Enclave and the attestation service.

Everybody else would trust the assertions encoded in the certificate issued by the attestation service. This indirection creates a lot of flexibility by allowing upgrades to the proof protocols that impact only the attestation service. With the certificate in hand, a well-known **Transport Level Security (TLS)** session can be established.

- The external entities could consume the assertion from the attestation service that states, roughly speaking, the *caller is in a secure Enclave owned by X*, but if it does so, the external entity needs to trust the attestation service, in addition to trusting the **identity provider** (**IdP**). It is simpler to trust one entity only, the IdP. The IdP itself can integrate with the attestation service and place the relevant claims (app running in secure Enclave) in the IdP-issued token. Then, the external entity can authorize the extra claim or have the IdP do the extra authorization using conditional access.

App on a confidential compute is shown, as follows:

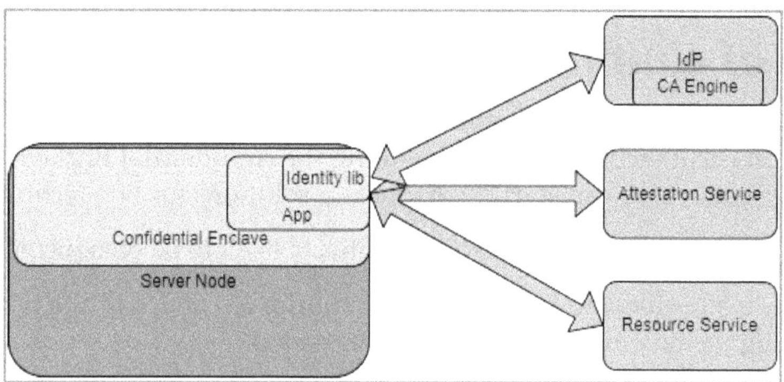

Figure 2.3: *App on a confidential compute*

There is a bit of complexity involved when the client must stitch together protocol elements coming from multiple services. Fortunately, the identity library (**Microsoft Services Authentication Library** (**MSAL**) is used by Azure) takes care of this complexity, so apps do not have to. Generally, using an identity library or component is highly preferred by app developers writing a protocol implementation. Protocols can be tricky to get right and are constantly evolving.

The *CA Engine* inside the IdP helps deliver authorization decisions of the type that *allow access only to applications running in confidential Enclaves that are owned by XYZ* (for example, Azure). This is to complement the authorization engine in the Resource Service, which likely implements authorization for end-user identities of the type *allow access to X*, where X is a user identity or a group of user identities.

There are three identities in play: that of the end user, the app, and the Enclave. More complex authorization expressions like *allow access to users X1..Xn when using apps Y1..Ym running in confidential Enclaves owned by Z*, are done by combining authorization done by the Resource Service with authorization done by the **conditional access (CA)** Engine.

It needs to be called out that authorization done by the CA Engine is **coarse-grained**, meaning that it applies to all items covered by the Resource Service. Say, access to all files under some folder needs to be authorized by the CA engine. This is not possible as the folder entity does not exist for the IdP. Only the storage service hosting all folders is visible. This is why this type of authorization is coarse-grained.

Sometimes, this is not sufficient. A common example is that there are items marked as **classified** and others that do not have the same requirements as those for the classified items. Access authorization can only be done by apps in secure Enclaves, where, for non-classified content, the app could be running anywhere.

One solution is to have multiple services, one serving classified content and one for **regular** items. Generally, there needs to be as many services as there are different CA policies. If we assume a distinct CA policy per item class, then the number of services should be equal to the number of classes. For example, if there are **classified1**, **classified2**, **and classified3**, then we need three services, one for each classified class. This would allow for three CA policies to be applied, one for each service.

Multiple services for multiple item classes, as shown in the following figure:

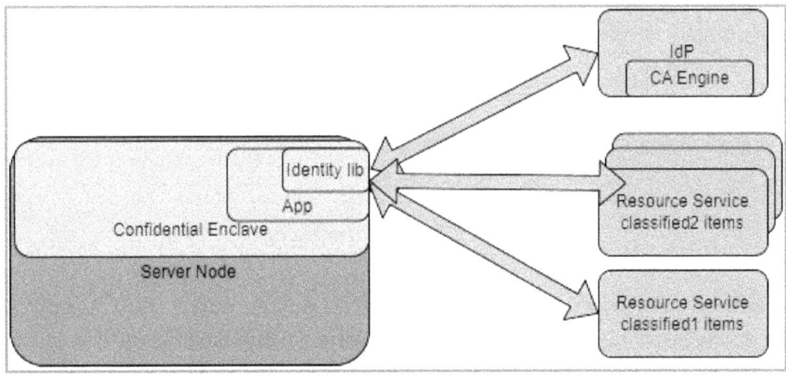

***Figure 2.4:** Multiple services for multiple item classes*

Bootstrapping Enclave proofs

It is evident that something (we call it proof) needs to be present in the Enclave to identify it as such to the attestation service. Let us assume that this something is a secret key (certificates are bound to keys as well). Further, consider that the key format is asymmetric, implying the existence of a public or private key pair. An external entity can associate the public key (the secret should never leave the Enclave) with some Enclave properties.

For example, the entity can record the public key **Kpub**, associated with the Enclave owned by Azure. However, for this to work, the channel from the Enclave for this external entity needs to be **trusted**, such that entities in the middle cannot record data of their choice. One can visualize a manufacturing process where the new item (Enclave) information is recorded.

Such registration is required to identify the Enclave. Some may argue that the alternative would be to give the Enclave a certificate during the manufacturing process. This, however, is a form of registration where the newly minted Enclave must request a certificate from the manufacturing **Certificate Authority** (**CA**).

Clean room setup

The clean room concept is about having a clean, meaning an uncompromised system, that can be used to bootstrap a system that can withstand a compromise at a later point in time. As illustrated, the confidential Enclave can be given a certificate by the registration authority in a clean room environment. Even if the environment gets polluted at some later point in time, the obtained certificate is still valid.

A few figures would help to illustrate the process. To start with, the Enclave is not proof-of-bootstrapping, as follows:

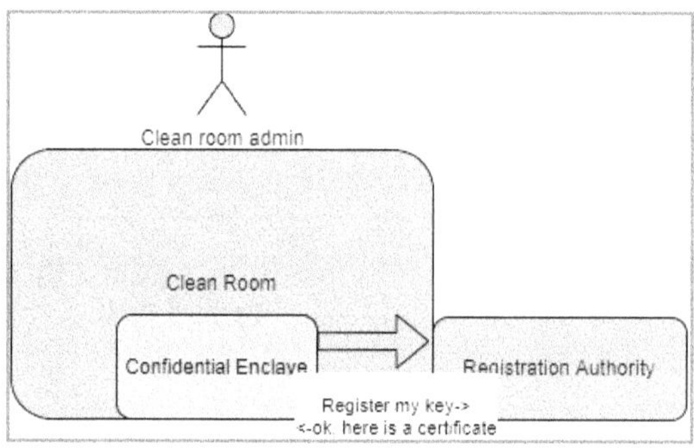

Figure 2.5: *Clean room setup*

At that stage, the environment needs to be trusted so we can trust the bootstrap process. The new persona would be the clean room admin. (S)he will have the power to register any key with the registration authority. If the admin is malicious, the registered key may not belong to an Enclave, but to the **adminb**.

State after bootstrapping is complete, as follows:

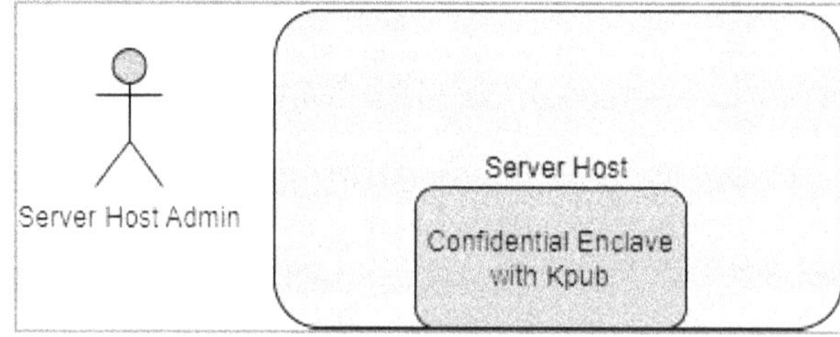

Figure 2.6: *Confidential Enclave in cloud server host*

The Enclave is represented by its (public) key. Rewinding some, the Enclave talked to the attestation service to get a certificate from it. Everybody else needs to trust the attestation service issuing the certificate. Let us consider how the attestation service can recognize that the requestor is an Enclave owned by some cloud. It needs to trust some artifacts identifying that the server belongs to some cloud and that the confidential Enclave belongs to that server.

The following are the important claims:

- This is a trusted Enclave
- Owner is XYZ cloud (for example, Azure)

Relying on these, the partner can decide whether to provide the requested service. An application, for example, can offer some services only to apps running in a secure Enclave.

Let us call out what is being achieved with this setup. There are **two personas**: clean room and server host admins. To compromise the app running in the Enclave, the attacker will have to compromise **both** admin identities.

The server host can hold secrets to **assert the app identity** (in Azure, these are called managed identities), and the Enclave can provide a secret for an identity of its own. Combining the two in the authorization logic eliminates the single point of failure caused by a single admin compromise.

However, failures can still happen. Either the app (server host admin) or the Enclave (clean room admin) or both can be compromised. Eliminating the single point of failure means that both entities need to be compromised to trick the authorization system into granting access. Although the probability has been reduced, compromises can happen, and there needs to be a way to revoke compromised secrets. Revoking app and Enclave keys would require different actions; app keys are revoked using IdP-specific gestures or APIs, and Enclave keys are revoked by the attestation service issued certificate, using attestation service APIs.

Identity provider for users, apps, and Enclaves

It is important to distinguish the various identities in place and consider authorization policies that could be authored based on those.

Refer to the following figure:

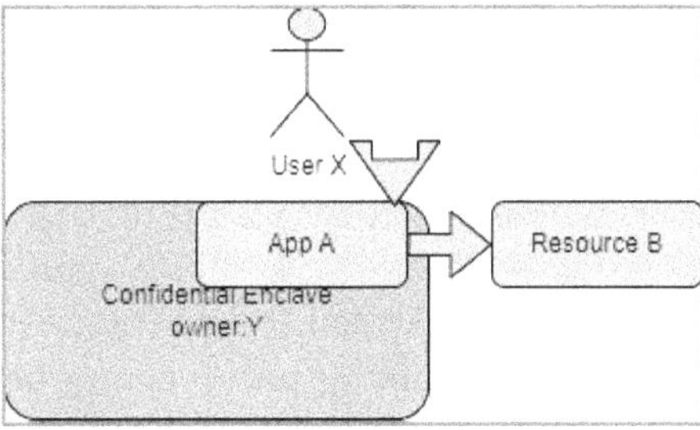

Figure 2.7: *Application in a confidential Enclave talking to a resource service*

Note: **The three identities at play here are those of User X, App A, and the Confidential Enclave owned by Y.**

Consider how we author authorization policies. Take the **role-based access control (RBAC) model,** commonly used as an example.

Let us discuss if we can assign roles to X, X on A, or X on A on Enclave owned by Y, or X using any app in the Enclave owned by Y.

These expressions can become arbitrarily complex, and most authorization systems, notably legacy ones, will not be able to deal with such complexity, as these requirements have emerged long after the systems were designed. Regardless, all the above are valid cases that need to be implemented with some acceptable admin experience. We need to accept that authorization systems are generally hard or impossible to change. If Resource B authorization cannot handle the multiple identity expressions, we need some alternate mechanism to implement authorization on the additional properties.

All said, it would be great to simplify the resource authorization system requirements so that roles are assigned to one identity without having to evaluate expressions on multiple identities' properties.

The IdP can issue tokens containing claims about all the identities involved, but it is also helpful to offload some of the authorization decisions from B's authorization system. This is known as **conditional access** or CA in Azure.

For example, B can enforce that X has access using its existing authorization, while the IdP can implement *issuing tokens only if the app is running in a secure Enclave owned by Y*, thus providing authorization on the additional properties. If one is to draw parallels, a secure Enclave owned by Y is like a *compliant device according to some policy set by Y*. The end-to-end flow is shown in *Figure 2.7.*

Compute and storage

In this chapter, we discuss confidential compute and CA. Cloud providers provide mainly *compute and storage services* to cloud apps. We should call out networking as well, though from a security point of view, we can assume a full interconnected mesh, meaning all services are connected to each other by default, and networking is assumed to have little to no security impact. That said, it would be very helpful to clearly articulate the authorization rules.

For example, storage could be available to App A running in a secure Enclave owned by Y. If the app is installed elsewhere, the storage will not be available. The authorization rule *running in a secure Enclave owned by Y* could be implemented as a conditional access policy by the IdP authenticating App A, without having the storage service know anything about secure Enclaves.

Compute and storage cloud offerings will be shown as follows:

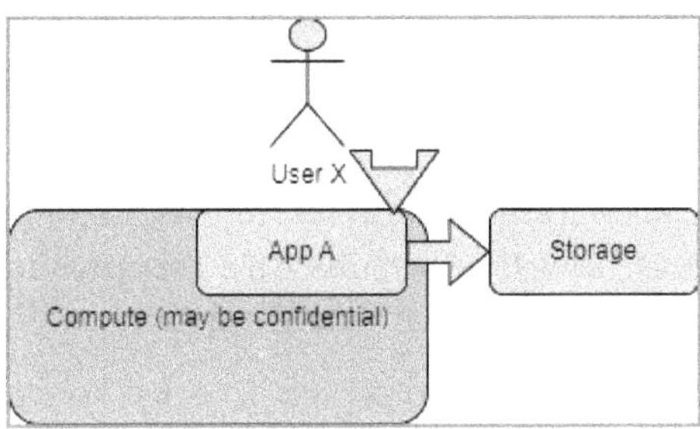

***Figure 2.8:** Compute and storage cloud offerings*

We need to discuss a small detail. Suppose there are item1 and item2 under the storage service. How do we apply policy P1 for item1 and P2 for item2? After all, the IdP implementing CA sees only the storage service, and not the items underneath it. A typical example is requiring a different policy for the items marked **classified**. What is classified and what is not can be expressed as a property of the item, called **classification** (**class** for short). There needs to be a mapping between the **classification** property and the required policy. We can express this mapping as follows:

```
item.class => IdP.PolicyID.
```

We previously discussed having a separate storage service for each **`item.class`**. But then, there needs to be a way for the app to figure out **`item.class`** for the item it needs to access.

One approach is to have **all storage** service that tells the client which storage service to contact for a specific item. For example, if **`item.class=classified`**, the item should be located behind the **`ClassifiedStorage`** service. To simplify, we can assume that all items under a specific storage service are of the same class, and if there are multiple classes, there will be multiple storage services, one for each class. Using the **classified** example, there must be **`ClassifiedStorage`** and **`NonClassifiedStorage`** services to serve items of the respective class, as follows:

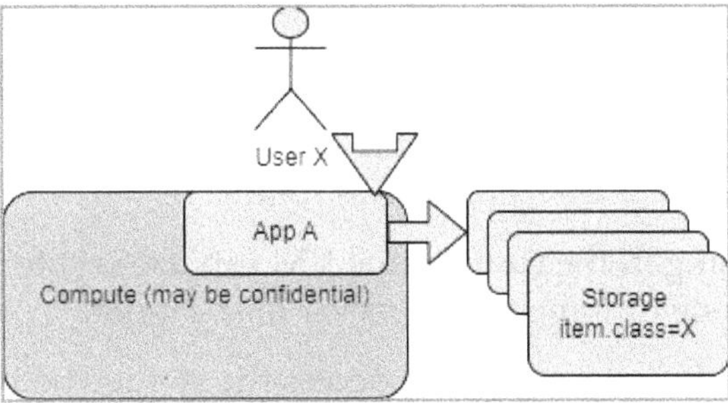

***Figure 2.9:** Using a classified example*

What is not shown is the mechanism used by the app to address the correct storage holding the item of interest. There are various methods that are legit to perform such a discovery. In the general case, the storage discovery service tells the client which specific storage service must be contacted to fetch the item the client is interested in.

Compute and storage architecture security considerations

The previous section introduces compute and storage as major cloud building blocks. With this in mind, we can discuss how this architecture can provide security to applications running in the cloud. Let us begin with some assumptions.

The app code is open source. There are no secrets in open source, and anyone can execute the code on their own computer. To formalize it, let us assume that the app exposes one **API**; it will be expressed as follows:

```
(output_i, state_i+1) = App.API(input_i, state_i)
```

Considering the app code is open source and input comes from the caller, the only thing that can be secret is the **`state,`** which comes from the storage services. To access this state, the app needs to access a secret. This secret cannot be part of the code, which is open source. If it were, it would not be a secret, which leaves Enclave, the server host, or the Enclave as secret custodians.

You can visualize the secret in the Enclave as follows:

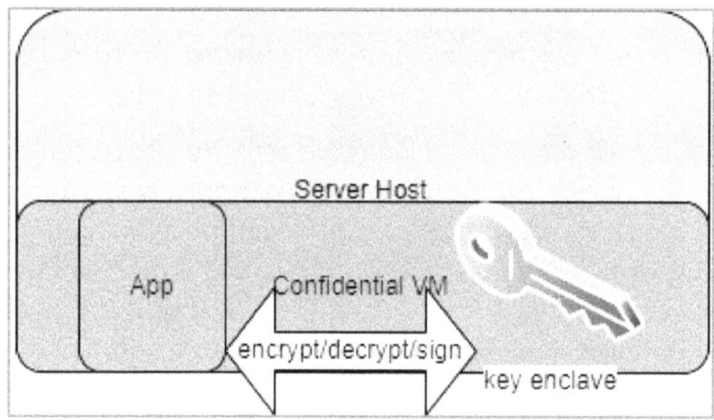

Figure 2.10: *Secret in the Enclave*

The confidential VM exposes the same crypto APIs as **regular** VM, so apps do not need to change. Security invariants or assertions are as follows:

- Only code running in the confidential VM can use crypto with the key inside the VM Enclave. Code running on the server host cannot.
- By extension, only code in VM can access the storage holding the persistent state (**`state_i`**) required for the computation.

To conclude, the host can get the app. There are no secrets in open source. What it cannot get is the persistent app state held in storage. It requires crypto operation using a key accessible only by code in the Enclave. An example of this would be, process running in the confidential VM.

Blockchain architectures

Blockchains do not have distinct compute and storage resources. The blockchain node provides both services, as follows:

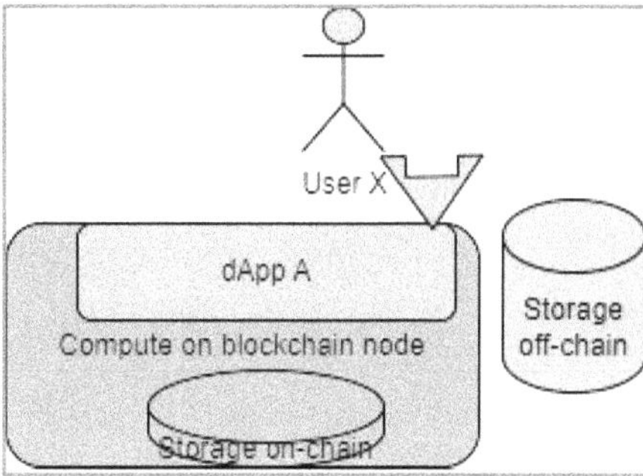

Figure 2.11: Blockchain node services

Note: **There is no explicit conditional access concept in blockchain authorization implementations.**

Authorization rules are computed within the blockchain node, and identities belong to the end user and the app. The missing **Enclave identity** should not be a surprise, given the public nature of blockchains. It could be argued that the blockchain virtual machine (EVM for Ethereum) could be the Enclave, though this is a stretch, given that there are no guarantees for EVM integrity, other than its open-source nature. It would be more precise to forgo the secure Enclave concept when discussing the blockchain execution environment. The overarching blockchain principle is that individual nodes are not trusted.

Another important point is that storage could be split such that the **main** on-chain store on the node holds a fingerprint (hash) of the data that can be stored at an arbitrary location. Integrity comes from the fact that any data changes would result in a hash change, and the hash cannot be changed once committed to the chain.

Features of Azure

Check the following documentation to see multiple Azure offerings in the area: **https://azure.microsoft.com/en-us/solutions/confidential-compute/?ef_id=_k_CjwKCAjw48-vBhBbEiwAzqrZVLgjrNJSJwSxLcSS__tWvDNYbLKjcC-A_4NAG3YNLwCUkimIgw8zMxoCKM8QAvD_BwE_k_&OCID=AIDcmme9zx2qiz_SEM__k_CjwKCAjw48-vBhBbEiwAzqrZVLgjrNJSJwSxLcSS__tWvDNYbLKjcC-A_4NAG3YNLwCUkimIgw8zMxoCKM8QAvD_BwE_k_&gad_source=1&gclid=CjwKCAjw48-vBhBbEiwAzqrZVLgjrNJSJwSxLcSS__tWvDNYbLKjcC-A_4NAG3YNLwCUkimIgw8zMxoCKM8QAvD_BwE**

While there are many choices to consider, there is some commonality among the various approaches.

The main feature advertised is that the compute node operator cannot **peek into** the secure Enclaves placed within the operator-owned compute nodes.

There is an implicit assumption here that a compromise happens because of **peeking**. Thus, by prohibiting peeking, compromise is prevented. However, another obvious approach is to have the operator (node owner) execute code of their choice within the Enclave. We will discuss what is preventing this. Simply put, the Enclave should be instructed to only execute images from a trusted (pre-defined) source. This would amount to mutual authentication. The image needs a way to assert (claim in token) that it is running in a special Enclave environment, and the Enclave needs to authorize the images it runs, as follows:

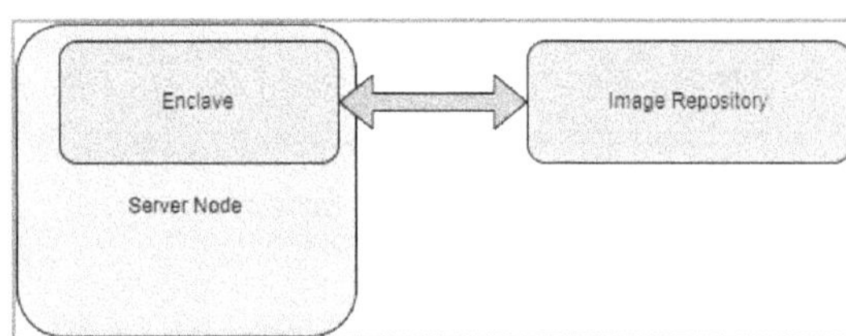

Figure 2.12: Authorizing images

The following are the assertions:

- Only images residing at the image repository are allowed to execute in the Enclave. An easier alternative would be to allow the file copy from the image repository only.
- Image or app executing in the Enclave can prove that fact to the partners they talk to. The mechanics for this are using tokens issued by the attestation service or claims in tokens issued by the IdP, refer to *Figure 2.4.*
- Enclave is protected from apps running on the server node. Someone needs to control what is being executed in the Enclave, but it cannot be the server node. According to requirements, the desire is to preserve Enclave integrity, even when the host is not trustworthy.

To see the view from the portal, navigate to: **https://portal.azure.com/#view/Microsoft_Azure_Marketplace/MarketplaceOffersBlade/selectedMenuItemId/home/searchQuery/confidential/searchInitiatedFrom/plusNewBladeSearchContext/suggestionCorrelationGuid/4e352574-0ad0-497c-bc2b-212aaf79e009/suggestionResponseRequestId/1e694861-fc1f-4f0e-8ca1-721565d61c54**

These are the AI-generated search results for **confidential**. There are many choices, but remember the assertions aforementioned describing what we want.

Types of Enclaves

As we discussed, there are **confidential VMs**, **confidential containers**, etc. in the Azure offerings.

For confidential VMs, see **Azure confidential virtual machines FAQ | Microsoft Learn**

Confidential containers, **Confidential containers on Azure Container Instances - Azure Container Instances | Microsoft Learn**

There seems to be a **confidential** counterpart for each compute resource offering. Then, what is the requirement for multiple offerings?

Most, if not all, existing apps target some **operating system (OS)** or container platforms, which are offered as cloud compute resources. So, delivering VMs or containers allows the apps to run without changes, aka the lift-and-shift approach. Making these **virtual machines (VMs)** or containers confidential does not change app requirements, as confidential VMs have the same properties as the **regular** ones, plus some additional ones.

As a practical matter, apps integrate with some identity library that knows how to assert the confidential platform to the IdP. The app integrates with the library and works the same way on any platform supported by the library.

Visualize the confidential offerings as follows:

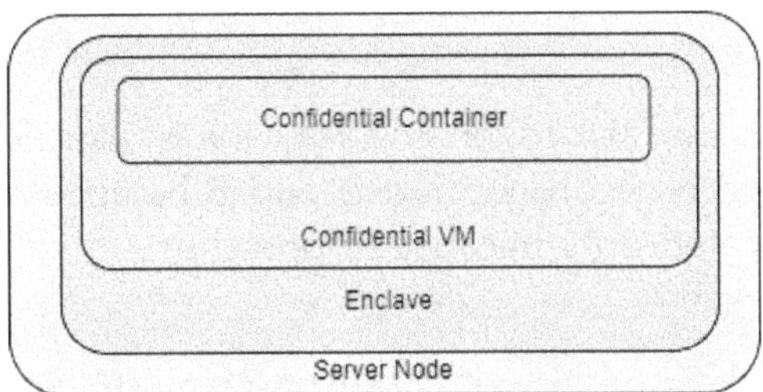

Figure 2.13: *Visualizing the confidential offerings*

Note: **In case of a serverless setup, let us not forget that serverless does not mean that there are no servers.**

As it was suggested in *Chapter 1, Introduction to Application and Cloud Security*, the future would most likely be serverless. However, Enclaves correlated to VMs, or containers, imply the existence of explicit server compute resources. In a serverless environment, the application is deployed to a cloud provider without reference to a specific server or VM compute resource. However, the abstraction is projected on actual VMs, which can be confidential, and would allow us to call the **serverless** abstraction **confidential** as well.

Different philosophies

In this section, we will highlight the contrast between the blockchain approach and the various cloud-supported secure computation setups. The question is, as usual, *who can be trusted.*

In the blockchain philosophy, there is no trust placed in individual compute nodes. Instead, trust is in the community of nodes. If more than half are **trustworthy**, then the result would be trustworthy. That said, the result is an integrity-protected ledger (or database), and there is no provision for confidentiality (encryption).

The different philosophies are illustrated as follows:

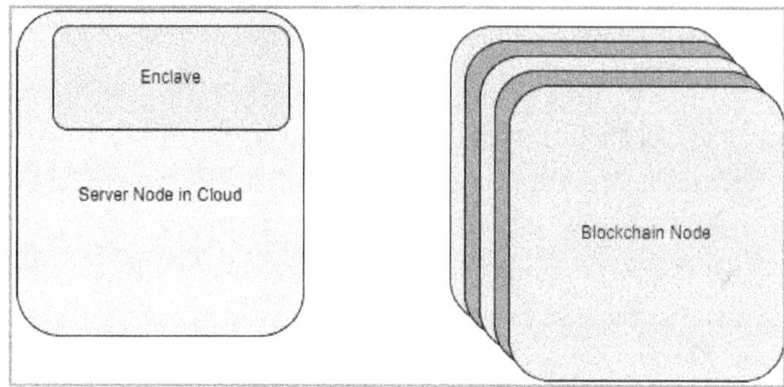

Figure 2.14: *Different philosophies*

Integrity is indeed super important, though confidentiality is often desired as well. (*Chapter 7, Encryption,* is dedicated to data encryption techniques). Some definitions with examples would also help.

Let us assume A wants to pay B 1 token and issues a transaction to this effect. Integrity means that the transaction is recorded, and A and B balances are updated accordingly. Further, balances are updated only because of processing a valid transaction. Any other update will break the integrity.

A practical example is how, in real-world ransomware attacks, the attackers modify or encrypt a legitimate app's data and then demand a ransom to give back or decrypt the data. With integrity enforcement, such attacks will not be possible as the attacker's encrypted data will not meet the integrity requirement checks, and, therefore, attackers will not be able to overwrite the legitimate app data with encrypted data.

Let us try to understand what should be kept confidential.

Using the same example, A wants to pay B 1 token, subject to confidentiality, are A's and B's balances, addresses, as well as transaction details about the number of tokens being sent.

Data can be kept confidential. One way to do this is to use encryption. Start by calling out the basics for implementing encryption for the confidential data.

To point out the obvious, encryption requires a key, and having blockchain nodes be public excludes the possibility of having a shared key, since anyone would be able to get it. But then, what can be done if the encryption or decryption key cannot reside with the node?

Multi-party compute paradigms hold some promise (nodes having different keys that work), but if anyone can join, the result would be the same as having a shared key. If we put a limit on the number of nodes that participate, then the chain cannot be called public.

The next chapter discusses the semantics behind public and private clouds.

Achieving public blockchain confidentiality

Confidentiality generally requires the data at rest to be encrypted, and encryption requires a key. Being public implies anyone can run a node, and if the key is to encrypt the data, it is to be maintained by the nodes, then it cannot be a secret. Consequently, we need to exclude the possibility of encryption by the blockchain nodes. Then, confidentiality should be achieved differently. Let us examine what needs to be confidential.

A typical transaction can be described as *A wants to send to B, X tokens*. To execute, a validator needs to know A and B balances, as well as the value of X. Denote as **`A.Bal`**, **`B.Bal,`** and **`X`**. The information, which could be valuable, is A and B addresses, balances, and X, which is the number of tokens being sent.

Next, will discuss some approaches to protecting this information.

Homomorphic encryption

Homomorphic encryption is the conversion of data into ciphertext that can be analyzed and worked with as if it were still in its original form. Homomorphic encryption enables complex mathematical operations to be performed on encrypted data without compromising the encryption.

To illustrate, assume that balances **`A.Bal`**, **`B.Bal,`** and **`X`** are encrypted with some form of homomorphic encryption, with the sender in possession of the key, such that:

```
Encrypted(A.Bal) - Encrypted(X) = Encrypted(A.Bal-X)

Encrypted(B.Bal) + Encrypted(Y) = Encrypted(B.Bal+X)
```

The - or + operations can be applied to the encrypted data with the same semantics as when we apply them to the clear text. Doing so protects **`X.Bal`** and **`X`** from being publicly revealed.

Having said that, addresses (**`A.Addr`** and **`B.Addr`**) are not protected. To find **`A.Bal`** and **`B.Bal`**, the nodes need to know **`A.Addr`** and **`B.Addr`**. To put it in simple terms, the fact that A sent something to B is not hidden. The actual amount is.

Often, the information about who sent something to whom is as important as the actual amount that was sent. Leaking this data would destroy the privacy claims in the eyes of many. With this restriction, homomorphic encryption alone will not qualify as a confidentiality method.

Another issue is that if the transaction details are to be revealed to authorized callers, there would be complications that necessitate re-encrypting the data to the authorized party key, such that the node invoking the operation remains agnostic to the data. Though devising such algorithms is possible, they may not exist, at least not to the author's **knowledge**.

Tumblers

A tumbler is an entity between A and B. Instead of sending X to B directly, A sends it to the tumbler, which forwards the amount to B in a way that the transaction cannot be attributed to A based on the blockchain transaction logs.

It is shown in *Figure 2.14*, as follows:

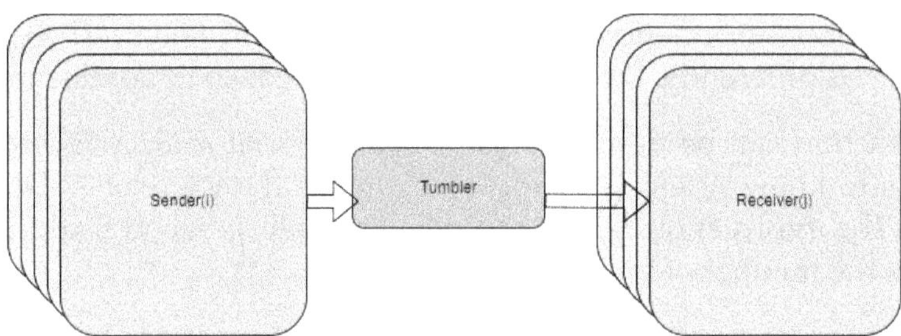

Figure 2.15: *Tumbler*

It seems like a promising idea utilized in a few confidential crypto networks, though there are a few issues with it that seem concerning, such as:

- The tumbler plays the role of a centralized service. It gets to see the private information, and we need to believe it keeps it secret. For this to be true, it needs to either drop the information on the floor or store it encrypted. In the latter case, the encryption or decryption key needs to be available to the tumbler, which means that the tumbler cannot be running on all blockchain nodes and, thus, cannot be public.
- In some cases, the private information could be needed, for example, A could need proof that it sent X tokens to B. This would require that the transaction details be kept around and revealed to authorized callers. This requirement would be put on the tumbler, which, again, would make it not suitable to be public.

These restrictions place a big question mark on the design suitability. Major chains like **Bitcoin** (**BTC**) and Etherium (ET0H do not employ tumblers).

At its core, it is a centralized service and carries all the negative sentiment that exists towards centralized services.

Other techniques

We should mention **Zero Knowledge Proofs** (**ZKP**) and **Multi-party Computation** (**MPC**) as areas attracting heavy research efforts.

While the motivation behind it is not focused squarely on solving the blockchain confidentiality issue, these methods are often touted as possible solutions based on the promise behind. It should be noted, though, that there is no clearly articulated concept showing how these methods can be used to achieve the desired blockchain confidentiality.

Blockchain architecture summary

Assuming that lack of confidentiality is inherent in public blockchains, then if confidentiality is a desired solution property, public blockchains will not be the tool of choice.

While there are various promising techniques being researched, the fact remains that major chains do not offer confidentiality. However, it would not be a surprise if a confidential blockchain takes off soon. It has not yet.

Conclusion

Desired isolation from malicious operators can be achieved by applying confidential compute techniques or by using blockchain architecture approaches. Either approach achieves the goal of ensuring that a malicious operator cannot affect applications running on the resources that can be accessed by these operators. The main points behind both approaches are highlighted in the *Points to remember section*.

In the next chapter, we will learn about public and private clouds.

Points to remember

The following are some of the main points to keep in mind:

- All clouds want to make their customers feel safe and secure. A common approach is to offer confidential compute choices and claim that even if the datacenter's physical security is compromised, the apps are still safe.
- Confidential compute implementations come as Enclaves that are isolated from the physical compute node in the sense that physical access to the node does not translate to Enclave access. For this to be an effective mitigation of the physical security breach concerns, the following are also needed:
    - Attestation service certifying the caller is running in an Enclave. There can be various proof types.
    - IdP that can consume the attestation service assertions.
    - IdP implementing CA supplemental authorization that allows configurations like *allowing access only to apps running in secure Enclaves owned by XYZ cloud provider(s)*.
    - An alternative to an IdP support is a resource authorization system that can consume complex claims issued by an IdP that refer to app and Enclave identities. It is also possible for the resource to consume the attestation service assertion directly vs. relying on IdP claims.
    - Either way, the best resource option is to integrate with an identity library. If running on Azure and/or using Entra IDs, see Entra ID libraries description.
- Blockchains offer a different philosophy that does not rely on having individual *secure* nodes.

- o Confidentiality on blockchains is, in general, not provided
  - Since most popular chains are public, this excludes the possibility of having a shared key on the public nodes.
- o Provided is data integrity, which is super important, but may not be sufficient for some customers.
  - Integrity is implemented using consensus algorithms that do not require a shared key among nodes.
- o Confidentiality implies having a private key to encrypt or decrypt ledger entries, but since anyone can run a node, there cannot be shared secrets.

As an app developer or owner, one must choose if the app is to run on a blockchain as *dApp*, in the cloud on regular or confidential compute node, or some combination of these. There are tradeoffs either way. What is it that we want to be true will be the main guiding principle.

Often, the answer to this question sells the application to discerning clients. There is a reason why hyper-scalers have invested heavily in confidential computing.

Exercises

1. Describe your app requirements regarding confidentiality. What, if anything, needs to be confidential? For example, there can be a requirement to identify the transaction and ledger entry owner who can authorize access. Normally, participating parties (referenced in the transaction) would have access to transaction content, or at least the parts that affect the participating state. If someone sends me X tokens, I need to have access to the relevant transaction data.
2. Defend why the app should be using confidential compute resources.

   Hint: Using confidential compute is likely more expensive, but the reduced probability of compromise should be worth the cost. It should be expected that the confidential compute price will go down. Soon, all computes could be confidential. In the meantime, the extra cost for confidential resources needs to be justified. It could very well be that app customers are demanding the extra features.
3. Should the app run in the cloud, on blockchains, or both? A lot will depend on consumers picking up dApp clients and respective wallets. Since this is a major paradigm and experience shift, it is hard to ascertain when this would happen. But when it does, apps would need to have a decentralized presence (dApps on public chains) to be relevant to consumers.

References

1. Entra ID libraries - **Microsoft identity platform authentication libraries - Microsoft identity platform | Microsoft Learn.**

CHAPTER 3
Public and Private Clouds

Introduction

In this chapter, we will discuss various cloud classifications. Public vs. private is the main one. There are also hybrid and multi-cloud concepts. We will examine how these affect the overall security posture, as well as call out other benefits. The topics also include internal app architectures when apps are deployed to major cloud providers. Special attention will be dedicated to microservices architecture types and related security implications when using those.

Not surprisingly, the tradeoff between security and availability will be identified, and approaches to address it will be presented.

Structure

This chapter includes the following topics:

- Understanding public and private clouds
- Multi-cloud setup
- Blockchain principles
- Public and private parts for Azure
- Canonical cloud architecture

Objectives

The concepts of public and private clouds have been actively used in discussions describing compute environments. This necessitated looking closely at the subject and providing the needed definitions. Without these definitions, the semantics would be left to the entities that make use of the concept. Not surprisingly, that leads to the same concept having different semantics depending on who is using it. In this context, the main objective would be to define the semantics, so confusion in interpretation is avoided.

Understanding public and private clouds

Let us start by discussing the semantics. The core definition would be defining the public cloud.

Definition and semantics of public cloud

There are two possible pivots that are classified based on the cloud provider or the cloud consumer.

If we are to draw parallels with the non-digital world, public entities, such as governments, offer public resources, like public transportation. An important property of these public resources is that the providers, the government in this case, are considered to be public as they are supported by the voting public forming the taxpayer body. The consumers having access to these resources are indeed public, though not necessarily the same as those who have elected the government supplying the resources. Here, we should note that a non-government organization can provide these resources to the general public, as long as doing so is a profitable endeavor. But oftentimes it is not, so governments have to provide these unprofitable services. Taking this point of view, the public transportation provided by governments is not public from the point of view of the provider. It is public from a consumer's point of view, as anyone is allowed to use it.

In the digital world, there are public blockchains that allow anyone to contribute computing resources and benefit from usage. Blockchains eliminate the resource provider as the **middleman**; there are no taxes supporting the providers, only usage fees that make participation in the blockchain protocol a worthwhile endeavor.

While this is the state at present, it would not be surprising if governments start providing **public cloud** compute facilities to the public, the way public transportation is provided. If this happens, expect these facilities to be partially funded, the way public transportation is.

From the cloud provider's point of view, all clouds are **private**, as only individual provider resources are offered to customers. For example, Azure cloud will not allow outside entities to add **public** resources.

Note: **Offerings like Azure Arc (used to be Azure Stack) provide for customers to add and consume their own resources (private), but do not contribute resources to the Azure cloud, to be used by other customers.**

This is true for other clouds as well, and this should not be surprising, as there are certain promises made to public customers, and it is easier to uphold those promises when the provider owns the building blocks (servers), vs. using building blocks contributed by someone else. The message is that using private servers is good when the servers are used by the organization's applications, but not by applications handling requests for other organizations. In this context, private means *brought in by the customer and managed by the provider*. There is also the concept of the provider giving out dedicated resources to customers vs. them bringing in their own, residing in some on-premise location, meaning a location owned by the company that owns the servers.

There is an economic angle worth mentioning here, though the economic levers would be discussed in a later chapter. Specifically, if resources could be added to the public cloud, take compute and / or storage, then the contributor should be rewarded for providing these resources. In the cloud provider business model, cloud customers pay for the resources that they have subscribed. These payments are in a certain national currency (say USD), which must be shared with resource contributors, as per the arrangement.

It is important to point out that if host security (control what can run on the host) is a requirement, then a viable option will be that hosts come from the cloud provider, as it can provide host security that meets customer expectations. If customers provide their own hosts (on-prem), they will be responsible for the host security. Naturally, cloud providers cannot take responsibility for the security of hosts provided by the customer. There is a physical aspect to the host security. Cloud providers can give out management agents to aid with host management, but cannot provide the needed security, as, barring having confidential compute setups, physical access to the host translates into the ability to run any software on it.

Note: **With confidential computing setups (*Chapter 2, Different Clouds and Confidential Compute Promise*), the host security is not a requirement.**

However, the Enclaves must meet cloud provider requirements. While hosts contributed by a third-party could be viable in this arrangement, it is of little practical importance as third parties are not likely to score better deals with host and Enclave manufacturers.

In blockchain setups (refer to the *blockchain* section), rewards are in the form of underlying network tokens, which are granted to nodes that **behave correctly**, in terms of executing the blockchain consensus protocol for maintaining data integrity. With blockchains, the hosts (called **nodes**) are not assumed to be secure. Having network token rewards is an important feature, as participants do not need to depend on cloud providers for participation rewards.

Definition and semantics of private clouds

In a private cloud, the owners of the resources also own the infrastructure or hosts below. When referring to a **private cloud**, we will consider the cloud consumer organization, and not the cloud provider.

For example, it would be meaningful to say that organization X has a private cloud with provider Y. Semantically, the infrastructure is owned by X, and host management is done by Y. The infrastructure (hosts) can be provided by anyone X trusts, including Y. The important feature is that X controls what runs on the infrastructure (hosts) it owns, which helps with ensuring host security posture, eliminating inside-out attack types, as shown in the following figure:

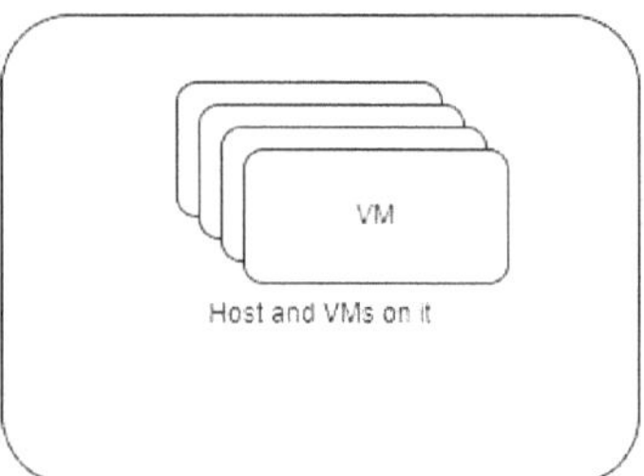

Figure 3.1: *Host with VMs*

Elaborating on the example, if the resource is a **virtual machine (VM)**, then the owner will have the physical server below it, and only VMs that belong to that owner will be created on that server.

The thought behind this is that, by owning the infrastructure (physical servers), certain classes of security issues are prevented. A common example is to point out bugs that allow **VM escape**, allowing the VM owner to take over the host, and from there, affect the VMs owned by others. Imagine a major company being taken over by someone who ran VMs with code and exploited that vulnerability.

In the general case, the resource owner must own the container where the resources are created. In the following VM example, the container is the VM host physical server:

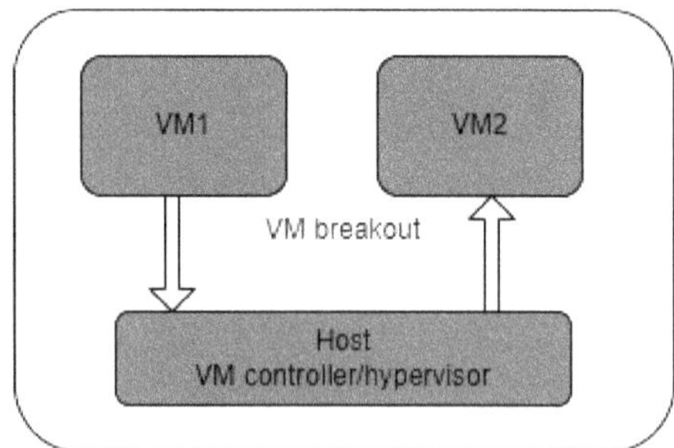

Figure 3.2: *VM breakout, Code in VM1 can break out to the host and from there take over VM2*

Let us reflect on this for a bit. While owning the immediate container has its benefits, there is still something left to be desired, as containers are usually stacked. Servers are placed in server racks, which go in server rooms, located in a datacenter, and so on. If a breakout occurs, the goal is to contain the breach within the container where it happened. For example, if one can write the code to take over a server host, then other servers should be protected. However, items in the compromised container are not protected, which causes various schemes, preventing container compromise from being invented.

While owning the physical server container addresses the attack vector caused by VM escape, it does not guarantee that the workload will not be compromised by using other vectors. However, we must recognize that the addressed attack vector is crucial when considering a cloud environment. It can be executed by other cloud customers who exploit some host vulnerability, allowing VM escapes. To reiterate, VM escape allows compromise of other VMs on the same host.

If we assume that container ownership translates into owning contained items, then container compromise cascades to all containers and items, owned directly or transitively.

Transitive ownership is as follows:

If A owns B, and B owns C, then A owns C

This means that, unless confidential compute or blockchain architectures are in place, physical security is a compromise vector, as shown in the following figure:

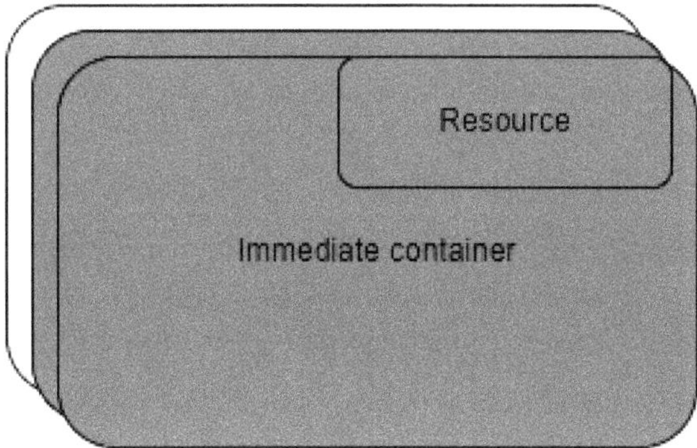

Figure 3.3: *Stacked containers, container compromise spreads to contained items*

The compromise scheme can be viewed as multiple stacked containers, where the compromise of one container affects all containers below. For example, the compromise of a server room affects all racks with servers in it. So, owning an individual server would not protect the owner from a room compromise. It does somewhat protect from server compromise through VM breakouts. This can be referred to as compromise direction, outside in, or inside out.

In addition to these two patterns, there is also a **lateral compromise** direction. If we take a physical server as the attack target, the attack vectors are as follows:

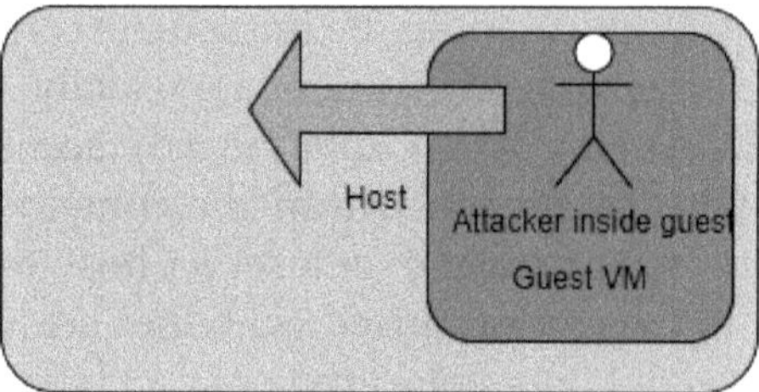

Figure 3.4: *Compromise from the inside*

This is a generalized model of the VM breakout case shown earlier. The pattern is that malicious code executing on the device cannot be contained and prevented from taking over.

The outside-in pattern shown in the following figure is the attacker using physical access to the device to take over it:

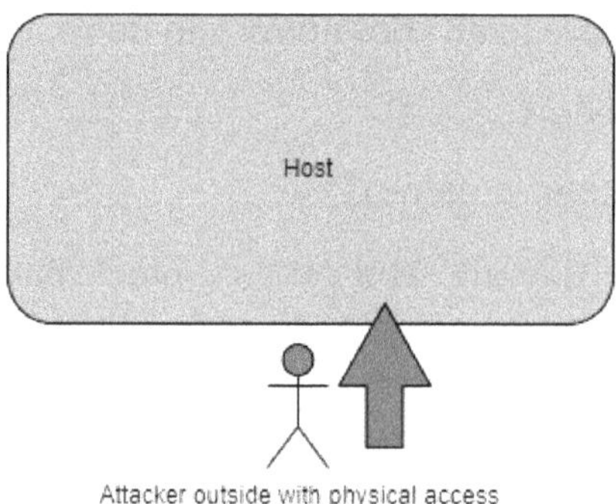

Figure 3.5: *From the outside*

This pattern is a manifestation of the compromised container issue discussed earlier. The rationale is that compute resources (the host) exist within some container, which could be under an attacker's control, thus providing physical access to the resource.

Another pattern of compromise can be labeled as a **lateral movement**, where the attacker does not have physical access to the host itself but does have access to the network the host resides, as shown in the following figure:

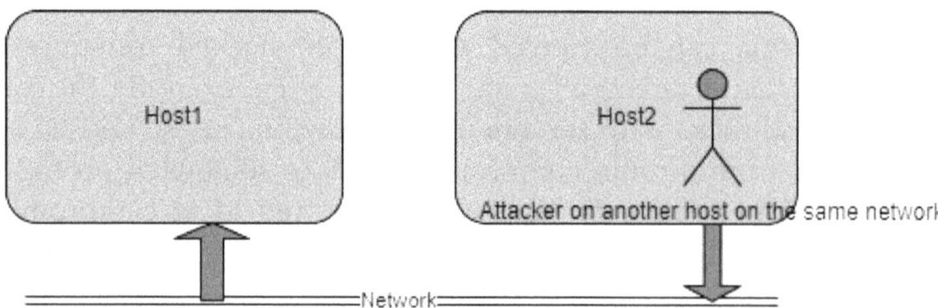

Figure 3.6: *Lateral movement, attacker on the same network*

In the lateral movement scenario, it is assumed that **host1** (the one getting compromised) has a vulnerable component listening to the network. In that regard, the flow is like the **inside-out** one, but instead of executing on a guest entity (VM or container), the attacker sits on a peer node and uses the network to issue specially crafted requests processed by vulnerable services, resulting in compromises.

It is useful to define the benefits of having a private cloud construct. These can be divided into two categories, security and availability.

Security benefits of private cloud

Private clouds giving out host ownership mitigate the compromise direction inside-out. As customers can control contained resource ownership, they can ensure that no malicious code runs there.

However, this type of private cloud does not quite mitigate compromises in other directions, unless some additional conditions are enforced. As an analogy, consider private cars and private roads. Having a private car is a protection against dangers posed by other users of public transit, but it does not protect against other users of the roads. Nor does it protect against dangers posed by the area's roads that run through. Additional **private ownership** conditions are needed to address those compromise vectors.

Having said that, it is important to understand what is being included in the private cloud. The conclusions from the previous paragraph assume that a private cloud consists of private compute nodes placed in some environment that is not private. If the host owner also owns the network connecting the hosts, then the lateral attack movement is also mitigated. But network ownership is hard to assert. It seems impossible to prove that a node is not teachable by unauthorized parties. The private network cloud offerings address networking for the guest VMs, and not for the network connecting the underlying hosts. The compromise of the guest VMs is the goal, so ownership of the guest VM network is a good offering. However, let us not forget that hosts need to be protected, as well as compromising a host can translate into hosted VM compromise.

Private cloud availability gains

A construct made available to cloud customers is allowing them to provide compute resources that can be used together with the ones that are given by the cloud provider.

A typical example is a customer providing resources (servers) at locations not reached by the cloud. This arrangement is somewhat different from building a private cloud using cloud provider hosts. Most of the major cloud providers can provide dedicated hosts to demanding customers, but this is not congruent with the cloud business model, which relies on shared hosts, as shown in the following figure (discussed further in the preceding sections):

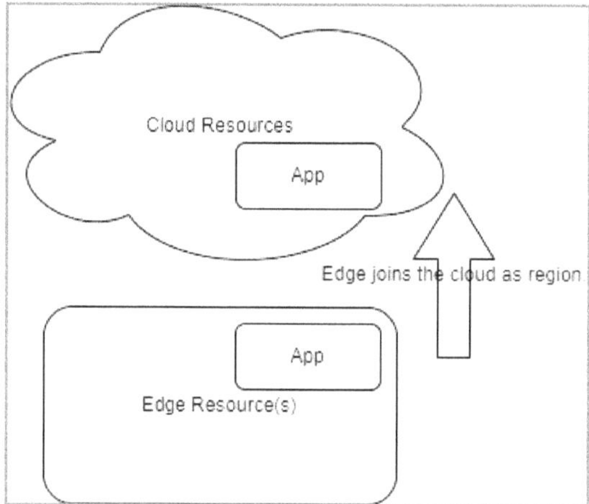

Figure 3.7: *Private resources for the edge*

The benefits of having customers provide their own edge resources, while also consuming cloud resources, come from having a unified view of all resources in the cloud.

Let us assume the cloud is partitioned by regions and that there is a region called **edge,** and (there can be many of those **edges**). While it is possible, in theory, for the cloud provider to add resources in all regions of interest, in practice, cloud providers allow customers to add their own compute resources in regions not served by the cloud provider (edges), as an extension of the set of resources from regions served by the cloud provider.

As an example, consider *Azure* compute resources in the *West US region*. These exist in one or more datacenters in the *West US*. A customer who needs resources in a specific (edge) location, say Eastern Oregon, can provide those. This way, the concepts using regions as building blocks for the cloud can be applied.

This is also illustrated in *Figure 3.7*. The benefit of using a single tool to see app deployments in all regions of interest is significant. It can be argued that app deployment on the edge can be separate from app deployment in the cloud, but then there should be two sets of tools, one for the edge and one for the cloud. If there are multiple edges (and realistically, there would be), the implication is having one tool instance per edge. A much simpler and intuitive approach is to have the edges connect to the cloud, present themselves as regions, and have one cloud tool to provide a unified view of the app deployment in all cloud regions, including the multiple edges.

The private cloud can exist within the cloud provider, excluding the customer's own private resources on the edge.

But then, there will be, theoretically, no availability gains as cloud resources, private or not, would have the same availability profile. For this not to be so, availability profiles (measured in some concrete terms) should be correlated with the private state of the resource. The resources offered as private should have higher availability scores than their public counterparts. The main reason why private resources increase availability is that customers can place those on the edge, where clients live. The availability gains come from clients and services being co-located. Extending the example we started with, a client in *Eastern Oregon* is likely to observe higher availability when connecting to an app service deployed in Eastern Oregon, vs. the same app service deployed elsewhere.

The following figure explains the concept:

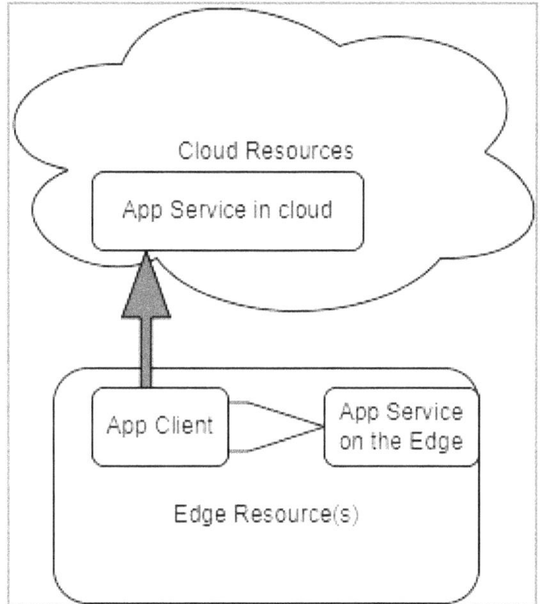

***Figure 3.8**: App on the edge connecting to service on the edge*

As shown in the preceding figure, an app living on the edge will experience higher availability when connecting to a service instance located on the same edge, compared to the same service instance located elsewhere, one of the cloud regions, for example. This comes to illustrate the benefits to the customer as they can provide edge resources.

The availability statement may not be 100% true as it assumes that location proximity is correlated to availability, which may not always be the case. However, we could assume the assertion is true for most customers, so placing services closer to clients increases overall availability, which depends on network availability, where the network is the path connecting the client to the service.

Clients in Eastern Oregon are expected to experience the highest network availability when connecting to services in the same region. Sure, clients in certain Eastern Oregon locations may experience higher availability when connecting to services deployed in *California* datacenters, but most clients would prefer services in the same region.

There is also the issue of network cost that would be covered when discussing the various economic models.

Hybrid clouds

According to *Google*, a hybrid cloud is a mix of public and private clouds. An app could be deployed in public, private, or both (hybrid).

As discussed, a private cloud brings security and availability benefits to justify the associated extra cost. It is important to know that the same security benefits would not be present in a hybrid cloud setup. The rationale is that the security posture is determined by the weakest (with the lowest security) link, which would be the public cloud piece in a hybrid cloud setup.

But the availability benefit is retained. An app running in a hybrid cloud will inherit the private cloud availability benefits. It is expected that the hybrid cloud would consist of private nodes on the edge and public nodes in the cloud, covering all regions outside the edge. Clients connect to the closest service instance, those on the edge connect to the edge instance, and others connect to an instance in the cloud. The following figure illustrates the idea:

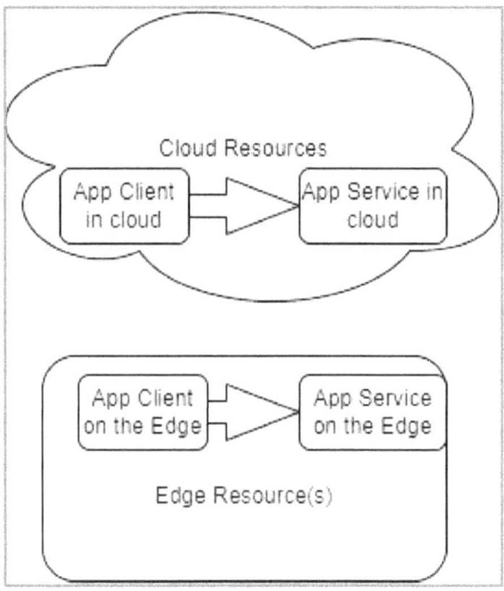

Figure 3.9: *Clients connecting to service instances in the same region*

To summarize, a client in each region connects to the service instance in the same region. The edge is viewed as a region populated by customer-provided resources.

Multi-cloud setup

In a multi-cloud setup, the app runs in multiple clouds. The main idea is to remove dependency on individual clouds. The suitable architecture for multi-cloud is shown in *Figure 3.10*. While it isolates the device app from the cloud specifics, the cloud app is still bound to individual cloud services.

If we isolate cloud apps from cloud-specific services, then a generic interface offered by cloud-specific connectors must be provided, as shown in the following figure:

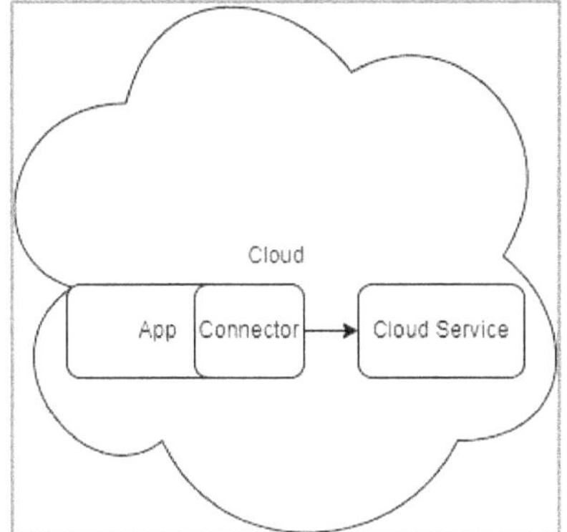

***Figure 3.10:** App with cloud-specific connectors*

The desired result is that the app can be deployed in any cloud for which cloud connectors exist. If a cloud becomes unavailable for some reason, app instances in other clouds continue to work, removing cloud dependency during runtime. While this is a great result, it must be pointed out that the cloud dependency still exists in app development (connectors) and deployment phases.

We have removed the runtime dependency, but there is still the issue of the app deployment ceremony involving multiple clouds. A cloud-independent deployment model is needed to facilitate deployment automation, as shown in the following figure:

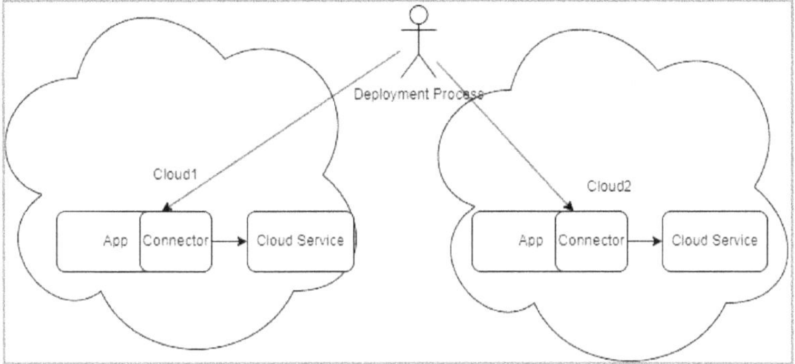

***Figure 3.11:** Deploying to multiple clouds*

Deployment may affect the app, connectors, or both. Ideally, only the app holding the business logic is deployed, while the connectors remain more static. The bottom line here is that a common deployment model is needed across clouds. In the same way, the app has cloud connectors to abstract cloud-specific implementations. Similarly, the deployment process has cloud-specific connectors to map generic deployment gestures to cloud-specific ones.

From a security point of view, security-related generic concepts should be translatable to cloud-specific ones, provided by all clouds that are part of the multi-cloud setup. For example, if the generic gesture is to create a resource in a private cloud, then a cloud-specific equivalent gesture should exist. For example, *Azure* has an API to create a dedicated server and VMs. The same should exist in other clouds that are part of the multi-cloud setup.

It would be a fair discussion to address cloud security in a multi-cloud world. Logically, if the app is deployed in multiple clouds (let us assume two for the sake of discussion), then the resulting cloud security level is the lower of the two. An attacker can choose which cloud offers better compromise conditions and would compromise the app there. Of course, if the security posture of both clouds is equivalent, then no harm is done as the effort to compromise either cloud would be the same.

As is often the case, the presented tradeoff is between security and availability. Running in multiple clouds may have a few availability benefits, but also security downsides. To reconcile, all clouds must provide some agreed-upon security level, which can be used as the lowest common denominator for multi-cloud deployments.

As discussed in *Chapter 1, Introduction to Application and Cloud Security,* security needs to use some metric to enable suitable comparisons. While it is clear how availability affects the bottom line, say each 9 in the availability metric (often quoted as number of 9s) is worth some dollar amount, it is not clear how security affects the bottom line, so these two are hard to compare. If both can be translated to some common metric, say dollar amounts, then comparison would be possible, and we can conclude whether running in multiple clouds is a worthwhile endeavor.

Multi-cloud deployment considerations

The mechanism depicted in *Figure 3.12* needs to be based on some multi-cloud control plane (the term is explained further in the chapter). There are two well-defined architectures to build that plane, which can be viewed as a set of APIs. The common multi-cloud (the words common and multi-cloud are used to carry the same semantics) API wraps the cloud-specific (control plane) APIs implemented by cloud1 and cloud2, and these architectures are as follows:

- Client library
- Cloud service in a common cloud

It is further explained in the following figure:

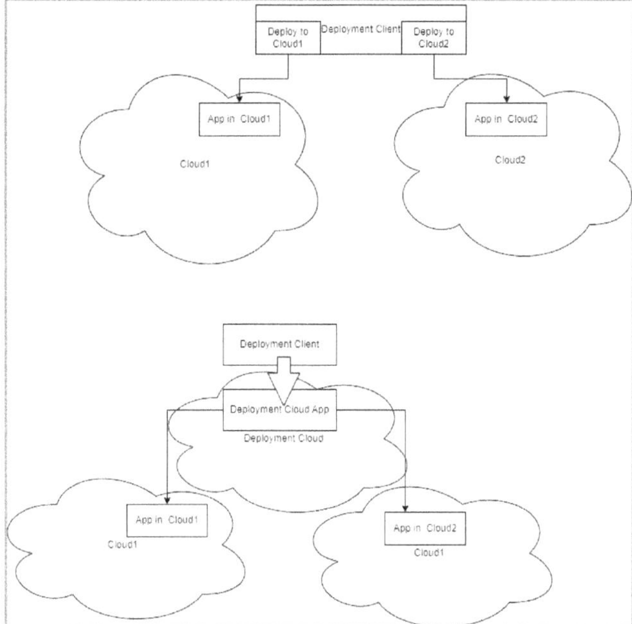

Figure 3.12: The multi-cloud control plane implementation options

As is the case with any wrapper implementation, some crown jewels of individual clouds would be lost, unless implemented by all.

Let us discuss the following pros and cons of the listed techniques:

- **Client library pros:**
    - o The apparent advantage of using a library is that no separate service is required
    - o It does not depend on any cloud availability
- **Client library cons:**
    - o Updates are hard to scale as the library must be distributed to multiple clients, unless implemented as a local service or microservice (discussed further in the chapter)
- **Cloud Service pros:**
    - o Makes the client simpler and easier to distribute
    - o Easier updates
    - o One version
- **Cloud Service cons:**
    - o Service needs to live somewhere. If this **somewhere** is a cloud, then the multi-cloud concept is compromised, as there is only one cloud setup for the deployment service; it cannot be multi-cloud.

While it is true that having the control plane API in a single cloud is a major downside, it needs to be considered that the control plane is the app configuration path, which does not need to be used frequently; only when the app configuration needs to change. Once deployed in multiple clouds, the app will continue to work even if the multi-cloud control plane does not.

It is important to know the goals behind the multi-cloud deployment. An apparent goal is availability, meaning that if a cloud goes down, the app instances in another cloud can take the load. While this is great, the goal can be expanded to address cloud regions. If a region is down, clients can connect to an app deployment in a different region of the same cloud, or to an app deployment in another cloud in a region that is closer to available regions of the current cloud. In this regard, having region mapping between clouds, so that the client knows that *cloud1.regionN* is overlapping with *cloud2.regionM*. But then, having such mapping available to clients would imply that clients are cloud aware, which is not something we want. If clients are not aware of clouds, then the service is discovered (say *service1.com*) using DNS. DNS will give back a set of networks (IP) addresses that correspond to *service1.com,* and these can point to service deployments on different clouds. In this scheme, cloud stickiness is not enforced, or rather, it is at the mercy of the platform networking stack handling DNS data. This means that requests from the same client to *service1.com* may end up going to IP addresses pointing to different clouds. To get consistent responses, the service instances in the different clouds need to be in the same state. This showcases another problem in multi-cloud deployments, which is the multi-cloud state replication. Compared to multi-region (same cloud), the multi-cloud problem has an order of magnitude greater complexity and requires some custom solutions. The same cloud, replication is usually addressed by the cloud provider's storage solution. Say for *Azure Xstore*, data is replicated by the Xstore implementation to all regions where the Xstore resource is installed. However, if the app is multi-cloud, for example, it runs in Azure and AWS, the data must be replicated back and forth from Xstore to some equivalent AWS storage solution (take S3). Special care must be taken to optimize the extra cost resulting from outside cloud network usage, as shown in the following figure:

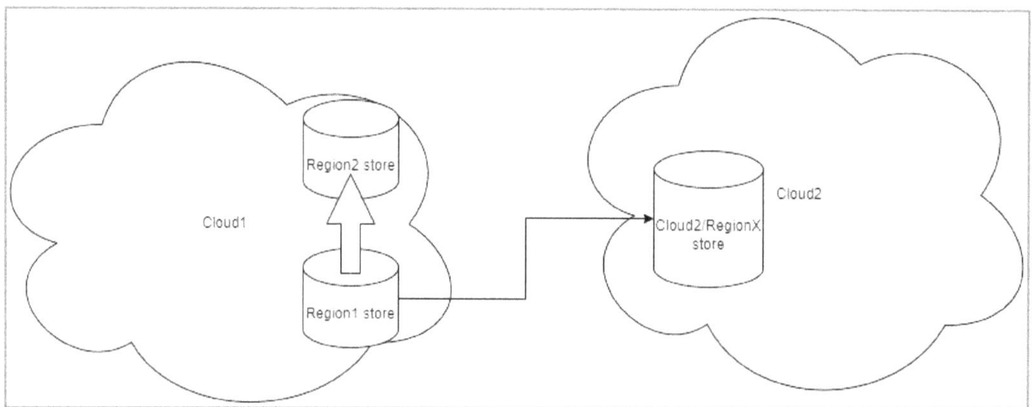

Figure 3.13: *Data replication within regions of the same cloud and cross-cloud*

Cross-cloud replication solutions are not that widespread. It would be reasonable to assume that cross-cloud replication will utilize a methodology different from the one employed when replicating within the same cloud, both within the region and across regions. The differences would show up in the replication schedule, as well as algorithms, both of which would be aimed at conserving network bandwidth while providing some acceptable latency.

The entity delivering the cross-cloud replication solution would likely be different from the participating cloud providers. The solution would likely be a complex one.

Consider that there is little incentive for the cloud providers to deliver complex solutions to help data replication to another provider's store. Providers would prefer to see customers stay entirely in their cloud. Yet another consideration is the commitment to data integrity and confidentiality. These commitments would be hard to stand by when data goes to cloud custody. This opens opportunities for third-party replication solutions. However, customers would have to investigate their needs to decide which solution fits best. There is a multi-cloud carrying the above-described complexity, a single cloud with major cloud providers and blockchains, which would likely meet most of the requirements, except for data confidentiality (refer to *Chapter 2, Different Clouds and Confidential Compute Promise).*

It would be natural to wonder if the added complexity is worth the projected availability gains. It needs to be taken into consideration that increased complexity equals increased costs, which should be subtracted from the gains resulting from the availability increase.

Multi-tenancy

It is another important concept and needs to be clearly defined.

Let us begin by looking at an example from the non-digital world.

Multi-tenancy is usually used to describe a model where a container houses multiple unique individual entities. The most common one is probably the multi-family building where the container is the building, and the entities housed are the families occupying it.

Now, let us consider a digital world example.

Consider an email service, and each email account offers email services. The email service is the container, and the email accounts are the tenants. For example, the email service for *<somename>@foo.com* is housed at *email.service.com*. There needs to be a mapping of the type *foo.com->email.service.com* to aid with email routing. The mapping is provided by DNS. It is worth pointing out that the mapping service is not secure (integrity protected). If an attacker gets to own the local DNS service, they also own the mapping, i.e., *<email domain name>-><email service domain>*. Resulting in clients routing emails to an attacker-chosen service. For DNS compromise attacks, whether the service is multi-tenant or not, does not matter.

An email service can be multi-tenant in several ways. It hosts emails for multiple accounts with the same domain suffix, as well as emails for accounts in multiple domains; if MX (short for Mail eXchange. refer to *DNS mapping* section, in this chapter) records point these domains to the email service. While it is possible (in theory) that accounts with the same domain name are hosted by different services, practically all accounts with the same domain name, e.g., *<name>@<email domain name>*, are hosted by the same email service. The mapping needed is *<email domain name>-><email service host domain name>*. This is exactly the mapping provided by DNS MX records.

To conclude, we can say that an email service is multi-tenant with respect to the accounts with the same domain name and could be multi-tenant for accounts with multiple domain names, if those domains have MX records that point to the same service. So, unless the email service serves a single account (unlikely), then it is multi-tenant by design. Here, it would be appropriate to point out that popular services, like Gmail, are multi-tenanted by design in both ways. One service serves multiple Gmail accounts and allows customers to bring in their own domains, vs. having to use Gmail (for further details, refer to **https://workspace.google.com**).

The following figure is the conceptual view of a multi-tenant service. In a classic environment, each customer installs a service instance of their own. In a multi-tenant environment (as shown in the following figure), a single service instance serves multiple customers:

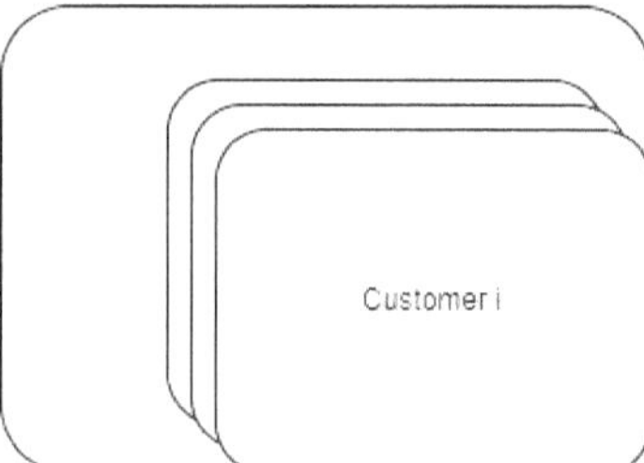

Figure 3.14: *Multi-tenant service, customers are identified by domain name*

A single customer service instance has the following conceptual view:

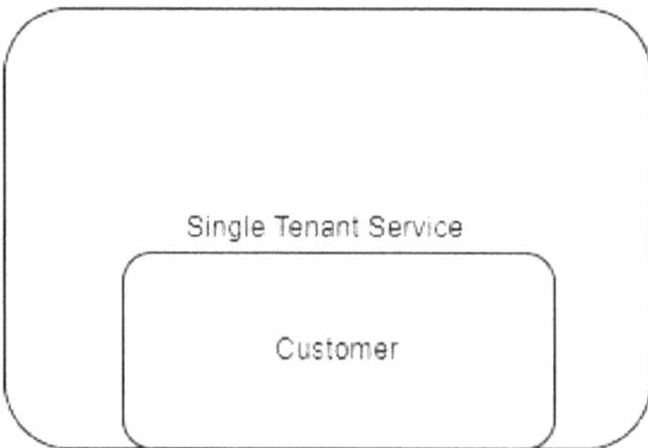

Figure 3.15: *Single-tenant service, a single (or fixed number) domain is served*

This is the **classic** service configuration where each service instance serves a single customer.

The multi-tenancy concept has been expanded to cloud resources, which could be viewed as services. In the private cloud setup, services are single-tenant and do not suffer from the noisy neighbor issues (discussed in the next section).

Noisy neighbor

In multi-tenant environments, entities housed (i.e., tenants) have neighbors. The role of the multi-tenant environment is to isolate tenants from each other. Such isolation is also achieved by having private clouds where the customer owns the physical servers hosting their service. The existence of private clouds speaks to the lack of success in convincing the tenants that isolation of their service from other tenants was achieved by other means.

It is fair to say that private clouds exist to address the noisy neighbor problem. The solution is to get rid of the neighbors, rather than providing sufficient neighbor isolation in the environment. One can hardly argue with the rationale behind this; one cannot get hurt by something that does not exist, which is why private cloud creation has been used to eliminate the noisy neighbor problem.

We will use the email service analogy we discussed earlier. If the email account holder can send or receive mail messages (or perform some other operation) that affect the performance of the email service (as seen by the other accounts), then we have the noisy neighbor type issue. To isolate, the other accounts can look for a **private** email service that is not susceptible to the noisy neighbor.

Blockchain principles

Blockchains are either public or private. From the point of view of who can contribute blockchain nodes, we call these entities **providers** or blockchain node providers. If anyone can contribute a blockchain node, then the blockchain is public.

A private blockchain is a decentralized distributed ledger operated by a single entity or a group of participants that can control access to the network. It has the power to determine who can view and create data on the blockchain, ensuring higher privacy and control, compared to public blockchains.

Blockchains can be considered not only as distributed ledgers, but also as execution environments, where the ledger provides the needed persistent state; it also has the compute capability to execute transactions, causing ledger modification, based on some rules.

We should set participation rules and define who can use the blockchain's store and compute capabilities, smart contracts, etc. Distinguish between allowing everyone vs. allowing certain entities only.

Considering that anyone can generate a key, the possession of a certain type of key cannot be used as a criterion to select participants when filtering is required. There needs to be some private ceremony to register the key, or some artifact based on the key (such as key hash) with the blockchain ledger, and then use authorization to grant access only to entities in possession of the secret key. Such a ceremony will allow only certain entities to register key artifacts. This creates a trust chain, where the root should be constant. To demonstrate, assume the root is key K1. An entity in possession of K1 can register K2, and grant it desired privileges, etc.

The alternative is to allow anyone, which would make the blockchain public from the point of view of the blockchain consumer. It can still be private from the point of view of the provider, who can add nodes to process consumer-generated transactions. This configuration can be compared to the various clouds that are private from the provider's point of view but offer services to public consumers.

Blockchains are classified as public or private, from the node provider's point of view. As a blockchain consumer, all blockchains can be public, as consumers cannot choose private nodes to isolate themselves from noisy neighbors.

Going back to the email service example, let us assume the service needs to be implemented as a *dApp* running on a blockchain. This dApp will have to serve all email domains, or need different apps or chains for different domains; this would, however, be a hard proposition. To compare with *regular* mail clients, a client (say Outlook) can be configured to serve mail for any domain. However, the mail services used can be different. Generally, the email domain name determines which mail service is used. Since dApp would be the email service, it will need to serve all domains, which will not allow it to interact with *classic* email clients, like Outlook (refer to *Chapter 4, Application Identities* for further details)

With respect to private cloud functions, such as isolation from attacks, blockchains do not subscribe to the theory of using isolation as a protection mechanism. They offer a different approach altogether, known as the consensus on state among nodes. The noisy neighbor problem is eliminated by having all nodes follow the consensus algorithm and ignoring those who do not.

The private cloud offers an option that is not generally available on public blockchains, where customers can choose to run on dedicated infrastructure (i.e., private clouds), which means no noisy neighbors are present.

There seems to be a demand among customers for this option (further discussed in the next section).

Public and private parts for Azure

The private cloud is defined as computing services offered either over the internet or a private internal network, and only to select users instead of the public. Private cloud computing (also called an internal or corporate cloud) gives businesses many of the benefits of a public cloud, including self-service, scalability, and elasticity, with additional control and customization available from dedicated resources over a computing infrastructure hosted on-premises. In addition, private clouds deliver a higher level of security and privacy through both company firewalls and internal hosting to ensure operations and sensitive data are not accessible to third-party providers. One drawback is that the company's IT department is held responsible for the cost and accountability of managing the private cloud. So private clouds require the same staffing, management, and maintenance expenses as a traditional datacenter ownership.

The assumption made above is that private cloud comprises on-premises (author's underline) compute resources, excluding the possibility of having cloud-hosted private compute resources. It does offer, however, the option of the customer providing their own private compute resources and having them managed by the cloud control plane. While Azure does offer dedicated hosts (cloud-hosted private compute infrastructure, it is a notable omission from the definition, suggesting a lack of interest in the model.

Now, let us discuss the on-premises label.

Compute physical resources and enclosing containers, including the datacenter building, are defined as on-premises.

We discussed earlier (refer to *Figure 3.3*) that resources are placed in containers, and if the container claimed ownership, so would be the resources in it. The on-premises construct is aimed at asserting ownership of the relevant containers, such that there is no top-level container, whose ownership by an entity other than the organization owning the host can translate into host or compute resource ownership. If the datacenter holding the servers exists in some country, the assertion is that country ownership (mostly government) does not translate into datacenter ownership, and from there into resource ownership. Even if it does, since these are customer-owned on-premises resources, the cloud provider will not be responsible for the physical security, just resource management, which requires providing visibility into those resources and enabling usage.

Note: **The customer is not offered proactively private resources from the Azure fleet. This is a good thing as it avoids having to promise certain security posture for those resources.**

However, the on-premises connection allows the customer to bring in their own private resources, which would be managed by the Azure control plane (explained further in the next section). One must admit that this is a well-thought-out decision by Azure. Customer resources (*Eastern Oregon)* can bring in the needed availability gains, while security advancements are addressed using other methods.

However, it is up to customers to choose networking solutions to protect their resources (but not the hosts) from network attacks. This is the **private part** that the cloud providers focus on, i.e., protecting cloud customer resources from the network.

Virtual private clouds and virtual networks

Most major cloud providers offer virtual private networks that connect customer resources. This is not the internal networking connecting the hosts, but networking offered to the hosted entities, customer VMs being a prime example. The rationale, from a security point of view, is that having controlled network access protects apps from malicious actors on the network. The semantics behind having a private cloud is shifted towards having resources on a private network vs. having resources on private hosts. The two approaches are complementary, as a resource can be attacked from both the network and the host (refer to the next section). Focusing on the latter (network) assumes that host attacks are addressed differently, as shown in the following figure:

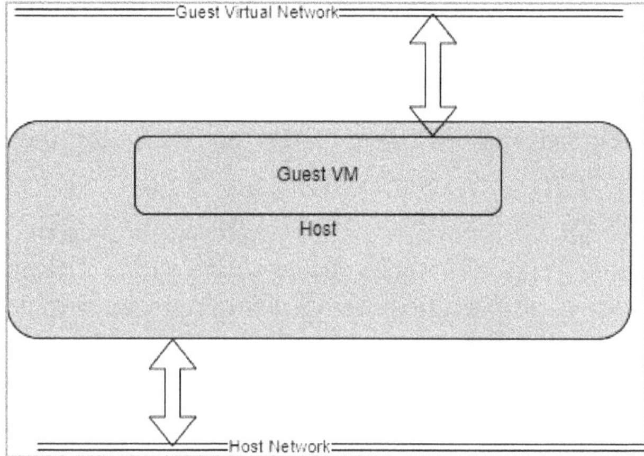

Figure 3.16: *Virtual (maybe private) network connecting guests*

Putting resources behind a private network is a good defense. However, the key concept is that the network cannot be relied on to be the only protection mechanism. While it can be easy to prove that the resource of interest can be reached on a given network, it will be almost impossible to prove that no bad actors have network access. So, making the network private does provide some peace of mind, but it should not be considered as a resource protection that resources can rely on.

The terms **virtual private cloud** (**VPC**) and virtual private network are often used interchangeably, generating some level of confusion. If the VPC is an implementation of private cloud (as defined earlier), then the role of networking is protection against certain lateral attacks on hosts. The virtual networking is offered to protect the guest VMs, not hosts.

Protecting the guests from peers on the network is different from protecting against host attacks. If a private cloud means owning the host, then owning the network for the guests is a different issue, though it should be mentioned that host compromise will also compromise the guest networks. Protecting against host compromise is a must. Once hosts are secure, attention can be shifted to guest networks.

To reiterate, designing and offering private or isolated networks is a great **defense-in-depth** feature. Though apps should not assume networks are secure, as only authorized and well-behaved parties are allowed access. To point out the obvious, computing network access and app access permissions are generally different tasks. It would be wrong to assume that one translates to the other, as recommended practice apps should assume that anyone is allowed on the network and do proper authorization to allow access to app resources (refer to *zero trust network access* for further explanation).

Protecting guests

Compute resources offered to customers by major cloud providers, including Azure, are in the form of some guest construct, implemented on a physical server of the provider's server fleet. We will assume this construct is a VM, though the conclusions would apply to anything that acts as a compute resource, like containers and serverless abstractions, as shown in the following figure:

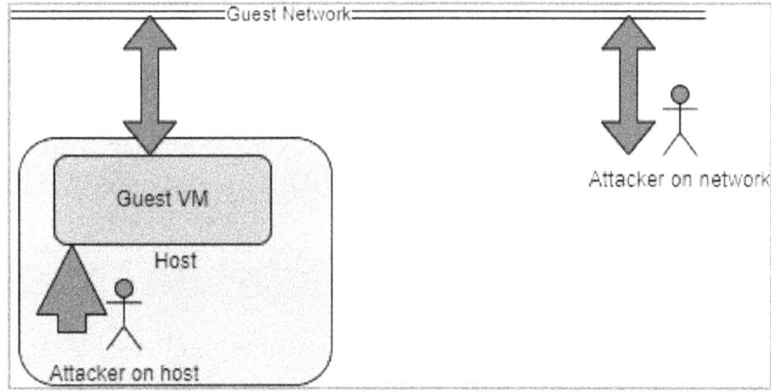

Figure 3.17: *Guest attack vectors; host and network*

Calling out the attack from the host, host attack vectors were called on earlier, from the inside (guests), outside (physical access), and lateral (from the network).

As shown in the preceding figure, guests can be attacked from the host or from the network. There can also be an attack where the attacker is already on the guest VM, running with a different privilege from the target. Since this privilege elevation is very much platform-dependent, it is excluded from the analysis. In the simplified model, the attacker running the code on the guest VM can be counted as a breach, no matter what privilege the code executes.

Guest valuables to protect

In this section, we will discuss the nature of the items being protected.

Firstly, the compute power of the guest can be considered a valuable resource. A common example is malware doing crypto mining on unsuspecting customers' hardware. Here, it is the compute capacity that is getting abused.

Besides compute power, apps have secrets that could be of interest to attackers. Using the previous example again, a cloud-based email app needs to be able to retrieve mail from storage, and for this, it needs a secret so that the storage service can recognize it. We will discuss the different authentication mechanisms (in the preceding chapters), but having an app secret is a common requirement. The major difference between a secret and a compute power is that the secret, if exposed in the clear, can be lifted and used elsewhere. However, the same is not true for compute power. The attacker must be on the compute resource to use it, and not take it home, i.e., use it from another location, as shown in the following figure:

Figure 3.18: *App valuables needing protection*

The protection needed must address the identified attack vectors, i.e., the host and network. A classic approach is to opt for **private** hosts and networks owned by the guest VM owner, hoping that an attack cannot originate from these trusted entities. However, such hopes have become less realistic in today's interconnected world.

Instead of searching for protection behind private entities, the recommended strategy is to assume that everything is public and accessible and try to find protection mechanisms in the public world. This may be considered a departure from the classic models, but it seems to be the only feasible approach.

Providing private hosts has become less feasible. However, it is still being offered as an option, refer to Azure dedicated host as an example, **https://azure.microsoft.com/en-us/products/virtual-machines/dedicated-host/?ef_id=_k_Cj0KCQjw_-GxBhC1ARIsADGgDjtz4fN-lhpfzRVacskoAQN0evMRVA4KFVF7aWxBs2nkTJRtXR5iJQ0aApXmEALw_wcB_k_&OCID=AIDcmm5edswduu_SEM__k_Cj0KCQjw_-GxBhC1ARIsADGgDjtz4fN-lhpfzRVacskoAQN0evMRVA4KFVF7aWxBs2nkTJRtXR5iJQ0aApXmEALw_wcB_k_&gad_source=1&gclid=Cj0KCQjw_-GxBhC1ARIsADGgDjtz4fN-lhpfzRVacskoAQN0evMRVA4KFVF7aWxBs2nkTJRtXR5iJQ0aApXmEALw_wcB**, though cloud providers prefer to advertise models based on private virtual networks labeling as VPC. This makes a lot of sense, as the cloud business models leverage resource sharing, but dedicated hosts cannot be shared. If the resource is virtual, it implies that the underlying physical device can hold multiple virtual resources and, hence, share them among customers who requested those resources. However, dedicated hosts are still needed to satisfy customer compliance requirements.

The view from the Azure portal, showing the dedicated host creation experience, is as follows:

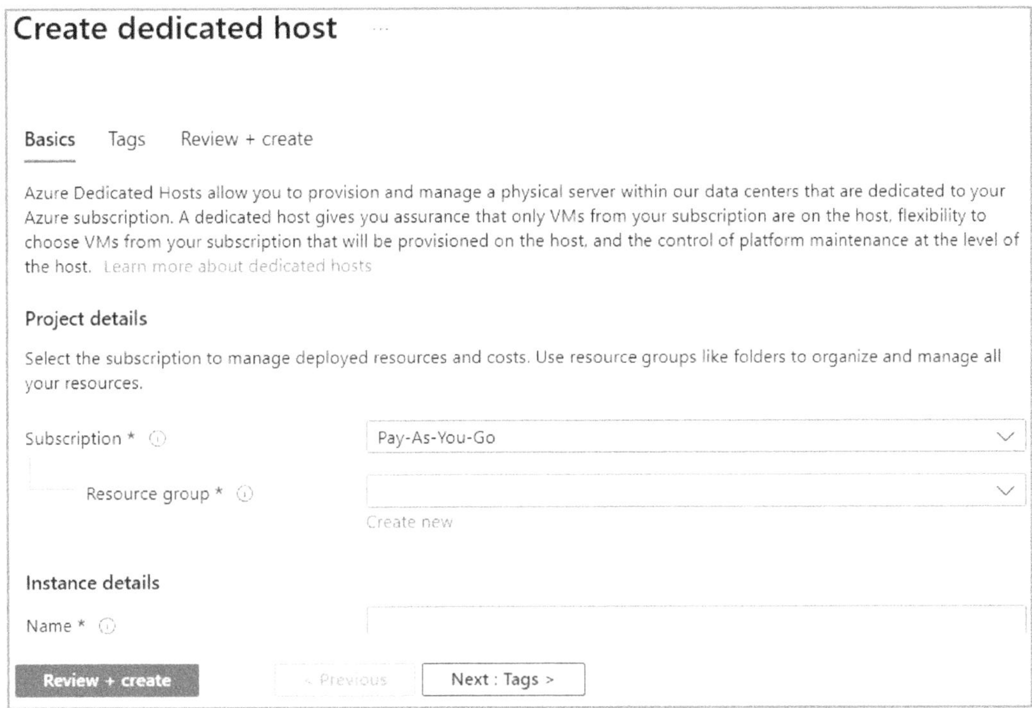

Figure 3.19: *Azure portal experience for creating dedicated hosts*

Azure allows the creation of dedicated hosts, where hosts are part of the Azure fleet. The resulting construct is quite different from using on-premises hosts owned by the customer. In this case, the host is owned by Azure. Customers can place their compute resources (mostly VMs) on these dedicated hosts. While this seems super valuable, the offer seems to be somewhat new, and the capability to place resources on dedicated hosts needs to be provided in the portal. In practice, the customer needs to be able to specify the **host Id** or **host group**, where the requested resources should be placed. No doubt that this experience will be added soon. The new Azure command line tool (i.e., Azure CLI) allows the host Id to be specified. The following figure shows the existing VM creation experience in the portal:

Note: **There are no fields for specifying the host Id and/or host group.**

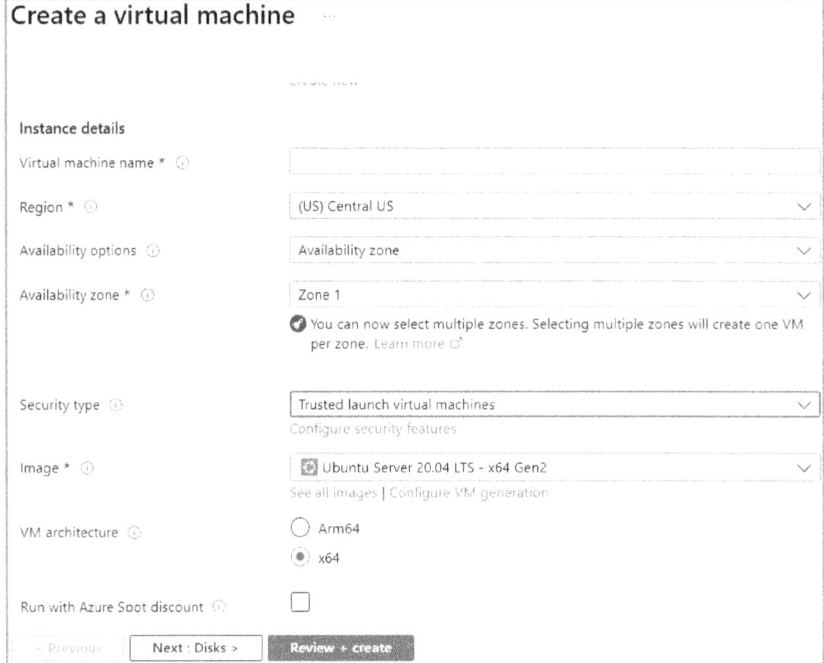

Figure 3.20: Azure VM creation in the portal

The portal experience could be missing the dedicated host details, but one can still use the command line (Azure CLI) app to specify the host Id, indicating the (dedicated) host, where the VM should be placed as follows:

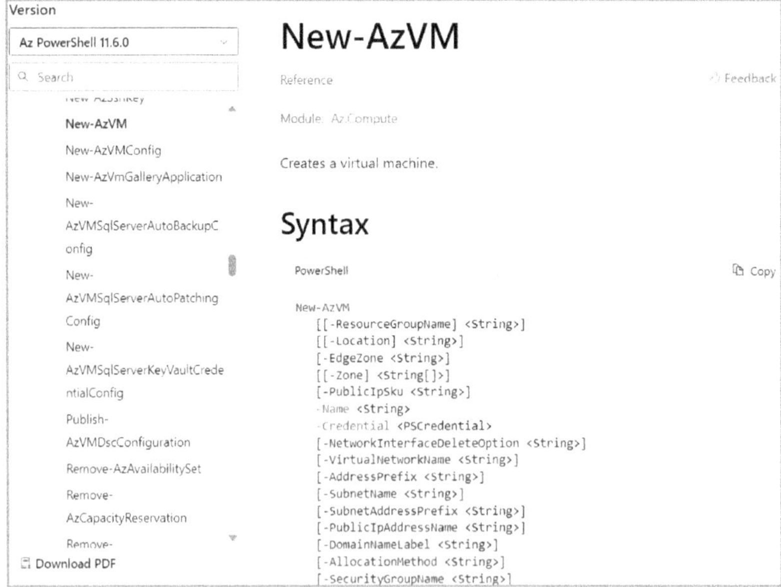

Figure 3.21: Azure VM creation from the command line

You can see the complete documentation on: **https://learn.microsoft.com/en-us/powershell/module/az.compute/new-azvm?view=azps-11.6.0**

Not surprisingly, it is the new **Azure CLI** command that offers the new options, specifying the host Id to be exact. Specifying hostgroup is still not available as an option (it probably will be soon). It is a much-needed flexibility, so that app owners do not have to track individual hosts.

Based on public information, it appears that the ability to put compute resources on dedicated hosts has been requested by customers for compliance reasons. And this makes a lot of sense, security-wise. Most reasons are listed in this chapter, the main one being eliminating inside-out attack classes.

We should also be aware that, even without using this new dedicated host feature, it is still possible to place the VM on a host that does not house any other VMs. The workaround is to specify a big enough VM size, such that the host cannot hold more than one VM.

Azure VMWare solution

This is another Azure offer that utilizes dedicated hosts. Based on the documentation, the procurement of these dedicated resources is somewhat cumbersome.

We can see the details here: **Request host quota for Azure VMware Solution - Azure VMware Solution | Microsoft Learn**

The view from the Azure portal is as follows:

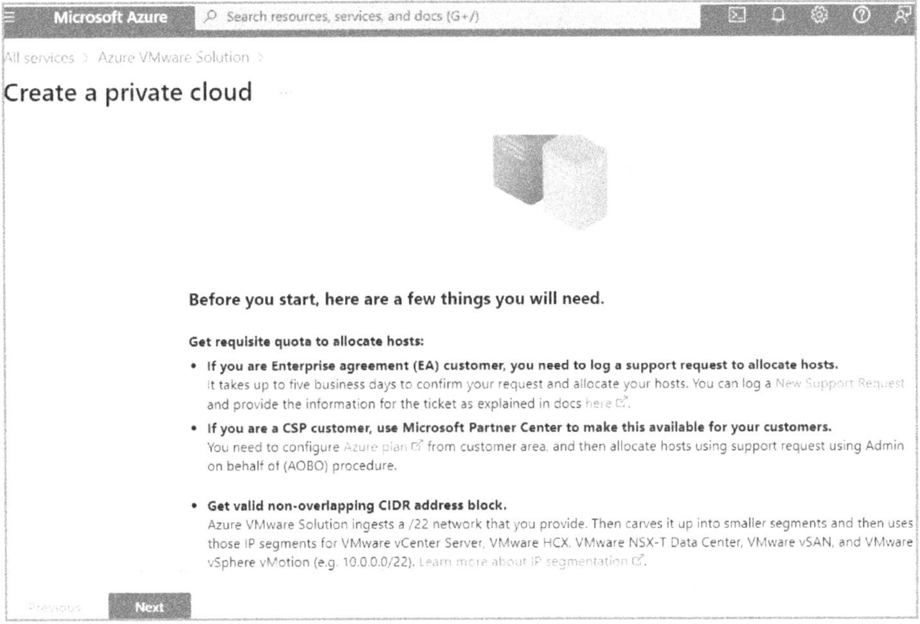

Figure 3.22: *Experience for private VMWare cloud creation in Azure*

Dedicated hosts creation is a time-consuming and cumbersome process. It can be done, though the cost of doing it is hard to estimate. However, it is highly likely that the dedicated hosts for VMWare VMs are needed to mitigate the various VM escape attacks discovered when using VMWare hypervisors. A hypervisor is the software that puts the VM on the physical server host.

Defense in depth

A foundational principle introduced in *Chapter 1, Introduction to Application and Cloud Security,* is that security should not have a single point of failure. This means that one entity compromise should not lead to a whole system compromise. In the context of private networks, this means that an attacker needs to do two things: find a vulnerability to exploit within a network-connected app and get on the network to exploit it. Either one of these (finding vulnerability and getting on the network) taken alone will not be sufficient to perform a successful attack on the guest.

Even with defense in depth, if all barriers can be breached by compromising a single identity, then the result is less than what was expected. Ideally, the same identity should not be authorized for resources used in defense-in-depth protection schemes.

It is hard to test who is authorized for what access. If we trust the authorization policies as an authoritative permission source and know what to test for, i.e., understand authorization semantics, then tasks like finding an identity authorized to perform certain actions in multiple authorization policies are relatively trivial. Having disparate authorization policies, as is often the case, makes such analysis hard to perform, as the analysis tool must be familiar with all policies involved in the authorization decisions.

Canonical cloud architecture

A typical architecture features control and data plane routes. These terms originate from the design of network routers, and it turns out they are applicable to cloud internal designs.

A control plane refers to the APIs used to configure the resources used by the app, and the data plane refers to APIs exposed to app customers.

Note: **A control plane is for the app owners, and a data plane is for the customers.**

Taking the email service example, the control plane would be the API used to configure the number of compute nodes used by the service, and the data plane would be the send, receive, or read mail APIs offered to the mail service clients. The data plane would normally take a lot more requests than the control plane, whose function is fixed, and a fixed number of resources can be allocated to it. By contrast, the data plane serves the heavy volume of customer requests. The cloud providers offer dynamic resource allocation for the app data plane routes, as shown in the following figure:

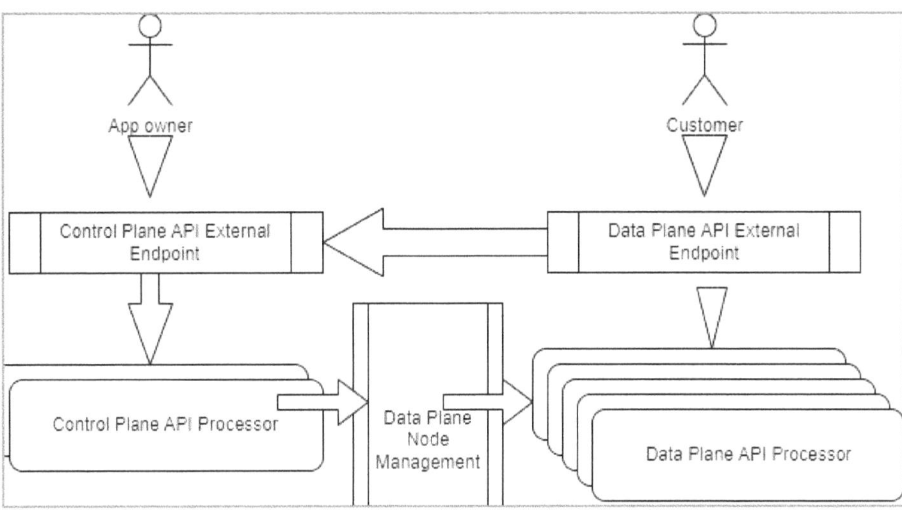

Figure 3.23: Control and data plane routes

A data plane is app-specific, so data plane compromise can be counted as app compromise (discussed in *Chapter 1, Introduction to Application and Cloud Security).*

The control plane is cloud-specific. A compromise there would affect app configuration with unpredictable results, ranging from app availability to app integrity breaches.

A typical use of the control plane would be allocating compute, storage, and network resources to the app.

Note: **The existence of a data plane | control plane | data plane control loop.**

It enables the data plane front door, seen as the data plane API external endpoint, to manage the data plane processing nodes, using the control plane loop. This arrangement enables the touted elasticity of the data plane, meaning that compute power is added on demand vs. having to pre-allocate it and bear the cost of unused capacity. One should allocate a capacity that meets the maximum demand. While having this elasticity is great for cost saving, there is a tradeoff with security. The ability to allocate data plane nodes on demand implies that the control plane has everything needed to run the app, so control plane compromise would equal app compromise (as discussed in the previous paragraph). It may be an acceptable risk, considering that cloud providers invest heavily in control plane protection, but nevertheless, the risk should be pointed out and quantified. It can be speculated that a control plane compromise can lead to app compromise without having the elasticity feature; in this case, one can claim that the elasticity *comes for free*. While this can very well be the case, seeing the proof would convince stakeholders that the tradeoff does not actually exist.

Note: **The data plane front door (external API endpoint) has sufficient privileges to interact with the control plane.**

Request anatomy

Only the router or front door is exposed to the public internet. The app sits on a private network, which is exposed (presumably) to the router only. All services the app talks to are on the internal network as well.

The following figure shows how app processing requests are forwarded by an API router:

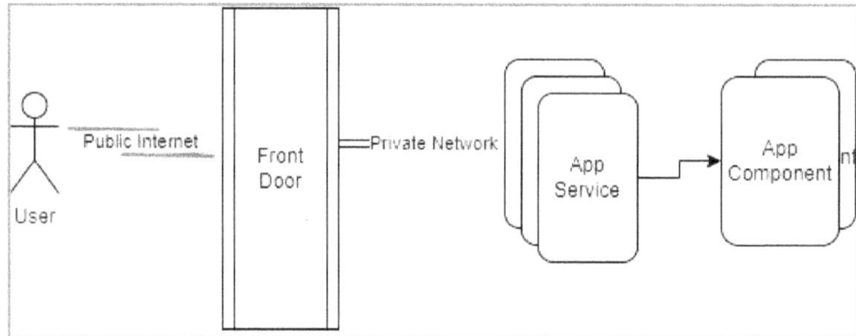

Figure 3.24: *Internal and external networks*

While the rationale for the preceding design is mostly clear, we need to discuss it a little further. A major component offered by cloud providers is the so-called **API gateway**. It plays multiple roles that can be implemented without knowing the API details, as follows:

- **Network segmentation:** The network is divided into public and private segments, meaning in front and behind the front door. The idea behind this is that, on a private network segment, the app will experience fewer network type attacks. This only applies to attackers on the public internet who exploit a vulnerability that exists outside the app's expected requests. To protect against attackers on the internal, private network, the application must take advantage of the virtual private networks offered by the cloud provider. A good example to consider would be the various services that expose a network interface, but since there is only one endpoint, let us assume it is the web server, which is of interest to external callers. Everything else is a liability and should remain hidden from the outsiders, as follows:

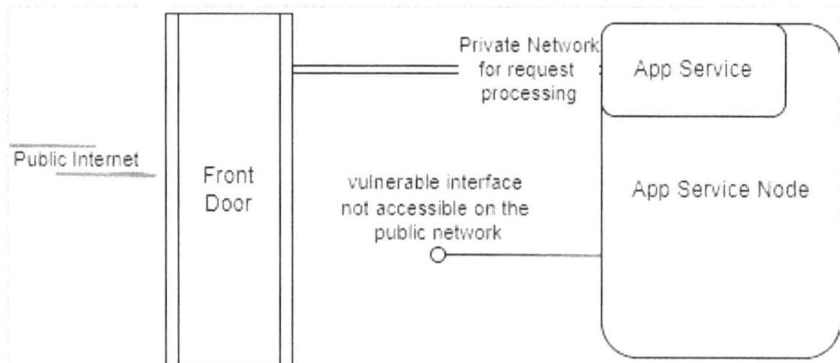

Figure 3.25: *App service with multiple interfaces*

- **Load balancing and capacity elasticity:** The app service is placed behind a set of internal **IPs**. The front door can check service load levels behind each internal IP and route the request to an instance of the service that is capable of handling it. If all instances are loaded, the front door can spin off new ones. If the ability to spin new nodes gives some special powers to the front door, then the front door can route the external request to a service of its choice, subject to **transport layer security (TLS)** termination logic.
- **Route translation:** Suppose, the request URL is, **https://myapp.servce.io/someapi,** the request is routed to **`<service internal ip>/someapi`**. The key consideration is ownership of the certificate and the corresponding private key, needed for TLS termination. Possible implementations are having the front door terminate TLS or having it act as a router only and terminate at the app service endpoint. The front door must be terminated if any type of request modification is required. The apparent downside of this approach is that the front door becomes a valuable target for compromise, as the attackers compromising the front door would be able to impersonate any service behind it. As a counterargument, consider that key protection done by a cloud provider service, such as the front door, would be stronger than that done by the apps. As usual, there is a tradeoff. Front door protection may be stronger, but it is also a more valuable target to attackers, meaning that it can be expected to have more resources allocated to attack it.

The following figure shows two services behind the front door, along with the TLS termination options:

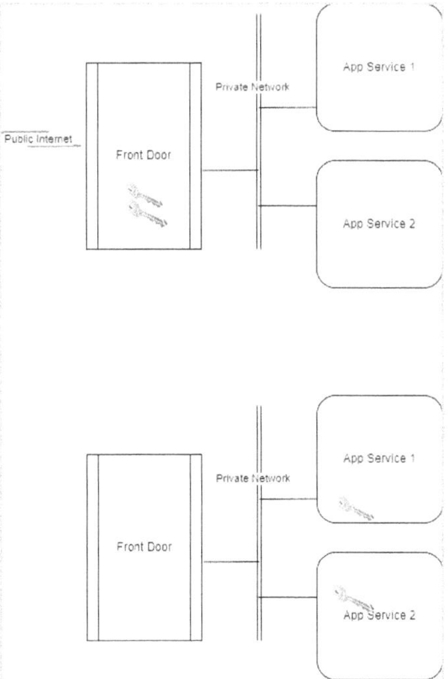

Figure 3.26: TLS termination options - front door or service behind

The front door provides listed services such as network segmentation, load balancing, and routing. With this, the common app architecture is enabled. For Azure front door service details, refer to **https://azure.microsoft.com/en-us/products/frontdoor/**.

For documentation, see the **command line** (**CLI**) reference using Azure PowerShell, **az afd | Microsoft Learn.** It is also illustrated in the following figure:

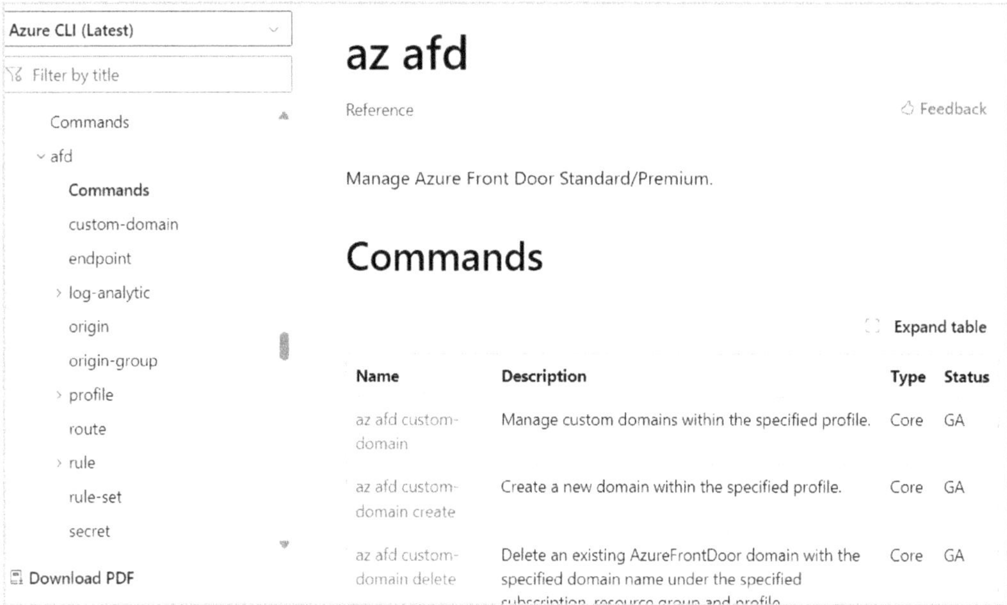

Figure 3.27: Azure front door configuration commands

One of the most advertised features of **Azure front door** (**AFD**), besides routing and network segmentation, is the ability to perform security analysis of the incoming traffic. To do this, it needs to be able to see the data, and this requires TLS termination at AFD. From the documentation content, it appears that AFD always terminates TLS. It is understandable, as not terminating will result in AFD only seeing encrypted traffic, and most of the functionality will not be available, as it requires the clear data to be seen, which requires TLS termination.

Another popular topic in service architectures is using microservices in place of components loaded in a single monolithic service. There are some differences in the two approaches, including security considerations that would be presented and discussed. As usual, the details play a major role when evaluating different approaches.

We will call the top-level process the **app** and the contained component the **comp**. The options listed refer to different ways the app can request services from the comp.

Historically, the most straightforward way to take advantage of component functionality was to load it in the same process as the consuming entity, as shown in the following figure:

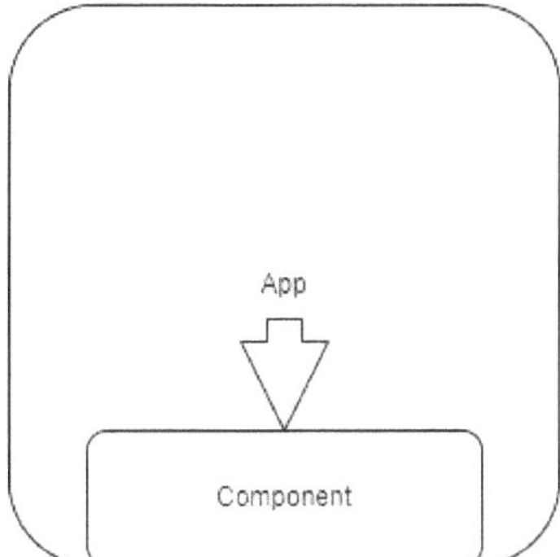

Figure 3.28: *App talking to a component in the same process*

While this is possibly the simplest, most straightforward approach, the downside is dealing with versioning and app process size bloat. The reasoning is that the *comp* must be loaded into every app that uses it. The downside summary is as follows:

- **Size:** Every app size will be increased by the comp size.
- **Versioning:** When a new version of the comp is released, apps will have to change to include the new version.
- **Security:** The component in the same process will inherit all security properties of the process, and if the component is malicious, these can be exploited.

These considerations are relevant when there are multiple apps using the same component, which is often the case in practice, as the reason to factor out functionality in components is code reuse.

The following are the upsides related to this:

- Simple architecture with few security issues caused by identity loss when calling the component. The component can inherit app identities and act as those. Every platform has ways to provide and query for the identities of the current process. The component does not have to do anything special to inherit these identities. Running in the app process is sufficient to take advantage of everything associated with the process, including identities. If the component is malicious, then it can exploit the app process identities, but if it is not, it is easier to use the existing in-process identities vs. having to transfer a subset for component use.
- The component does not need to scale separately as it is part of the app scaling process.
- No need to deploy the component separately from the app.

While most of these upsides are compelling, the downsides have weighed sufficiently to give birth to an alternate architecture. The following figure shows the most prominent ones:

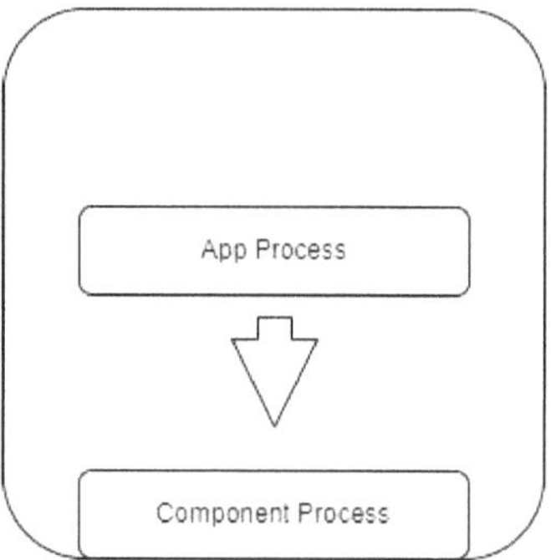

Figure 3.29: Components in different processes on the same compute node as the app

This architecture implies that the component and the app are co-located on the same compute nodes. There are certain benefits in doing so, such as:

- App deployment can also deploy the component as a service on the same node as the app. There is no need to have component-specific deployments.
- Platform-specific cross-process calls can be leveraged.
- Component is separated from the app and, if malicious, it cannot exploit app process identities.

Going further takes us to the following microservice architecture:

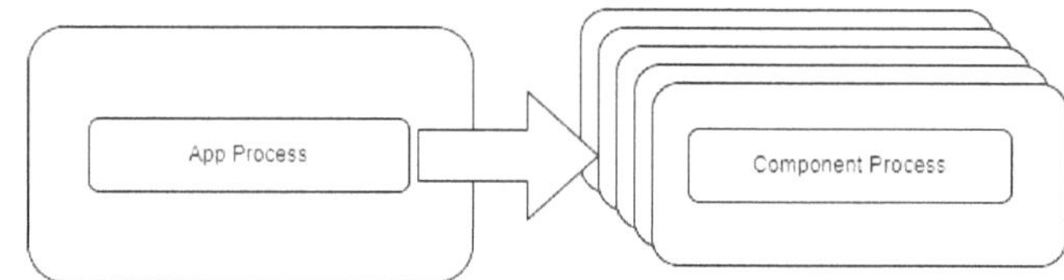

Figure 3.30: Components on compute resources that are network-connected

This is often described as **microservice architecture**. The difference with the previous one is that the service hosting the component does not need to be co-located with the app, just reachable over the network. For simplicity, we will assume the transport is HTTPS or TLS, though the conclusions would apply to any transport with such properties. The properties are as follows:

- Component service is authenticated. Semantics is that when the application calls the component service, there is an assurance that the request lands at the component service, rather than at some attacker-controlled entity. This is the server authentication concept in TLS. The server certificate provides needed authentication assertions.
- Traffic to the component service is encrypted, such that only the client and the authenticated service can see the content. TLS does this as well.

A complication in the implementation of this scheme would be assuming heterogeneous compute nodes. We cannot rely on the platform to carry the calling identity information as it was in the previous architecture, where the app and the component were co-located with the app on the same platform node. So, instead of relying on the platform, some identity authentication mechanism needs to be used to transfer caller identities to the component service.

When implemented correctly, the microservice architecture can be used to emulate the architecture calling, for running the component in a different process on the same node as the app. The difference is that with microservices, this process can be located on any network-connected compute device. So, it would be fair to say that microservices are a superset of the architecture where the component lives in a process different from that of the app. It does remove the co-location requirement.

Being a superset, the mechanism does inherit the upsides and downsides of the previous approach. Being outside the app process is, in fact, a great benefit.

Suppose the component microservices are offered to a single or multiple apps, and the authorization scheme is used. It is possible that the component authorizes app users or the apps themselves. Most likely, either scheme can be appropriate in each context. It is interesting to consider the authorization needed by chained components, assuming chaining is permitted, as it should be.

Cloud security features

Cloud hosting offers few security-related options, such as private clouds and confidential compute resources. There are also cloud-hosted services that can be subscribed to do a security analysis of the cloud-hosted app using some form of machine learning over the app activity logs. (Topics related to both are discussed at length in previous chapters, as well as in this chapter).

It is worth mentioning the different philosophies in play. The private clouds rely on compute host and/or network isolation to keep adversaries away. By contrast, the confidential compute approach assumes the host cannot be trusted and, instead of trying to protect it, focuses on protecting the hosted resources using Enclaves. Similar philosophy rules the blockchain designs, but instead of relying on Enclaves, blockchains use consensus algorithms to finalize state shared among untrusted nodes (refer to *Chapter 2, Different Clouds and Confidential Compute Promise* for details).

The realities of the digital world must be accepted, and security strategies chosen must fit these realities. This will reduce the reliance on **private** constructs.

Note: **Customer concerns should be addressed, even if it takes private clouds to address them.**

Conclusion

In the non-digital world, the word **private entities** has been associated with an increased level of security. The term private means *available to some users only*. The maxim that *we cannot be hurt by something that cannot reach us* has rung true over and over. As evidence, consider the efforts put into achieving isolation, building walls, for example. But unfortunately, or not, achieving isolation in the digital world has proven to be a lot more challenging, as there is a strong demand for interconnected entities. Not a day goes by without hearing about some exploitation carried out by hackers, sitting far away from the target. This happens due to the widespread network availability (internet), which eliminates protection based on reachability. While there are technologies to create private networks, the lines are getting blurred regarding what should be accessible by whom, in this interconnected environment.

To address this issue, initiatives like **zero trust network access** (**ZTNA**) have been created. At the core, these are meant to eliminate reliance on the network as a security protection, the main idea being that all networks should be considered open to anyone.

In practice, the efforts to protect the resources at the network level should be shifted to protecting entities within the compute resource. We should have identified compute power and secrets, and the network should be considered a hostile entity.

On a different note, the work and research behind confidential computing (see *Chapter 2, Different Clouds and Confidential Compute Promise*) eliminate the host server as a source of attack. The guest could be attacked from the network only, and if the apps running on it have a vulnerability (*Chapter 1, Introduction to Application and Cloud Security*), it would be independent of the host environment. Network segmentation provides some protection if the vulnerability is on an interface not exposed to customers.

Employing a private network can be a good defense-in-depth practice (refer to the previous section, *Defense in depth*) and must be used judiciously, evaluating potential benefits against incurred cost and complexity. A common rule of thumb would be that savings from eliminating some attacks must exceed the cost of the private network maintenance. If it comes for free, then even better.

The danger would be over-reliance on the private network security. Software must be developed considering hostile network environments. Running it in a well-behaved private network is a defense-in-depth approach. It can have performance benefits, but security should not rely on the network alone. In other words, the private network can be a factor in a multi-factor security scheme, but not the only factor to rely on. Speaking of multi-factor, more of this will be discussed in subsequent chapters. Most are familiar with multi factor authentication, but using multiple factors as a strategy can be applied to authorization as well.

Another issue that should be called out is that while it is relatively simple to prove that identity A is authorized to access a resource, it is not possible to prove the lack of such authorization. To take the private network as an example, where the network is the resource, identities are authorized to access. It is generally not possible to prove that the network cannot be accessed unless the app attempting the access acts as an authorized identity. Heuristics have been developed to deliver such proof. To mention a couple of those, one can test with randomly generated identities and expect not to have access, or penetration testing on the authorization logic can be done to prove the lack of authorization backdoors. Developers often create these for testing purposes and open later exploits.

Penetration testing, where code is examined by experts, is a great technique for discovering vulnerabilities and backdoors. Employing penetration testing must be encouraged. Having the code be open source is a form of such testing, as there will be many eyeballs on it, and backdoors are likely to be discovered by people across the globe reading the code. Code is hard to keep secret, so making it open source would be a good idea.

To conclude, if there is one most important takeaway from the discussion above is that the app cannot rely on the network for security services. It needs to do authentication and authorization using components under its control. The network protection can be a secondary defense, as explained in the *defense in depth* section. The overall picture is as follows:

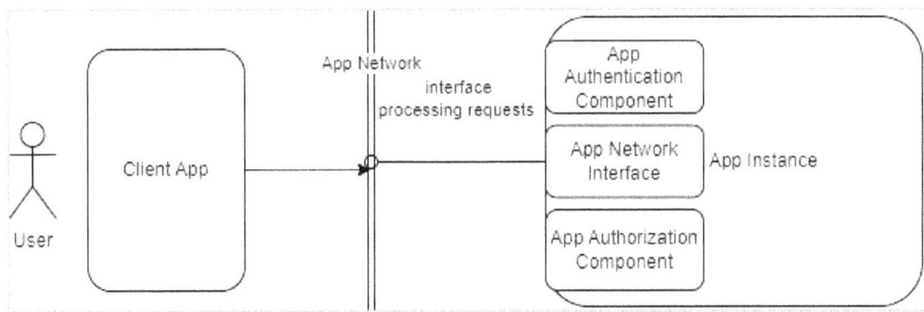

***Figure 3.31:** App with security components for authentication and authorization, as well as a network transport component*

It needs to be called out that no security function is outsourced to the network. Even if the network is hostile, app security should not be compromised. The app authentication and authorization components must be invoked on every request to perform needed duties. The network component would, generally, not know the identifier of the resource being accessed. For this to be the case, there needs to be a defined mapping of *resource name | network address*. The **REpresentational State Transfer** (**REST**) architectures are an attempt in this direction. It must be pointed out that, from an architectural point of view, coupling network names or addresses with app-specific resources is less than desirable.

It is natural to wonder why the authentication component can be included within the transport (network interface processing the incoming requests), but the authorization component cannot, or rather should not, be included. And the primary reason is that there are relatively few authentication protocols, where the resource variety and related authorization schemes are practically infinite. Naturally, it is much easier and within the realm of possibilities to integrate a few authentication protocol schemes compared to integrating authorization logic for generally unknown resource identifiers and policies. Unless a convention like REST is in use, the resource identifiers being accessed are unknown to the network interface component processing the incoming requests.

Exercises

Security is a feature that must resonate with customers. Understanding what customers care about most, and being able to see the potential impact on the ISV and customer business, determines what security features are needed.

The following questions are meant for the application product owner.

- Define the top 3 attack vectors your app must protect against and explain why. For example, it could be known attacks in the last 3 years that originated along those vectors. Knowing the vectors will help identify the approaches for mitigation. If the attacks are not infrastructure-based, then it may not be necessary to consider private clouds or other constructs aimed at protecting the infrastructure.
- What would be the approaches used? Private cloud, private networks, or confidential compute, and why?
- Do you need presence in areas or regions not covered by the cloud provider, and if so, how is this need addressed?
- Do you need a multi-cloud presence and why? Here, it is important to clearly articulate the reasons for using multi-cloud. For example, the maximum availability offered by cloud providers is 5 9s – meaning that 99.999% of the requests complete successfully, but app customers need 6 9s, and going multi-cloud would be a viable option to meet this need.
- What metrics should be used to evaluate the chosen strategy's success? For example, it may make sense to count detected breaches or consider finding them from penetration tests related to possible attacks that could materialize.
- Specify what compliance requirements, if any, are requested by customers (the dedicated host feature offered by Azure was driven by compliance requirements).

Join our Discord space

Join our Discord workspace for latest updates, offers, tech happenings around the world, new releases, and sessions with the authors:

https://discord.bpbonline.com

Chapter 4
Application Identities

Introduction

The notion of application identity helps consumers identify and trust the tools they are using daily. For example, users trust Microsoft Office, Gmail, and so on. These are **familiar names**, but there are also impostors pretending to be some app with a familiar name that has already obtained the user's trust. The main issue is about having easy-to-use tools that consumers can use to distinguish one application from another. Using names and logos will not do it, unless these are unique and authenticated items. Say the application store authenticates App1's name and does not let another application from the store use the same name.

For example, if an application says its name is **Outlook**, it would be great if the user could distinguish the **Outlook** app by Microsoft from the app with the name **Outlook**. Assuming any app can choose any name, the act of distinguishing by name will not be possible. The provider name could be included in the application name, think of **Microsoft/Outlook**, though that would lead to a similar problem as well as to a cognitive burden to consumers.

This is where application stores play a key role. These stores are usually associated with the device OS. There is an Android store maintained by Google, an iPhone Store by Apple, a Windows store by Microsoft, and so on. It could be argued that the downward pointing graph of Windows devices, see **https://gs.statcounter.com/os-market-share#monthly-201201-202411**, install base is caused to a large extent by the fact that most popular apps do not come from the Windows app store, but are installed from other locations, making it hard for the OS to assert the application identity.

No matter how many scary prompts users are presented with, warning that the application being installed can cause harm, these prompts will be considered as a part of the install experience and eventually ignored. The Windows experience for installing applications can be compared to the application install experience on Apple and Android platforms, where most major apps are sourced from the respective application store, and the user will go out of their normal experience to install an application from elsewhere. If we consider the inter-device communication between apps 1 and 2 (the same is true for cross-device), App1 wants to make sure it is talking to App2, and App2 needs to know that the client on the other side is App1. This is often referred to as **mutual authentication**. In any authentication arrangement, there needs to be a trusted authority to assert the participating identities. In the case of device-installed applications, this trusted authority is part of the device operating system. It is called **Local Security Authority** (**LSA**) on Windows devices.

The figure, illustrated in the *Applications in the Cloud* section, does not change much if we put app1 and app2 on different devices. There still needs to be a common security authority to assert app identities, and instead of relying on the local authority (same device), the authority service is moved to the network; the common authority is determined by association with the same public key.

Structure

In this chapter, we will learn the following topics:

- Application structure
- Names
- OAuth2 and OpenID Connect
- Role of OpenID Connect
- Applications on a blockchain dApps
- Azure applications
- Data partitioning patterns
- Implementing identity flows
- Putting it together in code

Objectives

The main objective is to provide a reference to architecture approaches for application authentication, or to put it another way, ways to make sure a block of code, constituting an application or an integral part of it, is used as intended. Common cases of misuse are having an application masquerade as another or having parts of an application being used by an unauthorized entity.

Application structure

Some of the application structure design patterns were presented in *Chapter 1, Introduction to Application and Cloud Security*. If we recall the figure shown in *Figure 1.3*, the app, installed on the user's device, fetches data from a cloud app. Showing the figure here again to provide context:

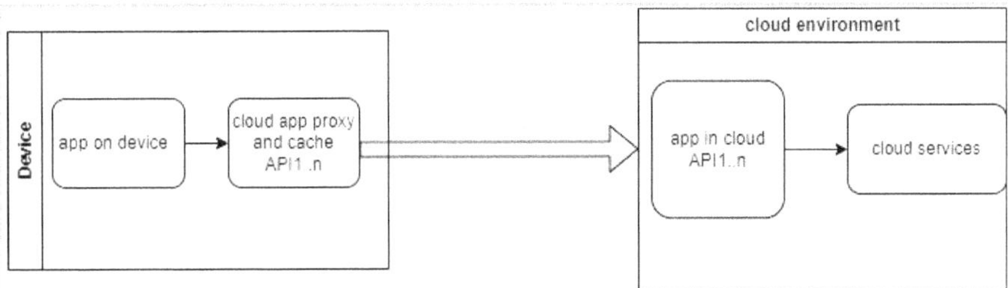

Figure 4.1: *Architecture showing cloud app and local cache*

Considering this, focus will be placed on application components on the device and in the cloud. When designing the application structure, an important concept would be whether the device and cloud parts should be treated as parts of the same application or different applications from the point of view of the **identity provider (IdP)** issuing the application identities.

Applications on devices

Applications installed on devices come from application stores connected to the device operating system. The process is shown in the following figure:

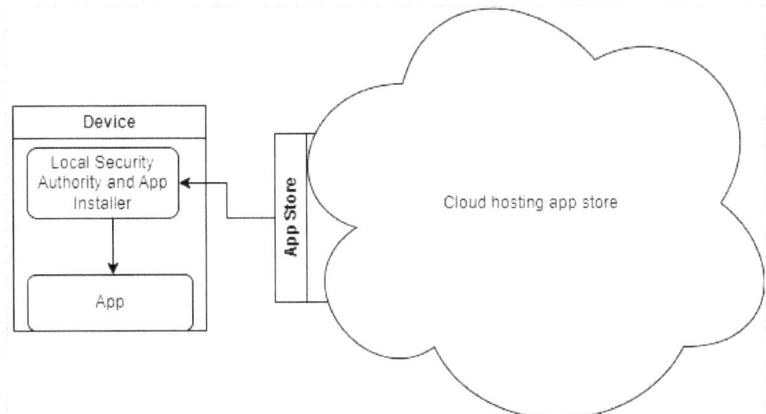

Figure 4.2: *Device app installed from device OS app store*

The most important aspect to note is that the integrity of the application is asserted by the application store, not by the owner of the device.

The identity of such a device-installed application is meaningful to other applications installed on the same device.

The process of asserting the application identity to other applications on the device is illustrated in the following figure:

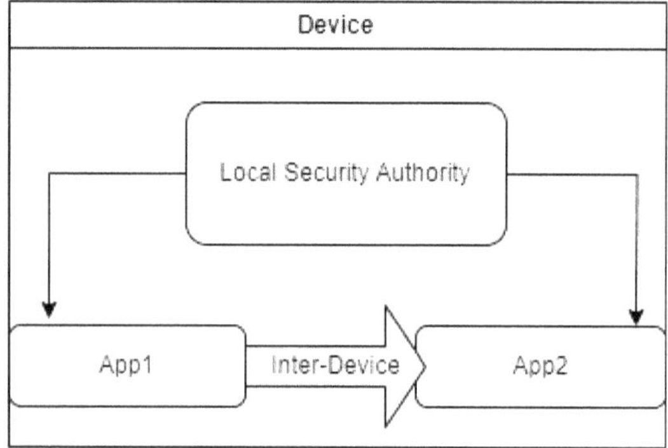

Figure 4.3: *App1 calling App2 on the same device*

Applications in the cloud

Clients trusting cloud applications can be other cloud applications or device applications. We should note that a network security authority (some call it NSA) asserts the identity of the called application.

The following figure illustrates the concept:

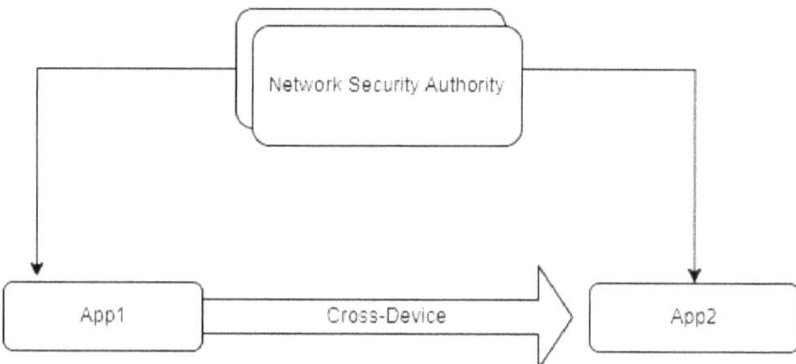

Figure 4.4: *App1 and App2 on different devices*

The main point here is that App1 and App2 need a common NSA to bootstrap the authentication between them.

While one can find pros and cons of either approach, namely using LSA or NSA to bootstrap the authentication process, having a fundamental position on the subject is useful. Having an LSA is not always possible. LSA implies that trust is based on location or some other property that is specific to the service, and cannot be (easily) faked, whereas in the NSA case, trust is key-based and the problem is reduced to that of key management.

It is the author's opinion that having different applications is a more flexible model, removing restrictions that could be placed on the application because of specifics found in some parts. As will be seen later in the chapter, the main issue with device applications is that there cannot exist a secret that allows these applications to authenticate themselves to cloud services. For the device pieces, there cannot be an assertion of the type **this is app X**. It can be **this is app X on device Y**. Since there can be a potentially very large number of devices (Y can have many values), the assertion **X on Y** is not very practical to consume. It is impossible to put meaningful semantics behind it. What could be useful? However, having assertions like **this is app X running on an Azure host**.

Note: **Y is being replaced by some distinguishing property (Azure host or other) that cloud apps can authorize on. Other options related to the entity (user) using the app are also very popular and will be examined in detail.**

A device application is depicted in the next figure:

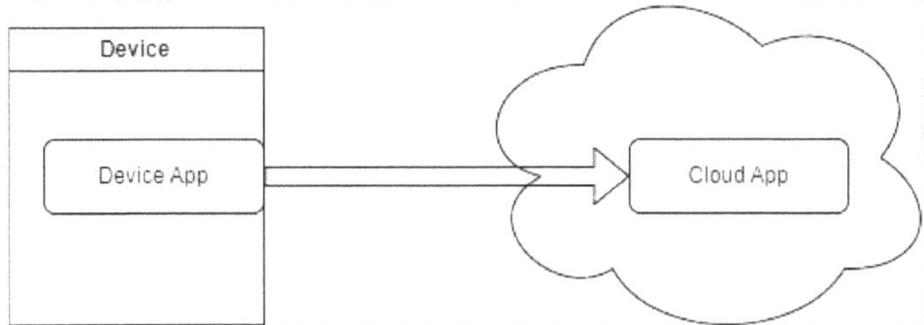

***Figure 4.5:** App on device talking to a cloud app*

If the app+device is not meaningful enough, then other options should be looked at. Historically, it has been user identities signing into the device apps and from there, to one or more cloud applications. Using the email application example introduced in *Chapter 1, Introduction to Application Security*, the cloud email app can be viewed as multi-tenant one, partitioned by user identifiers.

Partitioning an application on user identifiers is shown in the next figure:

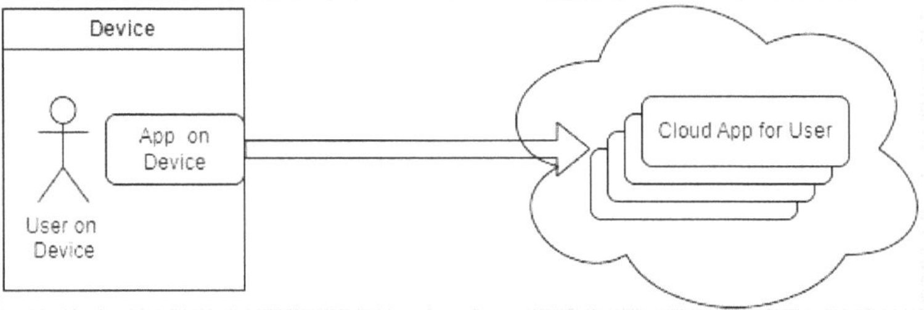

***Figure 4.6:** User+app on device calling into a cloud app*

It would be prudent to look into data and authorization logic in the cloud app. The identifiers from the authentication process can be used to derive resource identifiers and *must* be used to compute the effective access based on an authorization policy, resource identifier, and authenticated identifiers from the incoming request. While the authorization process and logic behind it will be examined deeply in the subsequent *Chapter 6, Authentication and Authorization*, here we will investigate aspects of authorization pertaining to application design, and the main decision to be made is whether the calling application needs to be authorized or the entity behind it. Taking it step by step, the following assertions can be made:

If the caller is an application on the user's device, the callee must authorize that the user using the application has access to the resource and that this access is delegated to the calling app.

The delegation requirement can be achieved using the OAuth2 protocol, see OAuth2 **Request for Comments (RFC) https://datatracker.ietf.org/doc/html/rfc6749,** which results in an access token containing the delegated permissions to the cloud app. Here is where mistakes can be made. The authorization process must first compute the direct permissions of the subject (user) and then intersect them with the delegated ones. For example, user A can consent (aka delegate) to app X to access user B's mail, but for this access to be authorized, user A must have the needed access to user B's email to start with. If the OAuth2 authorization is aware of the resource (user B's mail) authorization policy, then it should not allow user A to consent or delegate rights it does not have, but this is hardly the case in practice. The consent covers more coarse-grained permissions like **ReadMail**. This permission is coarse, meaning not specific, as it does not specify the actual mailbox to be read. The derived semantics can be read as the **user delegates her ReadMail to any resources to which the user has been granted these rights**.

As it was asserted earlier, if the requestor is a device app, the entity authorized is the user behind it. The component doing the authorization is the cloud app being called. Next, the state that would be examined is having the caller be another cloud app, as shown in the following:

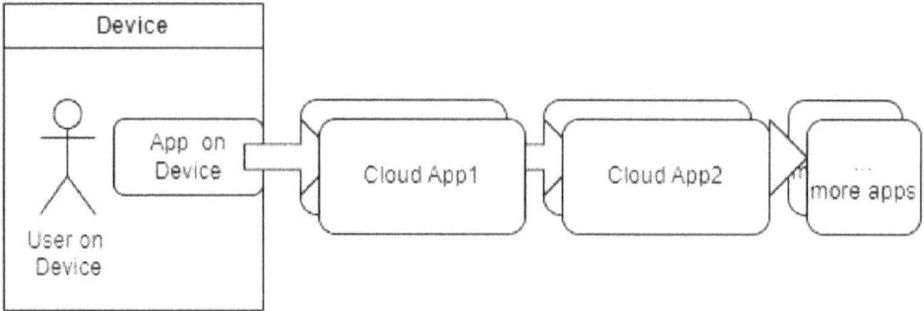

Figure 4.7: Multiple cloud apps

The choice presented to cloud app2, assuming all incoming identities are properly authenticated, if it should authorize app1 or the user on the device coming through app1. Both are viable options. Let us call out that if app1 (former case) is getting authorized, then app1's identity becomes a single point of failure. If app1 is compromised, so will the user data that app1 has access to. There is a subtle point here that needs some extra attention. This is the case of having an over-privileged app1, which has access to user data at app2 needed by other apps. App2 can tell that by analyzing authorization policies, though that is usually not the kind of analysis that is being done.

Note: **Expressing the assertion about the kind of authorization App1 needs to have, we can write as 'when App1 calls App2, it should only be authorized to access data it needs to satisfy the incoming user requests'.**

This is a way to express that App1 should not be overprivileged. This does not mean that App1's compromise cannot affect other apps.

Note: **For this to be true, we should assert that 'App1 should be authorized by App2 to access data that no other app can access'.**

This is easier said than done. The enforcement must be done by App2. A well-known approach is to designate a container (think folder) that each calling app is authorized to access. This does not always work, as there are valid use cases that require data to be shared among apps. As an example, consider a file system managed by App2. While we can assume the file system is dedicating a folder to each app using it, having shared files is a common practice.

It is suggested to use a simple rule formulated in the next paragraph. Alternatively, one can employ more complicated algorithms, but as the intent is to keep it simple, the assertion can be formulated this way.

If the service hosting the data (App2) is called by more than one client service, then it must authorize a single common entity interacting with the clients. This common entity is usually a user logging into the clients.

A user accessing data hosted by App2 through 2 apps named App1_1 and App1_2 is shown in the figure:

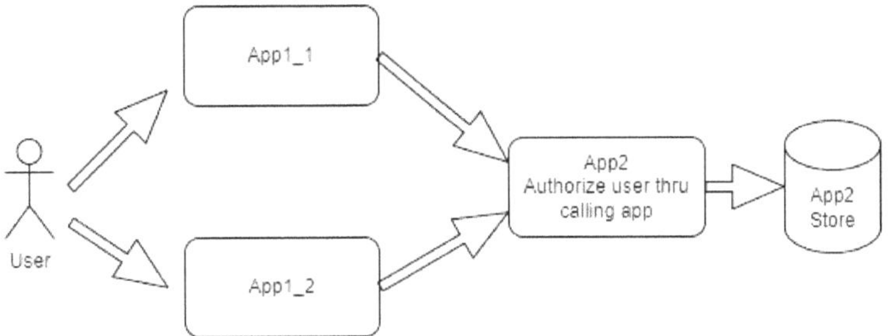

Figure 4.8: *Multiple clients calling App2*

It follows logically that if the App2 service accesses any data item only when called by a single client, then it may choose to authorize the calling application, instead of the entity (user). However, it would be hard to prove that only a single client is authorized, as there is no suitable proof to show how many identities (also known as security principals) are at App2. What is more, proof is needed that more than one entity cannot be authorized in the future. What we mean by that is that if App2_1 authorizes App1_1, there is no proof that other apps cannot be authorized. The point here is that even if one client is authorized now, there is a possibility that more clients will be authorized at some later point.

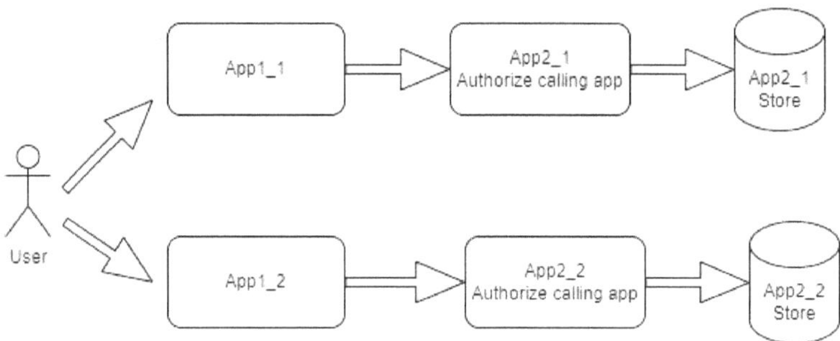

***Figure 4.9:** App2 dedicated to app1*

If we cannot easily prove that **dedication** exists, security issues may pop up later when someone decides to offer App2 services to multiple client apps. While doing so seems perfectly logical, the unexpected security implications remain hidden.

The best analogy from the operating systems world could be the concept of **containers**, where apps in the same container can be assumed to share resources that exist there. The reason that containers work on device operating systems is that there is some central authority to whom container and resource management is delegated. There is no such authority outside individual devices, let us call it the **networked world**, and it is generally hard, if not impossible, to say whether the two applications are in the same resource container or not.

Rules of thumb

To frame the discussion, consider the following figure:

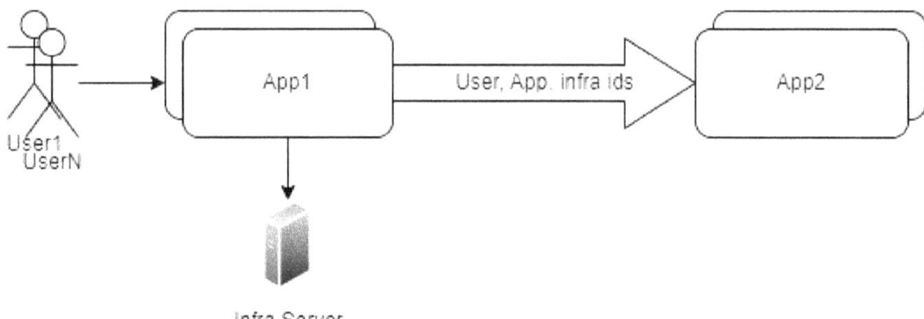

***Figure 4.10:** App1 calls App2 and passes on all known identities*

Some of the considerations presented in the previous section may sound complicated and hard to implement. To simplify, consider the following rules:

- **Rule #1:** App1 should communicate all authenticated identities to App2 in a way that is not spoofable in case App1's secret is compromised.

  What we mean by that is that, suppose user U calls into App1 and App1 calls App2 on behalf of U, communicating U's identity. If App1 is compromised, then App1 should **not** be able to call on behalf of U when U has not made a call to App1.

  Standards in the form of **Requests For Comments** (**RFCs**), in the context of OAuth2, have defined a **Token Exchange** protocol that would allow App1 to exchange an incoming token for a token destined for App2. This mechanism will meet the requirement of U's presence, as if U is not present, there will be no token containing U's identity to be exchanged. This exchange involves a network call to the entity doing the exchange, and such calls are undesirable from a performance and cost point of view.

  A major observation would be that App2 should trust the same IdP as the one asserting the identities incoming to App1. If the IdP is different, say IdP2, then App2 cannot see the identities asserted by IdP1.

  The needed IdP structure is shown in the following figure:

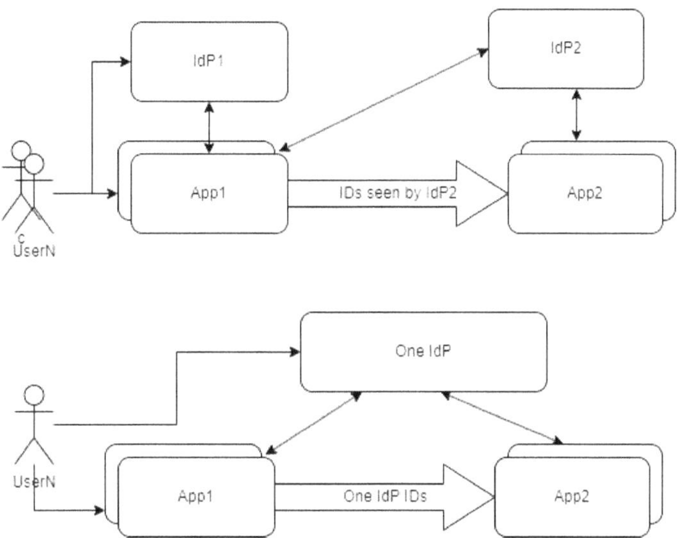

***Figure 4.11:** IdPs trusted by apps*

We can see that having a common OneIdp facilitates communicating identities between Apps using OneIdp. Big cloud providers, like Azure, discussed later in the chapter, do provide such a common IdP to apps that opt to use it. The catch (figuratively speaking) is that Apps must opt for using this common IdP. This may be an issue for Apps migrating to the cloud with their own IdP solution. Cloud IdPs make migrations easy by providing support for standard protocols likely to be used by the migrating app IdP solution.

- **Rule #2:** To simplify the decision making, App2 can authorize the identities incoming when asserted by the IdP; it trusts the labeled IdP2 in *Figure 4.11*. While trusting multiple IdPs is possible, the resulting complexity would be overwhelming. An additional benefit of only trusting IdP2 is having to deal with a consistent identifier format.
- **Rule #3:** The incoming identities must include a main identity called the **subject**. The subject could determine the name of the data resource accessed by App2. If it does, then the authorization system provides default **owner** rights to the subject.

  Although there is no rule provided to account for this, the **subject** entity could represent different physical entities, a user, an application, or some platform piece.

  An authorization implementation that takes the object type into account implicitly assumes that different object types, for example, applications and users asserted by the same provider, could have the same identifiers. Hence, the object type can be used as a distinguishing property, or the identifiers are used for different purposes based on the object type. For example, applications (**`objtype=app`**) could impersonate users, but other users cannot. Such assumptions are hard to justify and are bound to create a legacy that would be hard to change when the assumptions must change. So, it would be beneficial not to start with them. To put it straight, the object type should *not* be used for authorization, and should only be used with security identifiers. The term security identifier is explained in the next top-level heading. While objtype use in authorization policies may be counter-productive, using it in other contexts, like choosing authentication protocol flavor, would make sense. Authenticating an application would use a different protocol from that used for user authentication. The main consideration would be that application authentication is a non-interactive process, and while it could be tempting to introduce an interactive vs. non-interactive dichotomy, instead of dealing with objtype. Let us point out that authenticating the application and the platform piece it runs on are both non-interactive processes, but it would likely be a different non-interactive protocol authenticating the app than the one authenticating the platform piece server or some virtual abstraction the app is running on.

Protocols and libraries

Asking apps to implement standard protocols is a difficult task. It should be noted that protocols tend to evolve to address newly discovered issues, while the abstractions behind them tend to stay constant. It would be highly desirable to express these abstractions in library methods and objects without having to expose the actual protocols implementing them. Some important terms, like identity, are overloaded in the runtime of popular programming languages. For example, in Python, identity meanings are different from the identities we deal with in a security context. In security, identity refers to an entity with some rights defined in authorization policies, whereas in Python, identity is either a comparison operator, and to make this even more convoluted, a popular Python library defines identity matrix, see the link **https://numpy.org/doc/stable/reference/generated/numpy.identity.html.**

To disambiguate the identity semantics, we refer to the one defined for use in authorization, not the one used as a programming language construct or library function.

Using the term authentication avoids some of this ambiguity. Remember that authentication means asserting identities to someone who trusts the authentication provider.

Again, using Python as an example, authentication protocol implementation is available from the **AuthLib** library. A more generic version is shown in the following figure. Python syntax is then used to illustrate applications using the presented security authentication concepts.

The following figure shows an application using an HTTP server and client, HTTP being the most used transport:

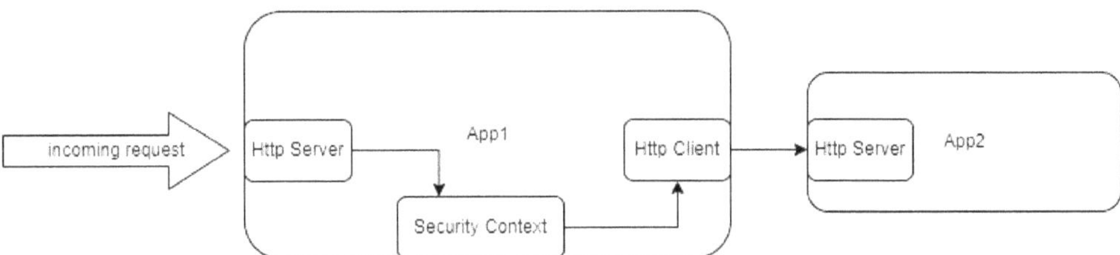

Figure 4.12: *Incoming and outgoing HTTP requests used by an app*

The components HTTP Server and HTTP Client are dependent on the language, libraries, and the platform used. The **security context** property may not always be available under this name. The important point is that there is a collection of authenticated identities that constitute a security context. For the incoming context, the one coming from HTTP Server, the identities need to be asserted by an authority trusted by App1, labeled as IdP1 in the previous figure depicted in *Figure 4.12.*

Some pseudo-code illustrating the flow is as follows:

```
// assume HttpServer is an existing object and HttpClient is a class that
can be instantiated
// using new operator and App2 Url
InComingHttpRequest IncomingRequest = HttpServer.GetRequest()
SecurityContext SecContextFromIncoming = IncomingRequest.
GetSecurityContext()

# instantiate an HttpClient object to send request to App2
HttpClient HttpClient = new HttpClient(App2.GetUrl() )
# get the request property of http client
```

```
# must be returned by reference, not copy
# as we are modifying it
OutgoingRequest OutgoingRequest = HttpClient.GetRequest()
# we want to impersonate the caller into the http server….
# the other option is to act as this app (app1) identity
OutgoingRequest.SetAuthenticationType(FromIncoming)
OutgoingRequest.SetSecurityContext(SecContextFromIncoming)
# … set other parameters needed in the outgoing request… then send it…
# …
```

This is a somewhat rough approximation for the logic in App1 used to call App2 and pass through the authenticated identities from the incoming request. The purpose here is to showcase passing through the security context. It is often the case that **`HttpClient`** and **`HttpServer`** objects are very different and owned by different teams, using different abstractions and so on. Above, it is demonstrated that both objects need to expose a **security context** as a property of their respective request objects. It is this common **security context** that allows the passing through of the incoming authenticated identities. An abstract **`SecurityContext`** class will look like the following:

```
# using python syntax
class SecurityContext(ABC):
      @abstractmethod
      def GetAuthenticationString(): …
      @abstractmethod
      def GetAuthenticationState(): …
…
```

This class is not found in common Python libraries. The issue of passing through the incoming identities has not yet been identified as something that needs a solution. The protocol support is there, but the **application program interface (API)** or object model implementation is not.

Names

Application is identified by consumers using some familiar names like **Outlook**, **Uber,** and so on, and one can choose their favorite app. The problem here is matching the name to the app instance that the user is interacting with. To see that, maybe, is obvious to most, but still worth calling out. If a name is managed by the underlying application entity, then it can choose any name for itself. It is like any application can claim to be **Outlook** or **Uber**.

If we are to trust the name or any other property identifying the application, it needs to be asserted by some trusted entity. On the device, this trusted entity is a core service (in Windows, it is called LSA) provided by the OS. The third service should be responsible for, among other things, enabling cross-process communication. The calling applications need to know they are calling into **Outlook,** and the applications that act as call recipients need to know who is calling, such as **Outlook**. We can take names as security identifiers if they are unique, immutable, and asserted by trusted entities. To put a stake in the ground for device applications, the identifiers would be unique within the device and be generated by the LSA.

Since this section is about names, it would be prudent to explain how names are correlated to identifiers. A name is an identifier, but not every identifier is a name. To be called a **security identifier,** the required properties are uniqueness and immutability. It can be assumed that the security authority is local or not; it ensures name uniqueness, along with some validation workflow, but then there is the question of immutability. This is hard to ensure, as most readable names need to be changed at some point; the most common reason would be a new branding effort that the application has to adhere to. To be clear, uniqueness and immutability are needed so the identifiers can be used in authorization policies. A simple proof is that, suppose identifiers used in the authorization policy are not unique or immutable. This would lead to inconsistent policies.

Non-unique identifiers

An identifier is associated with an item, let us call it an entity, within the IdP realm of supported objects, applications being one of those. If an identifier is not unique, then more than one entity is associated with it. An authorization policy binds an entity to roles, and the entity is identified by an identifier. If the same identifier is assigned to more than one entity, then it is ambiguous to determine which entity is assigned the rights in the authorization policy. To use an example, let us say that the identifier is the application's name, and each application can name itself, thus rendering the names non-unique, as uniqueness is not enforced. As a result, when granting access to an application named **Outlook**, it is unclear which application is referred to.

It should come as no surprise that uniqueness is a desired property when it comes to identifiers used in authorization policies.

Non-immutable identifiers

Mutability is a desired property for name identifiers. To put it simply, names must be able to change, as there are valid reasons for that. There is certainly a solution to handling name changes such that immutable identifiers are not required, but this is easier said than done. The resulting complexity is likely not acceptable to authorization systems, especially legacy ones. The issue is that within an authorization policy, identity identifiers are assigned rights (often packaged as roles) to resources, and if a mutable name identifier is assigned to a resource, then it is highly desirable that this resource can be accessible to entities using the new name. That may not be a big problem if there were a single or some fixed number of authorization policies that get notified when the name change occurs.

There could be an unbounded number of these policies. Yes, they could subscribe to some pub/sub service that broadcasts name changes, but that creates unwanted extra friction. Using immutable identifiers eliminates this friction and is a desirable property.

To illustrate the concepts presented, it is helpful to see an example authorization policy referring to application or other entity identifiers. More details on authorization policies will be presented in *Chapter 6, Authentication and Authorization.* The focus here is on identifier use.

An entity, such as an application, is referred to using an identifier. We can consider the identifier to be a property of the entity, and all references from other entities, in, say, policy documents, would use this identifier to refer to the entity in question. The closest analogy would be a pointer or reference to an object in a programming language. When referring to the object, we can use the reference, id1, in the following example:

```
Application store: entity->identifier (as example use id1)
```

```
Resource authorization policy: identifier (id1)->role(set of permissions)
```

If id1 changes to id2, an implementation can keep a record of the change, and all roles assigned to id1 are also assigned to id2. To make this possible, the authorization policy evaluation engine needs to consider the change record of the kind:

```
id1->id2
```

There are multiple possible implementations. It is of primary consideration to know if id1 is recycled and can be used by other entities or not. If yes, the new policy assignments for id1 must be distinguished from the existing ones.

If id1 is not reused, then it can be hardcoded in the application as an identifier to evaluate authorization. If it is reused, then there needs to be a computation producing the identifier for which authorization is to be computed.

As one can see, it is not hard to make security-related errors when implementing the rename logic. This is why it is highly preferable that the identifiers are immutable (can never change), so that such errors can be avoided.

For practical purposes, implementations use a level of indirection where names are mapped to immutable identifiers, which are then used in authorization policies and are carried in authentication artifacts. When the name changes, the mapping of the new name to the corresponding identifier is changed in one place.

A corollary is that unique names map to unique identifiers, which are assigned roles. The role of the identifier is to lessen the work that needs to be done by the authorization policy evaluator. The name, in string format, may not be unique and may require some additional processing to ensure uniqueness. Known methods are adding date and/or place of birth, or other characteristics known to the entity identified. Identifiers, on the other hand, are unique, which makes authorization processing less complex. Making the name unique has to be done only by the IdP, doing the mapping to a unique identifier:

```
Identity provider (IdP): name->identifier
Authorization policy: identifier->role
```

The mapping `name->`identifier is seen by the IdP only. It is stored in some identity store (often called a directory) accessed by the IdP during authentication. In Windows **Active Directory (AD),** these identifiers are called **Security IDentifier (SID).** In the cloud AD version, now called EntraID, the identifier format is a **Globally Unique Identifier (GUID)** residing in the **Object Identifier (ObjId)** property of the entity being authenticated.

To make things a bit more complex, applications have two unique identifiers, like **Application ID (AppID)** and ObjID. The former (AppID) identifies the application globally, across organizations. The latter (ObjID) is organization-specific. The same application, take Outlook for example, will have a different ObjID when installed in different organizations, but the AppID will remain the same. To illustrate, consider the app **outlook** and **outlook_<at_mycompany>**. The former maps logically to Outlook's AppId, while the latter is the ObjId of the **Outlook** installed at **<mycompany>.**

Cloud and device applications

Cloud applications can be seen as services running on a place other than the user's device, and we call this place the **cloud**.

To articulate a simple model, an application is either installed on one's device or not. If it is not installed, we will call it a **cloud application**.

The user interaction is always provided by a device application; the browser (Chrome, Edge, Safari, Opera, etc.) is the canonical device application.

The browser is the device application rendering the experience, though the actual experience content being rendered (html+jscript) comes from a server or cloud somewhere, rarely from the browser device, and when we refer to the device application, we usually refer to the html+jscript content rendered in browser, not to the browser itself.

In contrast, when content is rendered by some client app, other than a browser, then the application is the client app itself, even though the content could be the same as the one rendered by the browser, and the main reason for this distinction is that browsers are generic renderers where device applications aim to deliver specific user experience.

Public and confidential applications

This classification may sound similar to the previous section, cloud and device applications. It is true that device applications are usually public, and the cloud ones are confidential. Though the **Distributed Applications (dApps)** living on blockchains blur this distinction. For more details, see the *blockchain section.*

The most important application property determining whether it is public or confidential is its ability to hold a secret. Confidential applications can possess a secret, and public ones cannot. Secrets need to be placed in a secure location, which cannot be public, or the secret stops being a secret if it is in a public place. For practical purposes, secrets are handled by the underlying infrastructure. For example, applications running in the Azure cloud may use secrets stored in the Azure-provided infrastructure as Azure hosts.

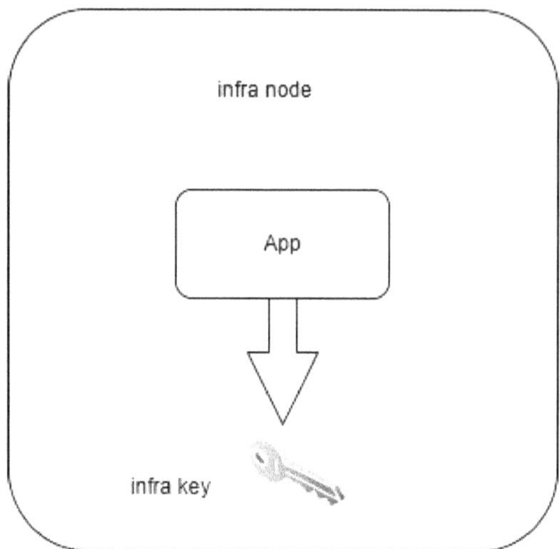

Figure 4.13: *Application secret managed by the infrastructure*

Corollary is that to be confidential, the application needs to run on infrastructure capable of managing secrets. Infrastructure offered by the cloud providers meets this requirement, but public blockchains do not. There can be no secrets on public blockchain nodes.

Role of certificates

To be specific, the focus is on `x509` encoded certificates. Encoding is not important for semantics, but since most available software expects `x509` certificate formats, you can use the following link: **https://www.itu.int/rec/T-REC-X.509**, and it will be assumed.

There can be multiple uses for x509 certificates. We will examine two use cases that pertain to application authentication**, Transport Level Security (TLS),** and code signing.

Before diving into these use cases, it would be prudent to provide a short description of the basic concepts behind the certificate ecosystem.

At its core, a certificate provides a mapping between a public key and one or more named properties. The mapping is endorsed by **a Certificate Authority** (**CA**) in the form of a signature validated using the CA's public key. This means that applications need to have a list of CA public keys available in order to do certificate validation. This list is usually maintained by the underlying platform, most often the OS. For example, on a Microsoft Windows device, one can launch **certmgr.msc** from the control panel to view configured **certificate authorities** (**CAs**).

The following figure presents an illustration:

- Certificates - Local Computer
  - Personal
  - Trusted Root Certification Authorities
    - Certificates
  - Enterprise Trust
  - Intermediate Certification Authorities
    - Certificate Revocation List
    - Certificates
  - Trusted Publishers
  - Untrusted Certificates
  - Third-Party Root Certification Authorities
  - Trusted People
  - Client Authentication Issuers
  - Preview Build Roots
  - Test Roots
  - AAD Token Issuer
  - eSIM Certification Authorities
  - Homegroup Machine Certificates
  - HpOneCertStore
  - Local NonRemovable Certificates
  - OEM eSIM Certification Authorities
  - Passpoint Trusted Roots
  - Certificate Enrollment Requests
  - Smart Card Trusted Roots
  - SMS
  - Trusted Packaged App Installation Authoritie

Issued To	Issued By	Expiration Date	Intended Purposes	Friendly Name
AAA Certificate Services	AAA Certificate Services	12/31/2028	Client Authentication, Code Signing, Encrypting File Syste...	Sectigo (AAA)
AddTrust External CA Root	AddTrust External CA Root	5/30/2020	Client Authentication, Code Signing, Encrypting File Syste...	Sectigo (AddTrust)
Baltimore CyberTrust Root	Baltimore CyberTrust Root	5/12/2025	Client Authentication, Code Signing, Secure Email, OCSP S...	DigiCert Baltimore ..
Certum CA	Certum CA	6/11/2027	Client Authentication, Code Signing, Secure Email, OCSP S...	Certum
Certum Trusted Network CA	Certum Trusted Network CA	12/31/2029	Client Authentication, Code Signing, Encrypting File Syste...	Certum Trusted Net.
Class 3 Public Primary Certificat...	Class 3 Public Primary Certificatio...	8/1/2028	Client Authentication, Code Signing, Secure Email, Server ...	VeriSign Class 3 Pu..
COMODO RSA Certification Au...	COMODO RSA Certification Auth...	1/18/2038	Client Authentication, Code Signing, Encrypting File Syste...	Sectigo (formerly C.
Copyright (c) 1997 Microsoft C...	Copyright (c) 1997 Microsoft Corp.	12/30/1999	Time Stamping	Microsoft Timesta...
DigiCert Assured ID Root CA	DigiCert Assured ID Root CA	11/9/2031	Client Authentication, Code Signing, Secure Email, Server ...	DigiCert
DigiCert CS RSA4096 Root G5	DigiCert CS RSA4096 Root G5	1/14/2046	Code Signing, Time Stamping	DigiCert CS RSA409.
DigiCert Global Root CA	DigiCert Global Root CA	11/9/2031	Client Authentication, Code Signing, Secure Email, Server ...	DigiCert
DigiCert Global Root G2	DigiCert Global Root G2	1/15/2038	<All>	<None>
DigiCert Global Root G2	DigiCert Global Root G2	1/15/2038	Client Authentication, Code Signing, Secure Email, Server ...	DigiCert Global Roo
DigiCert Global Root G3	DigiCert Global Root G3	1/15/2038	Client Authentication, Code Signing, Secure Email, Server ...	DigiCert Global Roo
DigiCert High Assurance EV Ro...	DigiCert High Assurance EV Root ...	11/9/2031	Client Authentication, Code Signing, Secure Email, Server ...	DigiCert
DigiCert Trusted Root G4	DigiCert Trusted Root G4	1/15/2038	Client Authentication, Code Signing, Secure Email, Server ...	DigiCert Trusted Ro.
DO_NOT_TRUST_FiddlerRoot	DO_NOT_TRUST_FiddlerRoot	7/6/2024	Server Authentication	<None>
DST Root CA X3	DST Root CA X3	9/30/2021	Client Authentication, Document Signing, Encrypting File ...	DST Root CA X3
Entrust Root Certification Auth...	Entrust Root Certification Authority	11/27/2026	Client Authentication, Code Signing, Encrypting File Syste...	Entrust
Entrust Root Certification Auth...	Entrust Root Certification Authori...	12/7/2030	Client Authentication, Code Signing, Encrypting File Syste...	Entrust.net
Entrust.net Certification Author...	Entrust.net Certification Authority...	7/24/2029	Client Authentication, Code Signing, Encrypting File Syste...	Entrust (2048)
GlobalSign	GlobalSign	3/18/2029	Client Authentication, Code Signing, Encrypting File Syste...	GlobalSign Root CA
GlobalSign	GlobalSign	12/9/2034	Client Authentication, Code Signing, Document Signing, E...	GlobalSign Root CA
GlobalSign Root CA	GlobalSign Root CA	1/28/2028	Client Authentication, Code Signing, Encrypting File Syste...	GlobalSign Root CA

Figure 4.14 (a): Root certificate authorities

The certificates shown represent root CAs. They sign intermediate authorities (intermediate CAs), shown in the next screenshot. The intermediate CAs sign individual certificates identifying applications or other entities. One can look at the certificate chain to see the full path. See the following example path in the figure:

Figure 4.14 (b): Certificate chain

A full list of intermediate authority certificates is shown in the following figure:

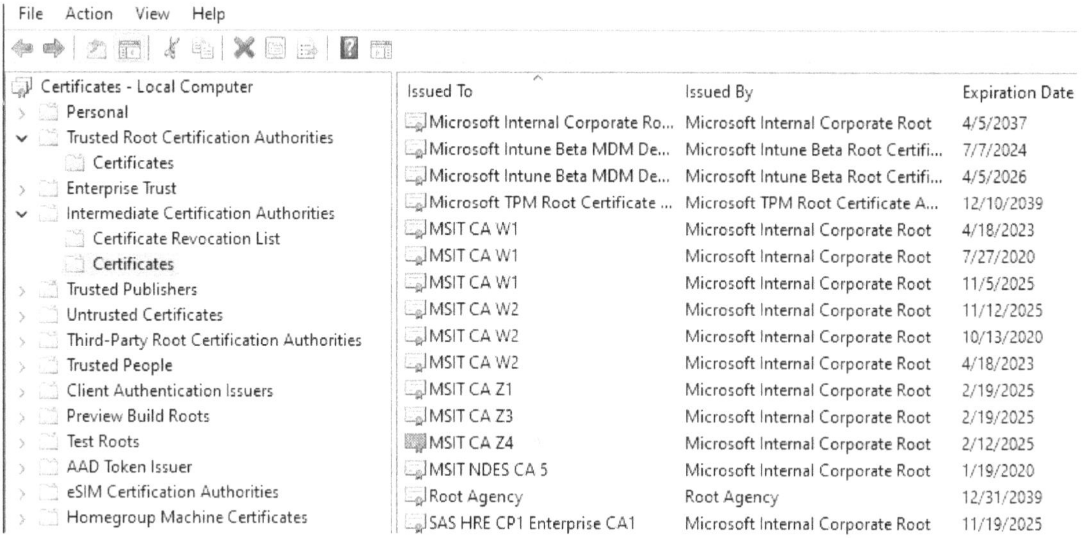

File Action View Help

Certificates - Local Computer
- Personal
- Trusted Root Certification Authorities
  - Certificates
- Enterprise Trust
- Intermediate Certification Authorities
  - Certificate Revocation List
  - Certificates
- Trusted Publishers
- Untrusted Certificates
- Third-Party Root Certification Authorities
- Trusted People
- Client Authentication Issuers
- Preview Build Roots
- Test Roots
- AAD Token Issuer
- eSIM Certification Authorities
- Homegroup Machine Certificates

Issued To	Issued By	Expiration Date
Microsoft Internal Corporate Ro...	Microsoft Internal Corporate Root	4/5/2037
Microsoft Intune Beta MDM De...	Microsoft Intune Beta Root Certifi...	7/7/2024
Microsoft Intune Beta MDM De...	Microsoft Intune Beta Root Certifi...	4/5/2026
Microsoft TPM Root Certificate ...	Microsoft TPM Root Certificate A...	12/10/2039
MSIT CA W1	Microsoft Internal Corporate Root	4/18/2023
MSIT CA W1	Microsoft Internal Corporate Root	7/27/2020
MSIT CA W1	Microsoft Internal Corporate Root	11/5/2025
MSIT CA W2	Microsoft Internal Corporate Root	11/12/2025
MSIT CA W2	Microsoft Internal Corporate Root	10/13/2020
MSIT CA W2	Microsoft Internal Corporate Root	4/18/2023
MSIT CA Z1	Microsoft Internal Corporate Root	2/19/2025
MSIT CA Z3	Microsoft Internal Corporate Root	2/19/2025
MSIT CA Z4	Microsoft Internal Corporate Root	2/12/2025
MSIT NDES CA 5	Microsoft Internal Corporate Root	1/19/2020
Root Agency	Root Agency	12/31/2039
SAS HRE CP1 Enterprise CA1	Microsoft Internal Corporate Root	11/19/2025

***Figure 4.15**: Intermediate CAs configured on a Windows device*

Shown above are both root and intermediate CAs configured on a Windows desktop. Leaf certificates, used for TLS (intended purpose is **server authentication**) and code signing, are issued or signed by the keys wrapped by the intermediate CAs, and the intermediate CAs are themselves signed by the keys from the root CA, thus creating the `chain Leaf->Intermediate->Root`.

Note: **Roots are the longest-lived, followed by the intermediate, then the leaf. The logic behind this is that roots are most secure and deserve to be long-lived. Additional considerations could be that having root certificates only sign intermediate CA certificates limits the number of signatures done with the root private key.**

It is delegated to the platform software vendor (Microsoft in this example) to maintain the list. The application can choose who to trust. Some applications, like Chrome browser (which will be discussed later), maintain their own list, but if the application has made the choice to run on a platform maintained by some software vendor (for example, Microsoft Windows), it may as well trust the platform to maintain a trusted CA list. There is a slight possibility that the platform does not have vulnerabilities other than those related to maintaining the trusted list, and while theoretically possible, it is not a real practical possibility. Platforms or OSs do have security issues, and the software maintaining a CA list may possibly have one of these, but it can hardly be the only possible security issue in the OS.

As mentioned earlier few major applications, like Google's Chrome, maintain their own list that is slightly different than the one maintained by the underlying OS (Windows in this case). To illustrate, see root and intermediate CAs used by Chrome on the same Windows desktop:

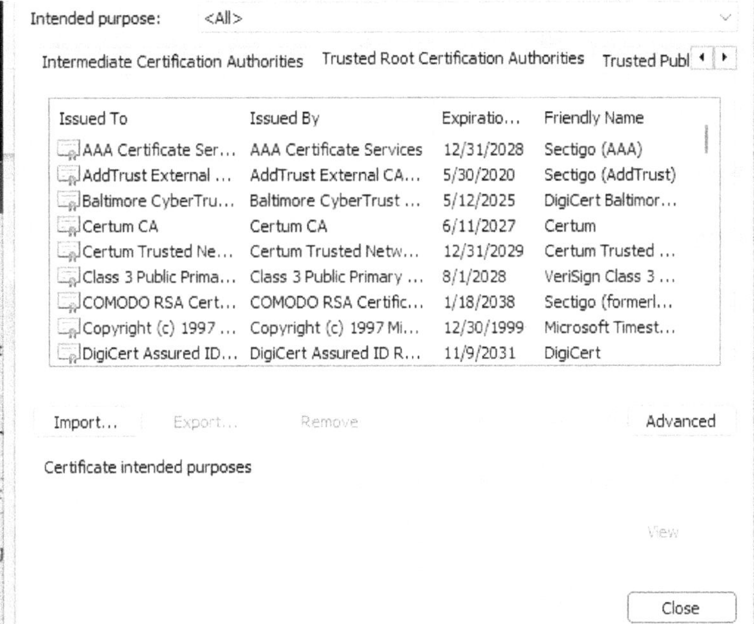

Figure 4.16: Root CAs in Chrome

The following and above figures show Google's Chrome browser view of CAs. While the model is the same as the one adopted by the underlying Windows operating system, meaning that both root and intermediate CAs are used in the content, it is slightly different in both configurations.

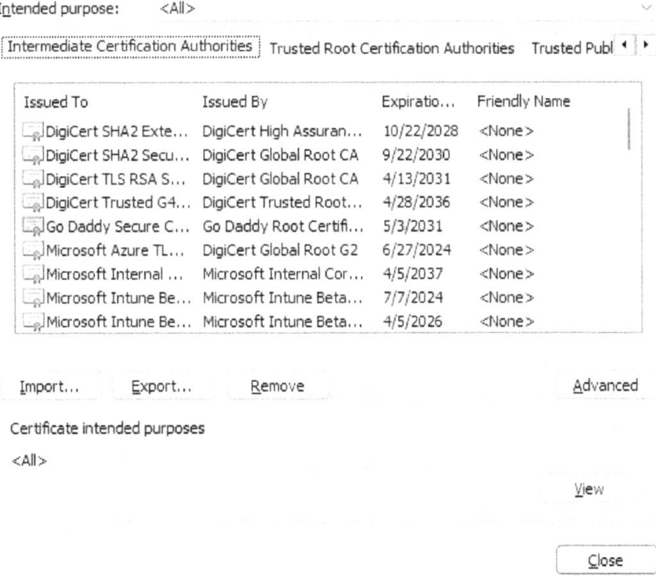

***Figure 4.17**: Intermediate CAs used by Chrome*

One can notice that the intermediate Chrome CAs are indeed slightly different from the Windows ones. Chrome may filter CAs differently from Windows. There are still root and intermediate CAs with the same semantics.

The Chrome-specific configuration illustrates that applications, especially major ones like the Chrome browser, can choose to trust CAs that are different than those configured by the OS vendor. The bigger point is that CAs constitute a central authority trusted by the application through the OS or not. There is a chain of trust that involves the entity maintaining the list. If somehow compromised, the successful attacker can replace the list with one of their choice, thus compromising the **Public Key Infrastructure (PKI)** ecosystem on the device that involves all applications that trust the CAs on the list.

Transport Level Security

Formerly known as SSL, a TLS certificate can be related to the server, a client, or both. This is also sometimes referred to as server authentication and client authentication. Server authentication is the cornerstone of TLS. There are a couple of assertions that TLS provides and should be called out as follows:

- The server certificate authenticates the service the client is talking to. For example, if the client talks to a service behind the URL **https://someservice.com/.../someapi**, the server certificate authenticates the name **someservice.com**. The certificate provides a mapping between the name **someservice.com** and a public key. The corresponding private key, or rather crypto functions based on it, is made accessible to the service behind the **someservice.com** domain name. It ensures that the service is the rightful owner of the certificate, asserting its name to clients.

  There is some name conflation going on here. Specifically, the network domain name someservice.com is conflated with the service name. One can imagine that the service, say named **someservice**, may need to run on an arbitrary network, which would be hard to accomplish if the service name is correlated with the network name, but then, it could also be argued that the name someservice.com identifies the service, not the network. Then we must assume that the **domain name service (DNS)** provides a service `name->network` address mapping. DNS calls the service name **a domain**, hence the name DNS.

  As it is the case in the physical world, or rather the old physical world, the address is semantically associated to the service behind. As an example, *Google search* is behind *google.com* address and the names Google (service name) and google.com (domain name translated to a network address by DNS and are often used interchangeably to mean the same thing.

  Securing the channel using TLS is shown in the figure:

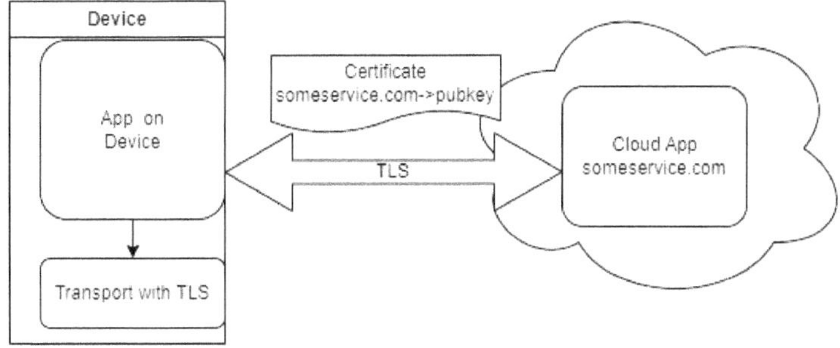

Figure 4.18: *Certificate authenticating a network service*

As it is shown above, the certificate presented by the cloud application has the application name to the public key mapping. Note that the application name **someservice.com** is conflated with the network name where the application is deployed, in the real world.

- Someone listening on the network cannot see or modify the data exchanged between the client and the service. This is often referred to as providing **confidentiality and integrity** of the exchange. To take this concept a bit further, there is a property of the TLS protocol called **Perfect Forward Secrecy (PFS).** It ensures that even if someone, at some point, gets the private key corresponding to the certificate wrapped public key in the certificate, they still cannot decrypt the messages exchanged over the encrypted channel. While this is a great property to have, it comes at a cost that many would find unacceptable: an extra network round-trip. This extra cost is paid on every new connection boasting the PFS property. And it needs to be balanced against the potential benefits of having it.

Code signing

While TLS uses the certificate-wrapped key to secure client or server communication channels, code signing uses the key to assert application authenticity via the publisher.

A code signing example is shown in the figure:

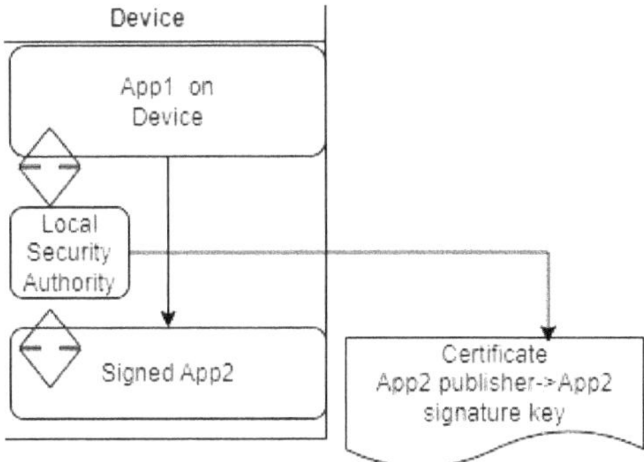

Figure 4.19: *Local security authority validates signed application*

In this context, it should be clear that certificates authenticate remote (or network) applications using the TLS protocol and local (or device) applications using code signing. It is also different entities doing the validation. For validating the remote application, the transport (using TLS) validates the server certificate. Validation is performed using the public keys of configured CAs. It should be fair to state that the entity in charge of maintaining the list of CA public keys, which can also be in the form of self-signed certificates, constitutes the root of trust. There can be multiple roots, maintaining different CA lists used by different transport implementations.

The same cannot be said, or rather cannot be said with the same conviction, about the process of validating code signatures. The difference with validating TLS certificates is that while an application can choose a transport to communicate over the network, it is the prerogative of the operating system to run applications and optionally validate application signatures. In contrast, this distinction may seem to be superfluous, as anyone could provide an app that runs other apps and thus be responsible for validating these other apps' signatures. It is very much relevant to ensuring the security of a platform, as running apps not using platform capabilities is considered to constitute an intentional bypass of platform-provided security features.

OAuth2 and OpenID Connect

These standards emerged in the last 10 to 20 years. The OAuth2 RFC was published in 2012, and it is important to call out that similar efforts have preceded it. OAuth2 came first as an authorization framework enabling delegated acçess where the application can act on the user's behalf. As it results in access tokens being given to the client application, people often refer to this pattern as token-based authorization.

The term token needs a definition. For example, *A token is a short-lived document carrying claims about the presenter and optionally about the rights the presenter has at the resource. These claims can be about the presenter's identity as well as about the presenter's authorization rights.*

Not to overcomplicate the definition, but there are a few more important details worth mentioning outside of it. All these pertain to security in the context of protecting against misuse of tokens. In the *Role of certificates* section, it is explained that the TLS protocol is well accepted and scrutinized, and can be considered secure. After all, the internet stands on it. Taking it a step further, a claim can be made that:

The token economy rests on TLS.

As a mental exercise, if we remove TLS from the environment, then using tokens as we do now will not be a feasible option. However, it should be reasonable to assume that TLS and associated certificates will stand the test of time, and if so, taking a dependency on TLS omnipresence is a defendable decision. A reasonable assumption should be that TLS is everywhere and can always be available.

While it is true that the token protocols can implement TLS-like functionality, the fact is that they have not. Considering that TLS is widely available, it is more practical to layer tokens on top of TLS instead of trying to re-implement what already exists. Also, consider that it took many years to weed out security issues of TLS implementation. Some issues are likely to surface when implementing similar concepts, and it is reasonable to expect to use some time to fix those.

To summarize, tokens are layered on top of TLS, and TLS provides needed message authentication, integrity, and confidentiality. In practical terms, when a client talks to **https://someservice.com/**, it is TLS that validates that the service on the other end presents a certificate matching the name. While we can say that a certificate can be viewed as a token for client authentication, the major difference is that clients can have one certificate to present to many services, where a distinct token would be required for each service the client authenticates to.

Role of OpenID Connect

While OAuth2 is considered an **authorization framework**, OpenID Connect is for authentication, defining how the identities are communicated to applications using tokens. In this context, the standard defines the ID token format. More details about ID tokens are provided in OpenID Connect specification as well as the next heading named ID tokens. One of the most important takeaways from the security point of view is that the OAuth2 access tokens and OpenID Connect ID tokens are intended to be consumed by an application identified in the token audience property, called **aud,** in **JSON Web Tokens** (**JWT**) formats. The audience must match the receiving application name or some value derived deterministically from the name, for example, appid, when there is a unique app `name->appid` mapping. The intent is that if the receiving application is somehow compromised, it should not be able to replay the received tokens to other applications, because if it could, the identities and permissions contained in the tokens would also be compromised, spreading the compromise to calling clients.

ID tokens

The name ID token is short for identity token. ID tokens essential identity properties refer to **https://openid.net/specs/openid-connect-core-1_0.html** for further details.

To summarize, an ID token is meant to deliver an identity identifier to an application. The encoding is the popular JSON format, and the tokens are referred to as **JWT, JSON Web Token**.

Access tokens in OAuth2

Access token could be viewed as an extension to id tokens, though historically speaking, the term access token came first. Access tokens are opaque to the client application and, in theory, do not need to be JWTs. Access to the token sent to a service is examined using the token introspection API defined in **rfc7662 http://tools.ietf.org/html/rfc7662**.

Looking at the claims defined in the output of the retrospection API, one can notice that the semantics overlap almost entirely with ID token claims, with the addition of the **scp** scopes claim, which has authorization semantics that define the rights the subject has delegated to the client application. More on this will be discussed in *Chapter 6, Authentication and Authorization.*

Applications on a blockchain dApps

To frame the discussion, the **ETH network (Etherium)** will be the focus when describing dApps. ETH is where most dApps are deployed. There are other networks as well, and it should be said that the concepts presented do not change. The principles stated are valid in all networks.

Blockchain applications

Unless stated otherwise explicitly, the blockchains will be assumed to be public in the sense that blockchain nodes can be run by anyone. This is true for the ETH network, as well as many others. As stated previously, ETH would be used as an example to demonstrate dApp properties.

These properties are:

- A dApp is identified by the fingerprint or hash of its bytecode executed by the blockchain virtual machine, known as Etherium Virtual Machine or EVM for short, describing the virtual machine on Etherium network compute nodes.
- The dApp does not have a secret. EVM plays the role of local security authority, asserting the dApp's identity to other dApps or external entities interacting with the dApp. There is a difference between asserting dApp identity to another dApp and convincing an external entity about dApp identity. In either case, it is the EVM playing the role of a trusted entity. It is either a local security authority or, a network authority trusted by the external entity. The assertion conveyed is **you are talking to dApp X**.

  More details about dApps on the ETH network can be found on the Etherium documents site **https://ethereum.org/en/developers/docs/dapps/**

To summarize, from a security and identity point of view, the dApp identity is asserted by the security authority within the EVM. In the section titled *dApp identity*, we look at a dApp identity from the client and service points of view.

The semantics of the dApp address need some discussion. While a **regular** app address is a URL with a distinct **domain name service (DNS)** name, for example, **https://someservice.com**, the dApp address is relative to the underlying blockchain network, where the dApp is deployed. There are **bridges** that connect dApps on one network to those on another. A dApp on the Etherium network has an address that can be expressed as `ETH\<dApp`

`bytecode hash>`, which is hard to visualize. The hash is a long string of hexadecimal, or base64, characters, making it hard to refer to or use. That is why most client applications present the dApps using some human-readable name and a logo. The same can be said about **regular** app addresses. Even though DNS names like *someservice.com* are considered by some to be usable, most would prefer to tap a familiar icon on their phone device and not enter a DNS name. Someone must **`do picture->app`** address mapping, which should be the same experience regardless of the underlying app address format. To simplify the procedure, we could assume the address is a URL that is not suitable for humans to type in. With the URL remaining hidden, users would be asked to tap on an icon to execute an app, which is the same experience regardless of the app type.

To illustrate, we will look at Chrome extensions representing dApp clients. The following figure shows the results returned when searching for extensions using the **web3** keyword:

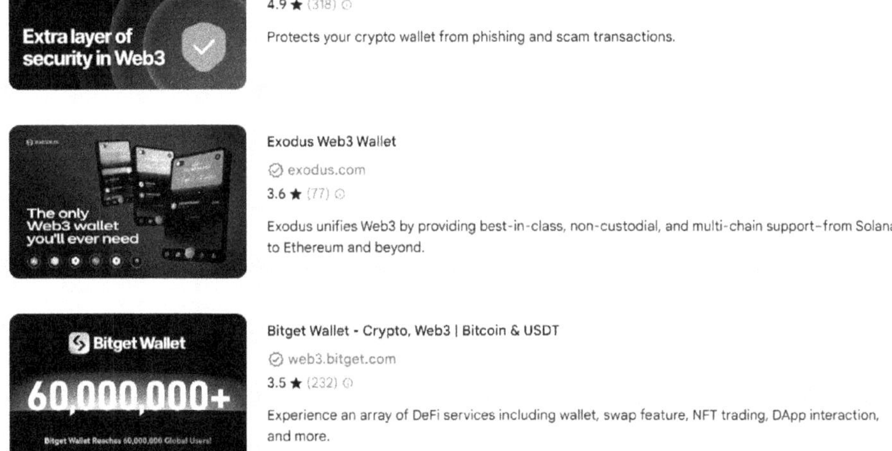

***Figure 4.20:** Chrome clients communicating with Web3 applications, dApps*

Like experiences offered by other device applications, the cloud, Web3, or dApp is not visible to the end user; only the device app is. The Web3 address or URL, while not usable by humans, is perfectly fine to be configured within the device client app. If we trust the device app and the device app trusts the cloud app, or dApp owns the address, then we have a complete trust chain.

Interactions are user to device app, device app to dApp1, and optionally dApp1 to dApp2, and then dApp2 to other dApps, etc., only the first interaction is visible. The integrity of the rest of the interaction depends on the client being able to validate the called app's identity. Blockchains and dApps, respectively, achieve client validation by passing signed transactions down the chain of calls, and by design, replaying the transaction back to the caller does not constitute a problem. This is different than just passing an identity where transaction modification is allowed. For example, let us say the transaction states that A sends to B X tokens. This transaction is safe to replay. An attacker cannot change A, B, X, or the transaction identifier used to eliminate duplicates.

These interactions are shown in the following figure:

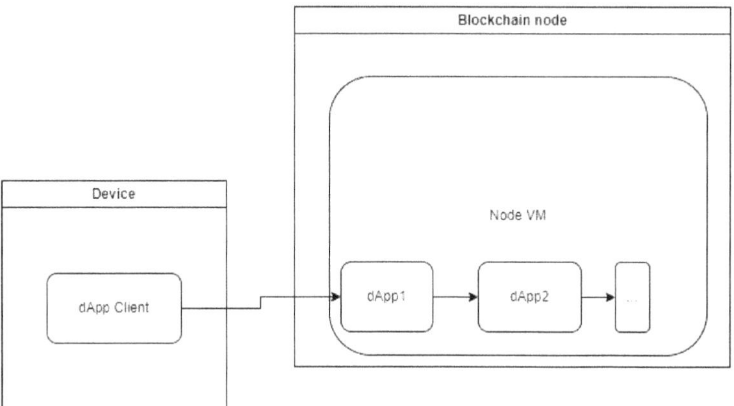

Figure 4.21: *App call-chain*

dApp identity

This chapter is about application identities. In **classic** environments, an application is either installed on a device owned by some individual referred to as a **user** or it is installed in the cloud and runs on compute nodes owned by a cloud provider. Blockchains introduce a new type of environment. Applications on the blockchain run on compute nodes that belong to the blockchain network, not by some cloud provider. Such a setup has elements of both device and cloud-installed applications.

Client dApp identity

The ETH implementation of client dApp identity, let us label it as dAppID, can be succinctly described as **`<fingerprint of dApp bytecode>`**. When dApp1 is calling dApp2, the identity seen by dApp2 is dApp1ID.

The assertion dApp2 gets is **dApp with dApp1ID is making the request**. dApp1 may or may not pass through the signed transaction it gets from the client app. This depends on the semantics of the call. If the call does not use any of the transaction properties, then passing the transaction is not necessary.

Service dApp identity

Service identity semantics is the opposite of the client identity described in the client dApp identity heading. dApp1 gets dApp2ID, where dApp2 is the request target. In other words, dApp1 needs to be convinced that it talks to dApp2. It can be important to have such assurance, as it allows dApp1 to trust the results it gets back from the call. For example, if the call is about getting a quote on the exchange rate, having the wrong value returned would be disastrous. If dApp2 can be trusted, the same applies to the responses it gives back.

The following are the advantages and disadvantages of using fingerprints as a distributed application identity:

- **Advantages:**
  - Simplicity
  - Client safety
- **Disadvantage:**
  - App updates are not supported

Explanation: An obvious advantage is the simplicity of the model. It is easy to implement and maintain. There is no need to manage and protect secret keys, and computing a hash is a straightforward task.

Another advantage is the creation of client safety, and by that, it is meant to express that:

- If a client calls into some dApp, keeping the dApp behavior, even if it may appear incorrect, immutable, makes the client's behavior predictable.
- We want to avoid situations where clients start breaking after an update is pushed to the service the apps call into, even if the update is needed to fix bugs or known problems. To illustrate, consider a client sending request X, getting a response Y, handling it successfully, and providing some reasonable user experience based on it. If the API starts returning Y instead of Y, the resulting user experience may not be acceptable.
- Each update results in a new app fingerprint, and clients need to change to call into the new service app version.

A harsh downside is creating a big hurdle in updating the app and preserving its identity. This is the same feature, called out as an upside above, but this time it is viewed as a downside. All apps need bug fixes and new features, which necessitate app changes. and having all clients change to call into the new service app version is a tall order and often presents an unrealistic expectation.

For example, consider the service app that exposes an API with semantics Add2and2. The API, for some reason, is implemented incorrectly and returns the wrong result, such as 5. It would be desirable to be able to fix the API without having to introduce a new version, call it Add2and2Fixed, and ask all clients to change and start calling the new version. It would be impossible to remove the old, buggy API, as doing so would break the clients that did not make the change.

One can point to cases where either behavior is needed. Eliminating the possibility of changing existing apps takes away some flexibility. Ideally, the app developer should decide if a change warrants having a new app version or not. Yes, developers will make mistakes if updates are allowed, then these mistakes would lead to breaking clients, but this could be an acceptable price to pay, depending on who we ask. In the dApp architecture, such mistakes would not be possible as changes are not allowed.

Azure applications

Azure applications are the ones running in the Azure cloud. Azure relies on EntraID **identity provider** (**IdP**) for authentication of its resources. Strictly speaking, the application identity could be asserted by any IdP, not only EntraID, but using EntraID has many benefits stemming from the same IdP authenticating users, applications, and infrastructure components; therefore, it is highly recommended.

One can register an application to represent a software service vendor, also known as an ISV. Certain applications, some shown in *Figure 4.22*, are offered to all Azure customers.

These are the applications advertised on the Azure portal at **https://portal.azure.com/#view/Microsoft_AAD_IAM/AppGalleryBladeV2**. Any Azure customer can add an application that can be used by other customers, but it will not be visible to them unless shown by the portal.

See a list of advertised applications in the figure shown in the following:

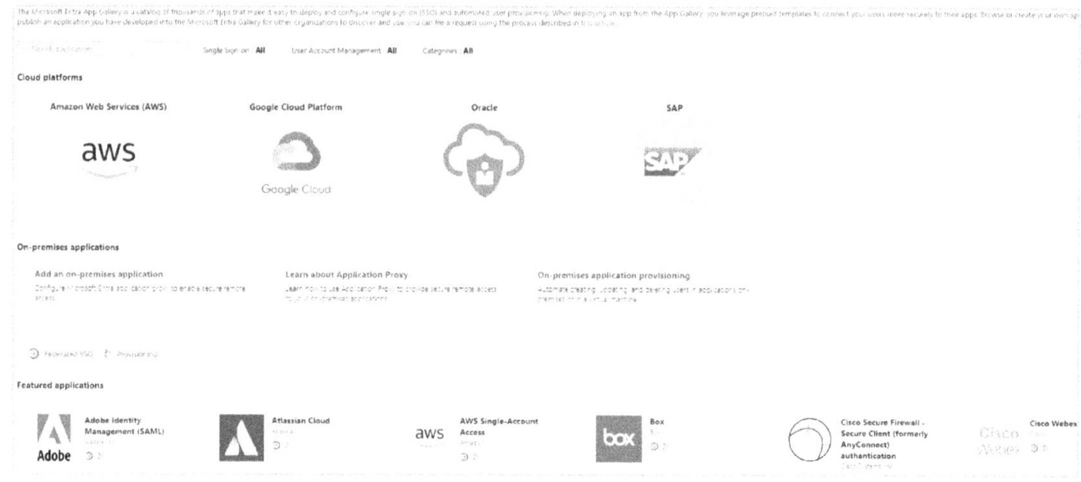

Figure 4.22: Choosing an application to register

There are many applications available in the app gallery. To use one, it has to be registered in the tenant directory. More on the tenancy model in the following section, *Application tenancy*.

If the customer has their own app or one not available in the app gallery, it can be registered as well. The experience is shown in the following:

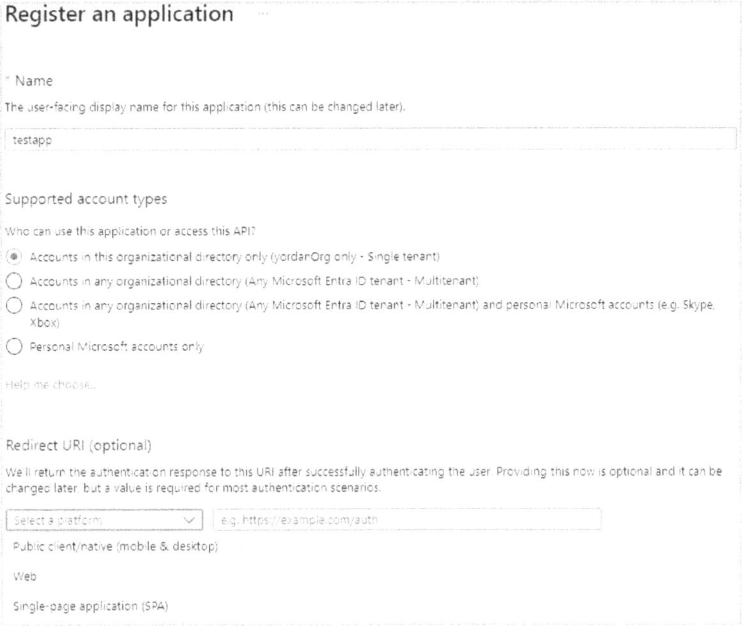

Register an application

* Name

The user-facing display name for this application (this can be changed later).

testapp

Supported account types

Who can use this application or access this API?

Accounts in this organizational directory only (yordanOrg only - Single tenant)

Accounts in any organizational directory (Any Microsoft Entra ID tenant - Multitenant)

Accounts in any organizational directory (Any Microsoft Entra ID tenant - Multitenant) and personal Microsoft accounts (e.g. Skype, Xbox)

Personal Microsoft accounts only

Help me choose...

Redirect URI (optional)

We'll return the authentication response to this URI after successfully authenticating the user. Providing this now is optional and it can be changed later, but a value is required for most authentication scenarios.

Select a platform | e.g. https://example.com/auth

Public client/native (mobile & desktop)

Web

Single-page application (SPA)

Figure 4.23: *Registering a custom application*

A few words on the application multi-tenancy property: an application is labeled as multi-tenant if the owner registers it in their own directory, and customers have the option to install it. The owner registers a single-tenant application if it is meant for a single customer.

The applications shown in *Figure 4.22* are all multi-tenant.

Application tenancy

There is the point of registering an application and instantiating it. For single-tenant apps, both actions occur in the same directory tenant. Multi-tenant apps are registered with the tenant of the app owner and instantiated with the customer tenant.

Focusing on the tenant term, a tenant represents a slice of an application dedicated to a specific customer. Analogously, a directory tenant is a directory dedicated to a customer, who is typically an organization. While there is a strong desire that application and directory tenants are aligned, this is not always the case in practice.

For example, there is an organization called **foo,** and multiple departments within the organization use an application called **bar**. The organization **foo** makes one tenant in the directory, and each department using **bar** makes one application tenant within **bar**. This is a prime example of directory and application tenants being misaligned. Azure forces the application tenant to be the same as the directory tenant, which in practice would mean all departments using a single **bar** and having to use some other way to disambiguate department-specific data.

The alternative would be for each department to be treated as a separate organization with its own directory tenant. While possible, such an approach is rather heavyweight as it creates the burden of multiple tenant management and makes it more difficult to manage inter-department relationships.

First party applications

The term **first party** is often used to describe some application property or behavior. For example, a Microsoft application should not be presenting a consent screen when acquiring a token to access another Microsoft application, which brought in the term **first party**. Attempting to provide a generic definition, it could be as follows:

- **The application has a property marking it as first party:** This is actually the case.
- **The application publisher is the same as the directory owner:** This is also true, though there is no such property (publisher) that can be checked.
- **The application is registered in a tenant owned by a specific entity:** While this may also be true, it also forces some restrictions on how and where the application is registered. The entity owning the tenant is also unclear. One way to untangle is to use registered domain names on the tenant object. For example, if a tenant registered domains contain names in some set, the application would be considered first party.
- **We can look at client and server applications owners:** If AppA requests a token for AppB, and AppA and AppB are registered in the same tenant, then AppA will behave like the first-party application. This is probably the most flexible model as it allows AppA to behave as a first party or not, depending on AppB. It also removes the consideration of specific owners when deciding if the application should behave as a first party or not. It is desirable to offer some first-party application behaviors, like not showing consent to all applications.

As it is shown above, the term **first party** is overloaded and could potentially have a different definition depending on context. The book will not define what the **first party** should or should not mean.

Data partitioning patterns

This is an important and often controversial topic. Partitioning techniques, sometimes called names like sharding, aim at reducing the storage capacity needed. To use an example, if there are a total of N objects and the current query can be made over N1, which is much lower than N, then the maximum storage capacity needed can be reduced to N1. There will be N partitions, let us label them p1 and pn, and each will hold roughly N and N1 objects. The challenge will be having a function that maps the query parameters to a partition number. Again, using an example, if the records contain user object properties, then the mapping function should map a property, say user name, to a partition number, and the query will be executed in the data store on this partition.

The patterns examined will be based on users, applications, and organization identifiers. This is a one-dimensional approach as there is a single property defining the partitioning axis. It should also be noted that partitioning is not always possible. A simple argument, if there is a query that can affect any two records in a table, then it is not possible to partition the table on any property. For example, in a blockchain architecture, anyone can send tokens to anyone else, and since records representing token owners are the building blocks of the blockchain store, it is not possible to partition these records since any two can be affected by a transaction.

Partitioning on users

Refer to the following figure for illustration:

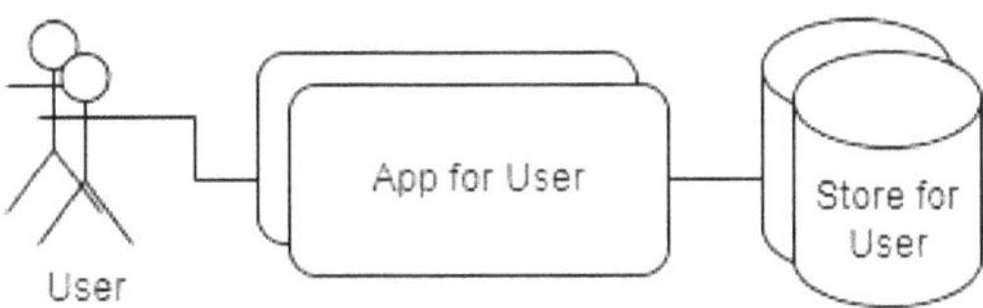

Figure 4.24: *Partitioning on users*

Each record in the store represents a user object. Given a user property, such as a user name, it is possible to compute the partition identifier where the user record is stored. This is a very common pattern, as most applications deal with user records. As it was shown earlier in the *Rule of thumbs* section, it is close to impossible, or rather very error prone, to ensure that there is no shared user data among applications, and that is why the recommendation would be to do authorization on authenticated user identities.

Partitioning on applications

App-based partitioning is illustrated in the following figure. The idea here is that storage belongs to the application, not to the user behind it:

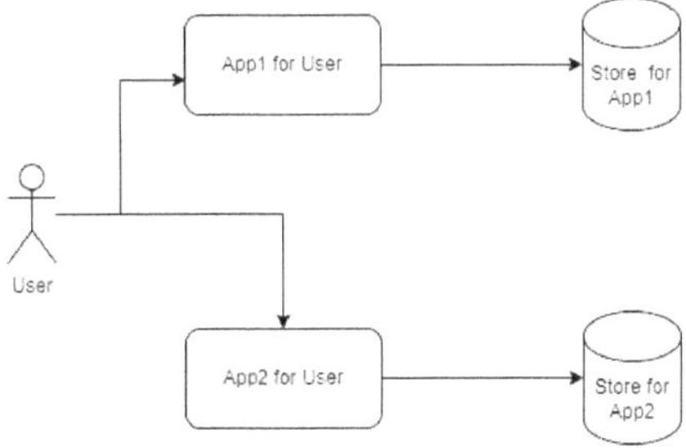

Figure 4.25: *Partitioning on apps*

As a callout, notice that each store belongs to an app. Access to the store data could be authorized on the app identity.

Partitioning within organization

Illustration of partitioning by orgs can be considered a mix of the previous two patterns. An organization can be viewed as a user property. The main idea is that users from the same organization get the same app instance and can share data. The model is shown in the following figure:

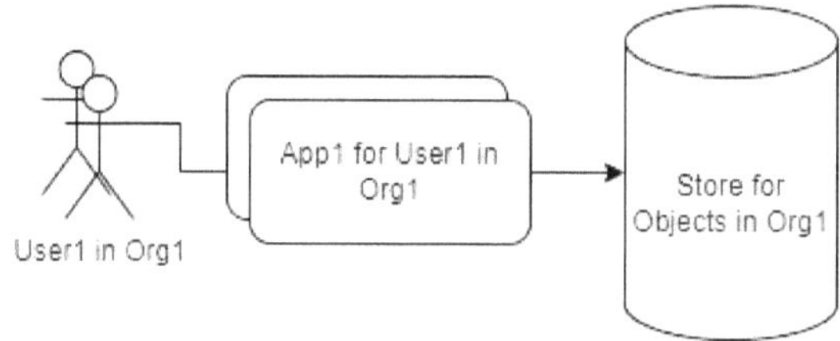

Figure 4.26: *Partitioning of organizations*

We see those different objects, apps, users, etc., end up in the same partition, provided that these objects belong to the same organization. Formally, we can write that the partition ID is derived in a deterministic way from the organization identifier.

The partition indicates the application instance:

```
partitionID = SomeDeterministicFunction(OrganizationID)
```

It would be important to note that the Entra ID object store is organized this way. Overall, it is a natural approach to partitioning objects. Those objects that belong to the same organization exhibit dependencies, like group memberships, which require that the objects stay together in order to compute them.

Implementing identity flows

Microsoft Entra ID would normally provide client and server libraries used to request and parse authentication tokens.

For different token descriptions, see **https://learn.microsoft.com/en-us/entra/identity-platform/security-tokens**.

Server libraries for parsing tokens and validating signatures used to exist, though at present, Microsoft offers guidance to applications describing how to do the validation. The code exists as a .NET package.

.NET packages are used in C# programs, holding common classes or functions used by the program.

https://learn.microsoft.com/en-us/dotnet/api/microsoft.identitymodel.jsonwebtokens?view=msal-web-dotnet-latest.

For details on validation, one can consult Microsoft documentation found at **https://learn.microsoft.com/en-us/entra/identity-platform/claims-validation**. The documentation focuses on validating claims issued by the Microsoft Cloud IdP Entra ID. For overall JWT validation, consult the JWT RFC, refer to **https://datatracker.ietf.org/doc/html/rfc7523**.

While web applications using .NET can validate the tokens using the provided .NET library, applications on other platforms have to opt in using the module suitable for the platform. For example, Python apps can use the PyJWT package for JWT token validation.

To show how the pattern described in the **application structure** can be implemented, see the on-behalf-of flow documentation **https://learn.microsoft.com/en-us/entra/identity-platform/v2-oauth2-on-behalf-of-flow**.

The desired architecture is shown in the following figure:

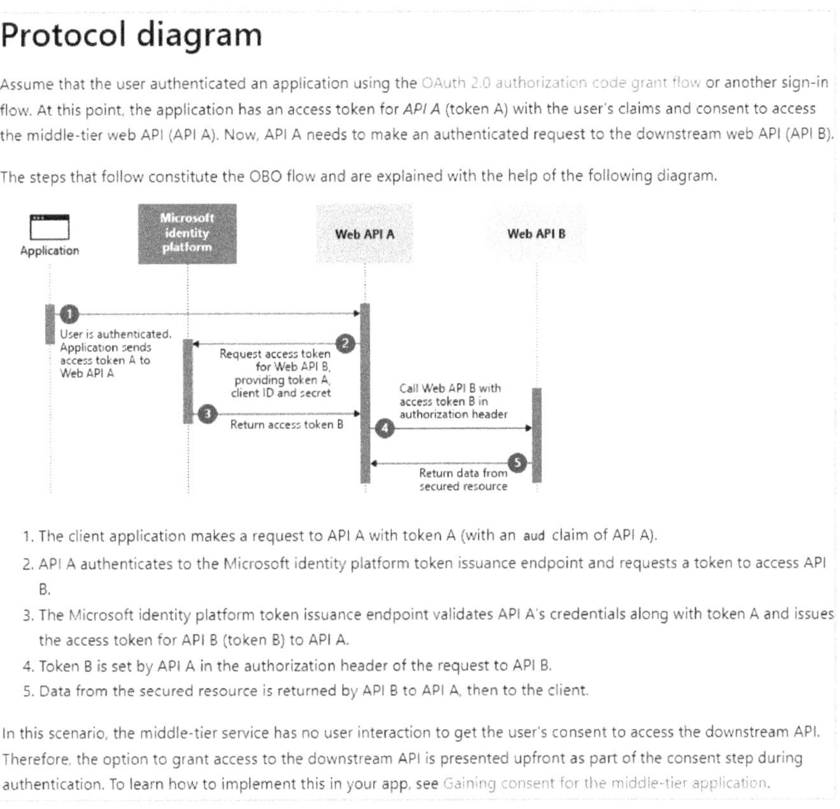

Protocol diagram

Assume that the user authenticated an application using the OAuth 2.0 authorization code grant flow or another sign-in flow. At this point, the application has an access token for *API A* (token A) with the user's claims and consent to access the middle-tier web API (API A). Now, API A needs to make an authenticated request to the downstream web API (API B).

The steps that follow constitute the OBO flow and are explained with the help of the following diagram.

1. The client application makes a request to API A with token A (with an aud claim of API A).
2. API A authenticates to the Microsoft identity platform token issuance endpoint and requests a token to access API B.
3. The Microsoft identity platform token issuance endpoint validates API A's credentials along with token A and issues the access token for API B (token B) to API A.
4. Token B is set by API A in the authorization header of the request to API B.
5. Data from the secured resource is returned by API B to API A, then to the client.

In this scenario, the middle-tier service has no user interaction to get the user's consent to access the downstream API. Therefore, the option to grant access to the downstream API is presented upfront as part of the consent step during authentication. To learn how to implement this in your app, see Gaining consent for the middle-tier application.

Figure 4.27: *Entra ID OAuth2 on-behalf-of flow*

One can notice the similarity of the on-behalf-of protocol to the flow shown in the multiple cloud apps figure, showing user context is being transferred along.

The Python code using the **Microsoft Authentication Library** (**MSAL**) client library is shown in the following figure. For complete details, refer to the link:

https://learn.microsoft.com/en-us/python/api/msal/msal.application.confidentialclientapplication?view=msal-py-latest.

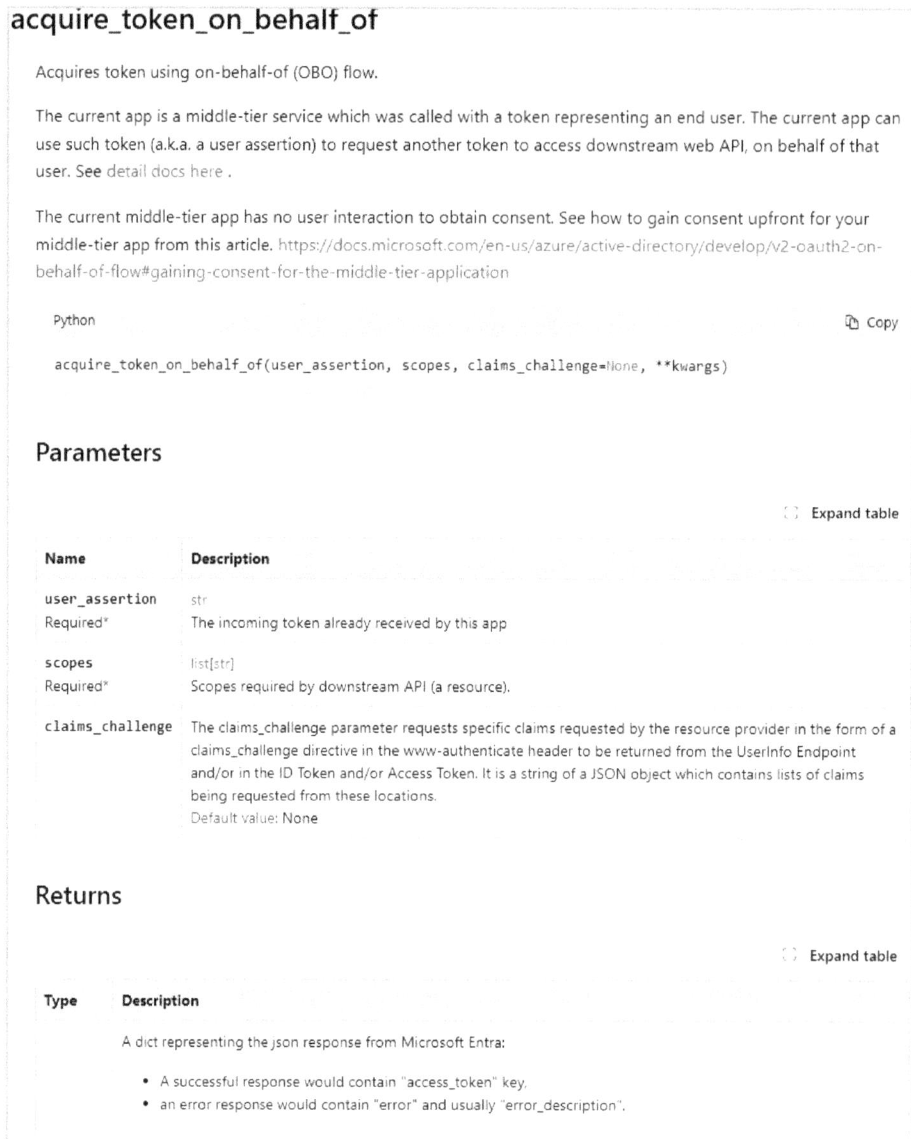

acquire_token_on_behalf_of

Acquires token using on-behalf-of (OBO) flow.

The current app is a middle-tier service which was called with a token representing an end user. The current app can use such token (a.k.a. a user assertion) to request another token to access downstream web API, on behalf of that user. See detail docs here .

The current middle-tier app has no user interaction to obtain consent. See how to gain consent upfront for your middle-tier app from this article. https://docs.microsoft.com/en-us/azure/active-directory/develop/v2-oauth2-on-behalf-of-flow#gaining-consent-for-the-middle-tier-application

Python Copy

```
acquire_token_on_behalf_of(user_assertion, scopes, claims_challenge=None, **kwargs)
```

Parameters

Expand table

Name	Description
user_assertion Required*	str The incoming token already received by this app
scopes Required*	list[str] Scopes required by downstream API (a resource).
claims_challenge	The claims_challenge parameter requests specific claims requested by the resource provider in the form of a claims_challenge directive in the www-authenticate header to be returned from the UserInfo Endpoint and/or in the ID Token and/or Access Token. It is a string of a JSON object which contains lists of claims being requested from these locations. Default value: None

Returns

Expand table

Type	Description
	A dict representing the json response from Microsoft Entra: • A successful response would contain "access_token" key, • an error response would contain "error" and usually "error_description".

***Figure 4.28:** Using MSAL Python to acquire tokens for downstream app*

It should be called out that the incoming token should be passed in as a string by the app, which necessitates that the app obtains the token from the header in the incoming HTTP request. Compare this to the abstractions suggested in the *Protocols and Libraries* heading. Instead of the application asking the HTTP server for a security context, it needs to get the token from the incoming HTTP authorization header. This approach assumes that the application is familiar with the header structure. It would be prudent to cover this specific information about transferring authentication state in headers using some library so the application does not need to take a dependency on the specific implementation.

The component figure would look something like the following:

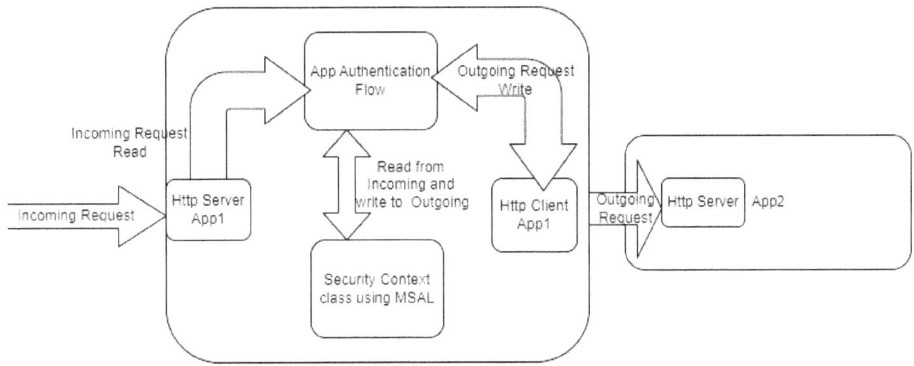

Figure 4.29: *Server authentication component extracting the state from the incoming request*

As it can be seen, the component figure is very close to the one shown earlier. The difference is that the security context class is now used in the app authentication flow component instead of the HTTP Server and client classes. This simplifies the HTTP transport implementation but complicates the app a bit, as it now needs to have an authentication flow component.

Putting it together in code

Like the code described earlier in the chapter, we can write the flow using the pseudo-code syntax easily transferable to Python.

The logic is as follows:

```
# Same as the code shown earlier, assume HttpServer is an existing object
and HttpClient is a class that can be instantiated
IncomingHttpRequest IncomingRequest = HttpServer.GetRequest()


# instantiate the object holding the incoming context
# IncomingContext is an abstract class that needs definition and
implementation
# its purpose is to hide from the application how the authentication state
# is carried in the incoming request
# also hide how the new authentication state is inserted in the outgoing
# request to App2
SecurityContext SecContext
# and initialize it from the incoming request
SecContext.Initialize(IncomingRequest)
```

```
# instantiate an HttpClient object to send request to App2
HttpClient HttpClient = new HttpClient(App2.GetUrl() )
# get the request property of http client
# must be returned by reference, not copy
# as we are modifying it
OutgoingRequest OutgoingRequest = HttpClient.GetRequest()
# we want to impersonate the caller into the http server….
# or the other option is to act as this app (app1) identity
# the option chosen is to impersonate
SecContext.SetOutgoingAuthenticationType(FromIncoming)
SecContext.SetAuthenticationHeaders(OutgoingRequest)
# … set other parameters needed in the outgoing request… then send it…
# …
```

Note: **There is no reference to the Python MSAL API within the code sample above. It is hidden in the SecurityContext class implementation.**

Conclusion

This chapter is about application identities and the ways these are used for authorization. Applications can be classified as running on a user device or a cloud compute node. While there are multiple classifications offered, the main property is the application's ability to keep a secret.

Applications have an identity asserted by some trusted authority. Applications on a user device are asserted to other applications on the same device by the local security authority, which is part of the operating system on the device.

Cloud application service identity is asserted by certificates. Certificates provide a mapping of a name or other property to a public key. To use the certificate in a TLS, the certificate owner also needs to own the private key matching the public key wrapped in the certificate.

OAuth2 and OpenID Connect are relatively new standards aimed at helping define authentication and authorization flows at the protocol level. OAuth2 combines authentication and authorization, whereas OpenID Connect is aimed purely at authentication. It is based on OAuth2, which makes the flows easier to explain and implement by teams and products familiar with OAuth2.

An important observation is that these new standards are layered on TLS, which in turn uses certificates (PKI) for authentication. Such layering makes a lot of sense, and it needs to be recognized. Without TLS, the security of OAuth2 or OpenID Connect would be weakened to the point that using these protocols, as defined, would not be feasible. The simplest argument could be that the metadata document, containing the keys used to validate tokens, is served over TLS.

We can talk about the concept of tokens and assertions, regardless of the type and state, that these can be used only when there is TLS implemented at the transport layer carrying the OAuth2 messages. Further, it can be stated that the equivalent of the audience (**aud** in JWTs) is required, and the audience value must be deterministically computed from the name found in the certificate used in the TLS session. This is to prevent token misuse by compromised recipients. The logic is that a token is accepted only by recipients with matching audiences and nobody else. Even if a recipient is compromised, its ability to spread the compromise to others would be limited, as the tokens received by the compromised recipient cannot be forwarded to others.

In the next chapter, we will discuss the building blocks offered by the cloud providers to the application developers, such as compute, storage, and networking.

Exercises

The goal of this section is to help application developers and product owners identify security needs and high-level approaches for meeting those.

1. Define application components. It should not matter how these components communicate with each other, but know what they are.

2. Define containment rules. Consider using the format.

   If A is breached, B should not be.

   Where A and B are components defined in #1.

   Then define semantics and how these desired outcomes would be achieved. For example, specify that A must pass the caller identity that would allow B to authorize the caller and limit the damage caused by A's compromise. To expand on the assertion above, if a user sends a request to a compromised app (A), the app can impersonate that user to other apps, but A cannot impersonate a user who did not contact it. Arguably, the total number of users is much bigger than those contacting A, so the compromise spread is limited.

3. Define remediation steps.

   If A is found to be compromised, it should be clear how to remediate the situation.

   It is a normal practice to have procedures for changing A's code and/or the secret, if A is a confidential cloud application. The secret, if there is one, would need to be rotated in any compromise event, and the code may or may not need to change depending on the nature of the compromise.

Join our Discord space

Join our Discord workspace for latest updates, offers, tech happenings around the world, new releases, and sessions with the authors:

https://discord.bpbonline.com

Chapter 5
Compute, Storage and Networking in the Cloud

Introduction

Compute, storage, and networking services are the crown jewels offered to customers by the many clouds. All applications need these, so it is not surprising that the cloud providers invest heavily in these areas. In this chapter, we will take an in-depth look at each of these and evaluate them from a security point of view.

To put some stakes in the ground, traditional software architectures employ the compute, storage, and networking paradigms to describe the environments in which applications exist. All three components are used by the application at runtime.

Modern architectures do not focus on these. We can trace back the origin of compute, storage, and networking components in the history of computing. Even now, computing devices are described by quoting the processor speed (compute), memory, and disk size (storage) as well as parameters of the networking equipment, like in and out transfer rates. In a server farm environment, the same considerations and resources are estimated considering compute power, storage capacity, and latency of transferring data to and from compute to storage.

For example, the provider may quote compute processing speed in some form, like processor instructions executed per second, storage capacity, and transfer speed to and from compute to storage, as well as transfer speed measuring network capacity that provides data links among internal and external components involved in application design:

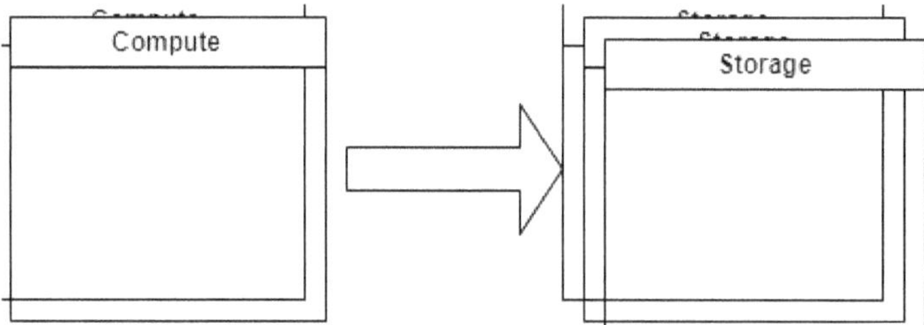

Figure 5.1: Scaling compute and storage

The main concept behind this architecture is the ability to scale compute and storage resources separately. There are applications consuming a lot of compute, storage, or both. The ability to scale compute and storage services separately would satisfy all types. While this is indeed an excellent observation, it rests on the traditional compute or storage architecture. Different architectures would be able to achieve the same but differently.

To state the goal directly, it would be an efficient use of the allocated or rented resources needed for executing the application. More concretely, the application owners would like to spend the minimum amount possible on renting compute and storage resources, also known as infrastructure, while maintaining needed performance characteristics.

Structure

In this chapter, we will discuss the following topics:

- Greenfield and brownfield
- Type of infrastructure
- Security angle
- Compute
- Storage
- Networking
- Historical perspective
- Blockchain architectures
- Cell architectures
- Serverless cloud architectures
- Assets to protect within compute and storage
- Azure
- Queues and asynchronous processing
- Kubernetes concepts
- Scaling architectures

Objectives

The main objective of the chapter is to provide a glimpse into cloud architectures and the historical perspective of the evolution of those architectures. Along the way, we introduce blockchain and serverless architectures, marking pivotal moments of this evolution.

Greenfield and brownfield

These terms refer to new applications that can be written assuming the cloud services and existing applications that were written without having the cloud in mind, but now need to be migrated to some cloud environment, called the lift-and-shift approach.

One can speculate that most existing applications can be classified as brownfield, which necessitates that the clouds implement seamless and easy-to-use lift-and-shift capabilities, meaning that it should be straightforward to move these applications to the cloud.

For example, suppose that an existing application is using a store of type X to read from and write to. It would be highly desirable that clouds offer an implementation of X, such that the existing application can migrate to the cloud without changing how it reads from and writes to X. As it is asserted next, cloud-provided store solutions carry many benefits, but using those is not always possible.

One can conjecture that at this early point in time, there exist a lot more applications that fall into the brownfield category, and to earn their business, the cloud providers have to offer tools that make it easy to lift-and-shift those applications to cloud environments. As applications get updated, the intent is to gradually replace external components, storage being a primary example, with cloud offerings. Using these will be much cheaper overall compared to using external products and running them on cloud-provided infrastructure.

Types of infrastructure

It is yet another important point to consider that some popular storage services require underlying infrastructure to meet certain performance criteria like minimum CPU speed rating, disk latency, and capacity. If applications deploy their own storage solution, the underlying infrastructure needs to meet the solution requirements, which could be an expensive proposition.

If, instead, the storage solution is provided by the cloud provider, it would be a lot cheaper, as the cloud provider is best positioned to use the cloud infrastructure resources efficiently. Other considerations would include auxiliary services like monitoring, reporting, etc. The cloud provider utilizes it to run the storage service it owns.

It is natural that the lift-and-shift types of solutions would exclude cloud-provided storage solutions, as all solutions employed by the application should be able to run anywhere, and the only dependency that is acceptable is the infrastructure on which the solution's software needs to run.

Security angle

From a security point of view, the question of containing the blast radius would most frequently be discussed in the event of compromise. Compromises do happen, and limiting the damage in case of one is a major part of the design for security exercises.

What we will do is assume a compromise of a compute or storage node and evaluate the expected effects. Nodes of interest are, of course, compute and storage.

Compute nodes interacting with storage are depicted in the following figure:

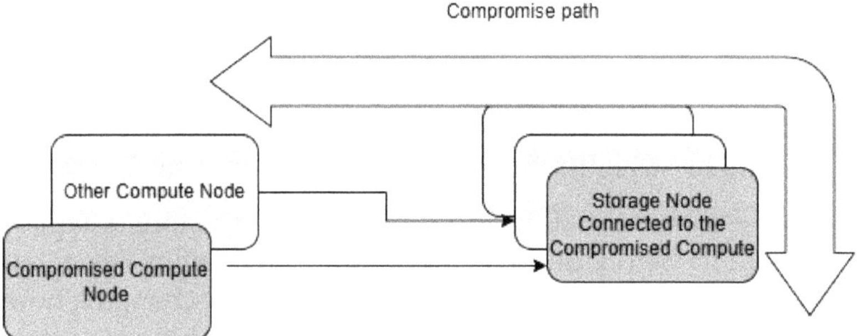

Figure 5.2: *Compromising compute node effects*

As we can see, since compute nodes need to access storage, compromising a single node gives the attacker who compromised the node access to the storage that the node had access to. We could assume this would affect all storage compute that has access to it, as shown in the above figure.

Compromising a storage node paints a bit of a different picture. Other storage nodes may get compromised depending on the replication topology. Other compute nodes, shown in lighter red in the above figure, may get compromised depending on how persistent state in storage is used. More details are given in the *Compute and Storage* section.

Compute

The definition is, *Compute refers to a set of resources that execute Customer applications.*

Formally, we could write that any compute would offer the following functions:

```
Output = ComputeFunction(input, code)
```

Internally, code is using and potentially modifying persistent state held in some storage. Modifying that persistent state can be written as:

```
Statei+1 = ComputeFunction(input, code, Statei)
```

Combining the above two equations, we can write the following:

```
(Output, Statei+1) = ComputeFunction(input, code, Statei)
```

To put it in words, the execution of an **application program interface (API)** behind the code symbol, takes as input API parameters labeled as input and current state labeled as `Statei`, returns an output result to the caller, and produces the next `Statei+1` that will be used the next time code is invoked.

The `State` values come from a storage service. There can be some multi-layered cache infrastructure in between, and the code running on the compute needs a key, or rather a crypto interface, to be able to perform authentication to the storage service.

The following figure shows the state of the storage node being used by the compute node:

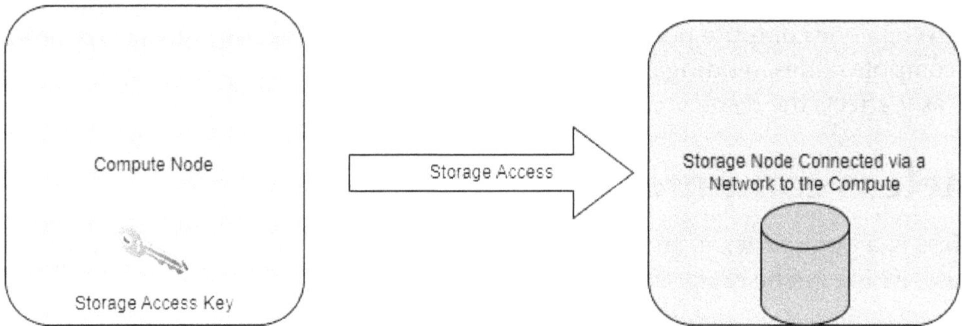

Figure 5.3: *Code on compute accessing storage*

Blast radius in the event of a compute node compromise spreads to all storage service nodes, considering that there must exist a replication service that pushes changes to all storage nodes. The thing to notice is the key that helps authenticate the compute to storage. In order to have access, one needs two things: physical access to the storage service exposed interface and the key to authenticate itself. The former (physical access) is provided by networking. As explained in the *Networking* section, it should not be used as the only authorization factor, and it should always be combined with identity-based authorization represented as access to key cryptography, which is independent of the physical access ability.

The perspective that the reader would notice is that the storage service may offer functionality very similar to the compute function described in the *Compute* section. The big difference is that the code parameter in a storage service is fixed to whatever code the service provider supports, like query, insert, etc. The compute is designed to run any application, where storage functionality is fixed.

Storage services have evolved to offer compute-like functionality in the form of stored procedures, which are often compared to function abstractions in popular programming languages.

The opposite, and seemingly stronger, trend is evolving the compute to offer storage-like services. The compute nodes being, generally, cheaper and more flexible, promote such an arrangement further.

It is here that we should point out the main trait of compute, and it is defined as its ability to execute customer applications. Executing customer applications can be used as another way to define semantics behind the code parameter in the compute function definition. It can be stated that the code is the customer application. Methods for distinguishing one application from another were discussed in *Chapter 4, Application Identities*.

To reiterate, the compute executes customer code that can be defined as a **Turing Complete System**. Translating this, the code can implement an arbitrary function that can map any combination of input and **`Statei`** to any tuple (output, **`Statei+1`**).

Another important thing to consider is the effect of the compromise on other compute nodes. While one compute node compromise does not always translate to compromising other compute nodes, sending polluted data to storage has an indirect effect on all compute nodes as it affects the results returned. More on this in the *Storage* section.

Stateless compute

Stateless is a popular term, so a more formal definition will be helpful. Most compute is stateless, which can be expressed formally as follows:

```
# stateless compute functions use a constant state
Statei = const
```

It is necessary to call out that any compute function can be made stateless by moving **`Statei`** to the input parameters. This would mean transferring the responsibility of maintaining the state to the caller. Yes, the function semantics would be simpler, but the caller logic would get more complex.

A common implementation is to have the compute node be stateless and have the state placed in storage. Compute nodes have a key that authorizes access to storage, and that key is the same, or rather has the same authorization, for all nodes. This way, the statelessness of the node is realized.

Storage

While the compute describes resources executing customer applications, *Storage refers to resources that hold customer data.*

From a security point of view, the objective would be to determine the blast radius in case a storage node is compromised.

We postulated that compromising a single compute node can affect all storage. The statement of fact is not quite the same when we consider the effects of compromising a single storage node. The first observation should be that compute nodes are not affected directly, meaning that we cannot consider compute nodes to be compromised in the sense of attackers having full control of the node functionality.

Whether or not other storage nodes get compromised, and by this, we mean populated with polluted data, depends on storage replication logic. Lacking integrity checks of the replicated data, and by integrity we mean proof that authorized parties modified data, we can assume that eventually, this **polluted** data would be replicated to all storage nodes, which would amount to all nodes being compromised.

Now, back to compute. If all storage nodes can be compromised, meaning serving bad data, then the persistent Statei read by the compute is also not to be trusted. That does not necessarily mean that the compute is compromised, as the attacker cannot run arbitrary code there; however, the result of running the compute code that depends on storage state, Statei, can be influenced by the attacker having control over Statei. Depending on the nature of the computation performed, influencing the result could be considered an act of compromise to those relying on the result integrity to control some high-value operation.

For example, the code may be computing the expected value of an asset based on prices read from storage, and compromising storage would lead to computing incorrect expected values.

Compute nodes accessing storage replicas look as follows:

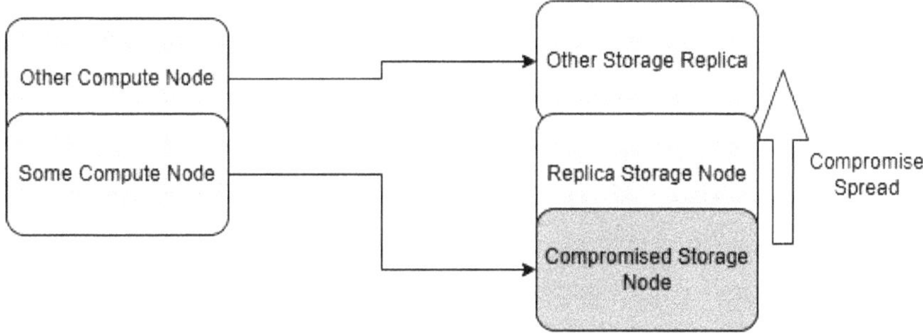

Figure 5.4: Compromised storage node effects

As shown above, compromising one storage node has cascading effects on others, marked as storage replicas, as well as effects on compute node states.

Compute nodes are shown to be in a **semi-compromised** state, which depends on the nature of the compute operations being performed and can be **fully compromised** for some functions where the persistent state held in storage can affect the results of the compute operation in a way fully controlled by the attacker.

An interesting and important detail concerning storage services is that the consuming application does not need to be deployed in the same cloud as the storage service. One could imagine a popular storage service being used by applications in multiple clouds.

Networking

The chapter, at first, was not going to include networking as it has little impact on the security posture, according to the authors.

As networking has become a major cloud offering, it deserves appropriate recognition and an in-depth look and analysis.

Using external and internal network segments is illustrated in the figure:

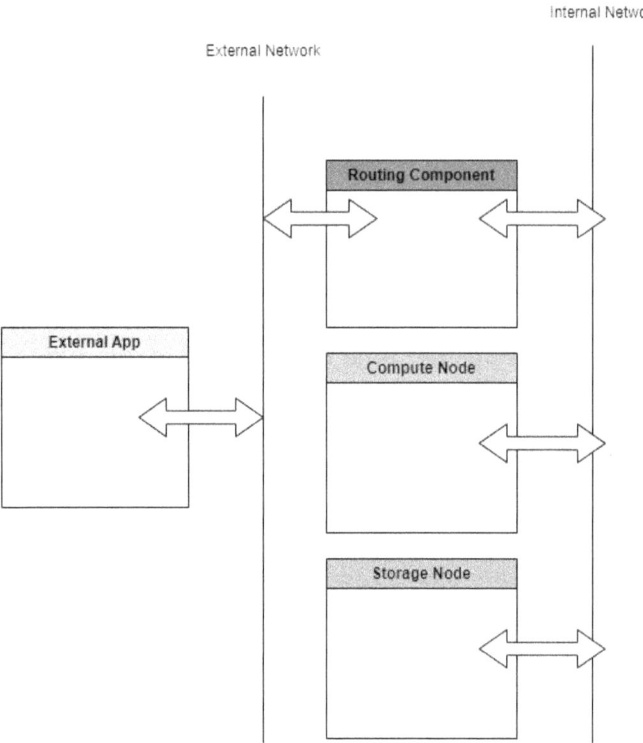

Figure 5.5: *Internal and external networks*

Shown in the above figure is a typical cloud service setup where one routing component is connected to internal and external networks, and valuable compute resources, and the storage resources connect to the internal network only, with the hope that internal networks provide protection against external threats.

Historically, in the following examples from the non-digital arrangements (consider airplane security provided by the **Transport Security Administration** (**TSA**) in the USA), networking was used as a means of letting only **trusted and vetted** entities have physical access to protected resources.

However, this approach falls short of delivering the needed authorization. Formally speaking, while it is relatively easy to prove that A has access to B, it is hard to prove that entities categorized as not A do not have access to B.

In general cases, there are an infinite number of (NOT A) entities, and lacking some additional information, constructing the proof (not A cannot access B) is a challenging exercise. For starters, all (NOT A) cases cannot be enumerated, so behavior can be tested as there is an infinite number of those (NOT A) entities. The testing methodologies must use approximations defined by grouping a class of (NOT A) entities together. For example, entities with names starting with A could be placed in the same group, and testing that one of those does not have access to B. This test, of course, is not 100% accurate, as other entities in the same group could have access.

While being on a network cannot be used as a primary factor for authorization, it could make an excellent second factor. To continue with the airline example, while one can be in a restricted area following the security check by TSA, having a boarding pass is still needed to get on the plane. A good heuristic would be to compare the number of breaches with and without the second authorization factor.

The other, maybe not so obvious, trait of networking is the performance measured in capacity, speed, and cost of transferring data from one location to another. The performance elements above do influence design decisions, which in turn have security implications, slow performance, and/or high cost, bringing in designs that try to minimize sending data, as doing so is cost-saving. However, minimizing the data sent may lead to security issues. There is a fine line in preserving security while controlling performance and cost.

Historical perspective

The computing architecture featuring compute, storage, and networking has deep roots in the history of computing. Looking at how the classic computer was built, there is a CPU (compute), storage in the form of memory as volatile and persistent, which is implemented on memory chips and disks, and finally, there needs to be something to serve as a connecting medium between compute and storage. In standalone computers, this **something** is usually some form of an internal bus that lets the bits flow from the storage to the compute and back.

Having this familiar picture in mind, it should not come as a surprise that cloud architectures have adopted this familiar model. The difference with the classic computer comes from using compute nodes to implement the compute, storage, or networking paradigms.

> Note: **The major difference if physical access to a standalone computer used to translate into ownership of the data on it, as well as compute capabilities. This is not true in today's interconnected world, where every compute and storage device is placed on some network and can be accessed from anywhere in the world.**

To promote security where access is only granted to authorized parties, one cannot rely on the network whose primary job is to provide access, not restrict it. This is not relying on physical access as a sole means of authorization, which is a major paradigm shift. It does bring the concepts of the **assume breach**, limiting the blast radius in case of a breach, and instituting processes for detection and remediation. To phrase it a bit differently, in the past, having physical access was the same as a security breach. This is no longer the case as network access is like physical access, which is assumed to be there for every resource of interest. So, one cannot say that having network access is the same as a breach.

Consider the following figure to visualize the architecture evolution:

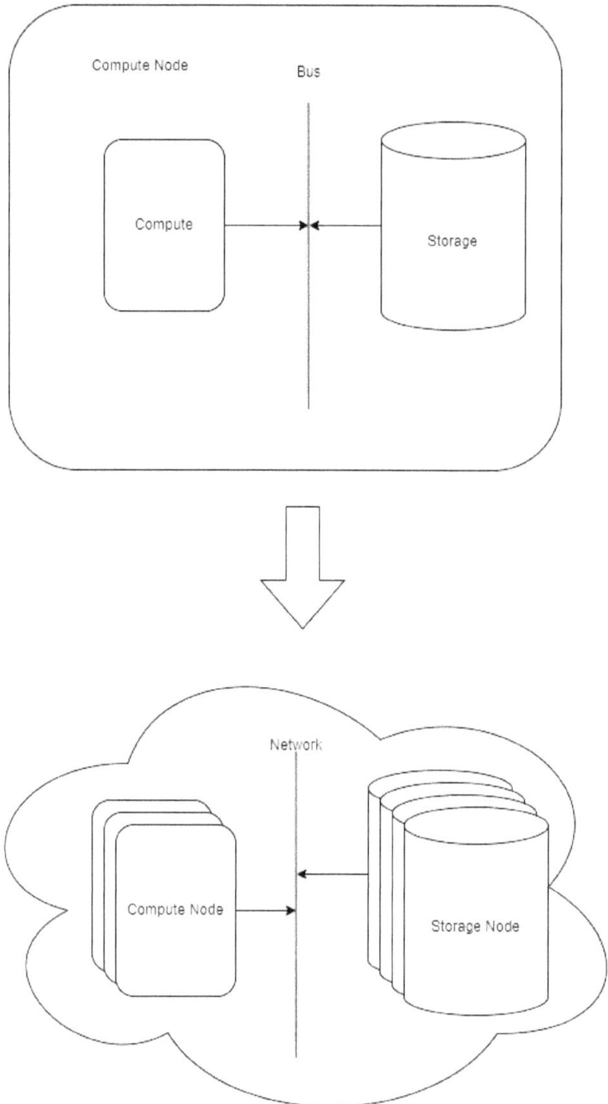

Figure 5.6: *Traditional computer architecture evolving to cloud*

The major difference coming from the evolution is the need for securing access when a network is used.

Blockchain architecture

When reviewing blockchain architectures, it could be argued that one of the major contributions of the architecture is providing assurance of data integrity.

In the traditional compute-storage architectures, modifying data in unauthorized ways (we call it polluting in this chapter) is hard to discover and prevent. It is certainly not possible, but the methods used are not cornerstone building blocks of the replication architecture, as with blockchains.

Data replication among storage replicas is usually a custom protocol specific to the storage solution that needs it. In blockchains, the block structure is standardized. Since replication propagates blocks from one node to another, the data format can also be considered standardized. While the actual protocol that moves blocks between nodes can evolve organically, the block data format must be agreed on and standardized, so transactions contained in a block can be applied by all nodes adhering to the standard.

Consider the following figure for illustration:

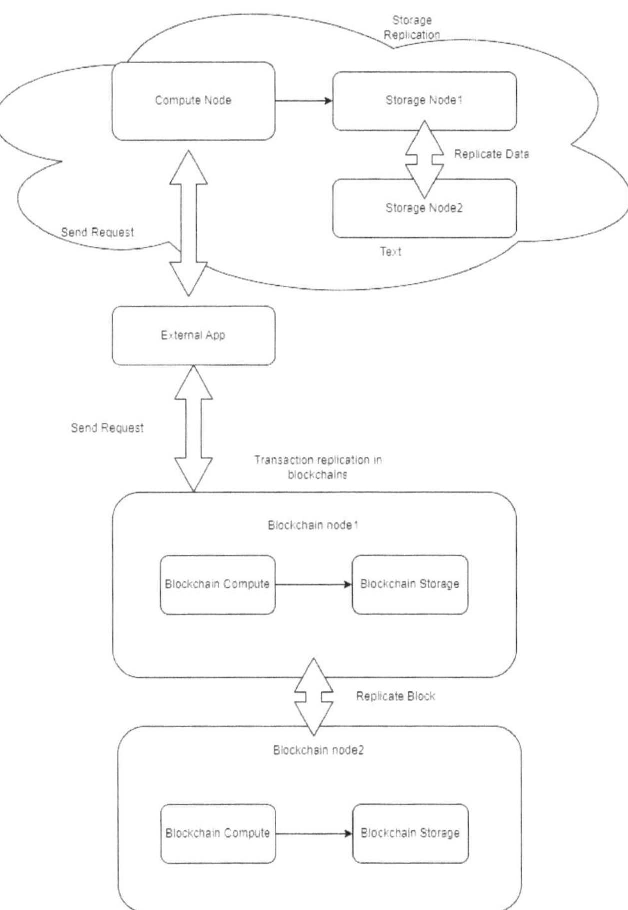

Figure 5.7: *Data replication architectures in storage and blockchains*

This could be one of the most important contributions of blockchain architectures to computing. Instead of replicating the state data, signed transactions are being replicated.

One can think of these transactions as instructions to replicate the state, including the authorization required for state changes.

Replicating data using implied authorization is tricky, as authorization rules are implied.

Specifically, if the transaction is signed with a key mapped to a blockchain storage record, then certain operations are authorized on this record. For example, changes that need such authorization would be decreasing the token balance field in the record being modified.

This authorization rule is subjective, specifically the authorization being applied only to decrease the subject token balance when processing a transaction signed with the subject's key. To point out a few examples of authorizations that can be controversial, seemingly, no authorization is required to increase the subject's balance. In other words, anyone can send tokens to the subject's account. While knowing that A sent some tokens to B could be harmless in most cases, there are some cases where it is not. This is especially true when the record could be correlated to some entity in the non-digital world. For example, if it is known that the blockchain record belongs to some well-known person, it could be disastrous to show that someone has sent tokens to it. Many would ask why tokens are being sent, and the person's reputation could be damaged by this knowledge. A relatively simple remedy would be to require that the recipient also sign a transaction authorizing the sender.

These authorization issues notwithstanding, the idea of replicating blocks to allow multiple nodes to apply the new transactions instead of replicating the storage data resulting from one node applying the new transactions has a lot of merit. It should be known that the authorization logic applied by the blockchain compute can vary. The issues called out apply to popular blockchains where, undoubtedly, the inflexible authorization rules were invented to promote simplicity for the basic operation of A sending tokens to B. The blockchain compute could apply more complex and flexible authorization, if so desired, without changing the blockchain architecture. It is still about replicating (or we can call the process propagating) blocks, wrapping transactions from one blockchain node to another. The change would be when these transactions are executed and applied to change the blockchain-secured data.

Cell architectures

A cell combines compute and storage and is, in a way, very similar to a blockchain node described in the previous heading. Entities, like other applications, communicate with a cell exposed by the target application. The overall picture is simplified as one needs to consider scaling cells, not compute and storage nodes. Arguably, it is easier to architect a construct where individual entities (cells) are being scaled versus having to scale multiple entity types like compute, storage, etc.

A cell combines compute and storage nodes in a structure like the one shown in the following figure:

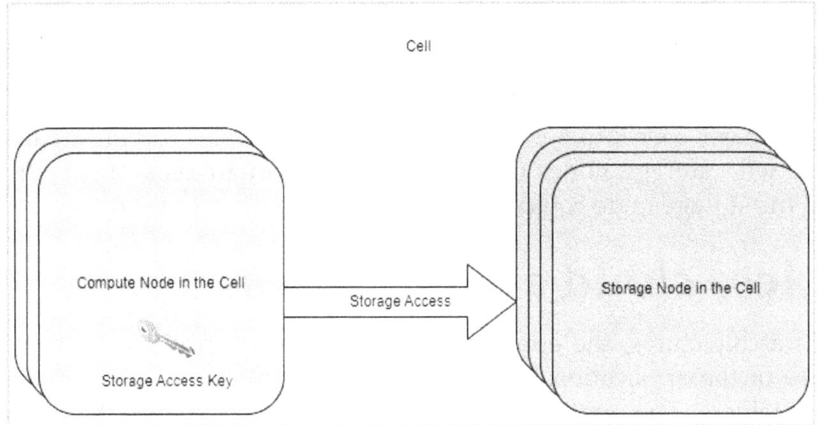

Figure 5.8: *A cell structure including compute and storage nodes*

A cell internally includes compute and storage components. However, the callers do not need to be concerned with those, only with the cell address where requests are being sent.

Having the concept of cells is a very useful abstraction. The cell is a component, like a blockchain node, that does all the needed processing within itself, utilizing the contained components. It could also be viewed as an instance of an application that can function on its own.

Using cells as application building blocks can be illustrated in the following figure:

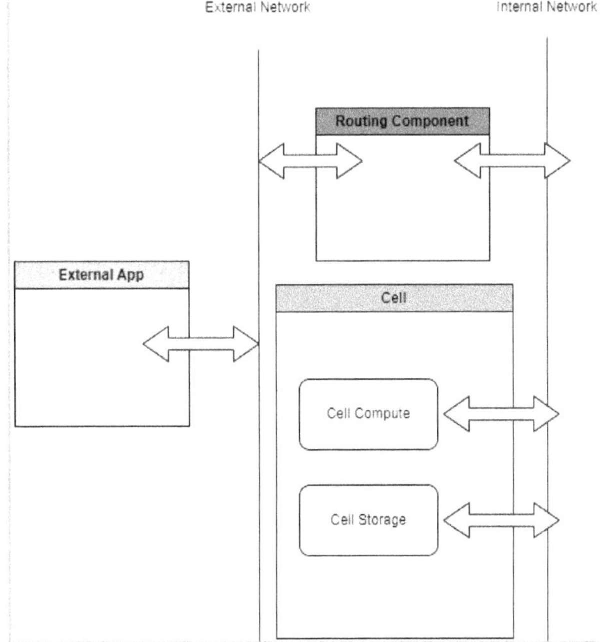

Figure 5.9: *A cell as an application building block*

As shown, the external routing component sees the cell as the application building block. Cell components are connected to the internal network, which includes cell compute and storage.

To call out the major conceptual change that comes with cells, a compute node can only communicate with storage nodes in the same cell. Without cells, this restriction is not present, and the storage node could be anywhere.

Serverless cloud architectures

In serverless architectures, the application owner is not concerned with managing the infrastructure of the application in the form of physical servers like **virtual machines** (**VMs**) or containers. The application needs a run time environment that supports the functionality it needs. Unsurprisingly, such an environment can be projected on the compute, storage, and networking components discussed in this chapter. The important point is that applications are not concerned with those. The requirements the application has, like processing a certain number of transactions per second while consuming a maximum of some storage amount, can be expressed without referring to a specific infrastructure.

Most often, serverless is used to describe compute architectures. Storage provides a persistent state to the compute functions. The persistent state used within a compute function could be implemented as part of the runtime environment or as a component of the application.

As a comparison between serverless and server-aware architectures, the following can be called out:

- Server-aware architectures focus on servers provided to customers by the cloud providers. As such, these are brownfield architectures that must exist to facilitate customer workloads moving to the cloud.
- Serverless architectures are meant to simplify customer application logic by removing the often complex task of managing the underlying servers on which the application runs.

Application components bring the complexity of sharing the same component among multiple applications while avoiding duplication and maintaining a degree of separation such that updates made by one application do not affect others. However, avoiding such duplication comes at the cost of engineering complexity. Installing the shared component needs special care to avoid conflicts arising from updates of the multiple applications using the component. For example, consider two applications, A and B, using a shared component C. If updating A results in updating C, then B could be broken as a result if not tested with the new C version. There are techniques to address this, but the resulting design is not trivial. It would be a lot simpler to dedicate the component to a single application.

Yet another issue of having a shared component is the need for security in terms of authentication and authorization. The component could have a separate state maintained for each application, which would considerably simplify the design model. This is a principle, but the problem is that it would be hard to test that it was upheld.

Assets to protect within compute and storage

This heading will investigate compute and storage resources that need protection, where the protection semantics are about authorizing access to these resources. If access is not being authorized, we can say that there is no protection.

It might be obvious to many, but still, it would be useful to spell out the reasons behind the need for asset protection.

If using an asset incurs cost for the asset owner, then this cost must be somehow recouped, or the owner will have no incentive to have the asset in a state ready to use. For example, consider the owner's server (S)he will have no incentive to keep the server in a good state and ready to use if anyone could use it without authorization.

There are other types of assets where the owner does not spend resources on keeping the asset in a state ready to use. For example, consider the computer codes, which take effort and resources to develop. Maintaining it in a state that is considered **ready to use** is another matter that can be very subjective. As opposed to other resource types, code can be used in pieces by the consumer. It allows for copying using a cut-and-paste type of technique, which does not need any type of maintenance, as once copied, the copy lives independently of the source.

That could be the primary reason why protecting code from unauthorized use is considered by many a futile exercise, and most code is now open source, which pretty much gives up the idea of protecting the code from unauthorized use by authorizing everybody to use it.

Then, if not by authorizing use, code asset owners need to find some other way to monetize the asset. More on this in a later chapter discussing the economic models and the role of security, considering that codes cannot be protected by authorization. Next, we will look at assets that need to be protected.

Compute assets to protect

An important asset in need of protection is the secret key used by the compute node, as shown in the following figure:

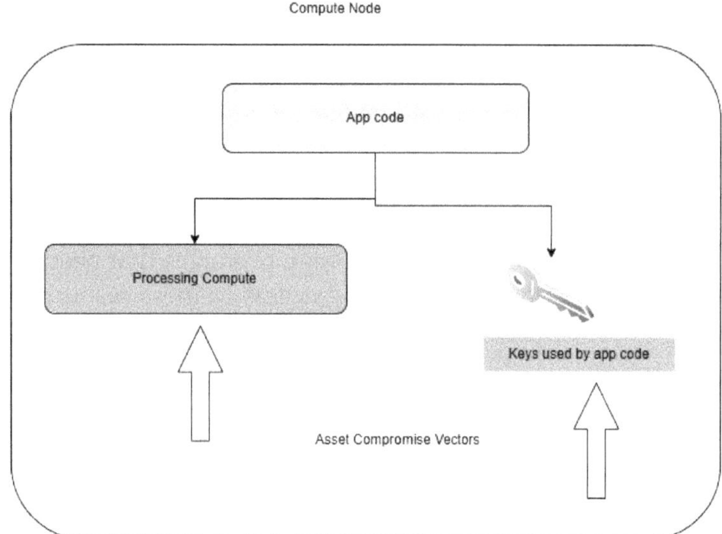

Figure 5.10: *Application code on compute resource*

Assets shown are the codes, the ability to execute (compute), as well as some data of limited size available to the code running on this specific compute resource.

The data is shown in the form of a key, which bootstraps access to storage that can hold data of arbitrary size and shape.

We can relate this to the real world of economics. Not accidentally, many valuable companies are in the business of designing and manufacturing compute, resources processors, servers, etc. Monetizing software takes some creativity, though it can prove to be a very valuable endeavor.

Storage assets to protect

While on the compute resource, the asset to protect is the ability to compute (visualize using processor horsepower), and the storage is mostly about the data it holds. It is somewhat similar, though not quite, to protecting the key on the compute node used to authorize compute to storage. The reason we are saying **not quite** is that getting the key alone may not be sufficient to access an arbitrary storage record within the storage service. The following the principle of limiting compromise blast radius, the key held in compute should *not* suffice to access an arbitrary storage record. As it was presented in the previous chapters, in addition to the key, the compute should present proof that the record owner authenticated to the compute node.

While it is true that a storage service could be abused for its capability to store large amounts of data, think of storing data for free. Most of the time, the data residing there is of more interest than the service's ability to store data. To use an email service as an example one more time, while it may also be true that using storage without having to pay for it is a benefit to an attacker who managed to do it, it is most often the case that being able to access someone's data in storage like reading emails that belong to another person and doing this without authorization, is more valuable than using storage services **for free**. In today's world, data is valuable as it can be monetized for many purposes.

Showing data as an asset targeted by attackers is shown in the following figure:

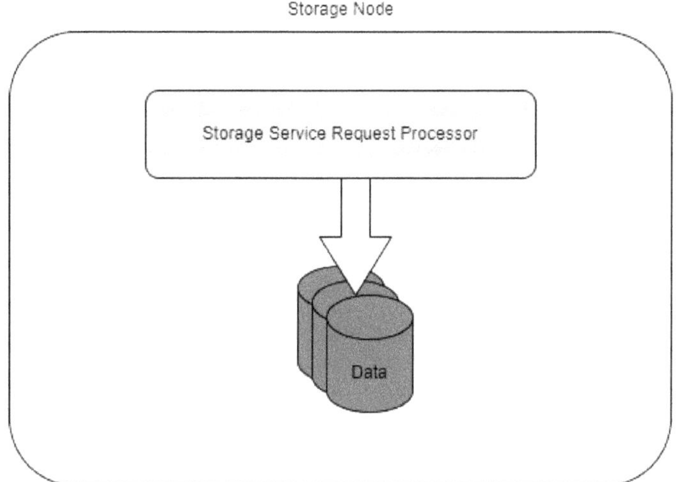

Figure 5.11: *Data is the most valuable storage asset*

As illustrated, the most valuable asset to protect on storage nodes is the data residing there. This is quite different than the compute where the assets are compute power as well as the ability to access storage.

Azure

Azure would serve as an example, cloud showcasing the compute, storage, and network resources it offers to its customers. Not surprisingly, both brownfield and greenfield customers will have plenty to choose from.

Azure compute

To give an idea, here is what the Azure compute selection of services looks like in the Azure documentation.

The reader can navigate to this link to see the picture **https://learn.microsoft.com/en-us/azure/architecture/guide/technology-choices/compute-decision-tree**

Choices of Azure compute services can be seen when navigating a browser to the link above. A glimpse is shown in the following figure:

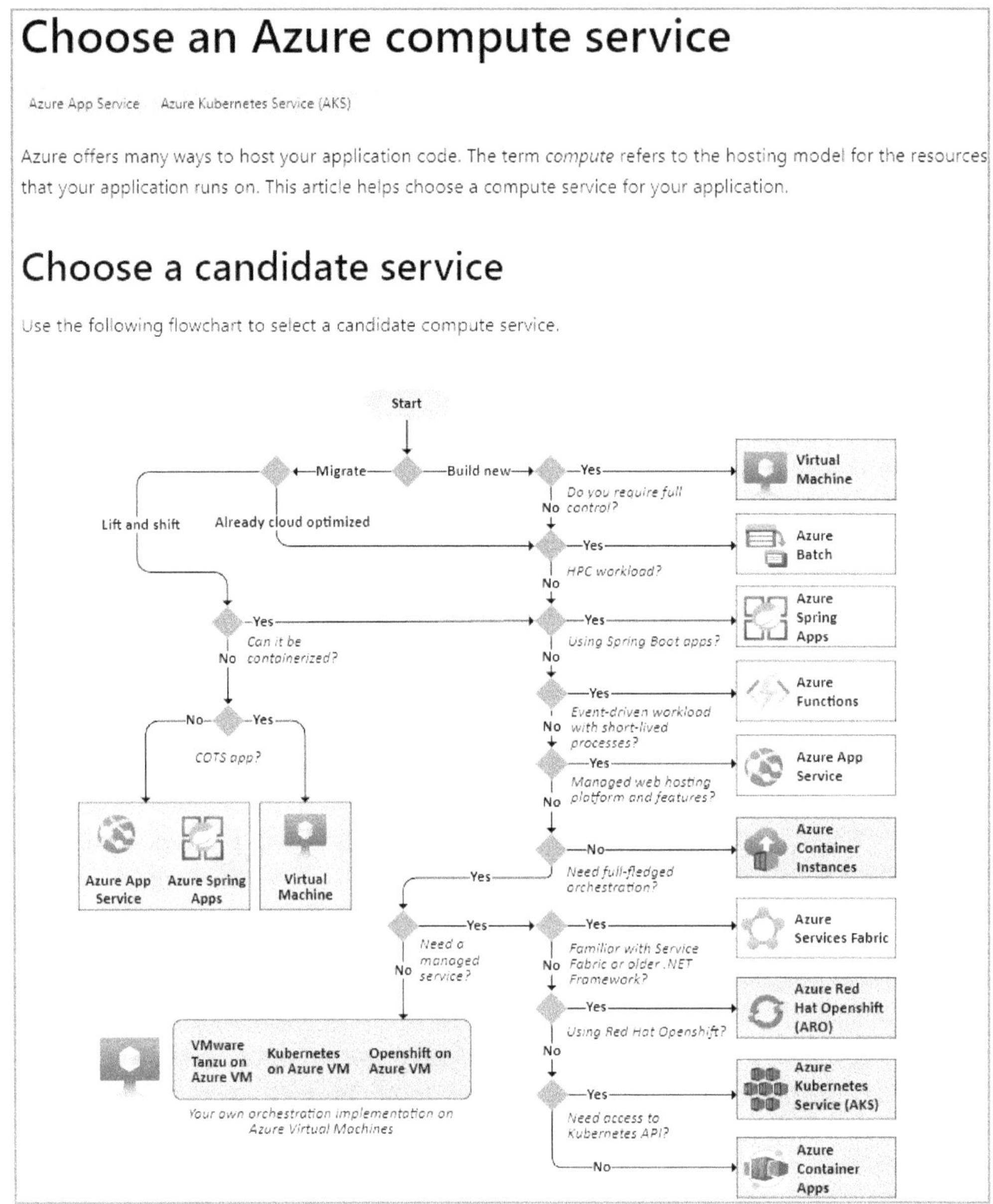

Figure 5.12: Azure compute services selection

Azure storage

There are plenty of storage options in Azure. The database offerings are separated from the rest of the storage in the Azure portal.

Selecting the needed storage service is in the experience shown in the following figure:

Figure 5.13: *Azure portal menu for choosing resources*

As one can see, there are many resource types. One of these is Azure storage. Selecting it takes us to the following screen:

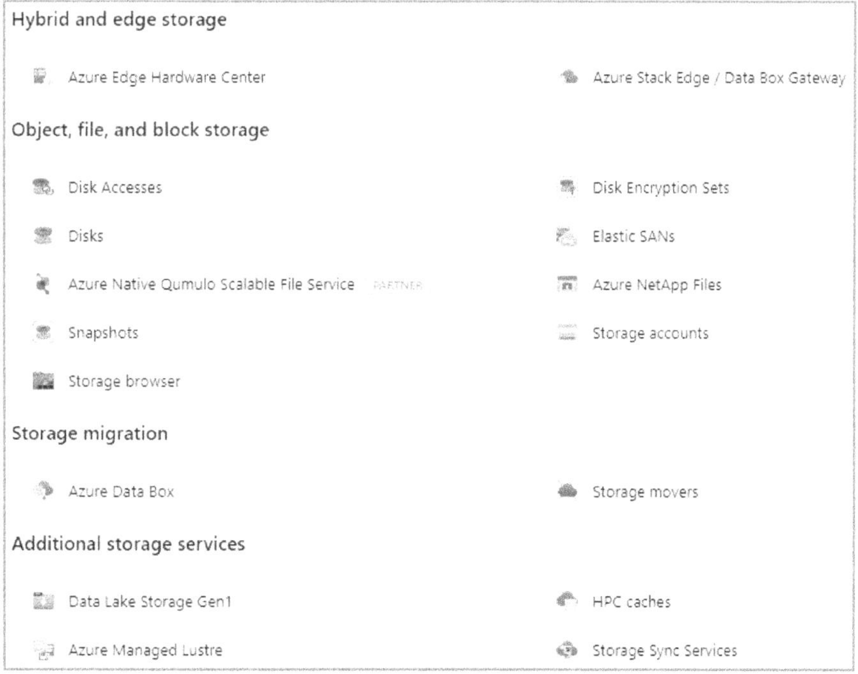

Figure 5.14: *Database and storage services*

As we said already, databases and storage are separate Azure services. This approach will resonate with customers looking for one or the other.

Navigating to the *Databases* section, we can see that the most popular databases are offered as services. A glimpse of the many choices offered to customers is shown in the figure:

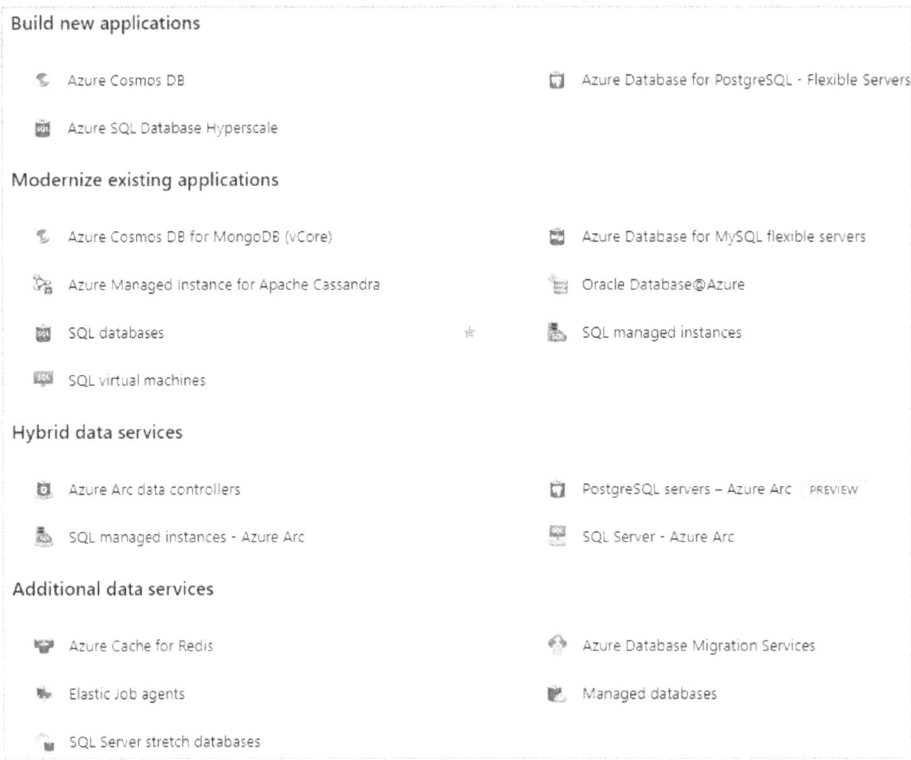

Figure 5.15: *Azure database offerings*

It is natural to have these. The relational databases have been very popular, and many applications have taken a dependency on one of those, so it is quite natural that major clouds, Azure being a prime example, have invested substantially in providing database services support for cloud applications.

Azure storage and database security

Azure storage has the concept of storage accounts that provide needed authentication and authorization to storage services. For complete details, refer to the link **https://learn.microsoft.com/en-us/azure/storage/common/storage-account-overview?toc=%2Fazure%2Fstorage%2Fblobs%2Ftoc.json&bc=%2Fazure%2Fstorage%2Fblobs%2Fbreadcrumb%2Ftoc.json**

Storage accounts in the Azure documentation can be seen when navigating to the link above. Partial content is shown in the following figure:

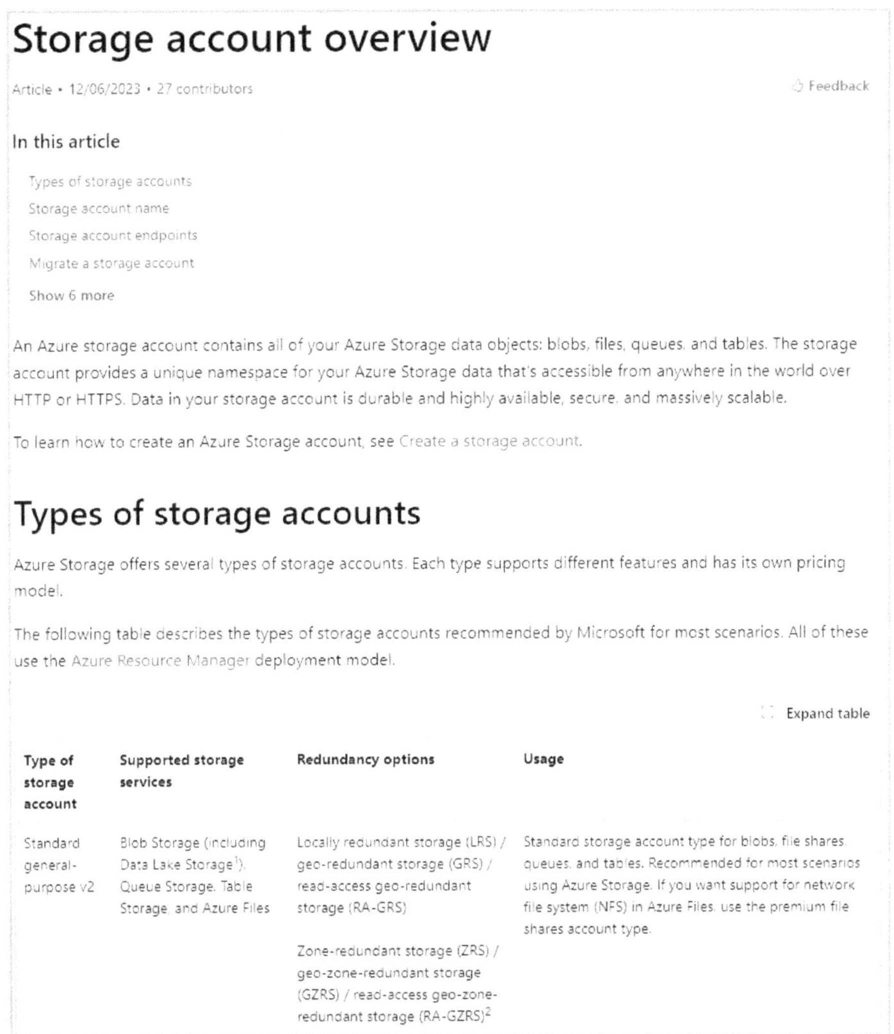

Storage account overview

Article • 12/06/2023 • 27 contributors

Feedback

In this article

Types of storage accounts
Storage account name
Storage account endpoints
Migrate a storage account
Show 6 more

An Azure storage account contains all of your Azure Storage data objects: blobs, files, queues, and tables. The storage account provides a unique namespace for your Azure Storage data that's accessible from anywhere in the world over HTTP or HTTPS. Data in your storage account is durable and highly available, secure, and massively scalable.

To learn how to create an Azure Storage account, see Create a storage account.

Types of storage accounts

Azure Storage offers several types of storage accounts. Each type supports different features and has its own pricing model.

The following table describes the types of storage accounts recommended by Microsoft for most scenarios. All of these use the Azure Resource Manager deployment model.

Expand table

Type of storage account	Supported storage services	Redundancy options	Usage
Standard general-purpose v2	Blob Storage (including Data Lake Storage[1]), Queue Storage, Table Storage, and Azure Files	Locally redundant storage (LRS) / geo-redundant storage (GRS) / read-access geo-redundant storage (RA-GRS) Zone-redundant storage (ZRS) / geo-zone-redundant storage (GZRS) / read-access geo-zone-redundant storage (RA-GZRS)[2]	Standard storage account type for blobs, file shares, queues, and tables. Recommended for most scenarios using Azure Storage. If you want support for network file system (NFS) in Azure Files, use the premium file shares account type.

Figure 5.16: *Azure storage accounts*

Using storage accounts to refer to storage resources and authenticate to them has plenty of benefits. The accounts provide naming for the resources that would need another mechanism if storage accounts were not used. The accounts also provide a natural and intuitive way to authenticate and authorize the storage resource. Simply, if one can authenticate the account, they can access the resources associated with it. From a security point of view, there is the issue of leaking the secret associated with the account. Using Entra IDs as a default mostly mitigates this concern, as a lot of effort has been made to protect Entra ID secrets, but the concern has not been eliminated. The storage accounts can also be used in **shared secret** mode, and management of this **shared secret** is handled by the application. The documentation explained how shared secrets can be enabled and disabled, which is the default. It could be that the brownfield application is using shared secrets and will continue to do so when migrating to the cloud. While this is well understood, it should also be pointed out that using shared secrets comes with a slew of security concerns. It is strongly recommended that the platform do the secret management and implement the needed authentication protocols. For Azure, it would be using Entra ID libraries and services. Note that Entra ID is the default authentication mechanism for storage services. Enabling other options, like shared secrets, requires configuration changes. To be consistent, it should be mentioned that using Entra IDs is another way of saying **using OAuth2 via Entra ID identity provider**, but saying just **using Entra ID** is simpler and clearer, and it is likely correct when we consider that protocols may change, but IDs are less likely to do so.

Azure networking services

Azure networking offers customers ways to configure so that a customer resource is only connected to other customer resources. As it was mentioned earlier, such a promise is hard, if not impossible, to prove. The feature is in high demand, nevertheless, and as such, should be given to customers.

Azure offers a variety of networking solutions covering all potential needs of applications deployed in the Azure cloud. This includes routing requests from external applications to cloud application endpoints, as well as connecting cloud application internal components that are not exposed externally.

A complete list of Azure Networking resources can be found at **https://azure.microsoft.com/en-us/products/category/networking**.

The following figure shows these top offerings:

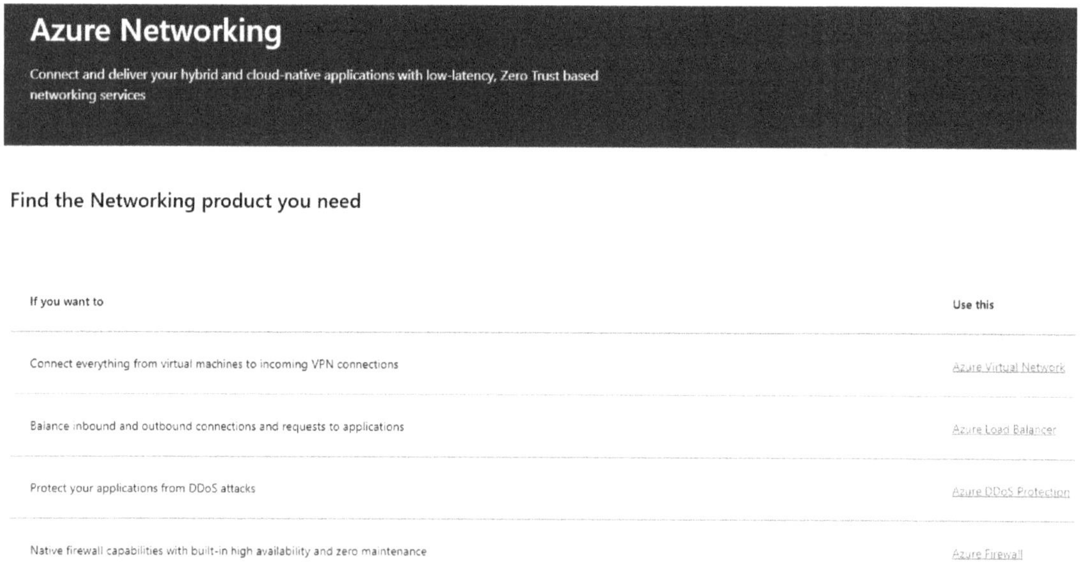

Azure Networking

Connect and deliver your hybrid and cloud-native applications with low-latency, Zero Trust based networking services

Find the Networking product you need

If you want to	Use this
Connect everything from virtual machines to incoming VPN connections	Azure Virtual Network
Balance inbound and outbound connections and requests to applications	Azure Load Balancer
Protect your applications from DDoS attacks	Azure DDoS Protection
Native firewall capabilities with built-in high availability and zero maintenance	Azure Firewall

Figure 5.17: *Azure networking products*

Note: **The variety of different offerings. What we need to call out as well are the smart defaults. The cloud provider does not expect its customers to be network experts. Given the many choices, it would be hard for one to choose the product they need. To simplify the process, consider the two vectors, which are new applications (greenfield) and existing applications (brownfield).**

Existing applications would most likely expect some networking environment with certain properties, and the cloud providers, Azure in this case, need to provide networking to meet application requirements, so that the application can move to the respective cloud. Since the application already exists in some environments, it is reasonable to expect that owners are intimately familiar with the application network requirements.

By contrast, greenfield applications have different requirements. For starters, one cannot expect that owners are intimately familiar with the application network requirements. That said, it would be perfectly reasonable to expect that owners have clear requirements regarding application performance, scalability, security, and so on. These need to be translated to network requirements by the cloud provider without burdening application owners with networking expertise. For example, it would be reasonable for the application owner to ask that the cloud provider run their Python application and guarantee some latency and throughput to users using defined device types in the defined internet environment, say a user in an internet café in region X must be able to use the application while observing so and so latency.

XYZ as a service

It has become very popular to advertise and offer almost anything as a service. While discussing compute, storage, and networking, it would be appropriate to address this subject as well. Since compute, storage, and networking are the main building blocks of any application, one can argue that they are also cornerstones of any service.

A starting observation would be that any compute function, as defined in the *Compute* section in the chapter, can function as a service of some kind.

The term **as a service** refers to delivering the desired functionality over the internet and without the need for physical access. For example, food cannot be offered as a service because there needs to be physical access to the food. However, orders for food can be made by a service because the order itself is not physical. Any processing pipeline consists of actions that may or may not require physical access. For those actions that do require physical access, like consuming food, the outcome can be encoded in a digital form.

If we are to visualize the **as a service** workflow, consider the following figure:

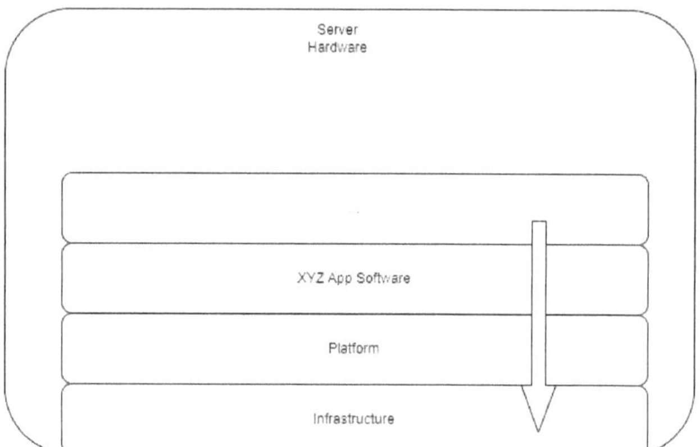

Figure 5.18: *XYZ as a service*

Some perspectives on the historical developments, as it all started with vendors offering **Software as a Service (SaaS)** products. Then we had **Infrastructure as a Service (IaaS)**, **Platform as a Service (PaaS)**, and eventually everything as a service (XYZ as a Service).

From a layering perspective, software needs a platform, which needs an Infrastructure to run on, as shown in the figure above. Such layering has produced SaaS, PaaS, and IaaS terms to verbalize the picture presented. There are a couple of points to point out:

- XYZ as a service and SaaS are semantically the same. XYZ is being more specific as it specifies, or at least it should, SaaS semantics.
- To uphold the layering, the infrastructure (IaaS) should only be used by the platform (PaaS) components. The SaaS (or XYZ) should only need to call into the PaaS exposed APIs. However, this may be wishful thinking as many SaaS providers would be tempted to call into IaaS directly, bypassing the PaaS layer for whatever reason.

Concrete implementation of the layers comes in the form of firmware, operating systems, and runtime libraries. To avoid difficult-to-diagnose and debug issues, it is strongly recommended that code in each layer calls only functions exposed by the layer below it.

From a security point of view, each layer must explicitly authorize the calls at the entry points exposed to the upper layers. While it could be better to allow anyone who has physical access to make the call, it could be reasonable in some situations. Being explicit about it is very useful as components are getting reused in new setups, and understanding the authorization rules will go a long way in staving off unexpected security issues.

It would be beneficial to look at and understand the similarities and differences between storage services and the XYZ app. There are applications that can function on their own, say an email service, and others whose primary use is as components of other applications, such as an Azure storage offering like a blob store. Indeed, the blob store, on its own, will not make sense to have as a standalone application, like the email service. This would be a major difference between the two services.

The corollary here is that storage applications are most appropriate as components of other applications, let us call the others XYZ. These other applications can either be components or act as user-facing applications that offer some form of **user interface (UI)** to enable user interaction. This interaction can be offered by a device-installed application using a device's native UI capabilities or by a generic browser rendering UI content received from the cloud app.

Other Azure services

Looking at the Azure portal and documentation content, we can notice that Azure (the same is true for all clouds) services are much richer than the compute, storage, and networking ones discussed in this chapter. All others can be classified as XYZ, as a service concept presented in the previous heading. While we put the focus on applications that run in the Azure cloud, it has to be pointed out that applications using some Azure XYZ service can run anywhere.

For example, a service running in some other cloud could be using an AI service offered by Azure. The services offered by Azure cannot be available in the cloud when the application is running.

The view of AI services from the Azure portal looks as follows:

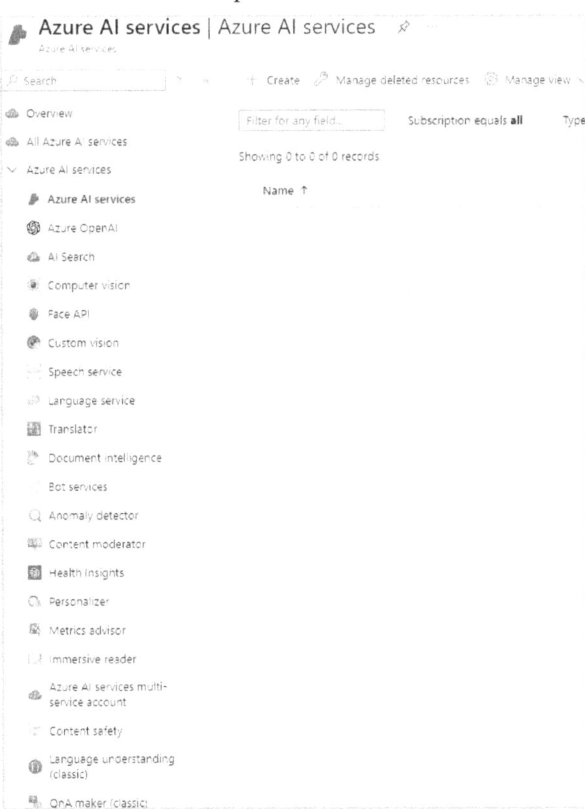

Figure 5.19: *Azure AI services*

The main things to call out are the following:

- Azure AI services are offered as Azure resources. This is the same model used for any Azure-managed service offered to customers.
- We can consider them to be Azure SaaS offerings or XYZ as a service offered by Azure.
- One needs to have an Azure subscription to subscribe to a given service. While this is not technically necessary, as subscriptions can be done using other means, Azure subscription services have a lot of benefits. To mention a few, it is popular, provides visibility, and is easy to onboard.
- As is the case for all Azure resources, authentication to the resource requires the caller to authenticate with their Entra ID, and the service will authorize usage using Azure **Role Based Access Control** (**RBAC**). More on this process in *Chapter 6, Authentication and Authorization.*

The above are some of the main points about offering a service as an Azure resource. The main takeaway should be that the consuming application does not normally need to run in the Azure cloud. While such a restriction could be introduced, it would make little sense to restrict the pool of potential customers.

Queues and asynchronous processing

In recent years, architecture patterns based on queues and asynchronous processing have gained considerable popularity, and for a good reason. The pattern promotes application simplicity and avoids common pitfalls.

The application logic looks like the following:

```
# application logic illustrated using sample code
# get an item from incoming queue, process it and put it in outgoing queue
of
# processed items
# start with importing needed apis
from myWorkQueue import Dequeue as DequeueWorkIem, Enqueue as ReportResult
from myAppRequestProcessor import ProcessRequest as ProcessRequest
# request processing loop
While (not End):
      RequestItem = DequeueWorkItem(IncomingQueue)
      Out = ProcessRequest(RequestItem)
      # End=True would indicate the item was the last one to process
# ...
```

The following figure illustrates the process:

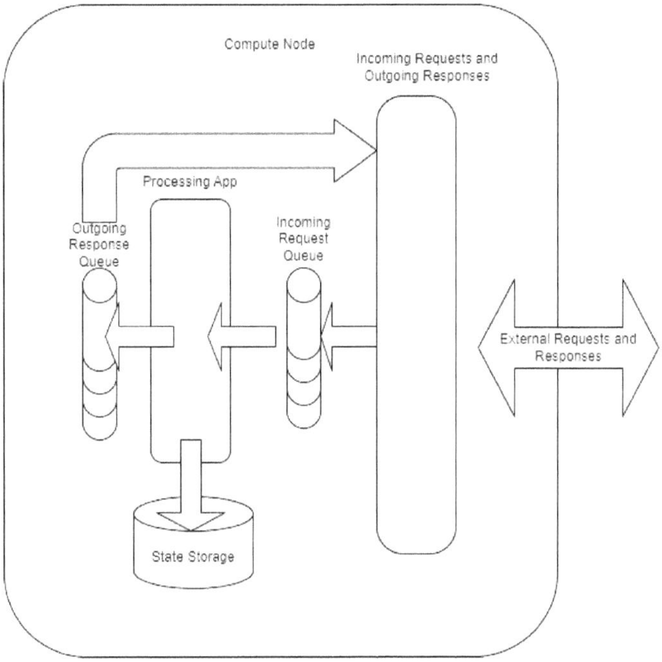

Figure 5.20: *Request and response queues*

The figure looks very similar to the blockchain architecture described earlier in the chapter. The issue would be, as it normally is, the security implications of implementing the architecture. Yes, it could be robust and convenient to implement, but the security issues still need to be called out. Specifically, the external request and response processor (the rightmost figure shown above) cannot authorize the entity that puts the response in the outgoing response queue. If an attacker gains access, somehow, to the queue, then they can manufacture a response of their choice. Fixing this issue would require that a response be accompanied by proof asserting the entity that generated the processing application in this picture.

Similarly, requests in the incoming queue must be protected from being faked. An attacker who gained unauthorized access to the queue should not be able to insert a request of their choice. Blockchain architectures accomplish this by having the requests (called transactions) signed by the key belonging to the entity that issued the request. The authorization system must support this. If the entity does not have a record in the state storage, then the request will not change any state changes, rendering the request processing an empty operation.

As mentioned above, the state storage needs to be protected. This was discussed in the *Storage* section.

Mechanisms for implementing desired authorization will be described in more detail in the next chapter. Here, we want to bring the reader's attention to the need for such authorization. It may look like a safe proposition to use internal data structures and think of request and response queues. However, these queues could get exposed to attackers, which can result in unexpected behavior.

Note: **The queue is accessed by more than one entity, which brings in the need to expose externally facing endpoints. In short, writing to the queues needs to be protected, and readers need a way to validate that whatever they got was produced by legitimate writers. We call this authorization.**

Kubernetes concepts

Many application owners want their applications to be cloud-agnostic. Using Kubernetes is a viable option. Kubernetes is a container orchestration system that can be viewed as managing the platform on which applications run. In a way, it constitutes a platform built on top of infrastructure provided by the cloud operator. Kubernetes architecture is described in the documentation behind this URL: Cluster Architecture | Kubernetes.

The underlying Kubernetes cluster architecture is shown in *Figure 5.21*:

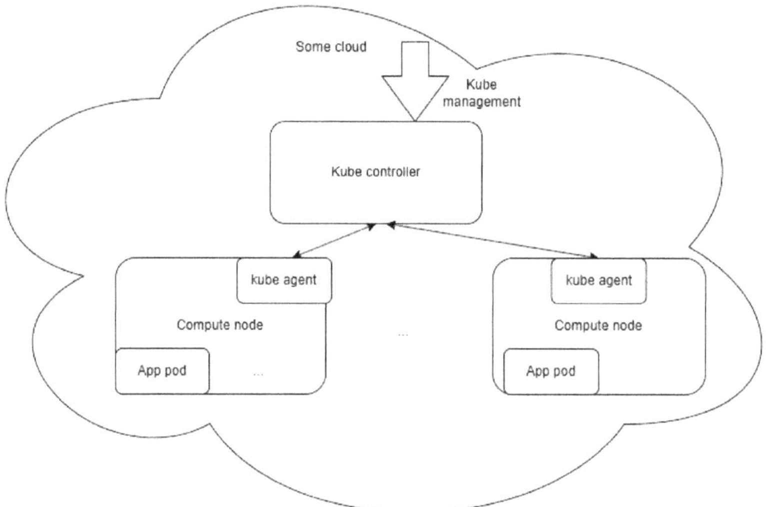

***Figure 5.21:** Kubernetes nodes architecture*

Using a unified platform on top of cloud-specific infrastructure is a great concept. It allows for managing applications in a cloud-agnostic way. The cloud-specific action is deploying the platform (Kubernetes in our case), which requires fewer updates relative to the updates required by individual applications. One still needs to be able to scale the cluster nodes to meet application needs. Kubernetes cluster cloud providers have provided such capabilities. Azure Cloud refers to this functionality as Kubernetes Autoscaler. Detailed Azure autoscaler documentation is at cluster autoscaling in AKS overview, Azure Kubernetes Service | Microsoft Learn.

It uses the concepts shown here:

Cluster autoscaling in **Azure Kubernetes Service** (**AKS**) overview, Azure Kubernetes Service I Microsoft Learn:

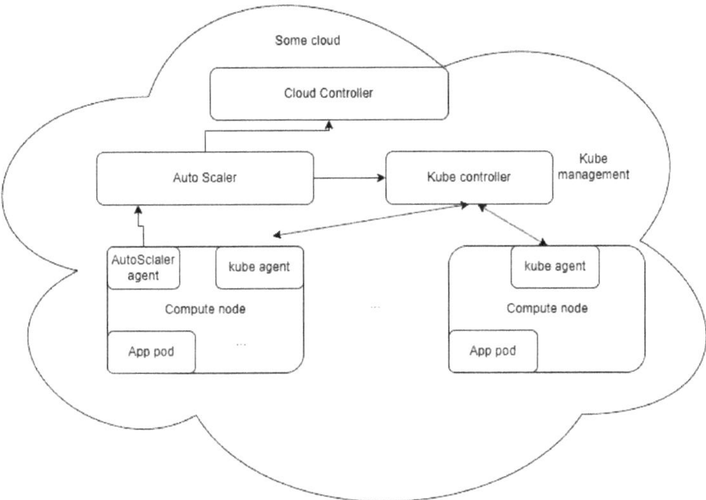

Figure 5.22: Azure auto-scale AKS cluster nodes

This autoscaling feature allows application owners to dynamically manage resources needed by the application based on usage.

Scaling architectures

The two notable architecture patterns examined here would be **Kubernetes Event-Driven Autoscaler** (**KEDA**) and Edge Computing.

Kubernetes Event-Driven Autoscaler

Details can be found at the **KEDA** website: **https://keda.sh/**. In a nutshell, KEDA is an iteration of the Autoscaler described in *Figure* 5.22. There is a level of indirection applied to make the model more usable. The Autoscaler agent can be replaced by a more generic monitoring agent that transmits monitoring values to some queue. KEDA can then apply logic to the events recorded in the queue.

Edge Computing

The idea behind it is to place some of the compute processing close to where the raw data is generated, thus reducing the amount of data that needs to be transmitted over the network to a compute node lying further from the source. This assumes that the network bandwidth needed to transmit data carries a cost that is higher than the cost needed to maintain compute bandwidth close to the data source. Although it may be practical to do so in some cases, if we assume the network is pervasive and available at some constant cost, the advantages of Edge Computing will disappear quickly. From a security point of view, any edge processing can be considered public. Benefits of improved performance would be available to anyone who has physical access to the edge network.

Conclusion

Traditional compute architectures are based on the compute, storage, and networking paradigms. Computers put these components together for applications to use. To understand the importance, it would be useful to look at the most valuable companies at the end of the 20th and beginning of the 21st centuries.

Cloud providers have implemented the same concepts, aiming to facilitate the cloud migration of existing applications, called **brownfield**. While the **brownfield** is expected to keep businesses afloat at the beginning, it would be the **greenfield** that should provide the expected explosive growth.

Greenfield applications would be **cloud native**, the semantics behind being that these applications were designed to run in the cloud and have accepted one or more dependencies on cloud services, providing storage and / or other functionality such as complex compute done using the application's data.

There is an important security consideration in this design. In classical applications, we rely on physical isolation for security. Cloud applications rely on authorization to figure out the requester's rights.

While there is little doubt that greenfield applications would be cloud native, it is still undecided which exact cloud these applications will be affiliated with. The desire would be to adopt cloud-agnostic management interfaces, like Kubernetes, that will enable resource management in any cloud.

Kubernetes nodes must be provided by someone. Cloud providers, like Azure, do it. There are **Azure Kubernetes Service (AKS)**, **Amazon Elastic Kubernetes** (EKS), **Google Kubernetes environment** (GKE), etc.

Note: The elasticity feature is offered by all clouds. In a nutshell, it boils down to provisioning new Kubernetes cluster nodes when certain conditions are met, mainly around resource utilization, like CPU running hot.

Clouds have invested a lot in automating the deployment of code from repositories to cloud compute resources. For Azure, refer to the content behind this link **https://learn.microsoft.com/en-us/azure/aks/learn/quick-kubernetes-automatic-deploy?pivots=azure-portal**

We need to call out the scaling feature that would automate cluster node provisioning. While Kubernetes, as designed, does not offer this auto-scaling capability, cloud providers implement it and offer it to customers.

There is a security-related downside to the auto-scaling feature. It should be true that the auto-scaler identity is authorized to deploy applications, along with the required secrets.

This means that if the auto-scaler gets compromised, the attacker will take advantage of the auto-scaler identity to access application secrets. Without the auto-scale, the design could be such that the admin who has access to application secrets must be compromised at the time of resource allocation to execute a successful secrets compromise.

The auto-scaling of Kubernetes clusters and asynchronous processing were the two main architecture examples used. Both had a profound effect on developer productivity, measured as the ability to deliver applications that solve important business problems at a low cost, measured by the number of nodes allocated to the application, thus removing the scalability concerns in application design.

While productivity has increased, there still exist security-related pitfalls that could derail application adoption and usage. These security-related concerns need to be addressed to ensure that trust with users is being created, which would result in more application usage.

The next chapter discusses **authentication and authorization** concepts and design patterns in detail.

Exercises

In this section, readers would be asked to look at the applications or applications they are considering to deploy from the lens of compute, storage, or networking paradigm.

1. Determine if the owned application falls into the brownfield or greenfield category. Most security-related activities would depend on this determination. If a brownfield is most often the case about migrating an existing application to the cloud, there would be very few choices to be made. The overriding concern would be doing the migration with minimum changes. If the application is using some storage by calling APIs from imported libraries, these need to be available and working in the cloud environment. A brownfield application does not have any cloud dependency since it was developed before clouds existed. It would be great to keep it this way, as introducing a cloud dependency would make it more difficult to migrate the application later to some other location, if required.

2. Determine storage needs by the application compute. This is assuming the application is classified as greenfield and cloud native. Needs can be expressed as functions with defined functionality. For example,

```
# expressing storage needs as functions. Use python's syntax
# to define an abstract class with methods defining the needed
operations on the data
# functions are methods on the abstract class. Shown are Query and
AddData functions.
# There could be others….
class StorageFuncs(ABC):
```

```
@abstractmethod
def Query(self, args) :
# query base implementation
# …
@abstractmethod
def AddData(self, args):
# AddData base implementation
#...
```

In the example above, the class **StorageFunc** isolates the application from the specific storage implementation details. The class providers should not forget to implement authentication for the storage service and handle authorization-related errors. This topic was discussed in more detail in *Chapter 4, Application Identities,* dedicated to application authentication.

For the **StorageFuncs** class to have visible access to the authentication state, it needs to have access to the security context.

```
# security context is now a property of StorageFunc
class StorageFuncs(ABC):
      # secContext type defined in the previous chapter
      # initializer
      def __init__(self, secContext):
      self.secContext = secContext
      # … other needed initializations …
      # … rest of the class defnitions …
```

3. Prioritize assets to protect. Consider assets contained within compute and storage resources provided by the cloud. Ask yourself the question needed to determine the most important assets. Refer to the previous chapter to learn about methods to partition the data and authorize access.

4. Define and implement protection schemes. In the general case, it would be the authorization of the caller that would be the protection scheme in use. Determine places in the code to do authorization. These need to be on every path starting at externally exposed endpoints.

   These tasks may look like common sense, but application writers often overlook them. Platform support in the form of libraries, classes, and APIs that the platform offers to the SaaS app goes a long way in promoting best practices.

   Using the sample code as an example, if the class implementing storage access promotes using the security context, then the application developer is more likely to use the request context as it is supposed to.

   Overall, the main idea here is that security designs must be a cornerstone of the underlying architecture, not something that feels like a bolt-on add-on.

Chapter 6
Authentication and Authorization

Introduction

Authentication and authorization are probably one of the most important issues in cyber (or not) security. In this chapter, we will examine in detail the main concepts behind these and the various techniques used to achieve desired results. As a matter of approaching the issues, the starting point would always be defining the desired results and then working back to define the techniques and processes used to achieve them.

It is a common assertion to state that some application or service is secure. What is meant by this statement is that known security weaknesses are not found in the application. As we stated in the first chapter, security issues fall into two main categories: remote code execution and improper authorization.

To put the concepts in a more understandable form, examples from the non-digital (some call it **real**) world would be used to illustrate. Authentication is about asserting some identity property:, such as name, age, nationality, and so on. On its own, authentication does not provide rights to anything. Authorization is about an entity's right to something. Some form of a ticket gives one the right to enter a venue at a certain time (for example, to see a concert or a movie) or use certain transportation services for a certain time. The ticket is the authorization needed to consume these services. Using a ticket can be visualized as presenting it to someone guarding the entrance to the venue, and gaining access to the person at the entrance, checking and approving ticket validity. Oftentimes, upon approving the ticket, the person checking the ticket would mark it somehow to indicate that an authorization has been performed. For single authorization scenarios (one admission), the mark is in the form of physically destroying the authorization artifact, like tearing the ticket used for authorization. This approach does not work in the digital realm, as it is relatively easy to produce an ideal copy of a digital artifact, so it is impossible to destroy it, considering that there can be an infinite number of copies. However, if instead of trying to destroy the ticket, the authority checking the authorization can record the usage in a lookaside data store. Then, the logic of computing authorization must consider ticket validity, as well as the number of times a ticket has been used. For the common **one admission** case mentioned above, this number is one.

Structure

In this chapter, we will cover the following topics:

- Concepts that support the authorization process
- Authentication mechanics
- Authorization process
- Blockchain implementations
- Cloud offerings with Azure

Objectives

Authentication and authorization constitute the basis of what is referred to as **computer security**. The primary objective of this chapter is to provide an in-depth examination of these fundamental processes, describing the existing architectures that support them. The main idea is that access to resources needs to be authorized, and authentication exists to aid such authorizations.

Concepts that support the authorization process

Performing the authorization in code would look like the following:

```
#
# There has to be a function that validates a ticket and one that records ticket has been used
# First, the string ticket initializes ticket object
TicketObject ticket(stringTicket)
def TicketUseAuthorize(ticket):
# the function recording usage would look like this
UsageCount = RecordUsage(ticket)
```

```
If ticket.IsValid() and RecordUsage(ticket) < MAX_USAGE
        return True
return False
```

To visualize the process, consider the following figure:

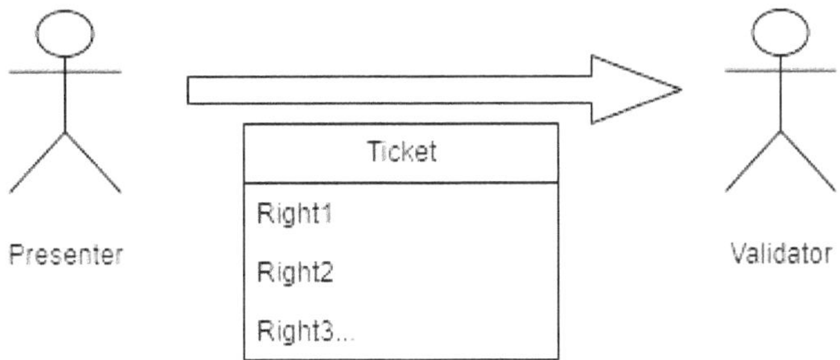

Figure 6.1: *Authorization ticket validation*

There are a few important things to call out here. Some of these will be discussed in more detail later in the chapter. To begin with, note that there is no reference to an authentication process or an identity to which the authorization ticket was issued. This does not need to be the case, but most often is, so it is taken for granted. The other thing to notice is that the authorization ticket is **bearer,** meaning that the possession of the ticket, alone, entitles the holder to the authorization rights encoded in the ticket. Again, this does not have to be the case. The ticket could be bound to a secret, and the presentation ceremony could include proof of the secret possession. Doing so would make the ticket secret-bound (also known as **proof-of-possession** (**PoP**) ticket) instead of bearer, so having possession of the ticket without the associated secret would not suffice to use it. While this is a great property to have, the benefits need to be weighed against the extra cost incurred by the complexity of implementing the PoP ceremony.

Such ceremonies are not straightforward to design and implement, though they may look so. One of the main factors bringing in complications is the need to agree on a protocol and data format of the proof that should be agreed upon, documented by some trusted authority, for example, the **Internet Engineering Task Force** (**IETF**), and implemented by the various vendors. In addition, the elements of negotiation are needed to reconcile different versions and ensure a level of interoperability.

Adding all this together amounts to a significant effort that is expected by many highly qualified engineers, which does not come cheap. Such a significant investment has to be justified. A big hyper-scaler company could do it and absorb the cost without affecting the bottom line in a significant way. But, even there, requiring a more complex ceremony for ticket presentation would affect third-party application integration.

For the decision to require a complex presentation, see the next heading for details that would rest upon estimating security benefits that come from demanding the extra complexity compared to the extra integration friction that needs to be introduced.

Tickets, tokens, assertions, and other artifacts

These terms are often used interchangeably. A ticket, also called sometimes a token, carries information that is used to authorize access to a resource by the entity presenting it.

Tickets can carry information about the presenter's identity, which can be used for authorization at the resource, or the ticket can carry authorization information and may not include claims describing the presenter's identity.

Either way, the ticket would be used to authorize access. This heading will not examine ticket types, but rather methods used to present the ticket to the resource service.

Bearer ticket presentation

This is likely the most common construct used in the non-digital world implementation of authorization tokens. A document issued by some trusted authority is the most recognized form. Consider, for example, a ticket that authorizes the holder to use a service or access a location. A ticket authorizing the use of public transport would be a good illustration of the bearer authorization concept.

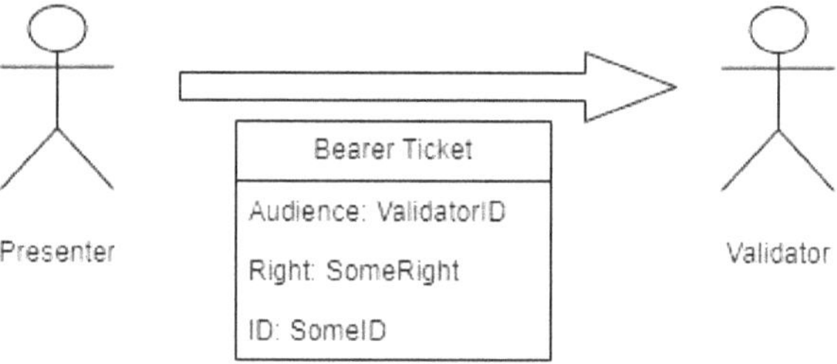

Figure 6.2: *Bearer token presentation*

To point out an obvious flaw with using bearer tokens, such a token can be used by anyone who gains possession. Since the token is transferred as is and gets handled by a variety of applications, opportunities to leak it are plentiful.

It should be assumed that with time, the probability of a token leak increases. The actual function of the increase is unknown; all we know is that it goes up. That is the primary reason why the most common mitigation against bearer token misuse is reducing the token lifetime. Logic is as follows: since the probability of a leak increases with time, reducing the token lifetime also reduces the probability of leaked token misuse, assuming the time it takes for the leaked token to make it to the attacker and be misused by them exceeds the token lifetime.

Another important property of the bearer token is the audience. It signifies who the token is meant for. Tokens with an audience set to A should not be accepted by validators whose IDs are different than A. The **identity provider** (**IdP**) dispensing the tokens keeps the validator token URL | validator ID mapping.

To conclude bearer token thoughts, we can see that using bearer tokens is justified in scenarios where the cost of upgrading the token presentation ceremony exceeds the benefits of preventing unauthorized resource use via leaked bearer tokens.

Proof-of-possession ticket presentation

This one is a bit more involved. To introduce the language describing the method in question, the term PoP.

Taking a step back to the goal is to protect the receiving party against a replay of leaked tokens. Binding the token to a PoP key in possession of the sender ensures that even when leaked, the token cannot be replayed without having access to the PoP key. To clarify the importance of such binding, it eliminates many of the downsides described when using bearer tokens. The token can be recorded without fear associated with recording a secret, as possession of the token alone will not be sufficient to use it as proof of anything.

In the non-digital world, identity documents often require some PoP binding. For example, consider the picture attached to some authority (government) issued identity document. The presentation ceremony requires that the checking entity compare the image in the picture to the face of the presenter. The picture (from there comes the term **picture ID**) plays the role of a PoP binding. This requires that the picture (the PoP) cannot be changed without invalidating the document. This approach can be compared to having a digital assertion, such as encoding, which should not be important, could be binary, **JavaScript Object Notation (JSON), Extensible Markup Language** (**XML**), or other formats, signed by a trusted issuer and carrying the PoP key.

Note: **Changing the PoP key, similarly to changing the picture in the picture ID document, would render the ticket invalid. Including the key artifact, say a public key, in the signed identity ticket would accomplish this.**

To illustrate a presentation with PoP, consider the following figure:

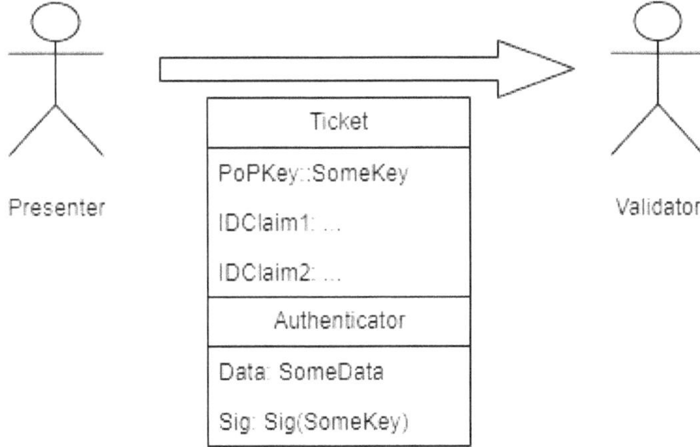

Figure 6.3: *PoP ticket presentation*

Though it may not be immediately obvious, constructing an authenticator normally involves data from the part where the token is presented, which involves an additional network round-trip. Since a round-trip was already performed to ensure security in the lower layers (TLS), doing it again would impose an unacceptable performance penalty. In the blockchain section, we will review how this can be done without requiring data from the relying party. If an authenticator can be constructed without this additional round-trip, then the concerns about the incurred additional network latency would be eliminated.

Non-repudiation

A definition, from the web search results, reads the following:

- **Nonrepudiation:** Nonrepudiation provides an assurance that the sender of data is provided with proof of delivery and the recipient is provided with proof of the sender's identity, so neither can later deny having processed the data. Further, this concept can apply to any activity, not just the sending and receiving of data. In a more general sense, it is a mechanism to prove that an activity was performed and by whom. Nonrepudiation is typically comprised of authentication, auditing or logging, and cryptography services. A common application of this service would be the digital signing of e-mail messages to prove that the message received was actually sent by the purported sender.

  Since access control and nonrepudiation share so many common components, they are frequently implemented together in controls or else closely interrelated. For example, once an access control function has been performed, it may provide sufficient data to facilitate nonrepudiation or at least partial nonrepudiation data.

  For complete details, see **https://www.sciencedirect.com/topics/computer-science/nonrepudiation#:~:text=Non%2Drepudiation%20is%20a%20security,fact%2C%20did%20or%20vice%20vers** for more.

  With bearer tokens, non-repudiation is hard to assert as the token can be easily lost and put into the **wrong** hands. Assuming the token carries the identity of the sender, it does not provide the desired non-repudiation since the sender can deny sending the request and claim someone used a stolen bearer token. In this line of thought, it should not come as a surprise that most identity documents have an associated PoP artifact.

- **Revocation:** Revocation is yet another feature to be considered. Every long-lived ticket, whether the presentation ceremony requires PoP or not, must be subject to revocation. Here, revocation means that validators should not accept revoked tickets. A common implementation of revocation is for the IdP to publish a revocation list containing identifiers of the revoked documents. A good example to look at is **Certificate Revocation List (CRL)** implementations. The entities validating certificates must download the CRL from the **Certificate Authority**

(**CA**) at regular intervals to account for revoked certificates. In the case of CRLs, the identifiers used are the certificate serial numbers, most likely matching some common non-digital world model, like using the passport or other identity document serial number to identify the specific document instance.

Most identity documents are long-lived and require a revocation mechanism. Granted that what can be considered long-lived is very much context-dependent, one can use some rules of thumb to determine if a ticket needs to be covered by a revocation mechanism. The most straightforward approach would be to offer revocation for tickets that live more than some pre-defined value X, but doing so, while straightforward to justify, brings in a lot of other issues. It is still resolvable, but it makes the logic a bit more complicated and brittle. For example, consider two tickets, which we will call t1 and t2. One is subject to revocation, and the other is not, in other words:

```
# t1 lifetime exceeds X which makes it subject for revocation. T2
lifetime is less than X and therefore, it cannot be revoked.
```

The issue here is the entity that decides if a ticket can be revoked or not. Since there are at least two entities that may have reasons to revoke a ticket, the determination of the ticket owner and ticket issuer is not unique. When the owner decides to ask the issuer to revoke a ticket, the issuer may refuse to say something to the effect **the ticket is not subject to revocation because its lifetime is too short,** and that is different than **ticket cannot be revoked because it was not issued by the authority asked to revoke it** and so on. Having clients parse all these errors and handle them accordingly would not be a reasonable request. What is more, it cannot be guaranteed, and the consequences of not handling the error according to some prescribed algorithm are generally unknown.

IdPs expose a token revocation endpoint, which is usually protocol-specific. The OAuth2 protocol has defined a revocation endpoint for the multiple token types used in the protocol. Refer to **RFC 7009 - https://oauth.net/2/token-revocation/**

This is somewhat settled behavior, and the **Request for Comments (RFC)** is about 10 years old. It allows clients to ask the authorization server to revoke a token that was issued to the client making the revocation request. This all makes good sense when we talk about confidential clients, such as the OAuth2 term describing entities that can keep a secret. On the other end of the spectrum are called public clients, and these, by virtue of being public, cannot be kept a secret. This makes it hard, if not impossible, to assert the identity of the entity making the revocation request.

Consider that there are three separate entities that can detect token compromise and ask for revocation, such as the client to which the token was sent, the token issuer, and finally, the access token recipient service, when the token was an access token. The quoted RFC specifies how access and refresh tokens can be revoked by the client. It does not specify that entities, other than the client, can detect conditions that warrant revocation. Another missing piece in the RFC is the mechanism of propagating the list of revoked tokens by the revoke API implementation, which lives with the authorization service, to the service consuming the access token. The services consuming access tokens must get notified about the tokens that were revoked. The most prominent example of such a process is propagating CRL from the CA to the entities accepting certificates issued by the CA.

Authentication mechanics

We call authentication the process of asserting an identity with properties, often called claims, to someone.

From the non-digital world, a good example will be using an identity document, like a passport, to assert name, date of birth, citizenship, and so on.

Authentication is done by an authentication provider, IdP. In the non-digital world, this would be the authority issuing the identity document. For example, country X issues passports for its citizens, and the passport contains passport authority-issued claims about the presenter's identity, such as name, passport number, address, and so on.

The main point about IdPs is that the identity properties asserted by an IdP are specific to the IdP issuing the identity document. One cannot compare identity properties asserted by different IdPs.

Multi factor authentication

A **multi factor authentication** (**MFA**), sometimes referred to as **two-factor authentication** (**2FA**), is an approach to combat password compromise as the main vector of identity compromise. The thinking behind this is that compromising multiple factors would be more difficult, and this way deters potential attackers.

In this heading, we will look at the available factors, calling out the advantages and disadvantages of each.

Factors in MFA:

Knowledge, possession, and biometrics

A few words for each factor. A more detailed description will follow:

- Knowledge
- Possession
- Biometrics

We devote a section to each where the factor is analyzed in detail.

MFA goals

The goal of MFA is to combat identity exposures caused by a single authentication factor compromise.

A common example is the effect of compromised passwords. There are many ways to get to know someone's password, such as through brute force, security breaches at another service where the same password was used, phishing, and so on.

If a password compromise easily leads to an identity compromise, and from there, a compromise of the resources the identity was granted access to.

Mitigating these consequences would mean that compromising a password alone will not be sufficient to compromise the identity to which the password belongs. This approach is in line with the spirit of eliminating single points of failure.

To summarize, authenticating the identity requires more than one factor to achieve the goal that compromising one will not lead to identity compromise, and while this sounds great on paper, there are a few pitfalls that should be pointed out.

The factors are known as knowledge (password, secret question or answer, pin, etc.), possession (my phone), and bio (for example, one's fingerprint). It is important to note that instituting multiple instances of the same factor, such as taking a password and a secret question or answer, does not translate into MFA. For authentication to be considered MFA, multiple factors must be used.

The MFA factors will be looked at in more detail in the following section.

Knowledge

This factor is sometimes referred to as **what you know**. Passwords, **Secret Answers** (**SAs**), and **Personal Identification Numbers** (**PINs**) fall into this category. This is the most traditional and well-understood factor, and at the same time, it happens to be the most disliked by the users. The main gripe is that ever-evolving requirements about password complexity make it practically impossible for a human to remember multiple passwords. And while complexity increases may help withstand brute-force attacks on password stores, the resulting drop in usability makes such increases hard to accept.

To formally name a few of the above-mentioned downsides, one of the most serious ones is, let us call it, **password proliferation**.

Applications ask that the password used be unique for the application being used. While the ask is reasonable from a security point of view, as it mitigates a class of attacks related to leaking stored passwords, the ask to use unique passwords per application is not reasonable from a usability point of view, considering users need to have multiple passwords to comply with this ask. Anecdotally, it is hard enough for users to remember one password, let alone multiple.

Enter password managers (also known as key rings) in the figure.

The following figure illustrates the concept:

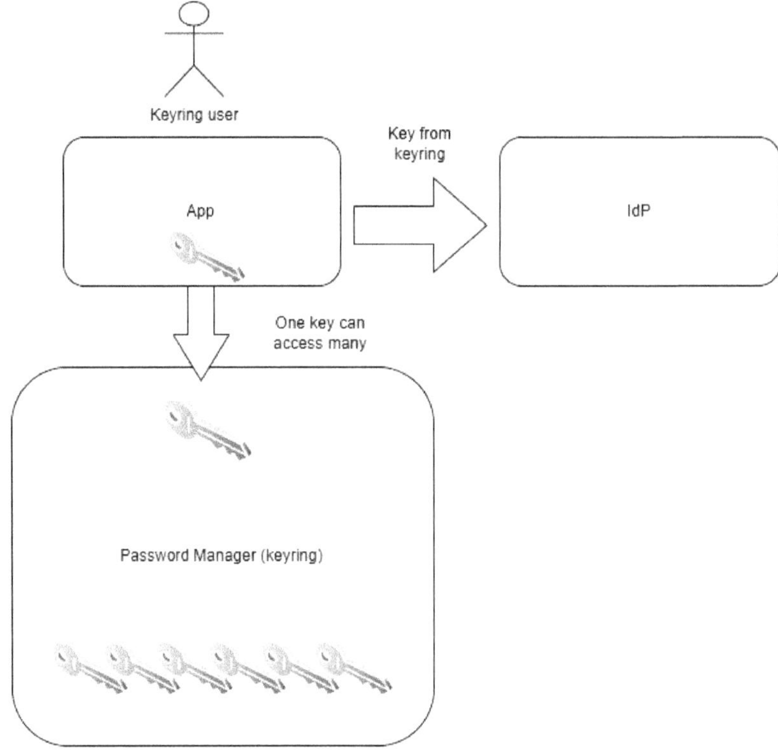

Figure 6.4 (a): *App interacting with a keyring*

While on this subject, it should be noted that, not surprisingly, big software companies have implemented password managers (also known as keyrings) integrated with the respective platforms they own. Doing so is understandable, considering that keyrings potentially can increase usability, and from there, user affiliation with the platform. To put it simply, if the platform can address the multiple passwords problem, app developers will tend to write more apps for that platform, which would translate to more users.

Possession

Possession relates to having a hardware device capable of holding a secret. Oftentimes, this device is the smartphone everybody, or almost everybody, owns these days. Generally, it could be any device the user has access to, including the device on which the application is installed. Some could require that the **possession device** is different than the **application device**, though the benefits of such requirements impose the need to distinguish these devices at the authentication provider side, and the benefits of having such a distinction need to be justified using some data. For example, it shows that the number of compromises of the possession factor goes down in some statistically significant way if the distinction is imposed. The other aspect is that requiring multiple devices will negatively affect MFA adoption, and if MFA is optional, as it is often the case, it would be less likely to be adopted.

The following figure shows possession factor usage:

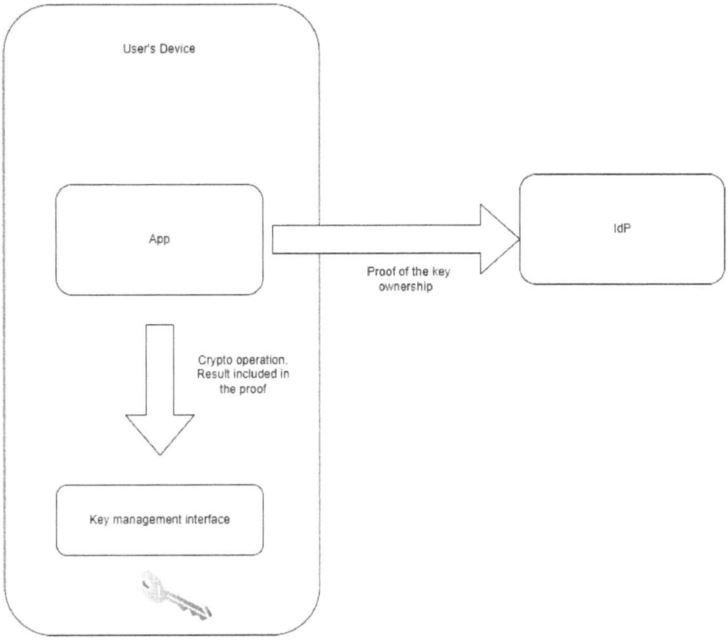

Figure 6.4(b): Possession factor

Recently, there has been an upsurge in passkey usage. Passkeys, by nature, are an implementation of the possession factor, as the key needs to reside somewhere. It is a great idea that would, hopefully, stick with users. As can be seen, possession can turn out to be the main, if not the only, factor for authentication to an IdP on the network. Having a model that resonates with the majority of the users would go a long way to strengthening the security posture of the authentication process.

Bio

The bio-factor carries a lot of promise. Common examples are using a fingerprint or retina scan, or a DNA sample. The difficulty of using these entities as a factor is that the bio cannot be changed for practical purposes. Once leaked, it becomes a public value and stops being a secret or a factor of authentication. Considering that with time, everything gets exposed, one can conclude that a bio factor, alone, cannot be used for authentication. It needs to elaborate on the semantics behind **alone**. Consider this example: one's fingerprint could be public information posted on some internet site. However, a fingerprint can still be used as proof of identity. The reason is that the sample is taken by a trusted device, possibly before witnesses, thus eliminating the possibility of the public sample being submitted as proof. The key to this is the availability of what we call a trusted device or sensor, guaranteeing that the sample was obtained following a due process, which eliminates or at least minimizes the possibility of an external sample being introduced.

Biosensor releasing a key is shown in the following figure:

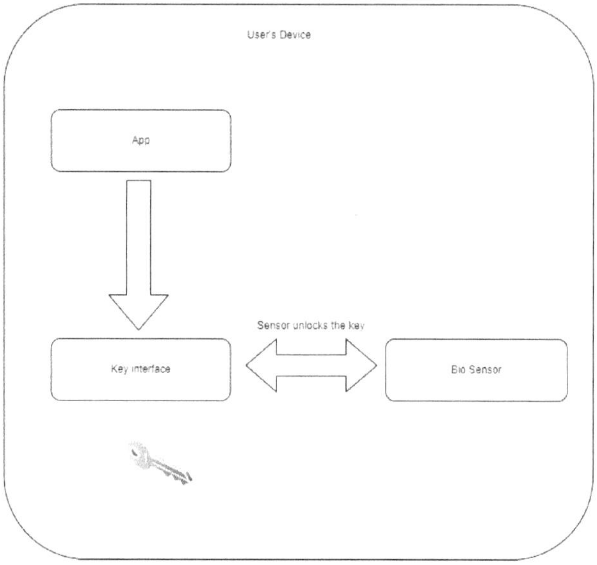

Figure 6.4(c): Bio sample taken by a trusted sensor

The task of determining what constitutes a **trusted sensor** in a network environment is not trivial. This is the reason for using a bio factor:

Phish-resistant authentication

As a starting point, consider that any user input is subject to phishing. For example, consider UI asking the user to enter a code she received over SMS. It can be a phishing attempt, the same way phishing UI is asking for a password. To make the authentication phish-resistant, it must be bound somehow to the server identity serving the UI. There have been efforts, albeit futile, to teach users how to distinguish UI coming from **trusted** servers. Someone can remember the green URL bar in the browser indicating the visited site has an **Extended Validation** (**EV**) certificate. Even if users are paying attention to it, a big if to start, there are many applications that insist on not showing the address bar, for perfectly valid UI design reasons, and this renders this line of defense indefensible.

The key statement is: *Any user input is subject to phishing.*

- To make it phish-resistant, the secret must **NOT** be provided by the user in the UI presented by the receiving application.
- If we look at the passkey designs, the user is not providing a secret for the application directly. Rather, the secret, or bio gesture, is provided to the local device where an application-specific secret is unlocked and sent to the IdP associated with the application. This approach eliminates most phishing possibilities as the secret is provided by a device component, and the user authorizes the secret's use in the UI presented by the component:

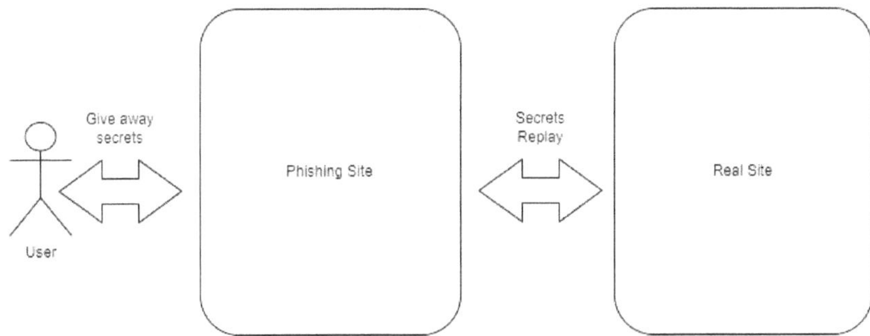

Figure 6.5: *General phishing model*

- The main takeaway is that phishing resistance implies not asking users to provide a secret in the application's provided UI. To go a step further, no secret used as proof is ever exposed to the user. If it is, someone will find a way to phish it. The main idea is that if the secret is never exposed to the user, then it cannot be phished, hence the phishing resistance.
- The secret is generated by some component on the device and protected with some gesture that is to be provided by the user's bio or knowledge factor. Users unlock access to the secret using the gesture.

> Note: **In this case, the bio factor is fine to use since access to the protected resource, a secret on the local device, also requires device possession. The bio factor, alone, is not useful without possessing the device with the secret.**

Using a passkey registered with an **Identity Service** is illustrated in the following figure:

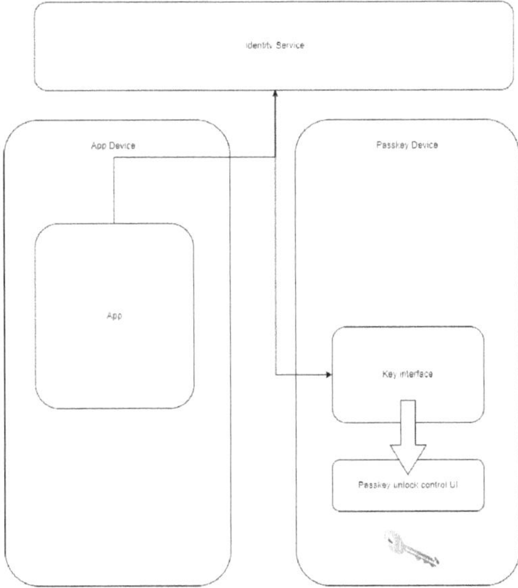

Figure 6.6: *Fighting phishing with passkeys*

Since there is no user to give away secrets and the passkey component would only give secrets salted with the site name found in the TLS certificate, the phishing site cannot steal users' secrets since the user's secret is not given away in any app provided UI. In fact, the user does not need to know their secret, so they cannot give it away.

- **The MFA promise:** What needs to be recognized here is that MFA is not a universal solution to all possible security problems. As was shown in the *Phish-resistant authentication* section. MFA factors could be subject to phishing, and if phishing is the main attack vector, then using non-phishing-resistant MFA factors will not move the needle much. Conversely, a non-MFA, single-factor approach could be phishing resistant and provide needed security benefits if phishing is the main attack vector.

  The other aspect related to MFA is that it must be recognized that the knowledge factor is required, which makes eliminating the problem passwords all but impossible. This is because the bio factor is, let us call it, **cloud problematic** because of the trusted sensor requirement, and this leaves knowledge and possession factors on the table. If knowledge is also removed, then possession remains the only option, and this is fine from the security point of view, but it is not MFA. Another term needs to be introduced. For example, something like **strong authentication** may work.

  The semantics behind the term would be that the authentication process is resistant to some known attack vectors. It may not be MFA, but it could still be **strong** in terms of attack resistance.

  Yet another axis to classify the authentication process is discussed next.

- **Mutual authentication:** The general picture looks like the following:

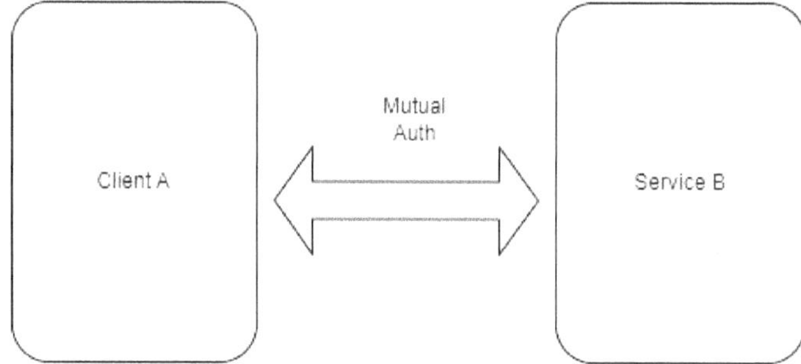

Figure 6.7: Client A talking to Service B

  Mutual authentication is often not intuitive to understand. When A is talking to B, there needs to be some assurance on each side regarding the other side's identity. Taking A as the client and B as the service, it is often the case that the service identity is implicitly assumed, where the client must present some explicit identity proof.

This phenomenon may have its roots in the non-digital world. As an example, consider the case of an individual at a border. The border patrol agents' identities are assumed by virtue of their being there and wearing some known uniform. The same cannot be said about the people who need to cross the border. Their identities cannot be assumed, and they need to present some identifying documents to the agents to get through. There is an apparent asymmetry here, and for a good reason. More on this subject can be found in the next section.

Symmetrical and asymmetrical models

These terms, symmetrical and asymmetrical, are used to describe the authentication protocols used to assert the client and the server identities. For example, a symmetrical protocol is **Transport Level Security** (**TLS**). It supports client and server certificates that enable client and server mutual authentication.

Other protocols (such as OAuth2) rely on tokens to deliver the identity and authorization delegated to the client.

Consider the following figure showing the different methods used to authenticate the client and service:

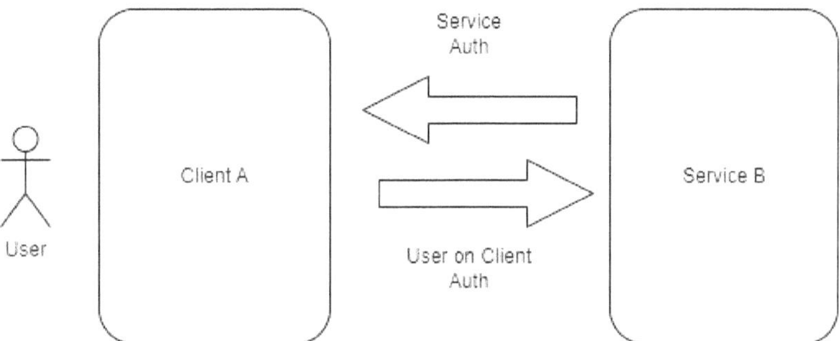

Figure 6.8: *Asymmetrical authentication*

In the figure above, the server authentication is over TLS. TLS also provides the integrity and confidentiality of the channel between the client and the server. The tokens authenticating the client are transmitted over this channel. It would be useful to reiterate the statement made in *Chapter 4, Application Identities.*

The token-based designs are layered on TLS transport that provides server authentication, as well as integrity and confidentiality (encryption) of the data transmitted over it. The token economy rests on TLS.

Without having TLS transport to step on, these designs would not be possible. A lot of recent design efforts, for example, OAuth2 and OpenID Connect, gravitate to the asymmetrical model. This is a natural consequence of the need to innovate, together with the difficulty of modifying TLS. It is a lot easier to innovate on top of some stable baseline.

The other important aspect to point out is that TLS is usually provided by the HTTP transport, and the user authentication comes from some package, module, or lib the application integrates with separately from the HTTP stack used. Such decoupling provides needed flexibility as user authentication protocols can evolve without having to change transports underlying TLS implementation.

Authorization process

The purpose of doing authentication is so that one can perform authorization on the authenticated identities. The reverse statement is not true, meaning that authorization can be performed without authentication. In fact, there are three distinct cases to consider:

- **Authorization without authentication:** Historically, this is probably the most common pattern. Easy to implement, use, and explain are the most appealing characteristics. Less glamorous is the relative ease of creating counterfeit copies of the authorization ticket. As a non-digital world example, consider the ticket one buys to gain access to a concert (substitute your favorite venue). The main point here is that possession of the ticket grants access by itself, without requiring any identity proof.

  Authorization ticket presentation is shown in the following figure:

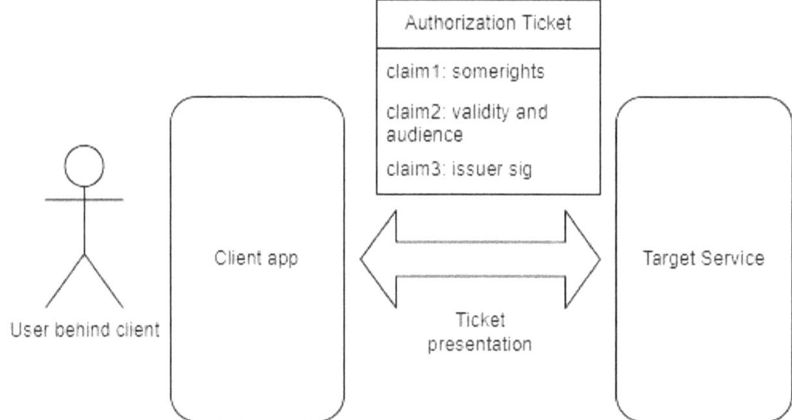

Figure 6.9: Ticket-based authorization

  In the figure above, if an attacker manages to steal or duplicate an authorization ticket, appropriate measures need to be taken to mitigate the impact of such actions. The tricky part is that the cost of these measures should be less than the cost of the damage inflicted by using the stolen or duplicated tickets.

- **Authorization weakly bound to authentication:** To illustrate the use case, consider this example: to be allowed into a concert venue, the individuals must have a ticket **AND** be over eighteen years old.

Sending both authorization and authentication tickets is shown in the following figure:

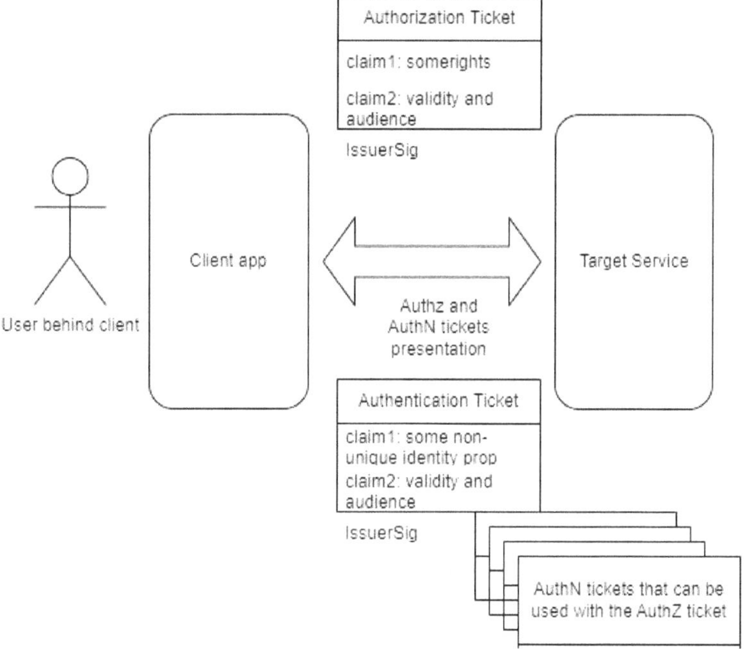

Figure 6.10 (a): *Weakly bound authorization ticket*

The main point illustrated above is that there can be multiple identity documents asserting the age of the presenter, and the claim of being over eighteen is not unique to any one identity document. The result is that the same authorization ticket can be used by many identities if the age can be computed to be over eighteen. There is the question of whether **over eighteen** claims should be part of the authorization ticket or not. A valid case can be made either way. In the example, we assume that the **over eighteen** identity claim is NOT part of the authorization ticket, meaning that the logic to accept such an authorization ticket only if accompanied by an identity ticket asserting the **over eighteen** claim is encapsulated entirely in the receiving service. There is nothing in the authorization ticket that restricts the identity of the presenter.

- **Authorization strongly bound to the authenticated identity:** Finally, we get to the strong binding meant to ensure that there is a one-to-one binding between authorization rights and the identity to which these rights are given.

  From the non-digital world, consider airline tickets. An identity document for the subject, matching the name on the ticket, is required for a person to be allowed on the plane.

  Like the previous figure, which illustrates the **strongly bound** identity concept, there is only one identity bound to the authorization.

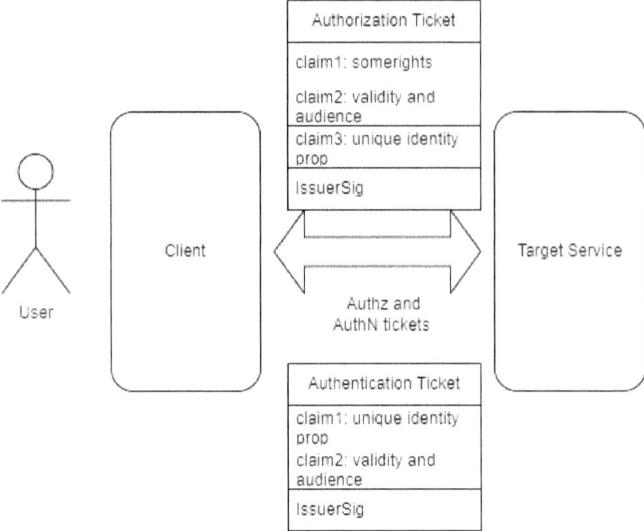

Figure 6.10 (b): *Authorization strongly bound to identity*

As opposed to the weakly bound identities, where the mapping of the authorization to identity is one-to-many, the strong binding requires a mapping that is one-to-one. This also allows for the authorization to be stored somewhere and not be carried as a ticket in the request. Only a ticket representing the identity is required.

The figure above shows how two tickets can be bound on some property, the unique identity property in this case. The strong binding semantics imply that there is one and only one identity possessing the unique property referenced above.

In the following, it is shown how binding can be done using one authentication ticket and data from the authorization policy document:

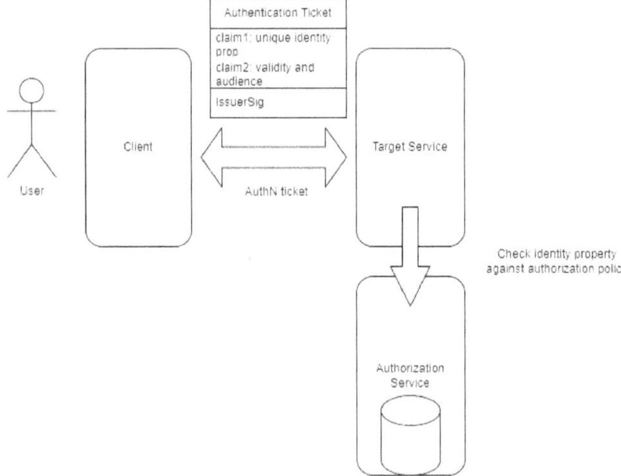

Figure 6.10 (c): *Strong binding with authentication ticket and authorization policy*

In this figure, the authorization policy comes from storage, not from the authorization ticket in the request.

To continue with the non-digital world analogy, the process of airline travel would typically include using both patterns described above. When checking in at the airline counter, the passenger provides an identity document. The name in the document (which plays the role of the unique identity property bound to the authorization) is matched against a name in the reservation system, and if a match is found, a boarding pass is issued to the passenger. This check has the same semantics as checking the identity property against the authorization policy. The boarding pass serves as an authorization ticket strongly bound to the identity document using the unique identity property. The two documents are checked for identity property match, and the boarding pass is checked for permission to board an airplane in the next N hours.

What should be called out is that these checks follow the patterns described in StronglyBoundTickets and StronglyBoundPolicy, *Figures 6.8 (a)* and *6.8 (b)*.

Delegation and impersonation

These concepts have a lot of practical relevance and warrant a more detailed definition:

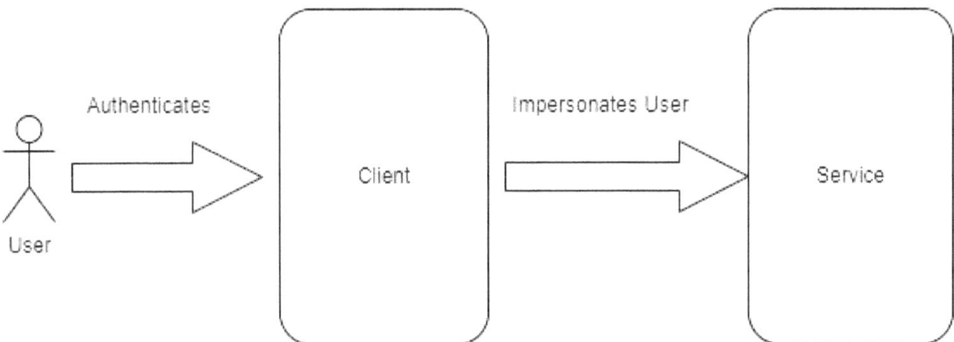

***Figure 6.11 (a)**: App impersonating a user*

The main thing to note about impersonation, as defined, is the unrestricted type of identity authentication, meaning that all rights assigned to the identity are automatically available to the entity impersonating it. We can also call this pattern **unrestricted delegation**.

Delegation, the more general term, involves delegating a subset of the identity rights to some entity. Doing so requires that the process of delegating be aware of identity rights. The delegation process is usually part of authentication, and identity rights are part of authorization, which implies that the authentication service knows about authorization models.

The delegation concept is shown in the following figure:

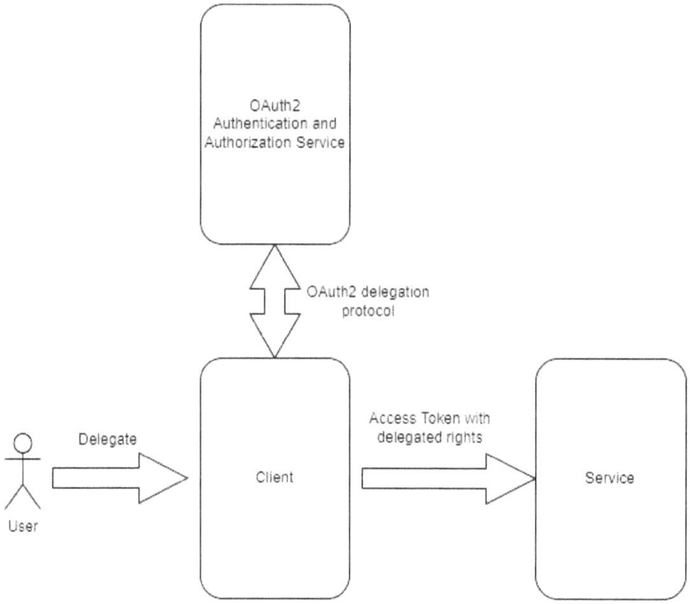

Figure 6.11 (b): *Delegating identity rights*

The most prominent example of delegation is the OAuth2 protocol. It performs authentication in a protocol-agnostic way and adds a consent experience to achieve delegation semantics so that the rights of the identity delegated to the application are restricted to whatever the delegating user has consented to. The benefit of using delegation is the protection achieved in the event of client compromise. If the client had full impersonation rights, then any resource authorized to the user identity could be potentially misused. With delegation, resources and operations on them are restricted to the set consented to by the user.

The tricky part about implementing delegation is combining authentication and authorization in the OAuth2 service. The service needs to know the rights the subject has so it can delegate some of them. The other option, chosen by Entra ID service, is to enable delegation consent experiences without checking if the rights are assigned to the subject. This works, though it requires that the authorization system in the service performs subject authorization and then restricts the subject's rights to what was delegated to the client. Doing so will ensure that the subject cannot delegate rights (s)he does not have.

Blockchains implementations

As it was stated previously, referring to *Chapter 4, Application Identities* blockchain examples are done assuming the blockchain is the Ethereum network. While the concepts are being used in multiple networks, choosing a specific one provides needed concreteness.

Blockchain's pattern is closest to the model described in *Figure 6.8 (a)* implies that a strongly bound pattern or authorization is only granted to a specific identity.

See detailed discussion in the *Authorization in Blockchains* section.

The canonical blockchain flow is shown in the following figure:

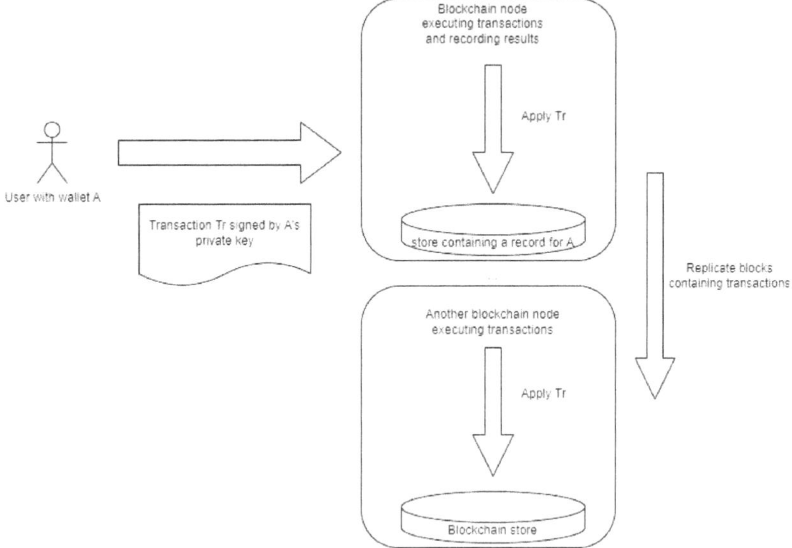

Figure 6.12: *Blockchain flow*

There are a few blockchain architecture details that should be called out. The client submits a transaction signed with the user identity key. This construct has a few distinguishing features:

- The most prominent one would be that requests, called transactions in blockchain terms, cannot be forged unless the attacker has access to the signing key. The blockchain nodes collaborate through some consensus mechanism to record the transaction and the results from execution, but a node cannot manufacture a transaction. Say the transaction says **A sends one token to B**. It is not possible to construct a different transaction, for example, **A sends one token to C** without having access to A's private key, also referred to as A's wallet.

- The nodes forming blocks, containing transactions, use some consensus algorithm to decide whose block to take. Well-known consensus mechanisms are proof-of-work, proof-of-stake, and proof-of-something. Basically, the nodes proposing a block must present some proof so that the rest of the nodes will agree to validate the proposal.

- The main point is that the nodes proposing blocks can only package transactions issued and signed by wallet holders. Other transactions would fail to be validated. As a reminder, the goal of this book is to examine the security implications of the various architectures. The details of blockchain consensus algorithms will not be examined in detail. Only the security properties of the mechanisms would be highlighted. Special attention would be given to possible failures that may lead to security breaches. In this context, the fact that nodes cannot manufacture transactions is important. Possible failures are not including a transaction, as well as trying to post the same transaction multiple times. The effect of this type of malfunction is different from the damage that would be possible if nodes could create transactions of their choice, and as it was shown earlier, the transaction **A sends N tokens to X** can only be created by A, or rather, signed by the private key that represents A's wallet. The nodes package transactions into blocks and use consensus to agree on block validity. The design efforts are directed to mitigating the effects of the failures caused by a node misbehaving, which can result in not including a transaction in a block or including it multiple times.

- Another significant observation is that the identity is derivable from the public key using some well-known function, such as a **hash,** for example. For illustration purposes, the derivation would be something like the following:

```
# identity is a function of the public key, call it DeriveIDfromKey
Identity = DeriveIDfromKey(pubKey)
```

This is an important callout. Specifically, the fact that the derivation function is purely computational and does not involve storage lookup. This can be seen as an advantage as the need to secure the lookup, and a disadvantage as there is nothing to lean on in a case where the key is lost or compromised. A new key means a new identity, which can be problematic when identity is used to authorize access to multiple resources. Re-authorizing access to all these resources could be hard, if not impossible. Blockchains typically have a single resource record authorized to such, let us call it a key-based identity, so such re-authorization is less of an issue. It boils down to creating a record in the blockchain store for the new identity that is identical to the old identity record. However, it should be noted that such a simplified model would only work for the simplest of scenarios. A few assumptions have been made along the way, and these assumptions are not always true. To be concrete, the first assumption is that an entity exists that gets notified when identity changes occur, such as changing the key from which the identity is derived.

The change notification function is outlined in the following:

- There exists an entity that is notified about identity key changes.

  The notification callback would look like the following:

```
# identity key changes notification callback
def CallbackForIdentityKeyChange(oldKey, newKey):
...
```

- The entity getting the notification should have permission to read and create records on the blockchain store.

The following section is about authentication and authorization implementations in blockchains.

Authentication in blockchains

The transaction signature constitutes the authentication. It serves as proof that the entity that submitted the transaction has access to the private key corresponding to the public key used to derive the identity. The important part characterizing this process is that the signature, let us call it proof of identity, cannot be used to authenticate a different transaction. As mentioned previously, the misbehavior one can worry about is the failure to execute the transaction and record the results on the immutable blockchain ledger. This may happen if the service the client is talking to is misbehaving or if the transaction processing software that runs an honest service has a bug that causes it not to behave correctly. Either way, verifying that the transaction is submitted to a valid blockchain node is a non-trivial exercise. Note that the transaction signature using the wallet private key serves as proof to validate the client's identity. There is no cryptographic key that can be linked to the service identity running on the node. The service identity, for example, the proof that the client is talking to a node on Etherium mainnet, must be provided differently. As far as authors know, there is no standardized way to assert the service identity.

The assertion that a compute node behind a network address belongs to some blockchain has to be based on trust:

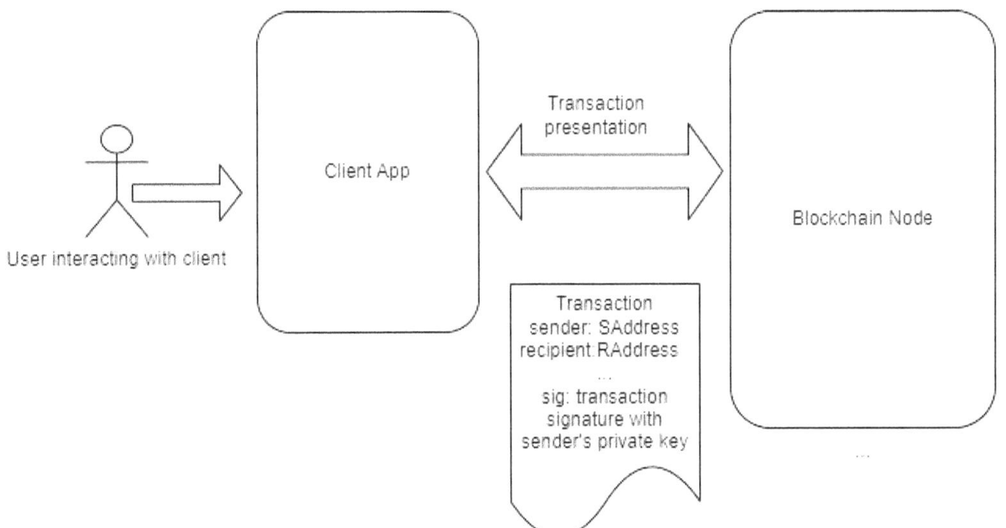

Figure 6.13: Client authentication in blockchains

Note: **The server authentication is not shown. There is implementation-specific server authentication, but it needs to be pointed out that for public chains, using key or certificate-based server authentication is not possible, since anyone can participate and gain access to the key or request a certificate. If anyone can become part of the chain, authenticating the participant is not useful for authorization purposes since the authorization rule is 'allow anyone'.**

It can be said that delegation is enabled for all since the implementation allows anyone to submit a transaction, but only the original sender can provide the signature. Once signed, the transaction becomes immutable.

Authorization in blockchains

Blockchain authorization uses, let us call it, **implied authorization rules**.

The basics are that the blockchain state is comprised of a collection of records where each record is identified by an address and a collection of properties.

An example record can be presented as follows:

Address of holder or ID	Property1	Property2
DeriveIDFromKey(HolderPubKey)	<some value>	<prop value>

Table 6.1: *Blockchain data item*

The implied authorization allows the PropertyN value to be changed by some function when executing a transaction signed with the holder's private key.

In the blockchain world, the most common example would be decreasing the account balance when tokens are being sent to another entity. To be concrete, the property is **`AccountBalance`**, and the operation is **decrease**. To execute the operation, the component doing the execution needs to have a transaction signed by the key associated with the holder ID. The asymmetry between increased and decreased authorization logic needs to be recognized here. It is the same **`AccountBalance`** property that gets changed, but depending on the nature of the change, authorization is different. The non-digital world example frequently given is comparing the holder ID to a bank account number. The observation is that the bank account number is not a secret, and while anyone can send money **TO** it, only the account holder can withdraw money, the same as the authorization rules applied when processing a transaction signed by the account holder's private key like sending tokens is authorized by the holder signature on the transaction while receiving tokens is authorized by any holder signature if the recipient in the transaction matches the account ID receiving the tokens whose balance gets incremented. The other rule to call out is that authorizing the sender must happen first. If the sender is not authorized for whatever reason, then recipient authorization must also fail.

These rules may look somewhat complex, but they are not hard to enforce given a transaction where the signer and recipient are known. The authorization is done by the blockchain virtual machine, such as EVM for Etherium, so applications can be agnostic about the authorization rules in play. A small caveat here is that the application may have its own storage, in addition to the blockchain store, and it would need to take on applying authorization for accessing records in its store.

Keys in blockchains

While the clouds, including Azure, could hold keys and make those available to applications and this way bootstrapping application authentication and data encryption, holding keys also presents a point of attack as the key holder receives privileges not available otherwise. Blockchains do not rely on secrets for implementing consensus algorithms. This is mostly true for proof-of-work algorithms, where the block proposer is selected because it was able to solve the computational puzzle (find a nonce value) fastest.

But even in this case, accessing the mining equipment (the one solving the puzzle) likely requires a key or some other form of authorization. The statement about not requiring a key is even less true for other consensus mechanisms, take proof-of-stake as an example, where the node selected to propose a block has to authenticate itself, and using keys is the only known authentication mechanism. In either of these algorithms, the keys might be used to manufacture a proof needed for node selection, but the keys are not used in the block structure. This allows for the nodes to hold different keys, not correlated with each other.

The scheme is represented in the following figure:

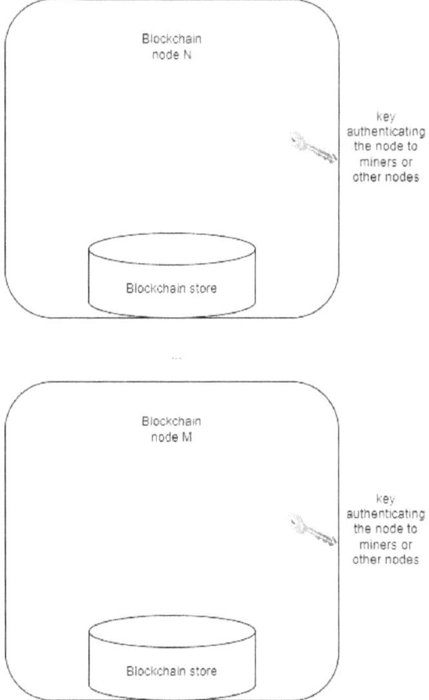

Figure 6.14: *Blockchain nodes having different keys*

The effect of this finding is that nodes can come and go, take their keys with them, and the blockchain will not be affected.

The main observation here is that keys are not part of the fundamental blockchain design, but rather an implementation of blockchain primitives related to peer-to-peer node communication.

Cloud offerings with Azure

Azure, and the same applies to other clouds, provides authorization services to cover resources offered to applications. With cloud providers, there are two aspects to consider: authorization given to the DevOps responsible for installing and running the application in the cloud, so they can provide the application with the cloud resources it needs.

The cloud resources, Azure, in this case, must trust someone to provide identifiers used for authorization. In the case of Azure, this someone is the EntraID service.

Azure authentication

Here, it needs to be discussed in detail, explaining EntraID usage in Azure. The most important and often misunderstood one is the EntraID (formerly Azure Active Directory) multi-tenancy architecture. It would become clear how it came to be when we follow the **Active Directory** (**AD**) evolution from on-premises to cloud:

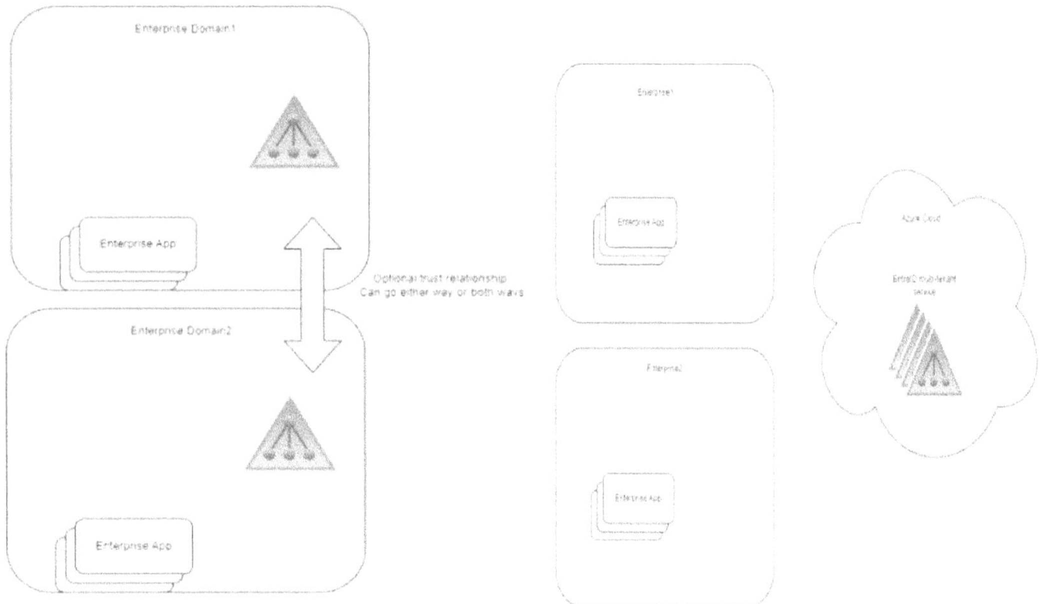

***Figure 6.15(a)**: Evolution of AD identity and authentication service from on-prem to cloud*

There is a bit of complexity here that is not obvious and deserves some explanation. In traditional AD architecture, the trust relationship must be explicitly established. It can be uni or bidirectional, with semantics defining who can authenticate to whom.

For example, if the trust relationship exists, users from enterprise domain1 can authenticate to applications in enterprise domain2.

In the cloud multi-tenant service configuration, there is no need to set up explicit trust relationships. However, users need to be invited into the organization to be able to authenticate to organization-installed applications

https://learn.microsoft.com/en-us/entra/external-id/b2b-quickstart-add-guest-users-portal.

Experience is described in the following Microsoft Entra documentation, excerpt shown in the following:

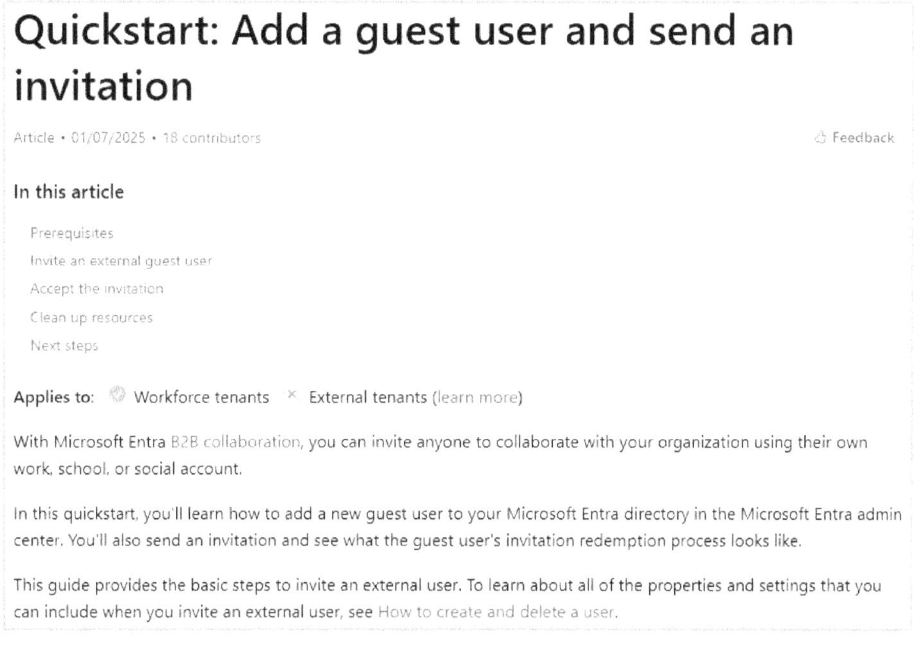
Quickstart: Add a guest user and send an invitation

Article • 01/07/2025 • 18 contributors

Feedback

In this article

Prerequisites
Invite an external guest user
Accept the invitation
Clean up resources
Next steps

Applies to: Workforce tenants × External tenants (learn more)

With Microsoft Entra B2B collaboration, you can invite anyone to collaborate with your organization using their own work, school, or social account.

In this quickstart, you'll learn how to add a new guest user to your Microsoft Entra directory in the Microsoft Entra admin center. You'll also send an invitation and see what the guest user's invitation redemption process looks like.

This guide provides the basic steps to invite an external user. To learn about all of the properties and settings that you can include when you invite an external user, see How to create and delete a user.

Figure 6.15 (b): *Entra ID guest invitations*

If we are to compare it to the on-prem AD experience, the explicit trust relationship creation could be viewed as inviting all directory objects from the foreign directory that are capable of authenticating themselves, also known as **security principals**. Let us call them **virtual**, and invitations do not result in physically instantiating the foreign objects as the invitations sent by Entra ID do, as shown above. The other important observation is that the Entra ID invitations work on users only. Other security principles are projected using other means.

It could be useful to discuss the reasons behind the discrepancy between Entra IDs and on-prem AD regarding the treatment of cross-organization collaboration, such as establishing trust relationships, sending invitations, and so on. The difference could be summarized as the format of the security identifiers used for authorization. Entra IDs, represented as

object ID property (oid), are in **Globally Unique Identifier (GUID)** format, where the **security identifiers (SIDs)** in AD are not present in the authority part of the identifier derived from the AD domain that issued it; see AD SIDs documentation. To emphasize that, given an Entra ID (GUID), one cannot determine who issued it. This design aimed to support authority changes without having to change the security identifiers issued by the old authority.

Note: **A compromised authority can issue tokens containing any security identifier and, in this way, affect the cross-organization collaboration between unrelated Entra ID organizations. However, Entra ID does not allow authorities, compromised or not, to mint security identifiers, so we are safe for now. It would feel safer if this assertion were made in the documentation, and appropriate controls were added to prevent such custom generation from happening.**

Azure authorization

Azure authorization is known as **Azure Role Based Access Control (Azure RBAC).** The authorization implementation relies on authenticated Entra IDs, which are needed to model the StrongBouldPolicy concept.

Details on Azure RBAC can be found in Microsoft documentation **https://learn.microsoft.com/en-us/azure/role-based-access-control/overview**.

Role definition experience documented behind the URL above is shown in the following figure:

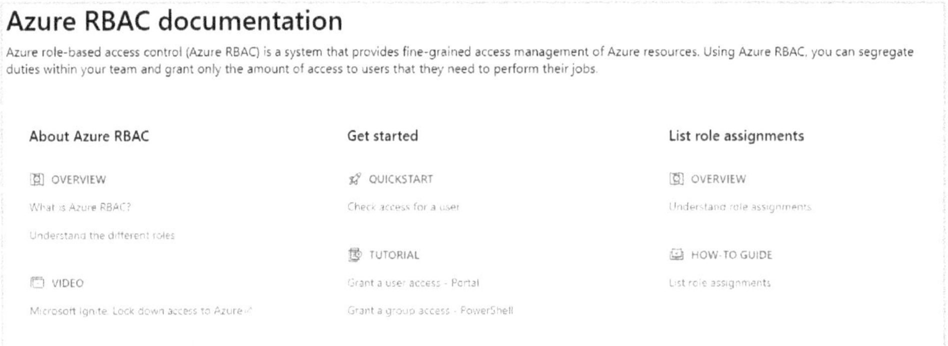

Figure 6.15 (c): Azure RBAC

Following are a few highlights:

- There is the **Azure Resource Manager (ARM)** that handles authentication and authorization for incoming requests. Resources behind trust ARM:

  `[arm handling authentication and authorization of incoming requests]`

  Figure 6.11 (b) ARM requests authentication and authorization.

- There is no delegation, probably not needed, meaning that ARM impersonates the authenticated identities to resources behind it.

  One can define custom roles. There is abundant documentation on how to do it. See **https://learn.microsoft.com/en-us/azure/role-based-access-control/custom-roles-portal**.

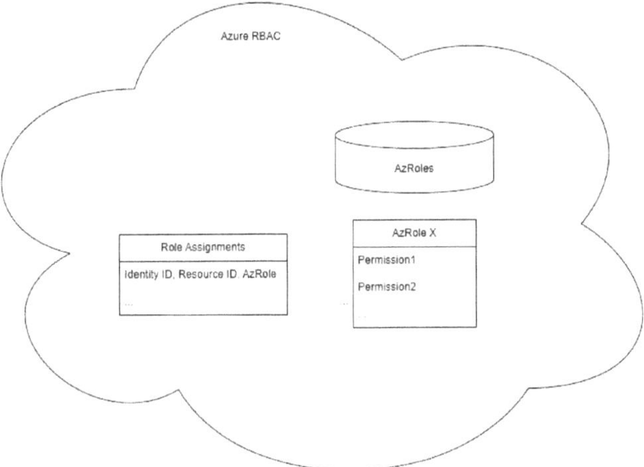

***Figure 6.15 (d)**: Azure roles*

- Each role represents a collection of permissions. However, creating permissions is not something one can do. Permissions are relative to the Azure resource providers, and resource provider services only come from Microsoft.

  For permissions details, see **https://learn.microsoft.com/en-us/azure/role-based-access-control/resource-provider-operations**.

  To visualize permissions, see the following figure:

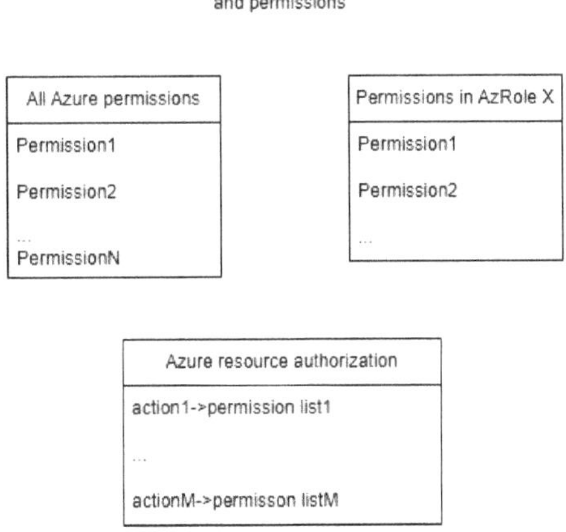

***Figure 6.15 (e)**: Azure permissions*

This structure is understandable from the cloud provider's point of view. However, applications running in the cloud need to have their own permission management system.

- Entra ID provides the authentication primitives. For authorization, it provides roles and permissions needed for managing Entra directory objects. See **https://learn.microsoft.com/en-us/entra/identity/role-based-access-control/permissions-reference**.

  There is some discrepancy between the authentication and authorization services available to applications by the Entra ID service. The authentication services are very rich. There is support for many protocols, device and application authentication, Windows desktop integration, and so on. By contrast, support for authorization is a lot less available. This is explainable. Most existing applications have authorization implementation and do not need one provided by the platform. This is not the case for new applications, where having authorization support will speed up time-to-market. It also shows that providing an authorization programming model to fit most applications' needs is a non-trivial task. There are both functionality requirements and performance considerations.

- A few words on attribute-based access control, also known as ABAC. Documentation is available at **https://learn.microsoft.com/en-us/azure/role-based-access-control/conditions-overview**.

  The following is an excerpt:

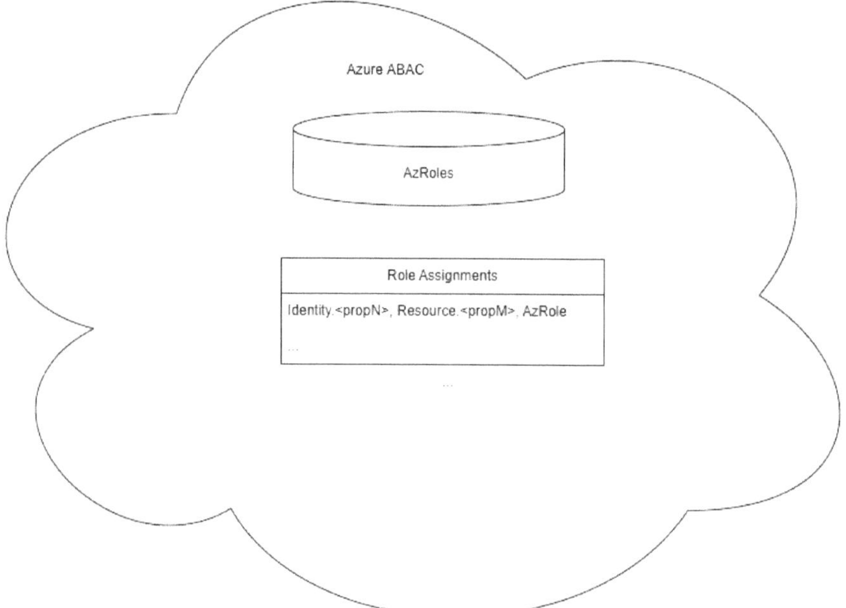

Figure 6.15 (f): ABAC documentation excerpt

A word of caution is that the attribute authorization used should only be mutated by the entity that owns the authorization policy. For example, suppose the attribute can be changed by the security principal it is a property of. Then, the security principal can set any value that authorizes access to the ABAC-protected resource, and if anyone can grant itself access, the authorization is not useful. These are subtle points, and mistakes can easily be made, resulting in security breaches. Some form of fail-safe procedures is needed to ensure this does not happen. For starters, it would be helpful to write down the desired outcomes and review how ABAC can help achieve them in the simplest and efficient way.

Conclusion

Authentication and authorization are the pillars on which application security is built. Many of the usage ideas originate from the non-digital world. The problem of authorizing resource usage is universal. One of the main findings presented is that authentication exists to help with the authorization process. Doing authentication without authorization is meaningless. But the reverse is not true. We can have authorization implemented without authentication, see authorization without authentication. The reason authentication exists is to make implementing authorization easier and avoid some of the pitfalls of misusing the authorization ticket.

Authentication itself is a complex subject. See the MFA for more in-depth discussion. It is a very important subject, keeping in mind that many of the security breaches are related to identity compromise, such as phishing, password database leaks, etc. All of these relate to identity compromise attacks. One of the main findings is that MFA, while being a very valuable tool, is not a universal protection against identity compromises. If phishing is the main attack vector, then phishing-resistant schemes, even if not MFA, can be very effective in combating the phishing threat. Recently, passkeys have been introduced by many applications as a **strong** authentication choice.

The next chapter is devoted to **encryption**. The main idea is that encryption is a form of authorization intended to protect data.

Subjects related to data confidentiality and integrity are discussed.

Exercises

The goal of these exercises is to raise the application security posture by providing needed visibility into the authentication and authorization workflows.

1. Authentication audit trail.

   For every request made, application owners should know the identity behind it. Even if the request is anonymous (unknown identity), the record should reflect that. A good report to have would be a list of all incoming identities with the request count and type for each.

Example record:

Identity	Request	Count ...

2. Authorization audit trail.

   Very similar to the above. Application owners would want to know what has been accessed, by whom, and how the request was authorized.

   Example record:

Resource id	Identity accessing it	Request id	Authz details...

3. Authorization techniques

   As it was described in the Authorization section, authorization can be performed with and without authentication. The question here is to spell out the authorization approach used by the application. It is strongly recommended that authentication be used as part of the solution. Existing applications will continue to use the authorization mechanism they have been using elsewhere, which may be the AuthZNoAuthN model. However, new applications should take a serious look at StronglyBoundPolicy as well as delegation mechanisms that protect services from client compromise events.

4. Authentication and authorization providers

   In most cases, it is not advisable that applications perform authorization and authentication of their own. Authentication and authorization providers, in the form of services and respective SDKs, are used. A service offering authentication APIs (implementing some public protocol) and / or authorization would also offer an SDK in common programming languages to developers, making it easy to integrate a developer application with the service.

CHAPTER 7
Encryption

Introduction

Encryption is being mandated by various compliance requirements. Take, for example, the **Health Insurance Portability and Accountability Act** (**HIPAA**) encryption requirements and **National Institute of Standards and Technology** (**NIST**) data encryption standards for encrypting data at rest and in transit.

From the HIPAA requirements document, one can find links to the NIST standards:

In addition to being significant requirements, when encryption solutions are implemented that comply with NIST SP 800-111 for data at rest and NIST SP 800-52 for data in transit, the encryption solutions contribute toward compliance with a recognized security framework as required by the 2021 amendment to the HITECH Act (HR 7898). For this reason, it can be worth spending time understanding the HIPAA encryption requirements.

The goal of this chapter is to dive into data encryption internals and examine what is being accomplished and what is not.

Encryption of data at rest and in transit will be reviewed in detail. Here, we start by stating the major goal of encryption, which is to protect data from unauthorized use. Since digital data can be copied easily, the goal can be restated as **protecting data from unauthorized exposure**.

The goal of encryption is to protect data from exposure to entities not authorized to see it.

To use other terms like encryption mitigates the single point of failure related to data access authorization. To see the unencrypted data, one needs access to the encrypted data and the decryption key. We can call this two-factor **authorization, as one needs to be authorized to access the data,** as well as the key it is encrypted with.

Data Encryption is an implementation of two-factor authorization.

Let us elaborate on the above statement. It is, if we can call it, **conditionally true,** and this needs an explanation. The encryption and decryption operations require a key. We will look at the decryption to be concrete. To gain access to the unencrypted data, one (let us call this one entity the attacker) needs access to the encrypted data and the decryption key.

It is also true that there is a case where the attacker does not have access to the encrypted data and decryption key mentioned above, but still gains access to the unencrypted data because some other entity exposed it.

Applying the data at rest or in transit encryption requirements recursively, the exposed data must be in one of these two states, such as at rest or in transit, and, therefore, must be encrypted. At this point, we need to address the question of handling and storing unencrypted data resulting from a decryption operation. Although not always true, we will assume that the process volatile memory is not available to the attacker. If it is, there will be much worse problems to worry about. If an attacker can peek into application memory, then nothing is safe. Attacker code can behave as the application since everything the application has is exposed.

Assuming that is true, if the decryption operation places the output result in the caller-supplied memory, then we can say that it is out of reach for the entities that, by definition, do not have access to the caller's memory. The data that must be protected with encryption resides in persistent memory (at rest) or network equipment devices (in transit).

The main point of having two-factor authorization is to mitigate the effects of compromised authorization operations. There is authorization to get to the encrypted data and authorization to get the decryption key. These authorization systems must be different for the two-factor to be effective. The goal is that an exploit that works on one system will not work on the other. This is hard to check. What can be said, though, is that if authorization systems are the same, then the same exploit will work on both. Taking the trivial case as an example, if the key and encrypted data are protected by the same authorization, then there cannot be a two-factor benefit. This would certainly be the case if the key and the data are placed in the same storage next to each other. Alternatively, the key and the data should be placed in different storage services using, presumably, different authorization services.

Structure

The chapter will discuss the following topics:

- Encryption of data at rest

- Key management
- Encryption options
- Encrypting data in transit
- Integrity and confidentiality of data
- Blockchains and encryption
- Azure storage option
- Key management
- Common pattern for data access

Objectives

The main objective is to clarify the role of encryption as a data protection technique. We dive into topics of encrypting data at rest, key management, encryption location, granularity, encrypting data in transit, cloud and blockchain approaches, and so on. Over time, encryption was looked upon as a panacea (catch-all cure) for data protection. However, as history teaches us, this is not exactly the case. A specific point is that the encrypted data can be considered to be as secure as the key used to decrypt it. The other important point highlighted is the difference between data integrity and data confidentiality.

Data encryption and decryption concepts

Separating key from data is illustrated in the following figure:

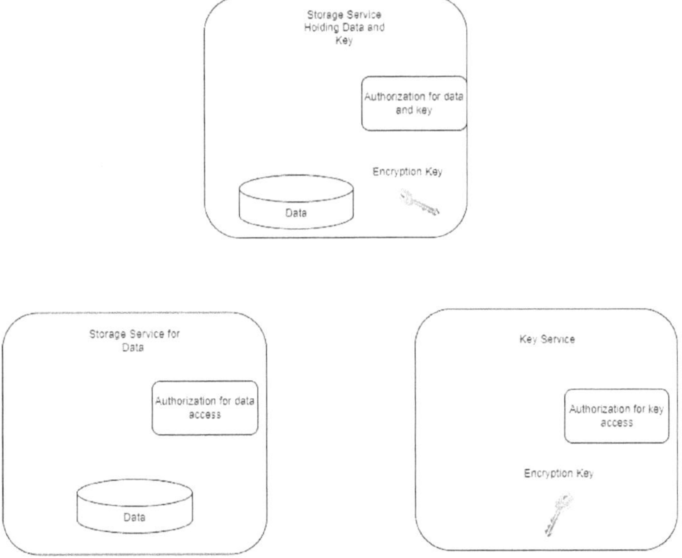

Figure 7.1: *Separating key and data*

It is interesting to note that identities authorized to access the key and the data may be the same or not. However, the authorization system has to be different. Yes, there is the issue of compromised identities that is addressed by upgrading credentials to include MFA and/or phish-resistant authentication methods, as discussed in *Chapter 6, Authentication and Authorization* If an identity is compromised, then any authorization will grant access to the protected resource. Here, we are considering the case where the identity is not compromised, but the authorization system is.

We will cover separately the encryption of data at rest and in transit. These may look similar, but there are a few major differences. These are related to decryption key availability. The key has to be available to decrypt when data is requested.

For data at rest, the timeframe for data availability is unknown. Once encrypted and placed in storage, the data should be retrievable, so the decryption key should be available. We will refer to both encryption and decryption keys as one entity called the **key**. This is to avoid terminology confusion. It does not make sense to have a key for encryption but not one for decryption or vice versa. In symmetric cryptography, encryption and decryption keys are the same, so this problem does not exist. Public key (or asymmetric) cryptography uses one key, which is not a secret, to do an encryption operation, and another private or secret key to do the reverse decryption operation.

Note: **It does not make sense to do one without the other, so both keys should be available or not. What is true, though, is that some entities only need to do encryption, and for those, using public keys relieves them from having to keep a secret. This may look appealing, but it is also an attack vector. The public key may not be a secret, but using the 'correct' public key has security implications. The entities doing encryption should somehow know that for operation X, public key Y needs to be used, and to illustrate, consider X to be the simplest case of writing raw data. For that, some integrity-protected store needs to provide X | Y mapping, providing the key, the raw data has to be encrypted before it is written to the data store. Such mapping can be expressed in a certificate signed by a trusted Certificate Authority.**

More on this subject can be found later in the chapter, as it is fundamental for encrypting data in transit designs.

Encrypting data at rest

Data at rest can also be called data in persistent storage. Since encryption and decryption require a key, key management becomes a major task.

See the NIST document on the subject as well. Most of the main points are covered there.

Another issue concerns identifying the entity doing encryption and decryption. There are a few options, each coming with some pros and cons. These options, along with their implications for each. The options are: doing encryption on the client handling the unencrypted data, the middle tier, the client talks to, and the storage service, the last one in the chain of calls.

See the various places where encryption and decryption can take place are shown in the [link to data encryption options] heading.

It is also necessary to consider the multiple interfaces exposed by a storage service, as shown in the figure:

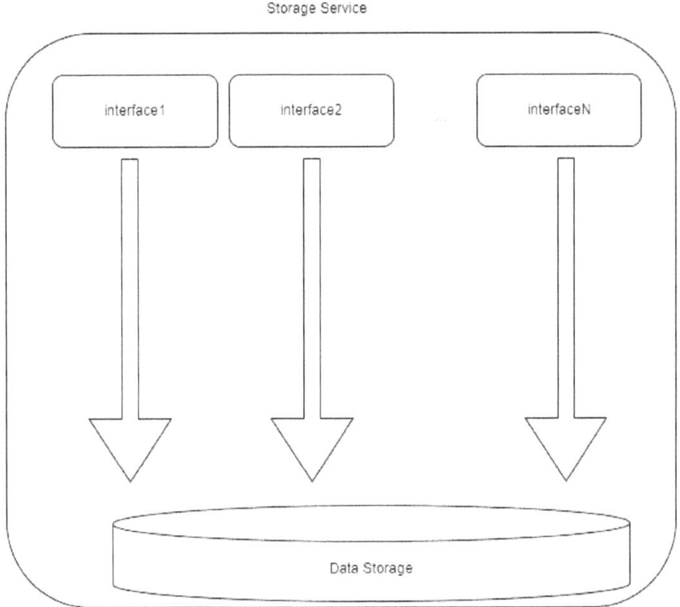

Figure 7.2 (a): Data could be accessed through multiple interfaces

An interesting problem is presented in the diagram above. Over time, the interfaces to access data proliferate as new technologies demand new ways to access data. However, the old interfaces are still present and do provide access to, let us call them **legacy**, applications.

One of these interfaces would be the physical access to the data. It can be described this way, so it fits other access patterns. The attack vector most stakeholders want to protect against is called the **take the disk home** threat. We can designate the physical access to the disk as an authorization method. In the spirit of using two-factor authorization, the attacker also has to be authorized to access the decryption key. Unless the key sits on the disk with the data, physical access will not do it.

Removing an interface is likely to cause an outage caused by some application error condition. In theory, it is possible to detect when an interface is no longer used and safe to remove. In practice, this is often a source of unexpected outages, and it is avoided for this reason as much as possible. Then, assuming all interfaces must be kept around, the problem can be formulated in relation to the many interfaces to the data stored. A new feature, like data encryption, could be made available to all or some of the data access interfaces.

Layering a new interface on top of an existing one is shown in the following figure:

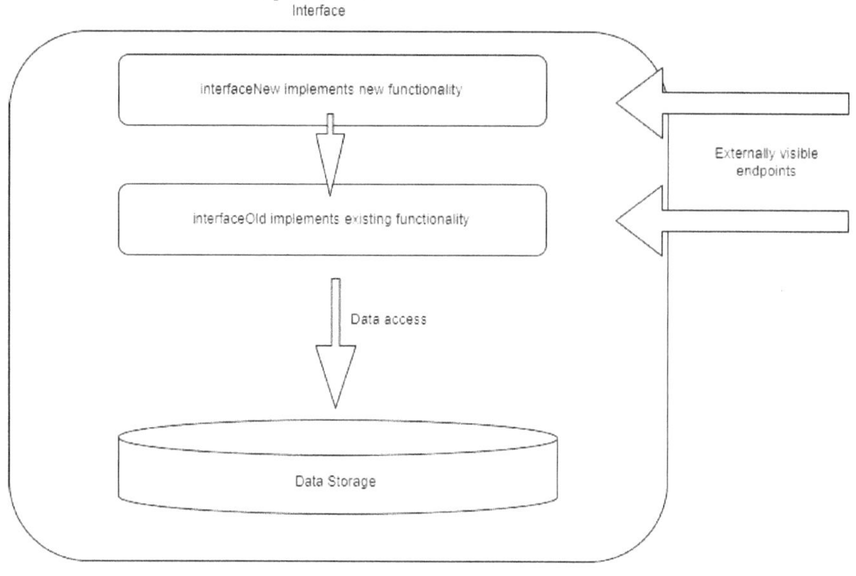

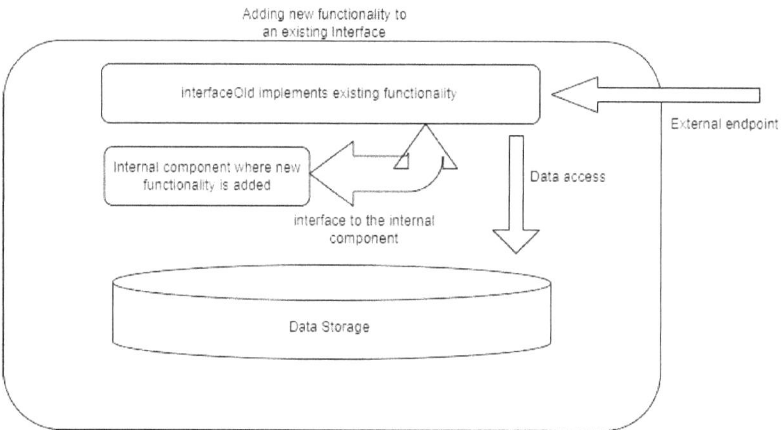

Figure 7.2 (b): Updating functionality when legacy interfaces are present - two patterns

The new functionality can be placed on top of or below existing interfaces. These are the two main options. If above, the new functionality is implemented in the new component, and the old can come from the existing one. The new component can also implement existing functionality instead of relying on an old interface. The interesting detail here is the need to decide if the new interface has to be different from an existing one. The new functionality may or may not require interface changes. For example, when data encryption is added, the caller may or may not be aware of the encryption functionality.

If they do, the interface may offer a parameter to reflect whether the desired data state is encrypted or not. It may also be needed that the caller provide a key or, rather, a crypto interface to be used when encrypting or decrypting the data.

If implemented in the figure, the existing components, then there needs to be an arrangement that the existing component calls some interface at a lower level (the upper picture), where the new functionality gets implemented. Doing so may seem convenient, but it also carries risks, as a bug in this low-level interface may affect multiple upper-level components.

For completeness, we need to mention a variant of the above, where calling the lower-level component is a configurable action that could be disabled if the component misbehaves. This approach could be called the pipeline pattern, as the configurable interfaces look like processing pipelines.

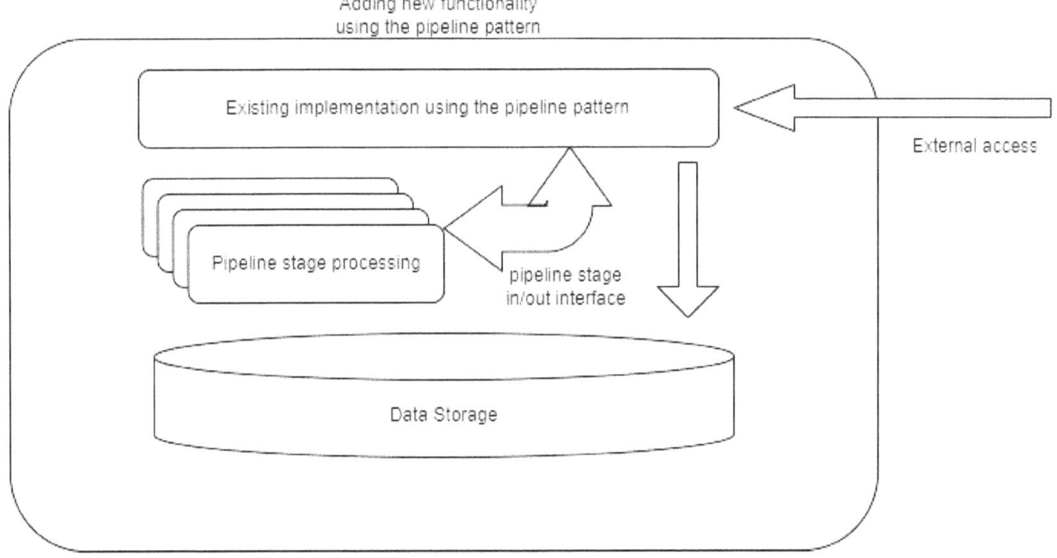

Figure 7.2 (c): *The pipeline pattern*

The difficult part of implementing this pattern is deciding what processing is required and what is optional, as well as defining the error handling logic that tells the caller what to do if the configurable interface misbehaves, such as crashing or returning an error. To illustrate, a stage in the pipeline could be doing data encryption before writing the data to storage. The controller code invokes pipeline processing.

Managing keys

Typical key management is shown in the following figure:

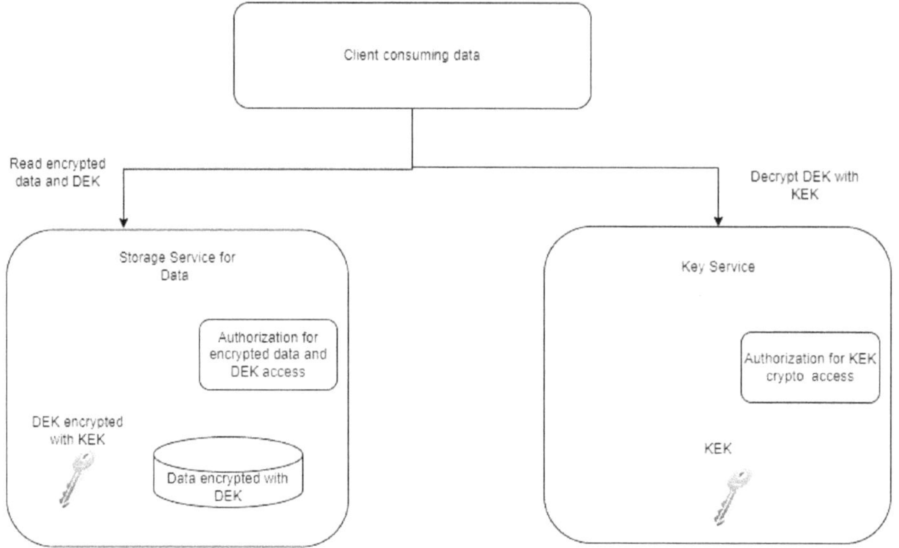

***Figure 7.3 (a):** Common key management architecture using DEK and KEK*

Data Encryption Key (**DEK**) is the key the data is encrypted with **Key Encryption Key** (**KEK**)**.** The key DEK is encrypted with a common design pattern is to have the encrypted DEK, possibly more than one, next to the data encrypted with it.

There is a good reason for the architecture depicted above, such as the DEK and KEK models. Compelling key management solutions like **Hardware Security Modules** (**HSMs**) do not release the key to the caller, but offer crypto operations using it. Doing it this way provides a guarantee that the key is not leaked outside the HSM. Consider the performance penalty if all data items have to be encrypted or decrypted by a remote HSM for every read and write operation. That would result in introducing an extra remote call for each of these operations, and this is likely to make them slow and expensive.

There is something to be said about the consideration expressed above. It could be argued, and rightfully so, that the DEK does not get the same level of protection as the KEK, and the astute attacker can target the DEK as compromising it will be sufficient to decrypt the protected data. Taking a more general look, there needs to be some key on the client that helps to authenticate it to the KEK key storage service, and compromising that key will enable the attacker to do KEK crypto operations, and decrypting the DEK is a KEK crypto operation. The difference between DEK decryption and data decryption is subtle. After all, if DEK can be used to decrypt the data, it appears that the effect of being able to get the DEK and decrypt the data is the same, and this is certainly true if we do not consider the auditing functionality. If decryption is only done in one place, for example, this place is the remote key storage service, then it can be audited, and it can be known who decrypted what and when. If the decrypted data is the DEK, then it is practically unknown how the DEK would be used, as the decryption operation will be performed outside the key storage solution, such as an HSM or similar.

This may not seem like a lot, and compared to the performance penalty of calling the remote key service for each crypto operation, it probably is not. We must assume that DEK encryption can be counted as the decryption of all the data encrypted with the DEK.

It should also be noted that using a DEK, stored encrypted, is not the only option to achieve the desired results. A DEK could be specified using an identifier and given to the caller by the remote key management device. This approach avoids having to deal with an encrypted DEK, though the goals accomplished are the same.

To restate the goals for clarity, in order to get access to the data, an entity needs to be authorized by two different authorization systems. The identity authorized by the two authorization systems used could be the same or different. In the implementations available, one needs to have access to the encrypted data and the decryption key. This access is authorized by two different authorization systems, thus achieving the stated goal. The entities protected by the authorization systems are the encrypted data with the DEK and KEK, respectively. If we move the DEK to the service protecting KEK and get rid of KEK, the authorization logic would be provided by the same system protecting the KEK, so the result would be equivalent. The difference is that the protected operation is importing a key with a given identifier, instead of decrypting a key and importing the result. Key decryption is shown in *Figure 7.3 (a),* depicting DEK and KEK usage.

The following figure shows a model using DEK only:

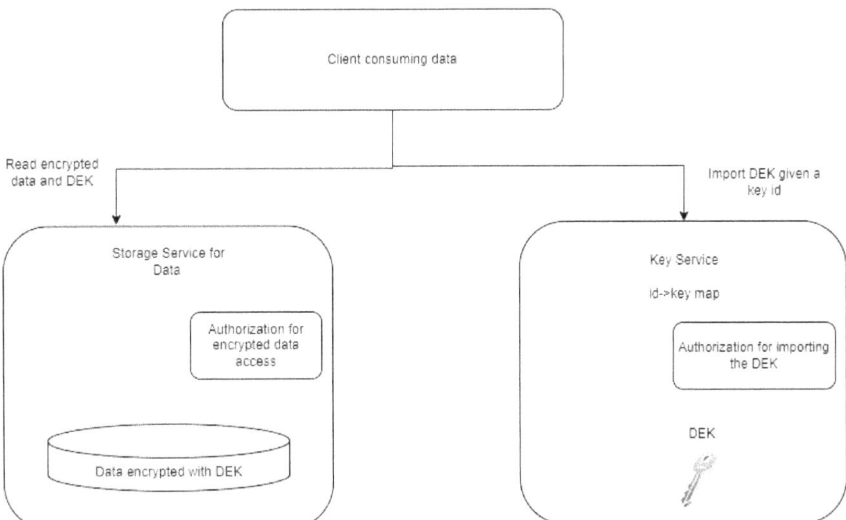

Figure 7.3 (b): Importing the DEK

Note: **There are various similarities with *Figure 7.3 (a)*. There are still two services providing encrypted data and a data decryption key (same as DEK), respectively. The difference comes from the method used by the key service to procure the DEK for the requestor.**

Storing the encrypted DEK next to the data it encrypts is a viable approach with solid historical roots. It is not hard to imagine that solving the encryption requirement requires a key, and storing that key along with the data it is meant to operate on made a lot of sense to implementors.

On the Question of Trust

There are a few quotes to frame the discussion, and these can be found on the US dollar bills. One can find the motto, *In God we trust*, which is also the official motto of the United States, and it sounds similar to the crypto circles, which says *In Code we trust*. This is semantics, which will be discussed shortly.

Another commonly used term is trustless. It deserves that we reflect on it for a bit.

The semantics of **trustless** need to be made clear to avoid different interpretations. In software development, trust is usually key (or secret) based. Saying that we **trust** someone means we trust that the party is in possession of some key, which they need to prove by producing a signature or other crypto artifact using the secret in their possession.

It would make sense to consider that **trustless** means **no key**, but then the key needs to be replaced by something. We could assume that this is code on the blockchain following the **In Code we trust** motto.

There are some analogies with the non-digital world that one can make. The trust has historically been placed in some authority figure. With time, authority selection has evolved, but no matter how it is selected, having one still implies a hierarchical structure where a single authority figure represents a number of entities, whether these entities support the authority position on the current subject or not.

This brings a few interesting issues into view. The code is public, not a secret. So, trusting the code is trusting something anyone can do, and there is practically no way to know what code anyone uses. So, saying that we **trust the code** is an assertion that is hard to prove, keeping in mind that the code is unknown. What could be possible is to lean on the algorithm the relying party code is executing, and instead of the motto **In Code we trust,** the motto could go by **in algorithm we trust** which may be more semantically correct, albeit it does not sound as catchy as the original version, but even that is not entirely correct. To produce a transaction, one needs to have a key. Recording the results of this transaction on the blockchain does not use a key and constitutes a trustless operation. The algorithm motto could be applied to the recording process. The integrity of the content recorded is asserted by the key signing of the transaction that caused the content to be changed.

To conclude, we can say that in the digital world, the motto is **In key we trust**, and blockchains use, instead, the saying **In algorithm we trust**.

Encryption options

As called out previously, data can be encrypted and then decrypted at various places. These can be classified as start, end, and middle of the data read and write calling chains. It makes a difference where the data is getting decrypted. It can be on the client, middle tier, or the storage service. In other words, start, middle, or end of the data flow as shown in the figure:

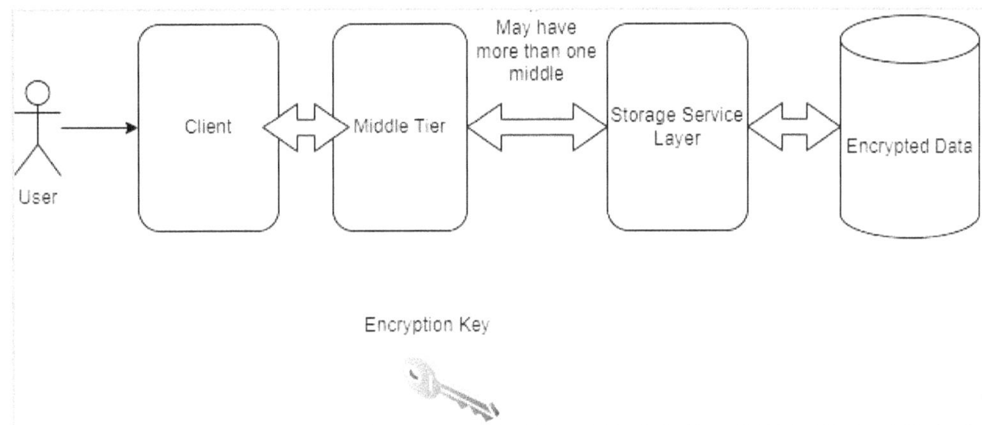

Figure 7.4 (a): Data encryption and decryption options

Suppose the operation requires access to the unencrypted data. In that case, the entity performing the operation also needs to be able to decrypt the data or get the decrypted data from someone.

As an example, consider the query: Give me all rows containing the field **eye color** with the value **blue**. To execute this query, one needs access to the unencrypted **eye color** or a way to perform the comparison to the value **blue** using the encrypted one. There is the homomorphic encryption concept where the encrypted data behaves as the unencrypted one in relation to the given operation, the operation being `StringCompare` in this case.

Expressed in mathematical notation, it should be true that:

```
# comparison needed to execute the query.
# same result using encrypted and unencrypted values
StringCompare(ValueofUnencrypted('eyecolor'),'blue')==
StringCompare(ValueofEncryped('eyecolor'), Encrypted('blue')
```

We should think about the key types that the value **blue** could be encrypted with. It could be a symmetric or an asymmetric key. If symmetric, then decryption and encryption keys are the same, and the entity encrypting the value will also be able to decrypt it. On the other hand, asymmetric key was used to encrypt, then assuming that the function `StringCompare` is homomorphic encryption compatible, then the encrypted value could be discovered by computing `StringCompare` for finite number of values encrypted with the known asymmetric public key The results will reveal the encrypted value, if there is a match, the value is the string **blue** in our example. If there is no match, we will know that the encrypted value is not present in the value set, but we will not know what it is other than it is not one of the known values. This is a good result, and it works great if the realm of possible values is infinite. This is not always the case. Eye color, for example, can take a value that is discrete, coming from a set of well-known values {blue, brown, etc.}. As a general observation, it can be stated that using homomorphic operations on encrypted data must be done with extreme care, with the goal that the operation should not leak information about the data that was encrypted.

The operation **StringCompare** used in the example does NOT do that. Information about the cleartext (unencrypted) value should not be given out to the entity applying the operation and seeing the results. It may not even be possible to know if the homomorphic operation is leaking information about the unencrypted data without knowing the set of possible values, and even then. In which case, it would be safer to assume that applying any operation on the data requires that the unencrypted version is available. In this case, having homomorphic encryption is not important. This may be a surprising result, but if the goal is to put security above all, then the conclusion would be reached naturally.

Encryption granularity and re-encryption

Granularity and re-encryption considerations will be reviewed separately. Here is an example to demonstrate the need for these:

Granularity: Although possible to use a single key for all data, it is a common practice to partition the data along some property and use a key specific to it. See more details in the *Encryption partitioning* section.

Re-encryption: the same key cannot be used forever. See the *Re-encryption* section further down where details of various re-encryption techniques are presented.

Encryption partitioning

It is important to understand the granularity of data being encrypted. There are multiple options, and the choice significantly affects the performance of the chosen solution.

A figure showing a storage service with multiple partitions and keys is shown in the following:

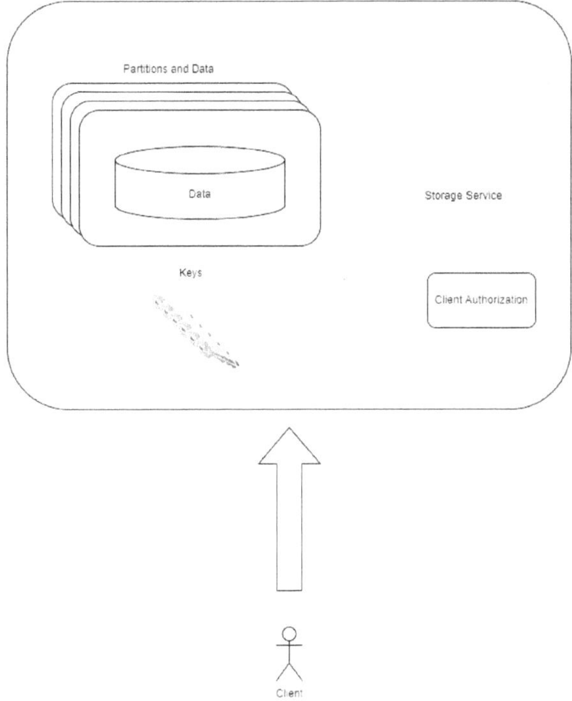

Figure 7.4 (b): Granularity of encryption options

We could call this partitioning for encryption. It may or may not be the same as partitioning for other purposes. It is important to recognize that data are partitioned, originally, for other purposes. The goals behind partitioning for encryption may or may not fit these other purposes. For example, one of the goals for encryption could be to have a key per location, but data may not be partitioned along the location property, which leads to data for access and data for encryption getting partitioned along different dimensions.

To provide a definition:

Portioning for encryption defines the granularity of data that is being encrypted or decrypted in one operation with a given key. As shown, data subject to encryption could be partitioned by location, table (if there is one), or record within a table. The unit of encryption granularity is generally the same as the granularity of the encrypted data read from the downstream service when there is one. To make matters more complicated, there is usually more than one dimension by which the data is partitioned. As shown next, there is a collection of objects that could be considered a partition as well as partitioning within the collection.

For example, the data, taking Azure storage as a showcase, is often partitioned by some identifier correlated to the identities authorized to access it. In the Azure storage case, this would be the storage account identifier. Within the storage account, data could also be partitioned along other dimensions. There are storage blob identifiers, and there could be more.

Re-encryption

Keys, even the best-protected ones, need to be changed on a regular basis, and key changes necessitate re-encrypting the data encrypted with the ones that are being changed. Assuming there is more than one unit of data that is encrypted, then there needs to be provisions to have more than one key active. Given a piece of encrypted data, there needs to be an algorithm to decide which of the active keys should be used. It could be a trial and error mechanism, or the encryption envelope could carry the key identifier or version of the key the data is encrypted with. Some overhead will be introduced either way.

In summary, data encryption introduces some overhead when considering both performance and code complexity. Implementors have to consider granularity in partitioning the data for encryption, as well as re-encryption options.

Encrypting data in transit

Let us start by giving an example from the non-digital world. Consider the post office; the packages sent are considered to be confidential, and the **proof** lies in the packaging. If the package appears to be intact, an assumption is made that the contents have remained confidential. This approach can be summarized as:

Secure the cargo, not the roads it travels on.

This approach makes a lot of sense. Securing all roads may not even be possible. It is also hard to prove that it is known what roads the cargo did and did not travel on, let alone to prove that these roads can be considered **secure** to protect the cargo traveling on them.

The digital world picture is shown in the following:

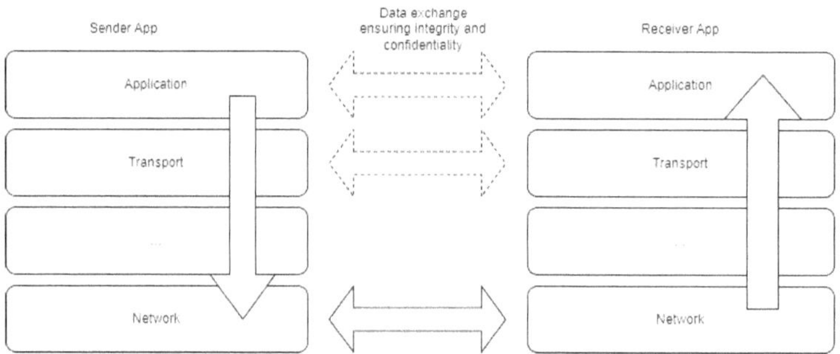

Figure 7.5: Encrypting data in transit

Note: **Once data is encrypted at some layer, it becomes protected from disclosure and tampering in lower layers. This is often referred to as providing integrity and confidentiality. Some will bring in the issue of duplicated functionality. Secure channels, featuring integrity and confidentiality, may be needed at multiple layers. This is addressed when the TLS protocol is discussed.**

The lower layers can affect the reliability of the channel by dropping data packets, but they cannot peek into the data or change what is being sent or received. Unreliable channels can be replaced, and oftentimes, there is more than one channel available to senders and receivers, so the lower-level channel's ability to affect communication channel effectiveness is constrained.

Most systems use a **Transport Level Security** (**TLS**) enabled transport to ensure the integrity and confidentiality of the data sent and received. The transport is most often HTTP, and the TLS-enabled version is often referred to as HTTPS. The wiki link above provides information on the rich history of the HTTP protocol evolution. It should be said that TLS is not strictly tied to HTTP, though the secured HTTP connection (once called HTTPS) is the most well-known TLS implementation. As the figure shows, the system design is comprised of multiple layers. The layer at the bottom does the actual data transmission, and the layers on top of it define data semantics. These semantics could be security-related or other; TLS is one of those layers. It needs a data transport layer below it to transfer the TLS messages. As mentioned, the most popular layer is HTTP, though it could be any transport capable of carrying TLS messages.

Applications, usually, do not implement the transport protocol on their own, but instead use a component provided by the platform they run on. This component implements the TLS transport integration, adding TLS messages to transport data parts.

Protocols, HTTP specifically, sit on secure transports like TLS, providing message integrity and confidentiality. To clarify terminology in some documentation, like the **Open System Interconnect** (**OSI**) model, HTTP is referred to as an application making use of transports. A prime example is the **transmission control protocol** (**TCP**) made available to the HTTP stack. To most, the term application carries the semantics of something providing unique functionality and experience to the end users. Saying that HTTP is at the application layer, hence an application, would be an unnatural message. Applications use an API to send and receive data from other applications or components. This API wraps some message exchange protocol commonly referred to as transport. We can call HTTP a transport from the point of view of applications using it to exchange data. To be precise, the applications need to have data exchange APIs to use. The transports used underneath are of little to no importance to the application using the API. There are some very valid points made within RFC 3439. Let us take the point about duplication of functionality across layers. To be super concrete, we will take the issue of providing message security expressed as message integrity and confidentiality. There could be a transport layer on the stack delivering those properties, or there could be a library made available to any transport on the stack. However, doing the latter brings in the duplication of functionality problem, as it becomes impossible to identify the layer providing message security, as multiple layers can take on that task.

The other option of having a layer providing message security is also not ideal. To point out a couple of challenges, the layers above will inherit the message security feature, but the layers below will not. If, for some reason, one has to integrate with the lower layer, then the message security feature will not be available. A related issue is that the message security layer needs to take a dependency on some other layer below it. This other layer may vary depending on the network configuration.

This leaves us with no good options for placing the network security component on the network stack.

In HTTP implementation, it is headers with authentication semantics, WWW-Authenticate and authorization provided by the server and client, respectively, that carry the server challenge and client identity context response to the challenge. The TLS channel provides the media through which those messages can be relayed.

It should be noted that the HTTP headers above are used to authenticate the client entity. The TLS channel, the HTTP transport (if we can call it that), sits on authenticates the server entity. TLS is also capable of authenticating the client using a client certificate. There can be more than one client identity, some authenticated with tokens carried in HTTP headers and some with client certificates over TLS. More on this can be found in *Chapter 6, Authentication and Authorization*. As the title suggests, it was dedicated to authentication and authorization techniques and architectures. Here, the focus will be on TLS as a provider of data integrity and confidentiality. The authentication capabilities will not be discussed at length, only mentioned in relation to the keys used to provide the desired channel security.

Transports featuring TLS

Architecture providing the security of the transport using a TLS provider layer is illustrated in the following figure:

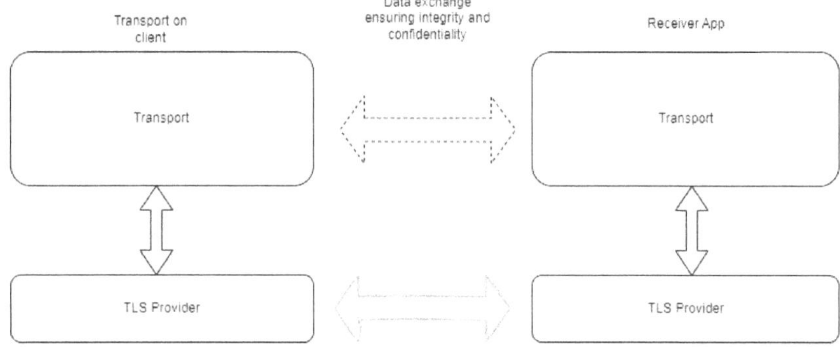

Figure 7.6: *Transport interacting with a TLS provider*

Let us point out here that both client and server need to have secret keys to implement the TLS protocol. The key could be auto-generated on demand or tied to a name using a certificate. The latter layers the benefits of integrity and confidentiality on top of authentication. If the key is tied to a name, X, for example, then we can make the statement that the **channel to X is secure**, and the key helps provide this security. Without the mapping, if we just have a key representing the party we are talking to, then we can say that the channel to our counterparty is secure, but we cannot say who that party is, lacking the authentication part. This opens the door to **Man-in-the-Middle** (**MITM**) attacks, where the channel can be secure, but if the counterparty is not, then all bets are off, since an insecure counterparty can compromise both the integrity and confidentiality of the data exchanged. Or, to put it in different words, the promise of TLS depends strongly on the counterparty authentication and authorization. The concept of mutual authentication was discussed in *Chapter 6, Authentication and Authorization*.

To elaborate, the TLS protocol ensures the integrity and confidentiality of the data exchanged, given that the communicating parties supply it with the respective keys. These keys are communicated to the other party over unencrypted and unauthenticated messages. See *TLS* **Request for Comments** (**RFC**) for details if interested **https://datatracker.ietf.org/doc/html/rfc8446**.

The keys are wrapped in certificates that provide an implementation for the name | key mapping. Without the certificate, the customers will encounter the situation described above; the channel is encrypted, but the party on the other end is unknown. This could be a problem if the data sent over the encrypted channel is sensitive.

Note: **The data may be encrypted, but the recipient is unknown. For example, if user passwords are being sent over, the recipient should be the only entity capable of making use of the password data. If not, the setup presents opportunities for MITM attacks where a password sent to a malicious entity, even over an encrypted channel, can be misused by the entity receiving it.**

Most setups use a certificate to assert the server key mapping to the service name. Having this prevents MITM attacks as clients cannot connect to the attacker site, unless the certificate signing key or the key the name in the certificate is mapped to gets compromised.

To summarize, applications accepting calls from outside should consider only using channels protected by TLS and configure a server certificate containing the application's name to support the TLS channel. The application should not accept calls on other, non-TLS-protected channels. There should be no need for these, and the risk of exposing unsecured endpoints is not justified.

Integrity and confidentiality of data

These terms are often used to describe data security posture, and providing respective definitions is useful for understanding the semantics behind them:

- **Integrity:** data is written only by authorized parties
- **Confidentiality:** data can be read only by authorized parties
- **Authorized parties:** identities authorized to read or write, or do whatever other operation is available on the data

Example from the non-digital world, the statement **A is married to B** can be characterized as being about integrity. If A or B does not agree that they are married to each other, then the statement of integrity is broken. It is less about confidentiality. Unless it is some kind of a secret marriage, then the relationship does not need to be kept secret.

Both integrity and confidentiality can be achieved using a secret key and performing some cryptographic operations with it. If there is a key attribute to A, then messages crypto-signed with that key can also be attributed to A. Assuming asymmetric key cryptography, a message encrypted with A's public key can be decrypted only if one has A's private (secret) key. Here, the main point is that having a secret key enables the holder to achieve both integrity and confidentiality of the data exchanged. Next, we can reflect on the options present in the absence of a secret. Achieving confidentiality is not an option, at least not to the author's knowledge. If something is confidential, the contents should only be available to authorized parties, and encryption using a key is only available to these authorized parties. However, achieving integrity is possible without a key. It is a premise that public blockchains operate on. Going back to the non-digital world example, the truthfulness of the statement that **A is married to B** can be asserted without using a key. There are some fine points here. To begin with, to make a statement, also known as submitting a transaction, one needs to have secret keys. In the blockchain (or crypto) world, these are the end-user account keys stored in the crypto wallet, but to record the statement, or transaction, if you will, there are no keys used. At this point, we need to point out that there is a difference between making a statement and recording it on the blockchain ledger. The former needs to be signed by the key that belongs to the entity issuing the statement. The latter needs a way to assure trust that the recording is genuine. Using a key to sign and putting the trust there is one way to do it.

Blockchains rely on consensus that does not necessarily involve using secrets, not secrets shared with other nodes for sure. To use a non-digital world analogy again, using a key is analogous to a centralized system where trust is placed in a central entity identified by having a secret in its possession and using that secret to sign statements others trust. The idea behind decentralization is to have multiple distinct entities agree that something is true, and they have to agree without sharing a secret. Recent advancements in blockchain technologies and algorithms have made this possible. However, this applies to assuring data integrity. Without a secret, confidentiality is not there, or to put it simply: Data on popular blockchains is not encrypted, at least not on popular ones like Bitcoin and Etherium. There have been attempts to encrypt the data on various networks. It is still not clear what key and key management should be used for the encryption. Assuming data is to be processed by multiple nodes, the choices are:

- All nodes should have access to encryption and decryption keys – could be one key if symmetrical encryption is used
- Operations could be performed on the encrypted data, and nodes do not need keys

There is one operation that needs keys for sure, and this is returning the unencrypted data to clients. This operation could be isolated, and only selected nodes would be trusted to perform it. This node segmentation is not evident, and it could be necessary to prevent unnecessary key exposure.

Few practical considerations

Asking applications to do key management and to perform data encryption with that key is a tall order that would most likely backfire. Instead, platform components owned by area experts take on these tasks. The application owners can configure a certificate and/or point to a key to be used, and it is often the case that this key is provided to the local key store by some key management service. It is the platform components that provide relevant experiences addressing key management. It is common to ask the customer to configure a certificate with a matching private key, or it could be a key without a certificate imported into a local key store.

It would be helpful to look at encryption at rest and encryption in transit separately, as there are nuances that make these unique.

Encryption in transit practical considerations

Data in transit must always be encrypted nowadays. It has become a de facto standard, and sending or receiving unencrypted data will not be acceptable to customers. Encryption is done in the vast majority of cases by a TLS-enabled transport. Transport configuration requires, if accepting connections, the customer to configure a certificate with a corresponding key for the endpoint accepting connections. Clients do not have to configure anything, as the keys needed to secure the channel are automatically generated. It does not matter what key values are, as long as they are random and it is computationally infeasible to discover them. Server keys, by contrast, need to be reflected in the configured certificate that maps the key to the service name.

The following figure depicts the process:

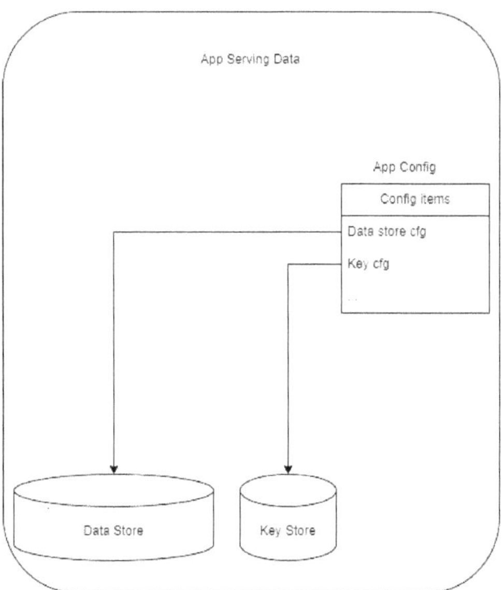

Figure 7.7: *Configuring a server certificate*

To articulate a few rules, a server, and this should be true for any server, accepting connections on some endpoint, physical or not, should allow a certificate to be configured on this endpoint to authenticate the service and encrypt data used to communicate with the client.

A certificate references a public key of the owner. To use the certificate, the corresponding private key has to be available to the application using it.

The applications would use a certificate and key configured on the compute node on which they run. There is a standardized data format to encode the certificate contents and the associated private key, most prominent being the PKCS12 format. The usual server configuration experience is that the entity configuring the server is asked to provide a reference to a certificate.

It has to be noted that the primary purpose of the certificate is to authenticate its owner. The ability to provide integrity and confidentiality of the channel is a byproduct of the authentication protocol. There can be a secure channel without authentication, but if authentication is performed, the secure channel should also be provided.

Consider a web server configuration setting. Taking the popular nginx server as an example, the configuration settings are depicted in the following figure. For complete details, see **https://nginx.org/en/docs/http/configuring_https_servers.html**.

Some of the content behind is shown in the following figure:

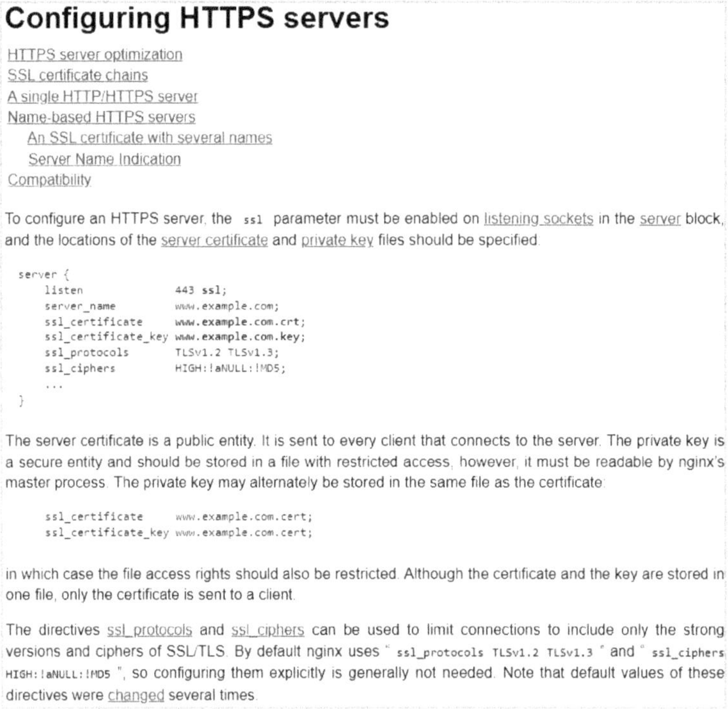

Configuring HTTPS servers

HTTPS server optimization
SSL certificate chains
A single HTTP/HTTPS server
Name-based HTTPS servers
    An SSL certificate with several names
    Server Name Indication
Compatibility

To configure an HTTPS server, the `ssl` parameter must be enabled on listening sockets in the server block, and the locations of the server certificate and private key files should be specified:

```
server {
    listen              443 ssl;
    server_name         www.example.com;
    ssl_certificate     www.example.com.crt;
    ssl_certificate_key www.example.com.key;
    ssl_protocols       TLSv1.2 TLSv1.3;
    ssl_ciphers         HIGH:!aNULL:!MD5;
    ...
}
```

The server certificate is a public entity. It is sent to every client that connects to the server. The private key is a secure entity and should be stored in a file with restricted access, however, it must be readable by nginx's master process. The private key may alternately be stored in the same file as the certificate:

```
    ssl_certificate     www.example.com.cert;
    ssl_certificate_key www.example.com.cert;
```

in which case the file access rights should also be restricted. Although the certificate and the key are stored in one file, only the certificate is sent to a client.

The directives ssl_protocols and ssl_ciphers can be used to limit connections to include only the strong versions and ciphers of SSL/TLS. By default nginx uses "`ssl_protocols TLSv1.2 TLSv1.3`" and "`ssl_ciphers HIGH:!aNULL:!MD5`", so configuring them explicitly is generally not needed. Note that default values of these directives were changed several times.

***Figure 7.8:** Web server configuration settings*

An interesting feature in the configuration shown above is that the certificate and the associated key are separate entries. This does not have to be the case, as the certificate content determines what key should be used without leaving room for having different keys. We could say that specifying the key separately is unnecessary, though it is also true that doing so creates clarity and helps underscore the point that authentication and channel security are distinct properties. As it happens, authentication can be leveraged to secure the channel. However, it is also true that the channel can be secured without having authentication, as there is an associated key used to bring desired integrity and confidentiality properties. To illustrate, we can think of unauthenticated but secure channels. *We do not know who we are talking to, but we know communication is secure.*

The above-stated premise can really work if applied with due consideration. We may not know who we are talking to, but with time and having many positive experiences, trust can be developed. There needs to be due diligence to prevent the revelation of sensitive data to an unknown entity.

This type of trust is based on prior outcomes, not on some central authority signature. The idea is modeled after non-digital world patterns. We could trust an entity because it has a reputation built on actions in prior times. This is different than trusting someone because they presented a signed document (called a certificate in the digital world) asserting some identity property, bootstrapping the trust.

Encryption at rest considerations

There are some important differences between properties required for encryption at rest and in transit. In transit, authentication plays an important role in determining the entity we are talking to. Then, keys are exchanged to construct what is often called a session key used to encrypt data in transit for the given session. As the name suggests, the session key is tied to a specific session. Sessions are short-lived, so it is not meaningful to have different versions. A re-negotiation will result in a different session key to be established and used on both sides of the communication channel. There is no point in time when multiple session keys are active. The same cannot be said about the keys used to encrypt data at rest. We can call the key DEK. It is possible to have multiple DEKs active due to re-encryption or partitioning considerations.

The application accessing data and keys, the data is encrypted with, is shown in the following figure:

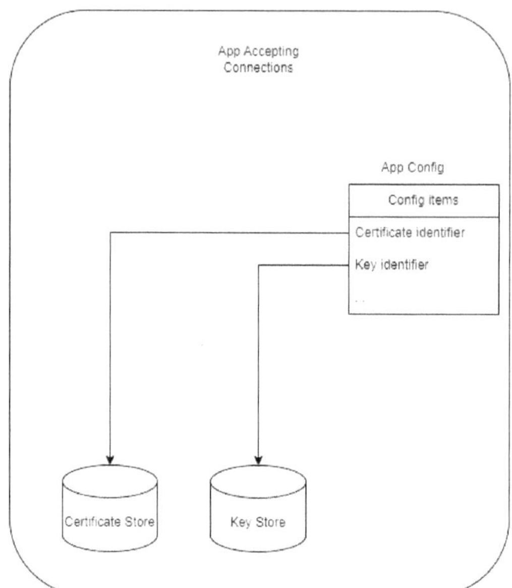

Figure 7.9: *Keys for encrypting data at rest*

In the opinion of the author, the best return will be achieved by letting the provider do encryption as they see appropriate. Having the customer provide the encryption keys creates a sense of control, though the actual benefit would be hard to quantify.

It would be a reasonable strategy to let the data storage provider do key management and data encryption and reap the resulting benefits. The alternative is to use **Customer Managed Keys (CMK)** if there is a strong reason to do so. Valid reasons could be compliance requirements where the CMK meets those, but the data provider-managed keys, called PMK, do not meet the compliance requirements. Although possible in theory, this situation is hard to encounter in practice. It can be argued that integrating with a CMK solution would require comparable, if not bigger, effort compared to the PMK one, and the effort is on both sides, such as the customer and the storage provider.

All said, encrypting data and the rest have more complicated problems to solve compared to encrypting data in transit. The complexity comes from the need to have multiple key versions active at the same time, the need to deploy a re-encryption algorithm, having to define partitioning for the encryption model, and so on.

It could be considered that not needing a certificate is a simplification of sorts, but that can be deceiving as well. In the case of encryption in transit, the certificate is needed to authenticate the counterparty that provides a public key used for session key derivation.

In the encryption at rest model, this counterparty does not exist, so the problem should go away. However, it should be noted that there is still authentication required to access the DEK in the key store. This authentication mechanism is not defined in the model, but it has to exist.

Blockchains and encryption

To start with the basics, Public blockchains do not provide confidentiality. The simple reason is that, by virtue of being public, the nodes constituting the blockchain network cannot share a secret key that could be used to encrypt the data on the blockchain.

The flow can be seen in the following figure:

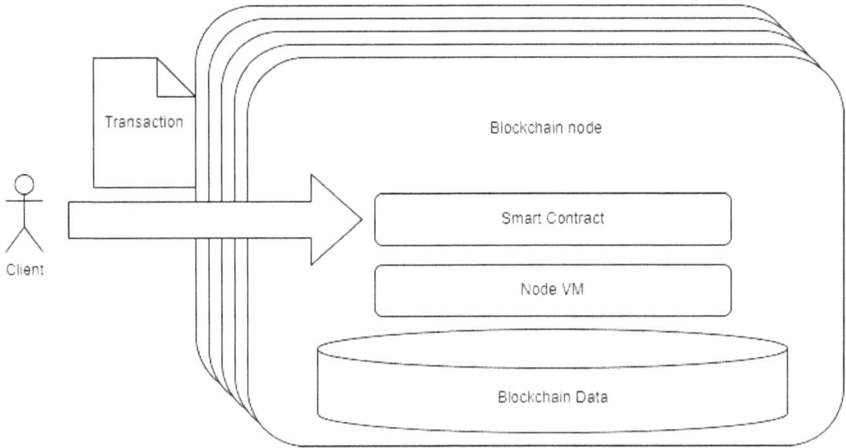

Figure 7.10: *Blockchain node*

Going back to our examples presented in the integrity and confidentiality of data section, blockchain designs focus on the integrity part. To illustrate, we can consider a statement to be true if the majority of blockchain nodes agree that it is. This agreement, known as a consensus algorithm, does not require that the parties (blockchain nodes) share a secret key.

As an analogy, consider a non-digital world setup where the truthfulness of a statement is asserted by many participating parties, like your neighbors, agreeing that the statement is true and not by some central authority vouching for the statement's truthfulness.

If we are to project the above into digital world terms, central authority vouching for something being true is like a signature on the statement fingerprint using a key in possession of the central authority, and majority agreement is like applying a decentralized protocol to reach a consensus without using a secret key.

In this setup, there is no provision for confidentiality. The neighbors can agree that the statement is true, but there is no way for them to keep it a secret.

There have been various attempts to hide the data contents, none of which have been successful to the author's knowledge.

If confidentiality is required, there needs to be a key to encrypt and decrypt the data. Access to this key has to be governed by some authorization system implementing the intent behind encrypting the data, which should define the authorized parties that should have access to the unencrypted content.

To put a somewhat different angle on this topic, the power of the majority is great to assert that something is true or to assure integrity, if you will. Speaking of the majority, it is not as effective when a secret needs to be kept, as we saw that having a secret is needed to achieve confidentiality. In fact, just the opposite can be said: the more entities are confided in with a secret, the less of a secret it becomes. As the probability of a secret disclosure increases as the secret is shared with more entities. As blockchain designs utilize the power of the majority, the algorithms behind them are really good at asserting data integrity.

Azure storage encryption

Details for Azure storage encryption can be found in Azure documentation **https://learn.microsoft.com/en-us/azure/storage/common/storage-service-encryption**

See the excerpt in the following figure:

Azure Storage encryption for data at rest

Article • 02/12/2023 • 20 contributors

Feedback

In this article

About Azure Storage service-side encryption
About encryption key management
Doubly encrypt data with infrastructure encryption
Client-side encryption for blobs and queues
Next steps

Azure Storage uses service-side encryption (SSE) to automatically encrypt your data when it's persisted to the cloud. Azure Storage encryption protects your data and helps you meet your organizational security and compliance commitments.

Microsoft recommends using service-side encryption to protect your data for most scenarios. However, the Azure Storage client libraries for Blob Storage and Queue Storage also provide client-side encryption for customers who need to encrypt data on the client. For more information, see Client-side encryption for blobs and queues.

Figure 7.11: *Azure storage encryption documentation*

Azure has a variety of storage services. The documentation above refers to the Azure blob storage. Similar concepts could be applied to any service, branded storage, or other. It is a gray area to decide if the service falls under the storage umbrella. It can be pointed out that any service uses some type of storage to hold state. This state is exposed to customers as results returned by the service APIs. These APIs to some processing on the data constituting the state in storage. One can use a heuristic to determine if the service can be considered to be called storage. An accepted way to do this could be to define a storage interface, and if the service implements it, it can be considered to be of type storage.

Encryption location

Earlier in the chapter, see *Data encryption options*, various locations where data could be encrypted and decrypted were called out. Azure storage offers all options to customers. Storage is offered as a service API, so encrypting in the middle does not make sense, and it is excluded as an option. Data could be encrypted on the client, which is customer code, or the Azure storage service. The components in the middle are not visible to customers. To them, encryption happens either on the client or the server side.

The following observation could be useful: if the data is encrypted on the client, then the service side does not need to know anything about the encryption process. It is also important to call out that client encryption will prevent most, if not all, operations on the data done at the service side. An exception can be found in the example showing homomorphic encryption in the *Data encryption options* section. As it was called out, it is hard to implement correctly and make sure that information about the unencrypted data is not leaked when an operation is performed on the encrypted data.

Granularity

Azure storage is partitioned using storage accounts. Naturally, the storage account also represents a partitioning dimension for encryption, or to put it in simple words, data associated with a storage account is encrypted in a certain way configured on the storage account. This is natural. It also creates a dependency between data and key partitioning.

If the key is data storage provider-managed, then it should be possible for the storage provider to use a different key partitioning scheme. For example, storage accounts having a given property, such as region affiliation, could get the same encryption key. But this is not something that can be counted on. The algorithm to choose an encryption key for a storage account belongs to the provider. One may assume that each storage account gets a unique key, even though the keys may not actually be different.

With CMKs, the control on what key to use for a given storage account is delegated to the storage account owner. It is reasonable to assume that different keys will be used to encrypt data that belongs to different accounts, but again, this is not guaranteed.

Key management

Managing keys used for various purposes is one of the major services offered by cloud providers. Generally speaking, keys can be managed by the cloud provider - Microsoft in the Azure case - or by the customer. There are CMKs that reside within a key vault service that provides general key management. Azure defines patterns for both customer and provider-managed keys. The provider manages keys as it sees appropriate. There are no assumptions to be made. CMKs fall into two categories such as client and service managed. As it was stated in the *encryption location section*, data encryption can happen on the client or server. If it happens on the client, then clearly the encryption key should be available to it. There is no work for the service in this case. The client encrypts the data and then writes it in the same way as the non-encrypted data. If encryption is done by the service, then there are various options for it to get the encryption key. Narrowing them down, the key could be provided by the client, a pattern known as **client-provided key,** or by a key provider like Azure key vault.

See the key management following figure showing the various options for providing encryption keys:

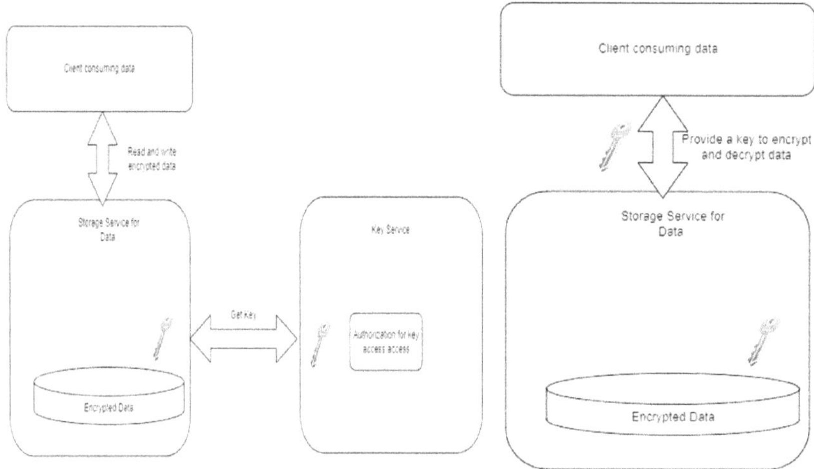

Figure 7.12: *Encryption key paths to the data service*

The path where the key is provided by the client is likely a legacy construct. It is not a good practice to communicate raw keys on any channel, and that is exactly how the pattern is designed to work. To support this claim, see the Azure documentation excerpt in the following:

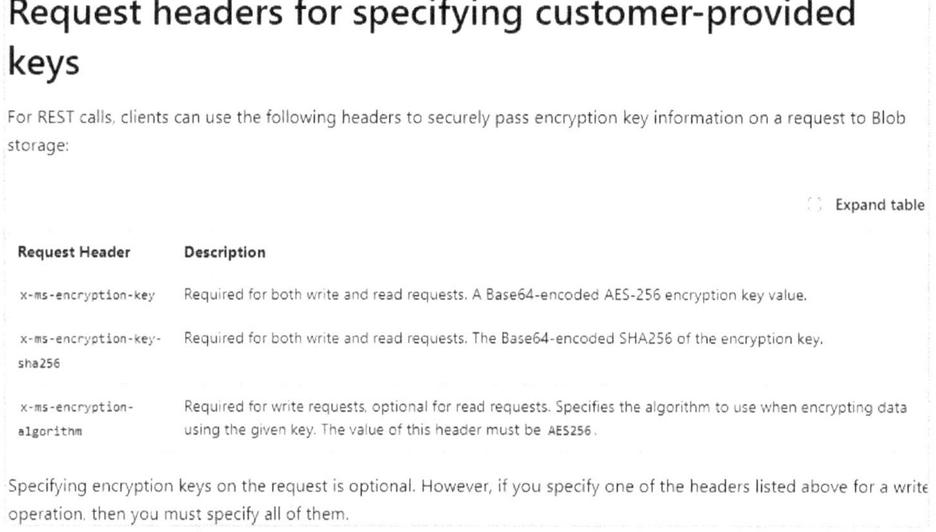

Request headers for specifying customer-provided keys

For REST calls, clients can use the following headers to securely pass encryption key information on a request to Blob storage:

Expand table

Request Header	Description
`x-ms-encryption-key`	Required for both write and read requests. A Base64-encoded AES-256 encryption key value.
`x-ms-encryption-key-sha256`	Required for both write and read requests. The Base64-encoded SHA256 of the encryption key.
`x-ms-encryption-algorithm`	Required for write requests, optional for read requests. Specifies the algorithm to use when encrypting data using the given key. The value of this header must be `AES256`.

Specifying encryption keys on the request is optional. However, if you specify one of the headers listed above for a write operation, then you must specify all of them.

Figure 7.13: *Client provided keys*

In the Azure documentation, the process is described here **https://learn.microsoft.com/en-us/azure/storage/blobs/encryption-customer-provided-keys**.

Here is a good place to elaborate on the subject of sending raw keys in headers or other constructs that are part of the input request. The request channel may very well be protected, but it is also a common practice to log request components. There is nothing more satisfying to an attacker than finding a valuable cleartext key in a seemingly innocuous log file. One way to avoid handing out such **gifts** to attackers is to adopt the principle of not sending out cleartext secrets on any communication channel. Encrypted or not.

It is important to note the difference between client-provided keys and CMKs. In the latter case, the key is provided by a key service as shown in the KeyService diagram. If the key is provided by the key service, it can be managed by various entities, such as the storage provider and storage customer, as two prominent examples that describe the offerings by Azure storage.

at **https://learn.microsoft.com/en-us/azure/storage/common/customer-managed-keys-overview?toc=%2Fazure%2Fstorage%2Fblobs%2Ftoc.json&bc=%2Fazure%2Fstorage%2Fblobs%2Fbreadcrumb%2Ftoc.json**.

The content is shown in the following figure:

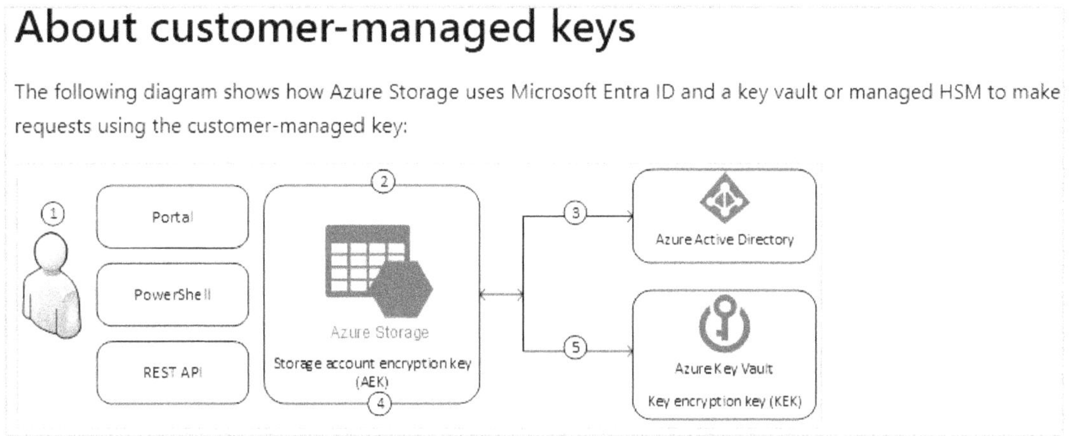

Figure 7.14: *Azure storage CMK implementation*

One of the main benefits of CMK is that it can be said that since the key is managed by the customer, a storage provider compromise does not directly cause data to be compromised. This assertion is rooted in the assumption that the customer would delegate key access to the storage provider in a way that the storage provider cannot utilize that access when compromised. This sounds great in theory, but there are a few practical considerations that will likely complicate implementation. The delegation of keys has to follow some rules that depend on the timing of the customer's access to the data. For example, if the customer is making an access request at time X, then the storage provider should be able to decrypt the data in some time window N, which is the time between X and X+N. If the storage provider is able to decrypt the data at any time, then a storage provider compromise will lead to data compromise. Then, we have the issue of designing a re-encryption algorithm with the constraint that keys are only available for a limited time window defined here as N. Having the key for decryption available only for a limited time makes re-encryption more challenging. The re-encryption discussion is in the *Re-Encryption* section. Such a design is not impossible, but it is also not trivial.

The other consideration is that the key management service usually comes from the same provider as the storage service. In the case of Azure, these are Azure key vault and Azure storage. While it is possible to imagine that storage is compromised and key vault is not, the possibility that if one is compromised, so is the other, is very real. There must be some correlation between the services offered by the same provider. Ideally, customers may ask that key management be done by other providers and that key management interfaces be standardized so that Azure storage can use keys from Azure key vault, as well as keys from other providers.

Considering this, the option of using encryption with provider-managed keys (Microsoft managed in the case of Azure) looks appealing, as it is not known how much Customer-Managed Keys increase the probability of the data remaining available only to authorized parties. Once the data is leaked, the consequences are irreversible.

The data could be re-encrypted with another key, but this will not fix the damage caused by the leaked data. It cannot be unseen. Re-encryption will help with preventing another leak, but will not fix past ones. If there is no significant difference when data is leaked, the effect of preventing future leaks does not add much value. The same cannot be said about preventing future breaches of data integrity. For example, a breach may cause a recording of a transaction claiming that A sent B one token. No matter how this happens, preventing the recording of future bad transactions is valuable.

All said, encryption at rest is complicated, and providers need to be very careful about the promises made to customers. It can be claimed that data is protected from certain attack types related to physical access, like the **take the disk home** pattern that can be performed by someone with physical access to the computer equipment where the data is stored.

As it is a common customer request, cloud providers like Azure must provide acceptable solutions. Another important wrinkle in the story is that encryption is often times a compliance requirement. Given these considerations, designs must account for it.

Common pattern for data access

While there are an infinite number of real-life patterns for data access, we can identify a common one that exists in all the above. And this common pattern can be described as applications accessing users' data.

An application accessing data on behalf of its users is shown in the following figure:

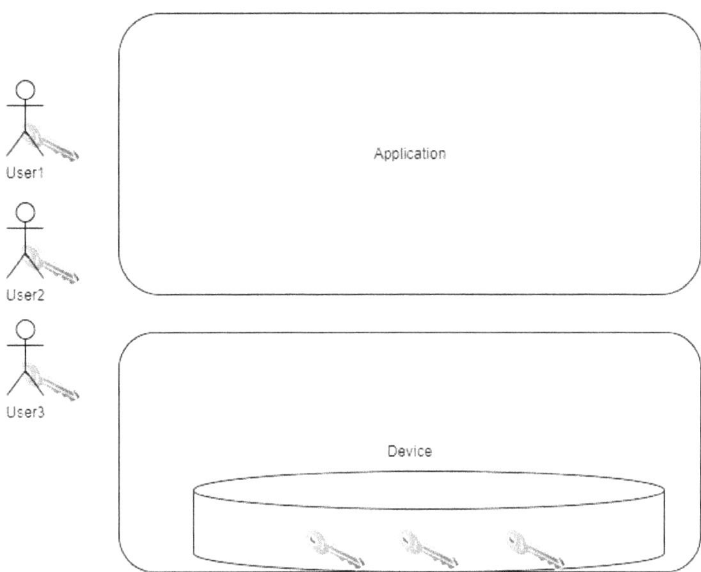

Figure 7.15: Secrets managed by end users and applications

Secrets that belong to end users come in different forms and can benefit from human properties. Humans can remember passwords, own devices, and produce unique fingerprints (actual fingerprints, retina scans, DNA samples, etc.). All these allow for innovative solutions for managing secrets that belong to an individual.

The same cannot be said about applications; neither of the human properties described above is inherent to applications. They cannot remember, own, or produce unique fingerprints, but we can connect humans to applications through compute-capable devices.

The logic is as follows: end users can own devices, and applications run on devices. An application running on a device owned by an end user can inherit access to the secrets on the device that the end-user has configured. We can also use application abilities to interact with end users through user agents such as browser controls. This allows user identities to be delegated to applications, and from there, applications can be enabled to access secrets that belong to end-users. This arrangement assumes application interactivity, and this is not always a valid assumption, as there are many non-interactive applications. Take well-known daemons, for example. These are non-interactive applications that should be able to function when the user is not present.

Conclusion

The chapter addresses data encryption approaches and requirements. As a starting point, it looks at the reasons for using encryption. The main reason identified is protecting data from unauthorized disclosure. This is a type of authorization, asserting that only authorized parties can see the data. Considering that there must already be authorization applied to the data read operation, encryption introduces an additional authorization layer used to access the data decryption key.

In this chapter, we also look at data confidentiality provided by encryption and data integrity, which may or may not require a key.

A common example from the non-digital world would be a marriage certificate asserting that A is married to B. The integrity of this statement is guaranteed by the authority issuing the certificate. It does so based on A and B providing their agreement in the form of signatures using their respective keys. In a **real-world** setting, A and B identify themselves before declaring their agreement. The process of identification and declaration of intent has to be acceptable to the authority issuing the certificate. Once the certificate is issued, it serves as proof of the A and B relationship. It needs to be noted that there is no encryption involved here. The marriage certificate can be read by anyone who is interested. The integrity is assured by the issuing authority, and there is no confidentiality to speak of. But integrity is there, and this is the required property of such certification. There is, in most circumstances, nothing to be kept secret.

The way the issuing authority provides integrity proof is by putting its signature on the certificate. In the digital world, producing signatures requires one to have a secret key. The situation is not much different in the non-digital world, where a secret is required to produce the equivalent of a digital signature. It is usually the case that this proof is a seal signifying that some authority vouches for the truthfulness of the data recorded in the certificate. Arguably, falsifying a seal is easier than forging a digital signature. The latter, forging a digital signature, can be done if the attacker has access to the secret key used to produce the signature. Without access to the key, producing a valid signature would require a brute force approach, given sufficient key length. This will not be a practical approach, given the computing resources available at present. The same cannot be said about forging a seal used in the non-digital world. It should be a relatively simple task, assuming the attacker has access to the materials used in seal production, and these cannot be kept secret, at least not for a long time. Eventually, the secret, if there was one, will leak out, and anyone with sufficient means will be able to produce a seal to their liking. Forging a seal is considered easier than forging a digital signature. To forge the signature, access to the signing key is needed, as mentioned above. There is no secret key in the seal case. To add to that, when the seal (integrity) is compromised, there is no suitable recourse. The seal could be changed, but the old one still has to be valid unless all documents signed with the old seal are reissued with signatures from the new one. Such drastic measures are not considered practical. The situation is the same if a digital signature key is compromised. The successful attacker can now sign documents with the compromised key, making it impossible to distinguish signatures done by the attacker after the compromise from signatures done by the trusted authority. As was the case with the compromised seal, the compromised key can be changed, though just changing the key does not fix the problem, as documents signed by the old key still need to be valid, or a re-signing process has to be in place. This is solved by the blockchain design that makes it practically impossible to issue back-dated documents and insert them in the blockchain.

It is important to consider the need for confidentiality along with the need for integrity. To achieve both integrity and confidentiality for data in transit, it is sufficient to configure a web server with a certificate carrying the name of the service and, of course, a corresponding private key. And it is important that all incoming requests are routed through the web server above and that it is configured to serve only requests over TLS. A typical architecture uses a gateway service, configured with a certificate and the key mentioned above, and then routes all requests through it.

Confidentiality for data at rest is not trivial to ensure, and while it can be claimed that data integrity is very important, let us call it fundamental to application security, but having confidentiality is not always required. As evidence, consider public blockchain designs, such as Bitcoin and Etherium chains, where confidentiality is not provided, but integrity is. Lack of confidentiality is a consequence of the inability to keep a secret on a public node. Integrity, on the other hand, can be achieved without a key by means of consensus, as it is done on public blockchains. This problem is mitigated to a great extent in cloud environments where the cloud provider gives out key management solutions, and keys for encryption and decryption are made available to applications running on the cloud provider's compute resources.

It is natural to question the need for confidentiality in cloud environments. After all, blockchains do not provide it, and applications on blockchain nodes are considered to be at the forefront of innovation, see *web3 apps link:* **https://www.blockchain-council.org/web-3/most-popular-web3-applications/**.

A lot of this is a consequence of the natural progression of technology in computing. Confidentiality implies encryption, and encryption needs a secret key. To have a secret, there must be someone to manage it and make it available to applications that do data encryption. This **person** can only be a cloud provider at present. More importantly, having a secret implies having some centralized authority behind managing it.

To state as a conclusion, the interactive application can make use of the identities of the users they are interacting with. Non-interactive applications make use of secrets configured on devices on which the application is running.

Indirectly, these are similar to the secrets on devices that are configured by users. However, the users configuring the secret on the device are not necessarily the same as the users interacting with the application. Using the common persona terminology, we can call these the application user persona and the application configuration persona.

We should also consider the purpose of the key. There are keys that provide data integrity and confidentiality for data at rest and for data in transit. These need to have different properties and levels of protection. Taking blockchains as an example, keys secure data in transit from one blockchain node to another. There are no keys used to secure the data written to the blockchain store, as this is done by the blockchain consensus mechanism.

In the next chapter, various economic models are examined with an emphasis on the perceived security guarantees in each.

Exercises

This section outlines, in the opinion of the author, the most important aspects related to data security that the application owners should decide on. There are three basic questions outlined below. And the answers to those will guide security investments needed to make the product successful with customers.

These are:

1. **Compliance requirements**

   It is often the case that data encryption requirements are driven by the need to be compliant with some regulation. In this case, it is very helpful to know the regulation and to require that all services used also meet the compliance requirement.

2. **Customer requirements**

   Customer requirements could be related to compliance or not. Customers have compliance requirements as well, and the technology they use must meet those requirements. On the other end, customers may demand features that are beyond compliance requirements. A common way to express these asks is to formulate a requirement of the type:

   If X happens, then Y should not occur as a consequence.

   For example, a common concern is the physical security of the data stores. So, it should not be surprising when the customer says:

   If physical access to data security is compromised, data contents should not be.

   To rephrase, the physical security should not be the only layer of data protection. It can be necessary, but not sufficient, to protect data contents.

   As mentioned multiple times in this chapter, data security is primarily concerned with ensuring data integrity and confidentiality. Both of these need to be considered when evaluating how customer requirements can be met.

3. **Technology choices**

   Technology choices will be a direct consequence of the requirements the application is set to meet. If storage technology meets compliance and customer requirements, it will make a reasonable technology choice for an application that must also meet these requirements.

Chapter 8
Economic Models

Introduction

Security has gained prominence in the digital age. Goal posts have shifted with advances in technology. Most effects have been caused by the development of communication media that have, on one side, brought people closer together, and on the other, have made it easier to reach assets and exploit weaknesses in defense mechanisms. This has made erecting Cybersecurity defenses a necessity. If such threats are ignored, then assets, including critical ones, will be compromised by remote attackers, causing damage to businesses relying on those assets to operate. Shifting the focus to economic models, the damage caused by the compromises has to be measured so it can be compared to the cost incurred by investing in security measures that prevent it. This is an area where having a cloud provider makes a lot of sense, as these providers can afford to invest in security features as the cost gets distributed among their many customers. This works because investments in security do scale well, in the sense that the cost is not proportional to the number of customers using the feature. There is a substantial cost during development, but then once developed, the feature will scale with minimal cost overhead with the number of customers. For simplicity, we could consider that the additional cost incurred with each new customer is zero.

Such calculations are common in software and other industries where a feature, security in this case, comes with a big up-front cost, but then the cost that comes with each new customer is negligible, and can be zero.

Structure

In this chapter, we will be discussing the following topics:

- Investigating in security
- Zero trust compliance initiative
- Economic models
- Devices and hardware model
- Software models
- Advertising model
- Cloud
- Blockchains
- Others models
- Azure Cloud example

Objectives

The main objective is to illustrate the role of security in making an economic model successful. There are common patterns identified. Security is examined from the point of view of product assets that need to be protected.

Investing in security

The investment will come down with time, as suggested in the graph shown in the following figure:

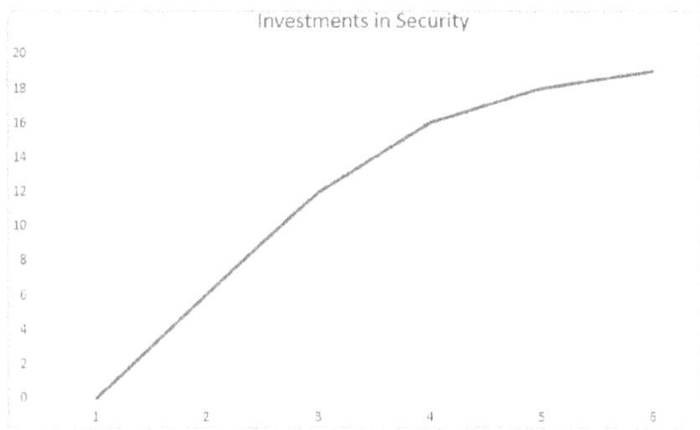

Figure 8.1: *Capital allocation for security*

The graph above depicts a sample of needed capital allocation to develop security features. Products are sold and advertised for features other than security, which appeal to customers. Security is often taken for granted and maybe it should. It should be noted that if not considered to be secure, the product will not sell, no matter what customer-pleasing features it may have.

The biggest impact on the product's success is generated by security incidents publicized in the media.

If there is a competitor product that is known to mitigate such incidents, it will gain significant market share with customers. The technical details are often obscure and hard to understand by the general public. The emphasis is always put on the end result. The more sensational, the better, and while it may not be possible to completely eliminate incidents, companies can reduce the probability of such events significantly by following security-minded design models, most of which were described in the earlier chapters.

There are a lot of compliance programs and related requirements. What must be called out, though, is that being compliant does not mitigate the consequences measured in lost business in the event of a publicized security breach. It helps, however, to grow the customer base in the absence of one, as being compliant with some respected regulatory standard carries the promise of a reduced security risk. If the author is to call out important compliance requirements, this would be the zero-trust compliance outlined in this document.

Zero trust compliance initiative

The zero trust documentation by Microsoft can be found here: **What do we mean by zero trust compliance? | Microsoft Learn**

It would be helpful to quote an excerpt from the above documentation to provide context for a discussion.

Refer to the following figure:

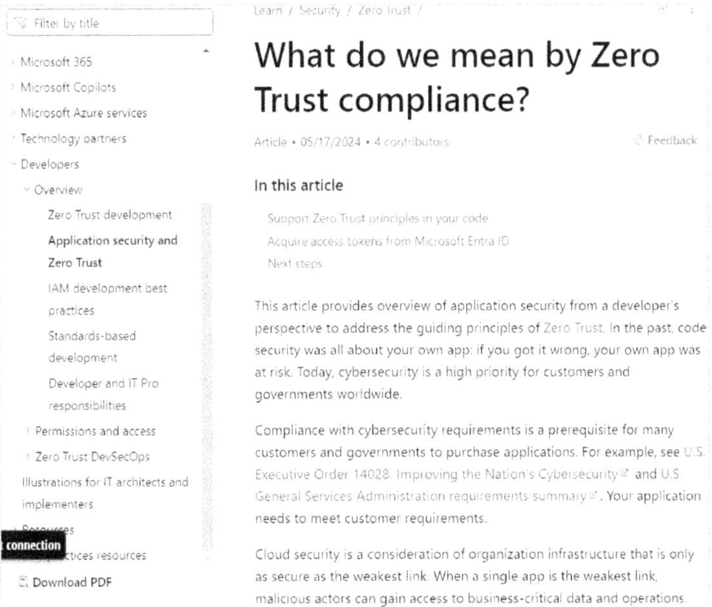

Figure 8.2: Zero trust compliance documentation

As we can see, there is a strong push for the zero trust principles to become foundational in computer systems development.

Fundamentally, the meaning behind these efforts is to reduce trust in external entities, as these could be compromised, resulting in the compromise of everything behind trusting them.

To re-emphasize an important point, a company cannot use its compliance posture to excuse its products from having security problems. However, in the absence of such problems, compliance provides customers with reassurance that product security is taken with the necessary care, or to put it in mathematical terms, compliance is necessary but not a sufficient product feature.

It should be said that the most important product feature, from the security point of view, is the lack of publicized security breaches. These can affect customer trust and, from there, product success in the marketplace. The compliance with a well-established security guideline carries the implicit promise that big security breaches are less probable.

Economic models

In software, there are multiple business models that enable companies to bring value to their customers and be profitable. Security posture is a cornerstone of all models.

Here, we will postulate that behind a security breach, there is an economic benefit to the successful attacker. Some will point out that not all breaches are motivated by an economic benefit. Attackers may have other reasons. And while this is true, the economic benefit would remain the main motivation and will be used as the primary lens to examine attack patterns.

Economic anatomy of an attack

Simply put, an attacker should stand to gain more than (s)he spends mounting the attack. We must also account for resources spent on unsuccessful attempts when computing the total cost to the attacker. To illustrate, suppose that on average one in ten attempts is successful and that each attempt costs a dollar. If a successful attempt brings more than ten dollars, then the effort is profitable.

A very similar calculation can be done on the defender side. Here again, the premise is that there should be an economic benefit to mount a defense. For example, it will not be worth spending a dollar to protect fifty-cent assets, but it makes a lot of sense to spend a dollar to protect a hundred-dollar worth of assets.

From another point of view, we should compare the defense to the attacks it is meant to protect against. If a dollar defense fails to protect against a fifty-cent attack, then it is not worth having. Consider that any asset worth being protected by one dollar is also worth the fifty cents spent by the attacker. This assumes that the asset has an equal asset value to both the attacker and the defender. Such an assumption is too simplistic, to say the least. However, if we make it, then some conclusions can be drawn. It could be said that the cost of the defense should not exceed the cost of the asset being defended. At the same time, the defense should withstand attacks costing less than the asset. Here, we also assume that defense costs less than the value of the asset. The defense does not need to cost less than the attack, but there is the issue of scale that requires defense costs to be less than the asset cost.

To elaborate on this, consider the following example: it costs a dollar to protect a hundred-dollar asset. It really does not matter what an attack will cost as long as the defense is effective against it. As the asset value grows, we could also grow (scale) the cost of the defense without changing the calculation semantics, as long as the ratio of defense cost to asset value does not grow. If it does, then we have a scaling issue. Say it may cost a dollar to protect a hundred-dollar asset, but it costs more than five dollars to protect a five-hundred-dollar asset.

A few words on the cases where economic realities are ignored, these require that the attacker will spend any amount required for a successful attack, and the defender will spend any amount on successful defense, no matter what the protected asset value might be. In this case, the defense should be capable of withstanding any attack, as the attacker's motives are unknown and success is worth it to them, no matter what the cost might be. In these cases, the value to the attacker goes beyond the asset that is being targeted. It is not the actual asset, but some derivative of it, that provides value to the attacker.

Next, we will discuss the most common business models used and the security posture impact on them.

Devices and hardware model

The most known example in this category is Apple and its plethora of products like iPhone, MacBooks, Macs, and so on.

We can add to this list devices from Samsung, servers from Dell, Windows laptops and workstations from various vendors, processors from Nvidia, AMD, Intel, and so on.

All of the above showcase the silicon capabilities. It can be said that the role of devices is to put easy-to-use computing power into the hands of users, both individual consumers and organizational entities, and in order to make this computing power usable and desired by the users, having device security is needed.

Device security

In order to have customers for these devices, having a good device security posture is required. Customers care most about authorizing access to the device capabilities so that only entities authorized by the customer can access those. In a similar fashion, customers care about protecting data managed by these devices. An obvious example would be that photos taken by an iPhone should only be available to the iPhone owner and authorized parties, not to anyone. A subtle point would be that physical access to the device should not suffice as authorization to access the digital content on it.

Another issue, maybe not as severe as the same one exhibited in the software model, is dealing with the problem of counterfeit hardware. The raw material devices are made of silicon, and silicon based products are becoming cheaper with time. The hardware business model relies on advanced design features that the products these companies offer on top of the silicon base.

Building these advanced features that are exciting to customers and difficult to duplicate is not a straightforward task. As we will see, there are popular business models that do not rely on leveraging the exciting customer feature, but instead lean on secondary properties, such as the ability of the company to manage configurations featuring the exciting product to customers that scale well.

Leaving these considerations aside for future discussion, the device security requires two main things:

- **Device owners** have some meaningful assurance that the device's compute and data are only exposed to authorized entities. This property will make the device appealing to customers who demand that their compute and data is only used by authorized party.
- **Device manufacturers** are protected against someone damaging the business model by creating device copies, like counterfeit iPhones produced and sold to consumers by someone who has not invested in the iPhone design. A top-of-mind strategy to achieve this is making device properties hard to duplicate so that the duplication effort will not be economically viable to the offenders. Moving critical functionality to the cloud is currently the accepted way to do this.

If we are to provide a historical perspective, the efforts have shifted more towards satisfying the former claim. Anecdotally, we are hearing less about counterfeit iPhones and more about attackers penetrating customer devices, iPhones, or other devices, and doing some unauthorized operations on them.

Trying not to prescribe any solutions, we can assume that there exists some acceptable resolution to the first issue that empowers the device business model. To summarize the outcome, the cost of manufacturing, marketing, and supporting counterfeit iPhones, all required to sell the product to customers, is prohibitive to the potential perpetrators. We can also say that the genuine device manufacturers, take Apple for example, did a great job making such efforts unprofitable, and this way discouraging willing counterfeiters.

We will do a similar analysis on the software model next. Copying software is even cheaper than copying a device. As a consequence, many of the conclusions regarding the device model are applicable to the software model and vice versa.

Software model

Here, the most prominent example is undoubtedly Microsoft and its rich portfolio of system and productivity software featuring Microsoft Windows, Office, and many others.

We can qualify software as a system or an application.

To provide a definition, a *system is software meant to support other 'application' software running on it.*

It serves the end user and does not run other software. The definition can bear some criticism as most software nowadays provides some programmability capabilities and, according to this definition, can be considered a system, as programmability implies there are programs, which we can view as applications that run within the application (or software) that provides the underlying programmability layer.

One can examine details about the application exposing the programmability layer to determine if it can be considered a **system**. To complicate matters further, this problem is recursive as applications sitting on the programmability layer provided by the hosting application can, themselves, provide for programmability that allows hosting other applications. To simplify the story, an application software is classified as either a system or not. System software exposes a programmability layer that allows other, known as hosted, programs to run on it.

The interesting observation about software is that it can be copied without being able to distinguish a copy from the genuine version. In this respect, similarities can be found to the device hardware discussed in the previous heading. Duplicating hardware may not be without cost, as duplicating software is considered to be, but it is still a lot cheaper than investing in genuine hardware design. The objective to distinguish the genuine one from the copied version is the same for devices or software models.

The software application must be able to run on any customer-owned device. The two models can be described as follows: the first model has different applications, branded the same way, representing one logical application on different devices. It may not come as a surprise that MS Word on Mac is a different application from MS Word running on Windows. The first model calls for utilizing a compatibility layer that the applications are written to, which remains constant regardless of the underlying device **operating system (OS).** In this model, the most common example is browser platforms capable of rendering HTML and running JavaScript code. Often quoted downside of such compatibility layers is that they need to implement and expose the lowest common denominator functionality that is available on all devices. This prevents devices from exposing device-specific advanced features if they fall outside of the compatibility layer's lowest common denominator definitions.

This observation applies to security features as well. A feature not exposed by the compatibility layer is device-specific and can be exposed to device-specific software only.

Oftentimes, we hear about the so-called native device features that can be very compelling, but are only available to applications targeted at specific devices and respective OSs. Making use of these device-specific features is a good thing as it showcases the device's advanced capabilities, but on the other hand, using device-specific features causes the proliferation of device-specific applications.

Figure 8.3 illustrates the compatibility layer concepts:

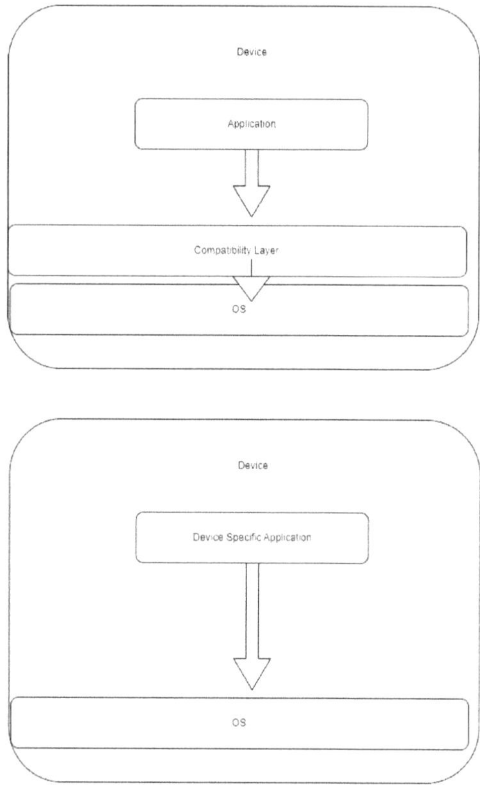

Figure 8.3: *Compatibility layer supporting cross-device applications*

Having a compatibility layer is a feature of the application platform. As called out earlier, browsers provide a compatibility layer to applications running in the browser, the language being JavaScript. Since all browsers offer a JavaScript execution engine, one can say that the browser acts as a compatibility layer built on top of the underlying OS. Applications targeting the browser platform can be agnostic of the device OS the browser is running on. The same idea underpins virtual machines supporting applications on various devices. We can point out the browser JavaScript execution engine, **Java Virtual Machine** (**JVM**), and **Etherium Virtual Machine** (**EVM**) as well-known examples.

In establishing a security context process, there exist primitives, if we can call them that, at multiple levels. Some are listed in the next section. It would be great to define an application-level interface exposing APIs for applications to integrate with.

There are cryptography, authentication, and authorization protocols, a user interface providing a user experience for entering credentials, workflows, and experiences for key management, and so on. It is desirable that the security gestures provided to end users are easy and straightforward for applications to implement. We want to avoid, as much as possible, applications that avoid the use of a security feature or implement it on their own because the feature did not meet some of the application's usability, ease of use, or other requirements. This is why having an application-level security interface is important, as providers can choose what to expose to applications. It can be argued that functionality like encryption and protocols should not be made available as there are other, dependent functionality that needs to be used to make these effective. To provide a glimpse into this, encryption is as effective as the key management, for the encrypted data can be decrypted with. Assuming symmetric keys, the same key is used to encrypt and decrypt. If the key is leaked, the benefits of encryption vanish. However, using encryption does not imply a specific key management method. That is why it could make sense not to expose the encryption interface on its own, as key management is an important dependency.

A few recommendations to conclude this section. Applications should not be exposed to specific cryptographic algorithms and protocols. For example, the application should not have to have explicit functionality to encrypt data, manage keys, or do any security-related operations. These actions should be wrapped in components used by the application. A typical example would be a storage component that encrypts the data stored or a communication component that encrypts data in transit. Other general abstractions can be exposed to the application while keeping in mind that these should not be possible to be misused in some way to cause a security issue. One such abstraction, shown in previous chapters, is the SecurityContext anchored by the authenticated identity the application is running as. Generally, there are three choices one can choose to act as the application, the identity signed into the application, or the identity making a remote call to the application and getting impersonated by it. One can call out that there is also the identity that belongs to the platform on which the application is running. This identity would be different than the ones mentioned above, but it can be considered to be secondary, and usage does not need to be affected by SecurityContext methods, which operate on the primary identity only. The secondary indicates additional information, which is the same no matter what the primary is.

We should say that the caller's identity matters only in the case of a remote call. If the call is locally served by a function within the same process, it should not matter what identity the caller runs as. The same identity is used to run the function.

Security context implementation guide

As a sample implementation, consider the one provided by the Python spring distribution. Refer to the link **https://docs.spring.io/spring-python/1.1.x/pydoc/springpython.security.context.html# SecurityContextHolderStrategy**

See a sample of the documentation shown in the following figure:

```
class SecurityContext(__builtin__.object)
    Methods defined here:

    __init__(self, authentication=<springpython.security.providers.Authentication instance>)

    __str__(self)

    Data descriptors defined here:

    __dict__
        dictionary for instance variables (if defined)

    __weakref__
        list of weak references to the object (if defined)
```

Figure 8.4: Python spring security context documentation

As shown, the implementation provides maximum flexibility by representing the context as a Python dictionary or a collection of arbitrary name-value pairs that allow any structure to be modeled. The context should carry a collection of identities that the application wishes to act as.

The concept of security context has been known for a long time. To show an example, recall the **Generic Security Service Application Programming Interface** (**GSSAPI**).

A good description can be found in the **Request for Comments** (**RFC**) dedicated to the GSSAPI: **https://datatracker.ietf.org/doc/html/rfc2743**.

GSSAPI uses the SecurityContext to describe the opaque data structure used to secure the communication between two entities. A view of the APIs defined in the GSSAPI RFC is as shown in the following:

```
CREDENTIAL MANAGEMENT

GSS_Acquire_cred             acquire credentials for use
GSS_Release_cred             release credentials after use
GSS_Inquire_cred             display information about
                             credentials




GSS_Add_cred                 construct credentials incrementally
GSS_Inquire_cred_by_mech     display per-mechanism credential
                               information

CONTEXT-LEVEL CALLS

GSS_Init_sec_context         initiate outbound security context
GSS_Accept_sec_context       accept inbound security context
GSS_Delete_sec_context       flush context when no longer needed
GSS_Process_context_token    process received control token on
                               context
GSS_Context_time             indicate validity time remaining on
                                  context
GSS_Inquire_context          display information about context
GSS_Wrap_size_limit          determine GSS_Wrap token size limit
GSS_Export_sec_context       transfer context to other process
GSS_Import_sec_context       import transferred context
```

Figure 8.5: GSSAPI methods

A few comments on the above. Technology, software specifically, has advanced significantly since the GSSAPI specification was created. Nowadays, the **Transport Level Security** (**TLS**) protocol has become a de facto standard for securing messages, and other protocols have faded. This phenomenon has reduced the importance of GSSAPI in the ecosystem. It does not make sense to support a generic API covering multiple protocols when we see that one protocol has clearly dominated in terms of market penetration, as software is concerned. To put it differently, if an application is using TLS for communication, it makes little sense to re-implement TLS functionality. And while the protocol used to secure communication between two parties may have settled, the question of client credentials and client identity has not. TLS requires a server identity encoded in a certificate to be present. The client certificate is optional. This means that the client identity does not participate in establishing the security context used to secure messages over the communication channel established between the two communicating entities. This topic is covered in detail in the chapter about encryption when encryption in transit is described.

The issue emphasized here is that the SecurityContext defined by the GSSAPI specification may not be the most understandable abstraction to describe the client identity being used. This is the reason why IdentityContext is introduced here. Instead of modeling message security, it is assumed that the underlying TLS transport protects messages, and the emphasis is placed on client identity used in TLD and modeled as IdentityContext.

Software security

Similar to device security software needs to meet certain security posture requirements to be considered acceptable to customers. Also similar to devices, software vendors need a way to protect their rights against software copies, which are easy to produce, as we called out in the device security heading. Also, software needs to offer some assurances to the customers that their data will be protected. We can assume that nobody, or rather very few, would be using an email client that exposes the content of customer emails to unauthorized third parties.

Application stores provide a partial solution to the problem above, as store owners can certify that the applications accepted in the store adequately protect customer data. Applications found to misbehave can be removed from the store and, sometimes, from customer devices. The details are not very clear and vary, as app store providers do not clearly call out if misbehaving applications that were admitted to the application store once will be removed from customer devices after discovering a security issue. This is a delicate business as once downloaded, the application is property of the customer and even if found to have security issues, removing it may cause some customers to oppose the process. If the provider is able to remove an application from a customer device, then a provider having an exploitable security issue will enable the successful attacker to affect all customer devices by changing the installed applications on them. Given this consideration, it is a little surprising that the application store providers are hesitant to implement drastic measures against applications found to have security vulnerabilities after the application has been admitted to the store and from there, installed on customer devices. This is a double-edged sword. Not taking action would let the compromised application run wild and exploit assets on the customer's machine. Taking action is also dangerous as it exposes the store in case it has an exploitable security issue, no matter how unlikely it is. One can think that letting the user take action on her own is a good solution, though it is not without pitfalls, as users may or may not take these actions.

Here, we have to discuss security needs when extending device software to the cloud. Devices need to be able to live without having an internet connection to the cloud. For using the full device functionality, having a network connection to the respective cloud has been determined to be an acceptable requirement.

About security, the content stored in the cloud has to be authorized to the user on the device. The topic about the nature of device identities is somewhat complex, and this is especially true for devices supporting multiple users. It is a common problem to determine if the cloud content belongs to the device or the user behind it. Going forward, we will operate under the assumption that it is the user behind that is authorized to access the cloud, not the device. And as is the case with any rules, there are some exceptions. User-independent content can be authorized to the device, though it will be fair to consider authorizing to any identity, or said in another way, not authorizing at all. Authorizing the device could make sense in backup-and-restore cases. Even there, it is highly questionable if user data should be made available without user authorization. We will need to assume the user has authorized the device to manage some of her data, and this must be offered via some meaningful user experiences that make it clear what is going on. This is easier said than done. Having some pre-conceived authorization semantics may be helpful. For example, instead of being asked for authorization to access some specific piece of data, the user could be asked to authorize access to all content created on the device. This is also tricky, as there is content that is being created on multiple devices. It would be much simpler and clearer not to allow the device access to any user content, and that also makes sense. Users can get to their content using their own identity.

In this context, the application role is to choose the primary identity under which it is operating. For the specific action being done, and for this to happen, the application security context has to be able to hold identities, which we saw it can do. It is missing, however, a method that enables the application to designate an identity to be primary.

An architecture based on this approach is depicted in the following figure:

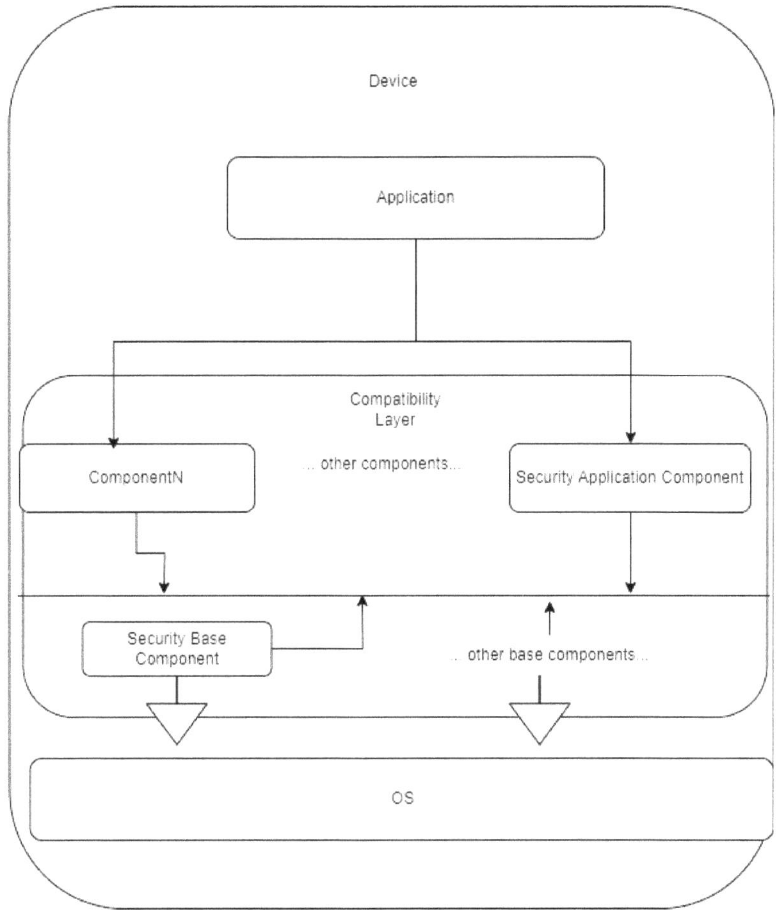

Figure 8.6: Breakdown of the compatibility layer

The intent is that the application interacts with the security component, modeled as a security context, to specify the primary identity to be used when interacting with the top-level components.

Note: **The reach needed by the application to call the base security component. To rectify this, the security component can be divided into two parts: base and application. The application part will hold objects, like the security context, that are visible to the application. The base part exposes objects and interfaces to application-visible components, but not to the applications.**

The resulting picture will look like the following figure:

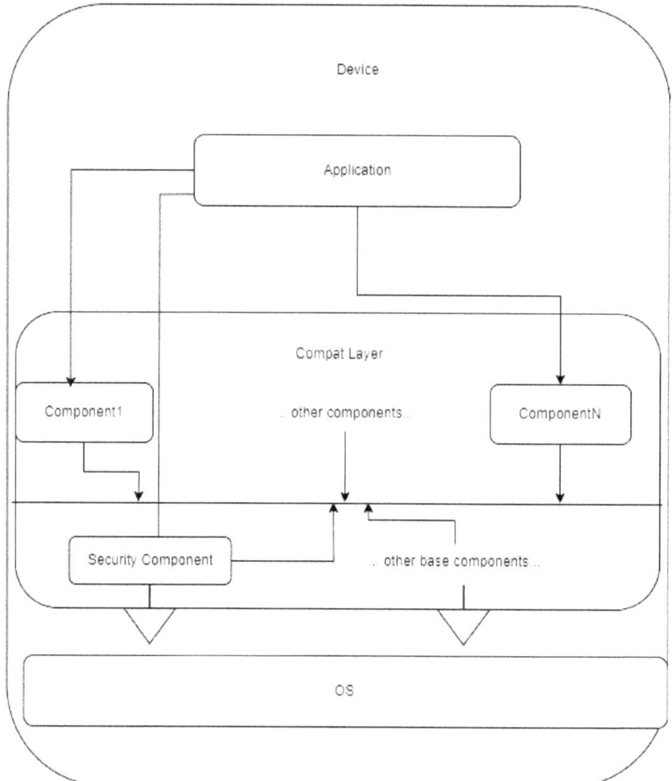

Figure 8.7: Splitting the security component

This approach is very much like having kernel and application modes in popular OSs, where the base components belong to the kernel. These kernels are OS concepts, and the goal here is to suggest a model for the security component that is OS independent.

The architectures possible can be based on a single or multi-layer compatibility component. The two-layer design shown above is an invariant of the multi-layer design, so it fits the second architectural pattern. The multi-layer compatibility layer architecture creates certain benefits for designers of components that fit there. It allows a component in the lower layer to be created that is not exposed to applications. Considering the security component, the base component in the lower layer does not need to be exposed to the application. This lower-level component could be the SecurityContext, preserving the GSSAPI semantics. The top-level security component is seen and used by applications. It could be spring's SecurityContext or another name to avoid name collisions and confusion. To put a stake in the ground, we will call the object an **`IdentityContext`** as suggested in the *summary* section. It needs to expose methods that allow the application to choose the identity context under which it is operating. And the choices are: the application identity, the identity under which the application is running, and finally, the identity using the application:

```
# outline in python syntax the identity context class
class IdentityContext:
    STARTEDID = 1
    APPLICATIONID = 2
    CALLERID = 3
    NONE = 0

    DefaultID = NONE

    def SwitchDefaultIdentity(ID):
        pass

    def GetDefaultID():
         pass

    # ... other methods …
```

The class above shows two methods to set and get the default identity for the application. It is a sample syntax to illustrate the concepts presented without implementing error handling and other details. We can recommend avoiding using this to switch identities. The default identity should be inferred from the way the application is invoked. If the application has to specify the identity, this could very well present an exploitable security issue. To mitigate potential security issues, the usage of the **`SwitchDefautIdentity`** method needs to be flagged and scrutinized.

Advertising model

Here, the most well-known company using this business model is Google. There are many other famous examples, such as Facebook/Meta, Amazon, Microsoft, and many others.

The goal we have here is not to analyze in detail the individual company's business model, but to illustrate the impact the security posture has on this model.

Advertising relies on the application attracting many users. The more users, the higher the value to advertisers.

To attract many users, the product needs to offer compelling features, with security being a very important one.

The most important point is that software is offered for no charge, and the business model relies on monetizing advertisers offering products that customers need to see. For that to happen, customers need to be attracted to the product, and having a good security posture is an important part of the story, promoting the product. Arguably, a product featuring poor security, as judged by customers, will be used less frequently compared to a product offering comparable features with a better security posture. There is a bit of fine print here regarding the comparative adjective. It does not mean the same. It is often the case that there is a compelling feature, let us call it **F**, desired by some customers. F is expensive, and the software vendor is faced with the choice of offering F versus features that contribute to enhancing the security posture. A consideration is also to take into account the meaning of F being expensive. It could be expensive to develop, expensive to run, or both. If it expensive to develop, once the development cost is assumed, then the feature is practically free to offer, but if it is expensive to run, say it consumes a lot of compute and storage resources, then the vendor has to consider the resource cost. There will be competition for resources needed to run security features, and the vendor needs to make a choice about what customers would need most – product features or security features consuming the resources.

Advertising security

On the surface, it appears that there are no security issues to worry about in the advertising business model. But this is only on the surface. A few will be pointed out in this heading. The issues are a bit more nuanced. It is the business model that is affected by the way the issues are addressed.

The first issue is about the default search engine (or similar functionality bootstrapping the advertising model) used on a device or application. The more popular the device or application, the more eyeballs will land on the advertising results. If an adversary can replace the default search engine with one of their own, then all advertising benefits will belong to the attacker without them having to invest in making the product popular with consumers. Imagine someone replacing Chrome browser default search with something else than Google's engine. Then, they can enjoy search advertising power without investments in Chrome, with many consumer-friendly features. This is similar to making counterfeit iPhones or Office packages and not having to invest in product design.

The other issue worth noting is that the products featuring the advertising component have to be compelling to customers, so usage is widespread to bring the volume needed to make the business model appealing to providers. A good example is the Android OS. It is free to use and open source. It took a lot of resources to develop and maintain. The reason that a big company, like Google, this is because the major OS investment supports its advertising-based business model. Without it, the advertising engine will be at the mercy of being included by other system software vendors. With Android being developed by the same vendor as the default advertising engine built in, the business model is to provide the OS free and rely on returns from advertising to achieve the desired business results. Since the returns grow exponentially with number of customers, as shown in the graph depicted in *Figure 8.8*.

To summarize, products based on the advertising business model have to be secure to ensure usage and, from there, advertising revenues.

This level of security has to be provided at some acceptable cost, which is less than the expected advertising revenue.

Cloud

The cloud business model is, in a way, very different. But it is also quite similar, as the major driving force behind it is efficient management of resources at scale. The cheaper it is to manage the resources, the higher the return as the price per source is reduced, and the profit from renting these is increased.

The model relies on the cloud provider managing resources for customers, see *Chapter 5, Compute, Storage and Networking in the Cloud* and offering these at a cost, smaller than the customer would pay if they managed the resources for themselves, while making a profit as the cost of managing these resources for many customers allows cost per customers to be sufficiently small to the cloud provider so the endeavor is profitable.

If we are to find similarities to other models, this will be the efficiency of managing resources at scale. At some point, the volume would generate enough profits to offset the upfront investments, and one of the major investments is about security posture.

The graph shows how investment and return change with time in the following figure:

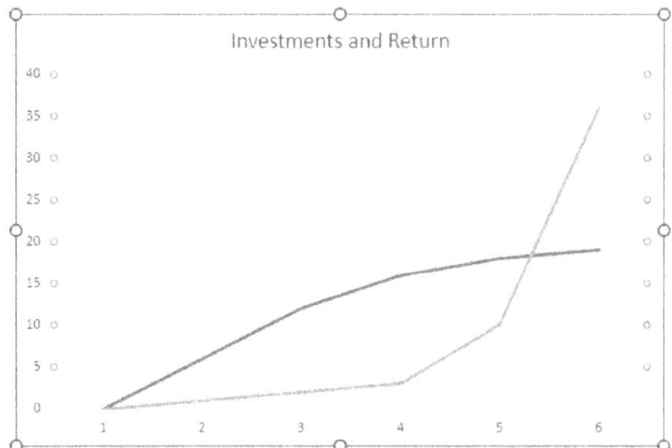

Figure 8.8: *Expenses for managing resources and resource count*

In this figure, note that expenses are big at the beginning and then taper off with time as the resource count increases. This phenomenon is known as profitable scaling since, as the number of resources managed grows at a certain rate, the expense of managing those resources grows at a lesser rate. If we assign a monetary value to each resource, then the two graphs can be compared as both x and y axes have the same semantics. The inflection point is where the two lines intersect. Before that point (Yret < Yinv at intersection), the investments exceed the return and the business is unprofitable, and after it, the business becomes profitable and the returns grow fast as x increases past the intersection point. This finding is not all that surprising and explains the strong motivation behind the efforts to acquire new customers.

Similar graphs are applicable to many business models. They come to prove that size, or number of customers, matters after all. As volume increases, so do profits. The other part of the equation is having the expenses grow more slowly as the number of customers spikes up faster. We call this efficiency in managing resources. A simple explanation is as follows: to serve a customer, some resources are needed, and as the number of customers goes up, so does the number of resources required to serve these customers. To have a successful business model, the profit from each customer has to exceed the resource expense for the resources required to serve them.

There is a natural advantage the cloud providers have, which allows them to invest heavily in cloud resource management, including providing security for these resources. As cloud resources are shared among customers, so is the management cost and other physical expenses incurred for managing these resources. If the customers need to pay this cost themselves, then a resource will cost them more than the same resource rented from a cloud provider.

There are many expenses here. Cloud providers ensure availability by supporting multiple datacenter and automatically directing traffic to a datacenter that can take the load. There are legal considerations related to managing datacenter in different countries; there is also a need to control cross-datacenter data replication, provide datacenter security, and so on.

This all makes sense, however, we need to point out that these advantages mostly disappear when we accept that there is a model under which compute and storage resources are infinite and distributed around the world. The managing software is free for anyone to use, and security is built into the management algorithms. There is no need to have secure datacenter, deal with legal issues, and other related activities. See the blockchains section that describes a model similar to the above. We can call it a global cloud as a reference term. Existing clouds are provided by individual companies and should, therefore, be **non-global**. This topic was discussed in an earlier chapter examining private and public cloud terms. To recall, there are consumers and providers, and when the providers advertise a cloud to be **public**, the semantics are that anyone can use it.

The term **global** is meant to distinguish it from the term public. Anyone can use a global cloud, just as with public clouds, and anyone can contribute resources to the global cloud, which is not true for public clouds. We can also call the opposite of global cloud a **company** cloud to be more specific. The intent is to distinguish it from **private** cloud, which relates to the cloud consumer, not the cloud provider. A company cloud describes the provider. The cloud, itself, can be public or private from the cloud consumer's point of view.

It is anyone's guess as to when the transition to the global cloud will happen. There are existing technical hurdles that prevent it from happening at a mass scale, performance and resource management efficiency being the top ones. However, it is very possible that a catalyst will appear and accelerate this transition, and it will not be surprising at all to see security as a major driving force behind such a transition. It takes a security issue or two in company clouds that are well publicized to persuade customers to look at the global cloud-based solutions. As it stands now, the company clouds offer many benefits and are positioned to be a good alternative to clouds made of individually managed nodes.

Cloud security

The goal of cloud security is not to allow **unauthorized** access to cloud applications and data. If we assume the application's logic is public, it would be data access that needs protection against unauthorized access.

The clouds want to claim that by moving applications from the datacenters they currently run in to datacenters comprising the respective cloud, security issues are not introduced, and some existing ones get mitigated. And this is probably true because, as discussed in previous chapters, the cloud providers can afford to make big investments in security due to the scale on which they operate. There also needs to be a metric to prove this is the case. Like blockchain claims that the *Bitcoin network has never been hacked*, the clouds need to be able to say *Cloud X has never been hacked*, or, for the more sophisticated customers, something like *Applications running in Cloud X are hacked less often*. The statement has to be true, backed by data, and appeal to customers.

As cost benefits become more and more evident and cloud providers' investments in security continue to grow, migration from private datacenter to the cloud would also continue to accelerate. The next phase would be migration to the **global** cloud.

As a natural conclusion, we can say that:

Cloud providers offer environments for their customer applications that boast security levels that are on the same level or better than the security levels at customer-managed clouds.

As to any rule, one can find exceptions to the above. Customers that are extremely security sensitive, such as financial institutions and credit card companies, may feature security levels at their own datacenters that are higher compared to the datacenter security offered by cloud providers. These examples could be rare, but they do exist.

To understand the issue in detail, it would be necessary to analyze the security measures available at these private datacenter and the effect on the applications running there. Same measures or better should be offered by the cloud providers.

Blockchains

Blockchains offer an intriguing alternative to the cloud compute which (the cloud compute) is based on **company** clouds. In the cloud, the business model is designed to support the cloud provider supplying compute, storage, and networking resources. In the blockchain scenario, there are network nodes that may come from individual consumers, cloud providers, or anywhere else, for that matter. Allowing infrastructure resources from anywhere democratizes the business by letting anyone who owns hardware capable of running a compute node participate in running the blockchain easily. The business model is supported by public and free software running on the compute nodes. This can be contrasted with software running on cloud nodes that belongs to the cloud provider. The software is free, in the blockchain case that is, but the resources it needs to run on are not, and to recoup the cost of providing these resources, the blockchain network node provider is rewarded with the blockchain native token. For example, nodes participating in running the bitcoin network are rewarded with bitcoins (BTC), those running the Etherium network get ETH tokens as a reward and so on.

The idea is very similar to the models described in the other section. It comes down to software facilitating maximum resource utilization and rewarding the resource providers accordingly, meaning that these providers cannot get better rewards elsewhere. The resources, like the blockchain network nodes, come from entities that are independent of the blockchain network.

Running this software on a blockchain network incurs some well-defined costs. We have to point out that there will be costs no matter where the software is run, blockchain, cloud, or the user's device, but it is not well-defined except when used to run blockchains. Cloud will tell you the cost that the customer charges, but they will not tell you their cost of supporting the underlying infrastructure. If the cost to the customer is 0 (free), this needs to be taken with a grain of salt, as the business model has to be meaningful for the provider to offer it. Free means that the customer is not paying the cost directly, but someone is, and there is a reason for doing it. That reason is, in economic terms, that the rewards for running the software exceed the cost of supplying and maintaining the hardware the software needs to run.

Security angle

There is a widespread perception that blockchains are secure, and there is a good reason for it. Major blockchains, like bitcoin, have been operating for more than ten years now without exploitable security breaches. A quick Google search can confirm the above statement. To quote a selected Coinbase article from the search results:

The bitcoin network has never been hacked. Its open-source code has been scrutinized by countless security experts and computer scientists. Bitcoin was also the first digital currency to solve the double-spend problem, making "trustless" peer-to-peer currencies a reality.

See the excellent article presented by Coinbase **https://www.coinbase.com/learn/crypto-basics/7-biggest-bitcoin-myths#:~:text=The%20Bitcoin%20network%20has%20never,to%2Dpeer%20currencies%20a%20reality.**

A view of a peer-to-peer blockchain network, which includes bitcoin is shown next:

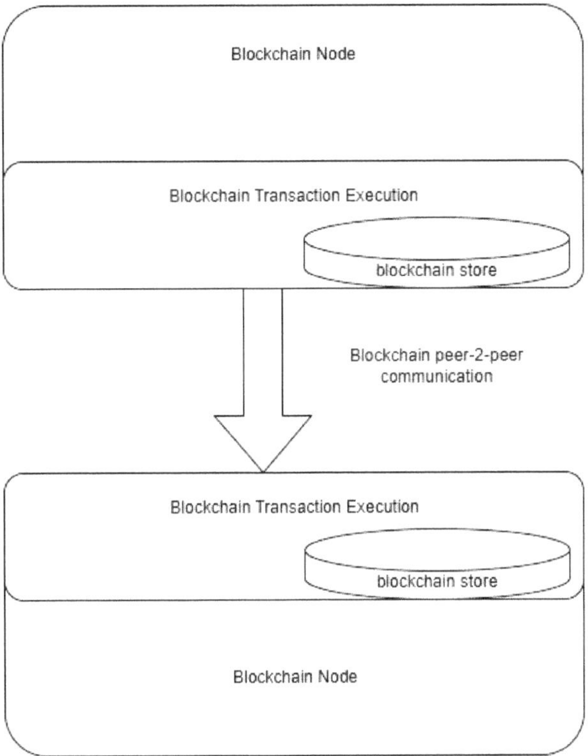

Figure 8.9: *Bitcoin network*

While this sounds great, we will try to put these statements in the appropriate context so that one can draw conclusions about the potential behind the bitcoin-influenced network architecture. We can also discuss blockchain architectures in general.

There are a few important observations regarding the design of the blockchain that should be mentioned. There is user security, or wallet security, and then there is network security, assuming the keys stored in the wallet are protected against unauthorized access. What is being claimed is that the network security has not been compromised for the bitcoin network. And on top of that, there is Crypto Exchange security.

A few words to explain the difference between network and user security. Using an example would be most illustrative. Consider a bank and its customers. If a customer's identity gets compromised, the attacker can impersonate that customer to the bank and misuse their assets. If, on the other hand, the bank itself gets compromised, then the attacker can misuse assets that belong to all bank customers. All customer assets exceed any individual user assets and the bank compromise event would be more damaging than individual user compromise.

There is an important difference related to customer identities between blockchains and banks, though, and it rarely gets talked about. If a bank customer's identity is compromised, the customer can use some mitigating actions to prove to the bank their identity and remedy the situation. There is no such option for blockchains. If a customer loses their private key, blockchain cannot help recover the account, as there are no recovery options available in the blockchain protocols. The recovery, if any, has to be handled by the wallet housing the customer's private key. This is a sensible arrangement as it separates the key management experience provided by the wallet from the key usage in the blockchain. Back to the bank example, the wallet-blockchain relationship is similar to what we have with the bank and authorities issuing the identity documents. The bank plays the role of the blockchain, and the wallet is represented by the identity documents issuing authority. Lost identities are handled by the issuing authority, not the bank same way as lost private keys are handled by the wallet, not the blockchain. There is a bit of fine print in this arrangement, as the situations are not exactly the same. Yes, the same private key could be recovered without affecting the blockchain designs, but issuing a new private key will be problematic. This problem does not exist for the issuing authority, as the identity document always has the same identity identifier. The key point here is that the identity identifier is not private. There can be a private key identifier in the identity document that connects the entity proving key ownership to the identity being asserted by the document. A picture ID connects the person whose face is in the picture to the name in the ID document. Faces change with time, but names do not.

Finally, we can talk about the concept of network security. The claim that the bitcoin network security has never been compromised is great, and we will take a closer look at its meaning.

As is the case with any statement, using some comparison to evaluate its importance would be very useful in creating confidence in it. To start with, we will try to establish a baseline. Assuming the bitcoin network has not been penetrated, it would be natural to understand what we are comparing it to and if this basis for comparison exhibits the same security characteristics delivered at a heftier price, or if the price is comparable, but the security is somehow lacking. If none of these are true, the claim about the bitcoin network's impenetrable security will not do the customer much good; they can get the same level of security, measured by the selected metric, *never been hacked,* and pay a lower price for it.

At this point, a few words about the selected metric would be in order. Whether or not the bitcoin network has been **hacked** is unknown. What we know is that a hack has not been reported in the mass media. And the same is true for the benchmark we are comparing to the blockchain network. If both the blockchain network and the benchmark, say a national bank, do not have security incidents reported, we can only conclude they are equivalent and go by the cost we, as customers, must absorb for the services we need. The lower the cost, the more likely we are to choose a service. This may not be very accurate, as a lack of reported incidents does not necessarily mean security posture is equivalent, but this is what most people will go by. Experts may consider individual security features and try to estimate the level of protection based on these. But most people are not security experts, and this estimation is an inexact science. Considering this, going by the public perception shaped by the mass media is a reasonable approach, and the results will not be far from optimal.

With all this said, the choice of underlying infrastructure that is decentralized blockchain or a centralized entity like a financial institution or a cloud provider will depend mostly on other factors, as security will be considered to be satisfactory in all the offerings. And the primary factor will be cost. Customers will choose a solution meeting their requirements at the lowest cost possible.

Here will be a good place to discuss tradeoffs between decentralized and centralized constructs. From a security point of view, decentralized algorithms rely on reaching a consensus about data integrity without the help of a trusted central entity. The same operation is performed on multiple nodes that must reach a consensus regarding the result. Centralized models rely on a central entity to guide towards the aforementioned consensus. Having a central entity is more efficient from a performance point of view when we consider the speed and the amount of computation needed. The tradeoff here, though it may not be evident, comes from the need to trust this central entity. The trust is key-based. If we consider public key cryptography, the secret private key is in possession of the central entity. Central entities have become good at managing secrets, but in the unlikely event of a secret compromise, the whole system that depends on that secret gets compromised. The decentralized architectures cannot have a secret that avoids trusting a central entity at the expense of increasing performance load. To summarize:

Decentralized architectures have to offer performance comparable to that of centralized ones to become a viable alternative to them.

As an example, consider the proof-of-work consensus algorithm used by the bitcoin network. It requires that participating nodes compute a hash value (mining), which is a computationally intensive operation that affects network performance.

As technology moves forward, the author has little doubt that this will eventually happen, though we do not know exactly when. Secrets are hard to keep and will eventually be revealed as a condition to participate in the network. This would be a controversial conclusion, as many resources have been spent on improving secret management. It may not be possible to completely eliminate secrets (or keys) from the security landscape, but the notion of unconditional trust based on secrets will be eliminated. Losing a secret should not lead to a compromise.

Other models

The models listed above constitute by no means a complete list. It is worth mentioning services that could be considered part of the cloud **Software as a Service** (**SaaS**) model, but can also be listed separately, as a service is not necessarily tied to a single cloud.

Typical service architecture is shown in the following figure:

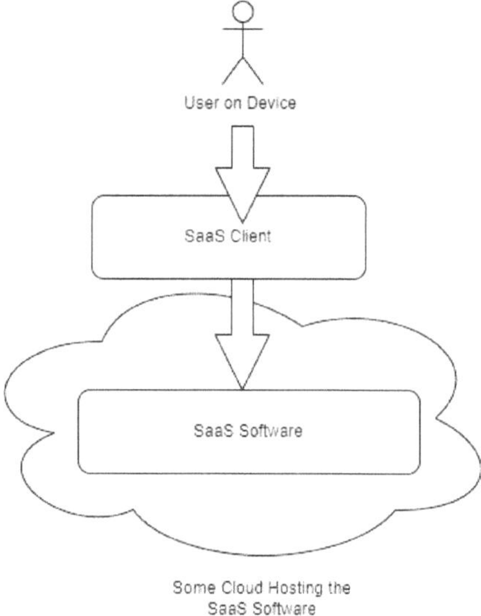

Figure 8.10: *The SaaS model*

A service can be viewed as a software component running on a cloud. As software, the service owners have to provide a defense against the two main threats listed in the software security heading. The major issues were protecting the customer data and other resources, and protecting the software from unauthorized use. The latter part is hard to accomplish, possible with some conditions, if the software is intended to be used by authorized users.

Note: **While user identity can be determined and authorized, the client identity cannot. But then, if a user is authorized, the client identity is not important. Meaning that using any client with the service software owner is acceptable.**

The prime example is to consider email clients. Any email client can access a user's email at any email provider. The user has to provide proof of his or her identity at some user interface rendered by the client.

The SaaS service provider will provide their own client with the intent to showcase an optimal experience while interacting with the service. The important thing is that the service cannot distinguish among clients. Any client can provide an experience of their choice on top of the SaaS service. As we said, authorization in the service is on the identity of the user, not that of the devices. There is a delegation flow that allows some of the user rights to be delegated to the device, but doing so requires a proof mechanism to assert device identity, and this is a non-trivial task assuming the device is not under centralized control. These are known as **public** applications in OAuth2 terms or applications running on user-owned devices. Being user-owned does not make the device public. However, the applications on it are. While the application is public and known to everyone, device+application as well as user+application is unique. We can remove application identities from these constructed identifiers, as public knowledge makes them superfluous, which leaves the user and device. Authorizing on device identity was discussed earlier in the chapter. Although it makes sense in certain scenarios, like backup-restore, there is the possibility of leaking user data unintentionally if the device key is compromised. If we choose to play it safe and avoid authorizing on device identities alone, this will leave users as the primary identity of choice to authorize on.

Security considerations

Most security considerations were called out in the model description paragraph. A brief summary would be the following:

The SaaS application should serve only authorized users.

It follows from the above that user identity needs to be authenticated by the client, SaaS, or other, and authorized by the service SaaS application. Details can be found in *Chapter 6, Authentication and Authorization.*

The main point to be called out is that authentication happens on the client, and the results of the authentication process are consumed by the service.

Business models evolution

It is important to point out the tendency for new business models to provide the logistics to manage resources, not the resources themselves. As an example, consider a rental car company. Following the traditional business model, the company owns both the rental cars and the management software.

The following figure illustrates the model:

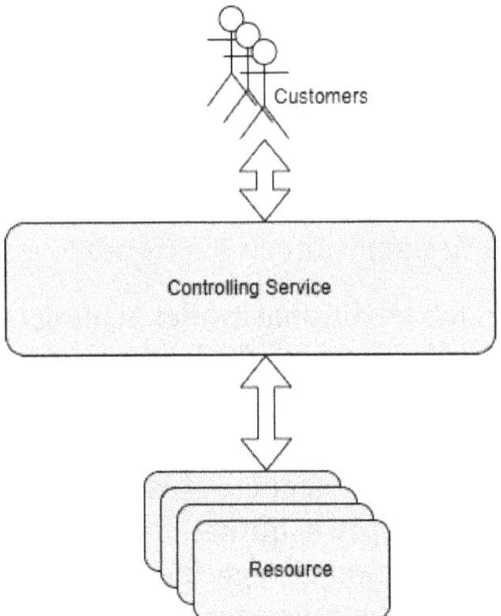

Figure 8.11: *Traditional model where a single entity owns both resources and management*

Owning both control service and resources gives the flexibility of defining the rules of how software is changed on each component. The downsides that can be called out are the proliferation of proprietary software that involves feature duplication and the need to define change management systems that can handle propagating security fixes, among other things.

Contemporary models brought by companies like Uber and Airbnb put management under company control, but the resources remain with customers. This creates two types of customers and related experiences: those providing resources and those consuming them.

The model is depicted in the following figure:

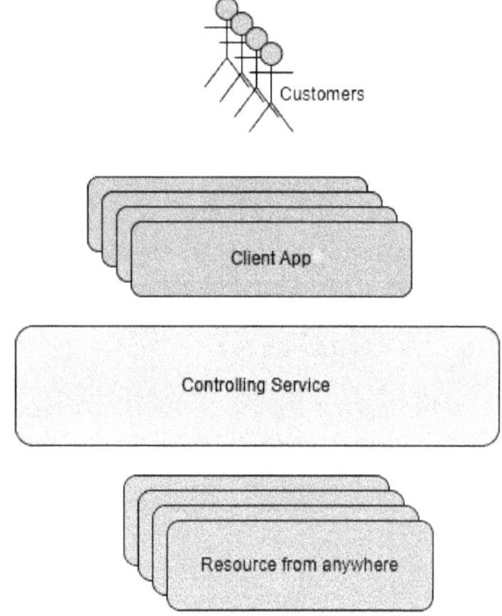

Figure 8.12: *Customers provide and consume resources*

This is often called a disruption of traditional business models as the provided flexibility and profit potential scale well with supply and demand. The controlling service can determine the price of resource usage, within some boundaries, thus promoting optimal resource usage and maximizing the profits of the resource provider.

It is worth pointing out that in the traditional model, scaling is limited by the sheer number of resources owned by the company running the business. In the contemporary model scale is theoretically infinite as customers offering resources to satisfy the increasing demand are expected to continue providing resources as prices go up with the demand. This is a way to satisfy the classic supply and demand balance. This is hard to impossible to implement in the traditional model where the supply is limited to company-owned resources. Once the resources are exhausted, there are no more regardless of the price consumers are willing to pay. And this creates inefficiencies and missed business opportunities that the new models are tapping into. Sure, it makes a lot of sense to offer a ride or to rent a room at high prices.

Azure Cloud example

Azure, same is true for other clouds, offers both system and application software to its customers. We will talk about both kinds. System applications, as defined earlier in the chapter, have the main function of providing runtime for other applications.

In *Chapter 5, Compute, Storage and Networking in the Cloud,* we examined services offered to applications by cloud providers. These services can be qualified as a system, since any application needs them to run. Clouds offer application software as well. This software does not need to run on system software, also known as a platform, built on infrastructure provided by the same cloud. What is true, though, is that these software services are offered using the same mechanism as the one used to offer software system services like compute, storage, and networking discussed earlier.

The cloud service model is illustrated in the following figure:

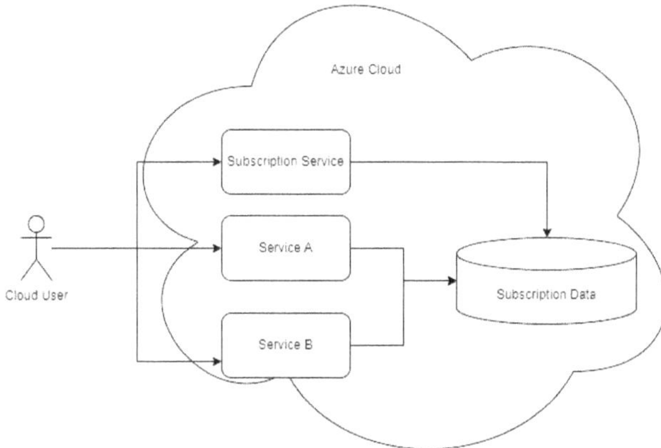

Figure 8.13: *Cloud services in Azure*

Customers subscribe in the same way to any cloud service. Take two cloud services and call them Service A and Service B. Service A can be a system software service that allows customers to use it to run their own software applications on it, and Service B can perform a fixed compute using parameters supplied by the caller.

Using programming language terminology, we can say that Service A acts as a function that takes as a parameter the known **Higher Order Function** (**HOF**) construct.

According to the definition, the HOF must either take another function as a parameter or return a function, or both. In the case we are examining, the former condition is satisfied, and another function is accepted as a parameter.

An important point to note here is that the function taken as a parameter to be executed does not have to be written in the same programming language as that of the executing function. For services, it is not even known what programming language the service was written in. This implies that the programming language must be specified so the callee can select the appropriate compiler or interpreter to execute the encoded program. More complex constructs call for installing a compiler or interpreter first and then supplying the program code to be compiled and executed or interpreted.

With these considerations in mind, it can be said that application and system software can be modeled using cloud services. Both can be represented as service functions exposed by the service as some remote call (g)RPC, REST, or other. In the case of system software service, the remote call supplies program code to be executed, similar to HOFs taking a function as a parameter.

Blockchain design

It is very useful to discuss the blockchain design pillars in order to extrapolate guiding forces behind new and upcoming business models. The clouds, Azure, and others are a natural evolution of traditional business models as they create extra flexibility and optimize resource utilization, creating extra profit potential in this way. Blockchains, on the other hand, may not be as sophisticated and still have a lot of room to grow. The important point, to the author's understanding, is that they push innovation and new business models in our world. The prime property of the new models is the disruption of the existing ones. Looking back, the new models have brought in many changes, and these changes are accelerating with time. Many would not remember that there were no iPhones before 2007, and now it is hard to imagine life without one, and all this happened relatively quickly. In this section, we will look at the main blockchain properties and their potential to disrupt traditional business models, and we will pay special attention to security features that are a big part of making blockchains an attractive alternative to many traditional models.

The following figure shows a typical blockchain architecture. We would like to bring the reader's attention to the two transaction types shown. There is a standard transaction processed by the node, and then, there is a custom transaction processed by the dApp running on it. Standard transactions are actions that are well-known and are executed by the core blockchain engine. A typical example would be A wants to send to B and N tokens. To unify the concepts, this can also be considered a transaction processed by the standard dApp in the engine:

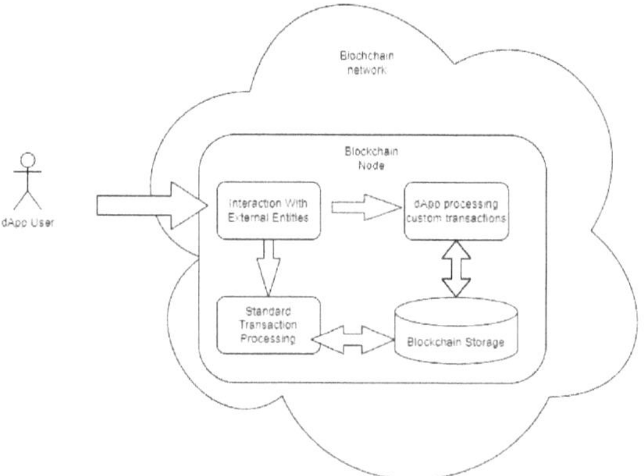

Figure 8.14: *Client interacting with a blockchain network*

The blockchains make the business model more transparent to users. It is evident that someone has to pay to have a piece of software execute on a blockchain node. And depending on the business model this someone could be the entity submitting the transaction, the entity executing it or even someone else. To make it work in economic terms, the benefit of executing the transaction has to exceed that cost. For example, paying with a credit card provides a convenience benefit, the perceived cost of which exceeds the cost paid to the network supporting the credit card transaction. Similarly, the benefit of executing the blockchain network transaction needs to exceed the cost of executing it. As we showed in the blockchain business model, the nodes participating in the blockchain network are rewarded with network tokens for their participation.

There is a standard defined network transaction and then transactions executed by smart contracts run by blockchain virtual machines on blockchain compute nodes.

To illustrate, consider the flow shown in this figure:

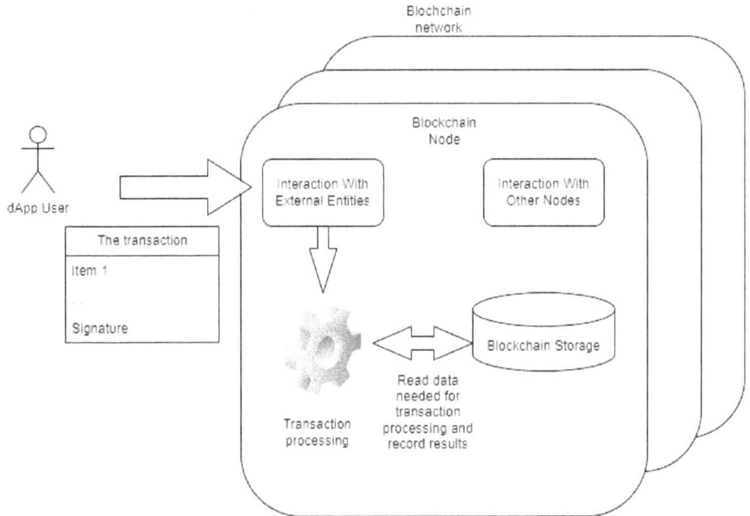

Figure 8.15: *Transaction execution on blockchain node*

There are a few important points that should be called out. There are two distinct reward systems in action that cover reward mechanisms. There are tokens minted by the network awarded to nodes who validate transactions, and then there are the so-called gas fees paid by clients submitting transactions for execution. With time, the load of rewarding nodes is shifted towards gas fees. We can interpret that as clients are being asked to pay for request execution and share less of this load with the network. This is a delicate balance as nodes have to be kept interested in approving transactions, and the clients have to be willing to send them. The economic incentives play an important role in maintaining this interest.

This, again, underscores the point that someone needs to pay the compute, storage and networking (resources used by the app) costs. The blockchain design makes these costs explicit.

Conclusion

The business models discussed were devices, software, advertising, cloud, and blockchain networks (cryptocurrencies being a big part of the latter). We also look at emerging models that disrupt traditional businesses in the *Other modules* section.

Detailed analysis was provided for the cloud, taking Azure as an example, and blockchains, with examples showing security features of the bitcoin network.

In this chapter, each section includes a subsection defining security properties that make a given business model viable. We consider what are known as **classical** models that still work, as well as provide a glimpse into contemporary ones pioneered by emerging businesses. Classical or contemporary, each model is supported by a solid security foundation, which is required to have success in the marketplace. It may not be the most glamorous feature advertised to customers, but without it, the product is not likely to be successful.

There is a lot of discussion going on about having security by design, from the ground up, and so on. This sounds great, and some of the practical considerations required to achieve this great goal are listed here. Applications need to use a well-established cross-platform runtime or compatibility layer that offers the security abstractions needed. Applications need to have a minimum need to provide security features like encryption and authentication of their own. Instead, the prerogative to supply those falls on the components supplied by runtimes, which should be much fewer than the number of applications using them. The top-level, or user-visible, applications deal with clear concepts that are difficult, if not impossible, to get wrong. The concept of a primary identity is one example. Each application needs to identify who it needs to act as. We should call out here that application developers can easily misconfigure the identity needed, so the fewer security-related decisions they need to make, the higher the resulting security posture of the application will be. Platform providers must give useful defaults that do not need to be changed in the vast majority of cases. If a default needs to be changed, the reason for doing so must be made clear. To use an example, oftentimes developers make an API call to work around some problems and make the program work. The issue is that this API call may cause security issues, and the proper course of action should be to investigate the reasons behind the observed problem and not try to work around it. To take the example further, suppose that some API call returns an **access denied** error with the current identity context but works when the context is changed; let us say to signify the acting identity is that of the application. Here, we can point out two things:

#1 A developer may easily forget to change the identity back to what it was prior to the call

#2 The application identity may be public or not as secure as the identity the application was running prior to the call

With this in mind, we can see how that call may cause unforeseen security issues. Looking at the failing API authorization logic and the identities available to the application, the solution can be identified. The main point being made here is that if we make it very easy for the developers to go wrong, then someone will. The author will stop short of recommending techniques to make it harder to make mistakes. These are well-known. However, it needs to be noted that complicating the programming model is a double-edged sword. On the one hand, there is a desire to make programming very easy to do, and on the other, we want certain things to be hard and prevent mistakes that impact product security. Something has to give in this picture. If the author is to draw parallels to similar phenomena, we can call out the emergence of new programming languages where mistakes leading to security issues are all but impossible at the expense of making programming harder.

This is an interesting tradeoff. The desired state is that programming should be **easy,** but mistakes leading to security issues should be **hard** to make. And the curious reader would wonder if there are any mistakes, not only security-related ones, that should not be **hard** to make. The answer most would like to see is probably **no**. Any mistake should be **hard** to make. If so, we should brainstorm ways to accomplish this goal. One way to approach this is to sound an alarm when a sensitive API is being used. There could be good reasons to do so, but the use case deserves to be looked at closely, and having the alarm will help with that.

The next chapter provides a summary of the main ideas presented in all preceding chapters.

Exercises

1. Describe the business model that is targeted. Create clarity on the business value that is contributed by each feature, security-related or not.

2. Describe the desired security posture. Vocabulary is important here. Consider using assertions of the type: *X should (not) be possible,* and assigning some numeric values to measure security levels that are meaningful to the customer.

3. Determine the cost allocated to security investments relative to the overall cost of developing and placing the product with customers. There are fixed upfront costs and ongoing costs incurred for product support, maintenance, and runtime resources. These are referred to as CapEx and OpEx, standing for capital and operating expenses, on businesses' balance sheets. The part allocated to security would be different. The OpEx part is very small, but difficult to estimate. Consider that the resources needed to investigate and remediate real or suspected security issues have to come from the OpEx budget.

4. Formulate an assumption about the security features customers care about most. Then focus on delivering the top ones that are absolutely needed to make the product successful.

Join our Discord space

Join our Discord workspace for latest updates, offers, tech happenings around the world, new releases, and sessions with the authors:

https://discord.bpbonline.com

CHAPTER 9
Summary

Introduction

In this final chapter, a brief overview of the topics discussed previously will be presented. We will revisit the main points in each of the earlier chapters and try to point out the underlying ideas supporting them. While there is a wealth of information to be absorbed, the main ideas should be simple and understandable, at least in the author's opinion.

It would be natural to get lost in the many details presented within the book's chapters. The purpose of this final chapter is to help bring that clarity to the reader. The effort would go to synthesize the presented concepts in one diagram and/or statement that is meaningful and can leave an impression to guide future decisions. As this book is about security, this topic will be emphasized, and examples from both non-digital and digital life will be used to illustrate the concepts being presented.

Structure

In this chapter, we will be discussing the following topics:

- Chapter 1: Introduction to Application and Cloud Security
- Chapter 2: Different Clouds and Confidential Compute Promise
- Chapter 3: Public and Private Clouds
- Chapter 4: Application Identities

- Chapter 5: Compute, Storage and Networking in the Cloud
- Chapter 6: Authentication and Authorization
- Chapter 7: Encryption
- Chapter 8: Economic Models

Objectives

The objective in this chapter is to capture the main ideas presented in the previous chapters. Some of the ideas and concepts are further expanded in the summary. Most of the idea expansion can be found in the first chapter summary. The issue with having well-defined and understood security metrics is still an unresolved problem. The presented content can be used to define metrics, but adopting those is altogether a different issue.

Chapter 1: Introduction to Application and Cloud Security

A popular quote states:

You cannot control what you cannot measure.

It was presented in the opening chapter as well. Providing it here as a context to frame the discussion. It should be fair to say that while it could be argued that the statement above is not always true, it is also hard to argue that without an accepted metric, improvement or a step backward is difficult, if not impossible, to identify. And this is especially true for advances in complex fields, such as computer security. The author has advocated for defining and using a metric, as imperfect as it can be, to put a value on existing security posture. It also provides a way to estimate how new features will affect this posture and be used as a guideline for product investments.

To refresh the discussion main points, it was suggested that breach probability in the next one year be used as the metric main ingredient for determining the security level of the product - the suggested formula:

```
SecLevel = 10 - BreachPobabilityIn1Year/10 - this formula assumes the
breach probability is measured in percentages which come from the set of
real numbers between 0 and 100. Dividing by 10 yields 10 base number to use
versus 100 base if percentages are used.
```

The other important point was that the **SecLevel** defined above is assigned to each individual security feature, which, we hope, reduces breach probability. The cumulative security level is defined as the sum of the security levels of all features. And this sum should not exceed some level, less than the maximum allowed, the number is ten (10) in the sample case. The number chosen is 9.5, which would be the maximum level of security an application may have. If we write it down, the equation would look like this:

```
AppSecLevel = min(9.5, sum(1..n, SecurityFeatureSecLevel(Feature_i) * w_i))
```

Where **`w_i`** represents the feature weight. Weight values fall into [0..1] range.

There is still a problem with this representation. And it is that according to the equation above, the sum is monotonically increasing with adding more features. And since the function is capped at some maximum value (9.5 in the example), adding more features would stop bringing extra value at some point. To add to that, as experience with security issues shows, not plugging a single hole would lead to a breach, as it can be assumed that a determined attacker would try to exploit all known holes. To address this, we define features that mitigate known vulnerabilities and those aimed at mitigating potential new vulnerabilities. If it cannot be asserted that all known vulnerabilities have been mitigated, then the security level is at the minimal level. No matter what extra features are present. If all known vulnerabilities have been mitigated, then a base security level has been achieved. In code, using Python notation, the concept can be represented like this:

```
# define constants for the min, max and base seclevels
MIN_SECLEVEL = 0
MAX_SECLEVEL = 9.5
BASE_SECLEVEL = 5
# base level is determined by the known security issues
# that are covered by security features. This can change when a new issue
is discovered
# It may be covered or not by existing security feature.
# the function below models known issues coverage - evaluates to basic or 0
def KnownIssuesSecLevel():
      If (KnownIssuesCovered())
            return BASE_SECLEVEL
      return MIN_SECLEVEL
# start with the base or zero
MinPositiveSecLevel = min(BASE_SECLEVEL, min(KnownIssuesSecLevel(), 0))
# add seclevel of other features
ExtraFeatureSecLevel = sum(n..m, SecLevel(Feature_i)*weight_i)
# then add extra security contributed by optional security features
AppSecLevel = min(MAX_SECLEVEL, FeaturesSecLevel)
def FeaturesSecLevel():
     If(MinPostiveSecLevel > 0):
return MinPositiveSecLevel + ExtraFeatureSecLevel
                  else
return MinPositiveSecLevel
```

The algorithm implementing the **`AppSecLevel`** computation may be different than the one shown above, but it should be true that a value for measuring application security level must be computable given the application security features and the minimum value of this security level must be agreed upon by stakeholders. And there is always a perception about the product security level, even if this perception is not explicitly stated. And the issue is that this perception may be different for the point of view of the different stakeholders. This is where having agreed upon metric can help align stakeholder's view on the product security level. A graph illustrating a sample security function behavior is shown below:

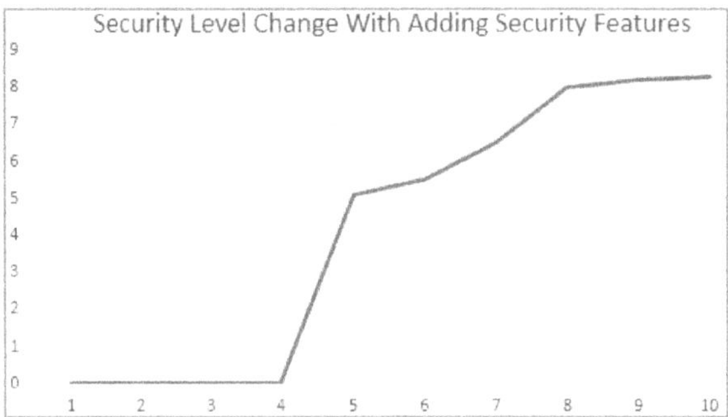

***Figure 9.1:** Security level of an application*

As the graph above depicts, the security level of an application has a value above zero only when all known security holes are being plugged. There are no meaningful values between zero and the basic level, shown to be five for illustration purposes, as the basic level suggests that all known vulnerabilities have been covered. Once the basics are covered, the security level increases by adding more security features following a custom function. We can say that the function is monotonically increasing, meaning that as security features are added, the resulting security level increases and its value is limited by the maximum security level possible.

As takeaways, we can say the following:

- There is a basic security level that serves to protect the application against known exploits. Anything less will enable an attacker to use a known exploit to compromise the application. We can assume that tools enabling such exploits are available.
- The application security can go above and beyond protecting against known exploits by implementing and/or integrating with security features that do not protect against known exploits, but instead mitigate weaknesses that could be exploited with some probability. The exploit may not be known, and the probability may not be one hundred percent, but the exploit is still possible, albeit the exact sequence of events leading to it may remain unknown.
- A similar technique is being employed in blockchain proof-of-stake consensus algorithms where participating nodes pledge a stake in exchange for the right to propose and approve blockchain blocks that consist of a set of transactions. If the heuristic used to approve a transaction deviates from the accepted rules,

this deviation will be caught by other nodes confirming transaction validity. The penalty applied is appropriating the stake and removing the right to propose and approve blocks. The thinking being that any possible exploit must include the node exhibiting one of the protocol deviations that can be detected by other nodes.

Chapter 2: Different Clouds and Confidential Compute Promise

We like to say things like **the cloud**, but the clouds are many and not necessarily the same. There is Azure from Microsoft, and then there are clouds from Amazon, Google, Oracle, and so on. An application would choose the cloud on which to run. The application could choose to be present in multiple clouds for the purpose of resilience. A cloud goes down for some reason, but the application is still alive in the other clouds. From the point of view of the outside world, it does not matter what cloud the application is running in. The interfaces it offers would look the same to outside entities. But application internals would differ to accommodate cloud specifics. This would be the case if the application depends on cloud-specific services accessed via cloud-specific interfaces.

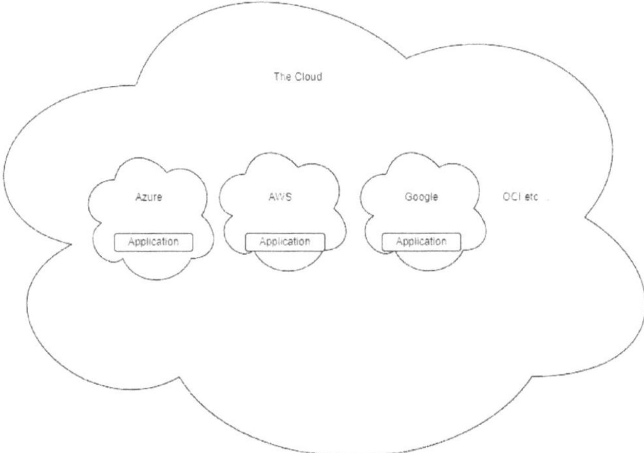

***Figure 9.2:** Multi-cloud application*

We could say here that the core application logic could be cloud agnostic if no cloud-specific services are being used. For example, if all the application needs is a network-connected **virtual machine** (**VM**) to run on, then the core application logic has no cloud-specific functionality to depend on. The process of installing and managing the application is still cloud-specific, but not the application logic itself. Consider an application written in Python. To run, it needs a Python language interpreter and the Python libraries it depends on. The specific cloud is not important if the requirements above are met. Then, the workflows for managing the application in this environment must be cloud-specific, as individual clouds offer their own programming to manage resources and applications running in the cloud.

The multi-cloud strategy is popular with applications as it provides increased application availability, removing the dependency on individual cloud availability. At the same time, security issues coming from the cloud are magnified as it is the cloud with the weakest security posture that determines the overall security exposure, since the application relies on the security of all clouds it is deployed in. That minimum common security level brought by the multi-cloud strategy will negate individual cloud advanced security features that do not have equivalents in other clouds.

Chapter 3: Public and Private Clouds

Private clouds have been popular with customers. The idea behind them comes from historical constructs from the non-digital world. It is that private resources are not shared with other customers and therefore offer a higher level of security. This notion, while true in general, is often misleading, as some components of the service are shared even if the service itself is advertised as being private.

Some notable examples would be shared public roads, airspace, and anything that is managed by a public entity, such as a government. The definition of a public entity would be one that is supported by the public and serves the public in various forms, so that anyone can use it. Not necessarily for free, but there are no restrictions on identities using the resource. It would be clearer to call the resource usage shared instead of public. And while it should be true that a private vehicle offers more protection to customers compared to a public one, it is also true that both vehicles travel on public roads that have the same level of security in relation to the road, regardless of what vehicles travel on it. To take it a step further, any private entity exists in an environment that is not private. So, it is natural to think about how using a private component affects the security level of the application.

Consider the following figure as an illustration of private components in public environments. Shown is a private cloud construct.

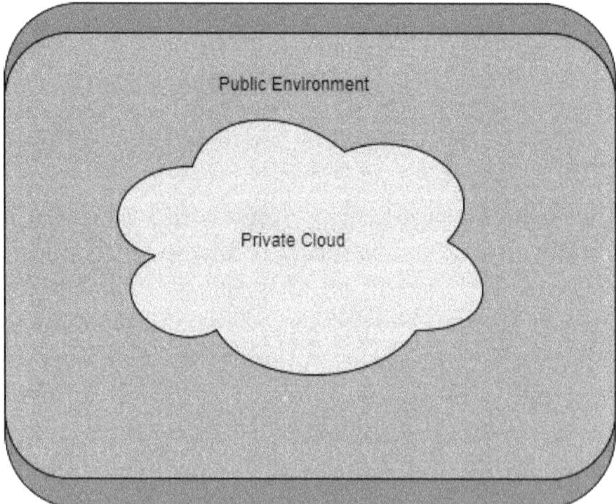

Figure 9.3: *Private components in a public environment*

The approach to adopt is to assume that any environment is hostile, meaning that any type of attack can be launched from it, and all the security defense mechanisms must exist within the component; it can be private or not.

It is reasonable to assume that private components must withstand fewer threats compared to public ones. The threats coming from the outside, represented by the hostile environment, are the same, but those from the inside are not. And fewer threats will result in fewer security features required to combat those threats. This said, the cost incurred to own a private component must be less than the cost of running and potentially developing security features that protect the customer from threats caused by using shared components. This is often not the case. The private component cost exceeds the cost of developing and running those security features. This is even more true in cloud environments where feature cost per customer is minimized with the increasing number of customers, but the cost of physical components cannot be absorbed the same way, unless the component can be shared with many of those customers.

Chapter 4: Application Identities

To re-emphasize the main point in the chapter:

Applications should be trusted.

Users provide their private data to an endpoint provided by the application. These data are private, and the applications that see them should be trusted to safeguard the user data and not expose it to unauthorized parties. The chapter is dedicated to authenticating applications, which enables experiences for distinguishing one application from another.

The following figure shows the two different application types and authorities that are trusted to assert the application name:

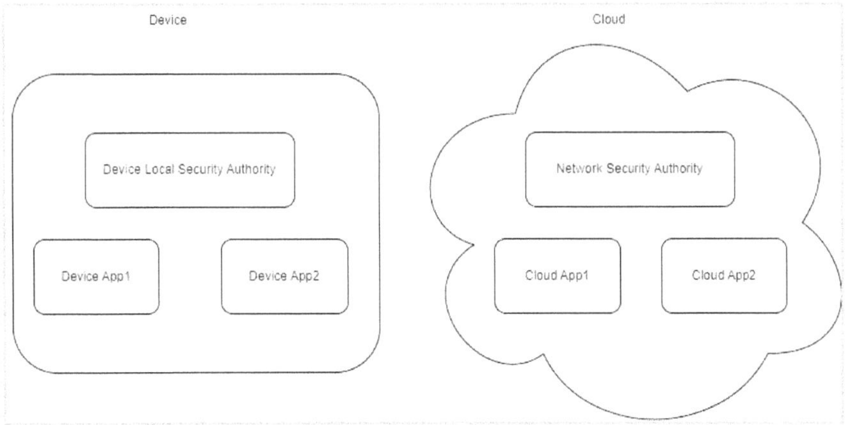

***Figure 9.4:** Device and cloud applications*

The figure above demonstrates the different implementations for asserting application identities for device and cloud applications. Device application identity is available to other applications on the device, as well as the user (human entity) interacting with it. The same is not true for applications on other devices. As an example, it is not possible to prove to an application outside the device that the entity communicating with it is application X (imagine your favorite application) to a user on some other device, unless we trust the authority asserting X. The simple reason is that applications and authorities on user devices cannot keep a secret. By contrast, cloud applications can keep a secret and authenticate themselves to other entities. This difference is expressed in the diagram with different authorities. The local **security authority** (**SA**) is trusted by users and applications on the same device. It asserts identities of local device applications. The network authority can be trusted on multiple devices. A common format to express this trust is to use certificates signed by a **Certificate Authority** (**CA**) key that is configured on the device. To be precise, the public key of the CA is configured, and it allows devices to verify signatures. To produce a signature, this key is only available to the CA. In this context, it is common to talk about certificates signed by a CA. A common conundrum in this architecture is making the decision whether the calling application needs to be authorized or the entity using the application. This entity is most often a human user, but it does not have to be. The entity identity, user or other, is communicated to the target resource, which can authorize it.

A suggested heuristic was to authorize application identity only if the service is to be used by a single application. A common example would be storage serving a one application. If there is more than one application using the same storage, then authorization should use the identity of the entity using the application.

Another important point relates to the SA trusted by the application, which is not necessarily the same as the SA that authenticated the identity of the user. This arrangement implies there is a trust relationship between the security authorities used by the caller and the resource. Such a relationship is often called a **federated identity**, implying that an identity authenticated by one SA is recognized by another. This relationship can be transitive. If a SA1 is trusted by SA2 and SA2 is trusted by SA3, then identities authenticated by SA1 could be recognized by SA3. Note that we are saying could, not must. Whether or not the identities are recognized depends on SA2 sending them to SA3 and SA3 accepting them. There is an inherent complexity created by this transitivity property. If SA3 trusts SA1, then there are two possible federation paths for an identity authenticated by SA1 to be asserted to a resource trusting SA3. One path goes through SA2 and the other does not. To make matters worse, the identifier asserted to SA3 could be different depending on the chosen path, which will make it hard, if not impossible, for SA3 to figure out that the same identity is authenticated, but the path is different. To avoid such mishaps, it is highly recommended by the author that such transitivity be avoided. Ways to do this are very much dependent on the trust relationship establishment ceremony semantics. The desired property can be summarized as **Give me only identities that are authenticated using a secret. Federated ones are not accepted**. The second part of the statement asking for **no federated identities** may seem to be a repetition of the first part that asks for **only identities authenticated using a secret**. The federated identities are also authenticated using a secret, but that secret belongs to the federation partner, not the individual identity.

The full condition should therefore be stated as: *Secret known only to the entity being authenticated* and since it is practically impossible to assert who the secret is known to, the second part saying that *Federated Identities are not accepted* implies that another SA cannot authenticate the incoming identity using its own secret.

That said, such statements are difficult to rationalize, implement, and popularize. It is also difficult to determine if the consumer of the federated identity intends to re-issue it to its own consumers. Even worse, an identity can be federated or not depending on the authentication scheme used. And it would be incredibly confusing to users if sometimes identity authentication works and sometimes it does not, depending on the destination. Using a public key as an identity (to be exact, the identifier used is a hash of the key value) is a solution employed by blockchain wallets. Federated identity is eliminated as a possible solution, as the only credential possible is a signature produced by the private key corresponding to the identity's public key. The apparent downside of this approach is that key changes need to be handled by all entities that recognize the key being changed. In a federated identity setup, the key is known by a single SA that is associated with the identity. The authority, then, issues an identity document that is recognized by other authorities. A non-digital world example of such a federation arrangement would be an identity document issued by country X being recognized as an identity proof by authorities in country Y.

Such a federation setup is not meaningful in blockchain networks or a decentralized architecture.

Federation is centralized.

In a decentralized identity architecture, there cannot be an intermediary, in the form of a centralized entity, vouching for the identity being authenticated. The advantage of such an approach is that there is not a single key whose compromise may lead to compromising multiple identities. The identity proof is the private key held on the wallet, and there is a separate key used to authenticate each identity. The model is shown in the following diagram:

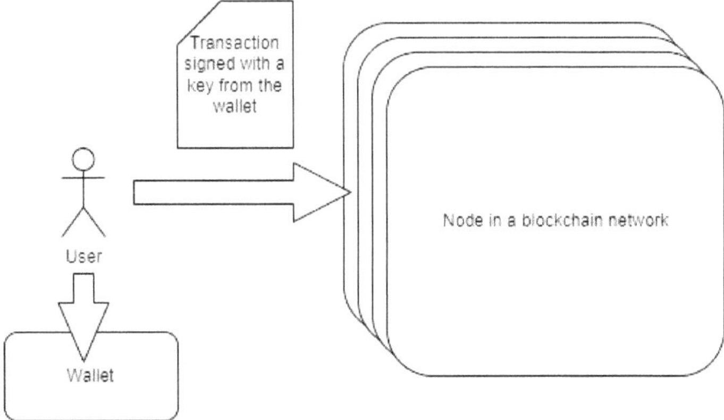

***Figure 9.5:** User interacting with a blockchain network using keys from a wallet*

Although not necessary for known good reasons, in practice, different blockchain networks require different public keys and associated identities. Having an identity key associated with a network has some advantages as well as a few disadvantages. To use an example to illustrate the point, consider that the wallet key used as an address in the Bitcoin network is different than the one used as an address in the Etherium network. As an advantage, it can be noted that using different keys for different networks allows for managing these keys independently. In other words, compromising a key used in the Bitcoin network will not affect the state in the Etherium network. End users are familiar with wallets holding multiple identity documents, so the resulting experience should be familiar and acceptable.

To point out disadvantages, the same things can be called out. A key serving as an address for a single network implies having multiple keys for multiple networks. If the wallet or keys in it are lost or compromised, keys will need to be recovered following each network accepted ceremony. It could be argued that it is preferable, from a usability point of view, to have the option to recover all keys in one shot versus having to restore each one separately.

Chapter 5: Compute, Storage and Networking in the Cloud

Cloud resources are utilized by cloud customers' applications running in the respective cloud. Focusing on Compute, storage, and networking services, excluding SaaS applications offered by the clouds. This simplifies the model and concepts behind it. In the content presented, it is shown how an application utilizes compute, storage, and networking resources of the cloud provider. More importantly, the argument is made that any cloud SaaS service fits into the models storage services provide to the applications.

The model is shown in the next figure:

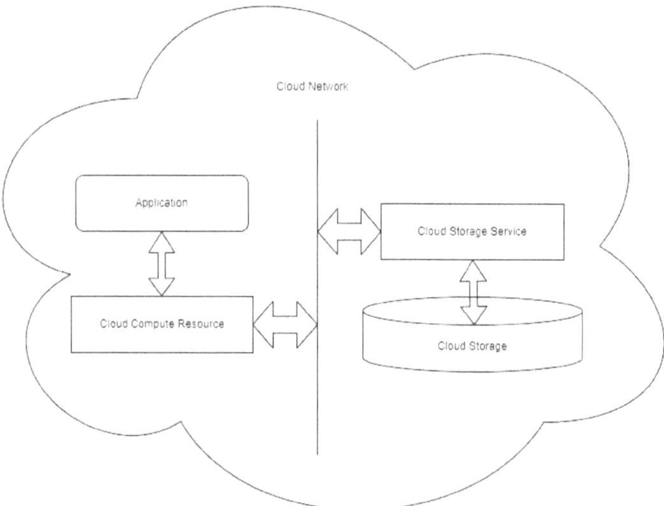

Figure 9.6: *Compute, storage, and network cloud resources*

As shown, the cloud application runs on a cloud compute, relies on cloud storage for keeping persistent state, and on cloud networking for communication with internal and external entities. There are two important points to note.

It should be noted that networking has become ubiquitous. From a security point of view, one can assume that anything is reachable over the network, whether the owner configured such access. This is a guiding principle in **zero trust network Access** (**ZTNA**). Any access has to be authenticated and authorized. We can expect that configuring networking to provide access will not be needed. If everything is accessible, there should be no need to explicitly configure such accessibility. Maybe there is a case to be made that, from a performance point of view, some minimum values for parameters like latency and/or data transmission capacity can be guaranteed with network ownership, but there cannot be security guarantees. We cannot say that requests over a network are safe. On the contrary, every request originating from the outside must be authorized. In this context from the outside and from the network can be used interchangeably.

The other important point to call out relates to the storage service. In fact, there are multiple points to be made. To start with, the storage service can be accessed by an application running on any compute. To take matters to the extreme, imagine that an application running on compute provided by cloud X may choose to access storage in a different cloud. And the issue to be resolved for having such an arrangement is not connectivity, which can be assumed, but rather the ability to authorize the caller. There is also a cost consideration. We can expect that the cloud provider will provide incentives to applications using compute resources from the same cloud. Next, let us call out that all points related to the storage service can be applied to all services exposed to applications. The storage service provides specific semantics related to reading and writing data, authorizing the application and/or the entity using it. From a security point of view, the model is the same for any service, providing services with storage semantics, **artificial intelligence** (**AI**), or other.

The blockchain model is similar, though some differences do exist. A **classic** application, call it App1, can live in any cloud or on-premises. It exposes interfaces or endpoints, calls an example endpoint EpN to clients, and these are addressed as **App1/EpN.** An application on a blockchain network, NetX is addressed using the network component, in addition to the application and endpoint names. Using the previously mentioned identifiers, an example name would be **NetX/App1/EpN**. Compared to the name used for the 'classic' application, the name of the application on the blockchain network includes the network name. A natural conclusion in this case would be that all **classic** applications run on one network, so including the network name would be unnecessary and useless. The mental model is that 'classic' applications are deployed on a global network, and blockchain applications go to the blockchain network.

The blockchain network discussed above is a logical entity that can be layered on top of any physical network. The global network of **classic** applications run on can also be considered a logical entity that is layered on one or more physical networks.

The following figure illustrates the design:

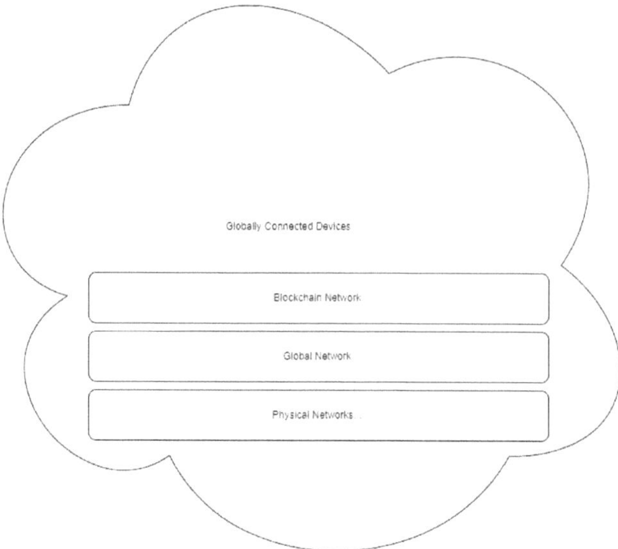

Figure 9.7: *Global and blockchain network layers*

We need to say a few words about the most commonly used global network known as TCP/IP. The history behind and many details can be found in various places, including a Wikipedia article on the subject. It must be pointed out that the layering principle is used in the design philosophy. The **Internet Protocol** (**IP**) provides the addressing and the fundamental data transport services to the **transmission control protocol** (**TCP**) and other protocol constructs above it, like the **HyperText Transfer Protocol** (**HTTP**). All these are, in the terminology used here, global networks. The address translation, say from a **Universal Resource Locator** (**URL**) domain name to an IP address, is provided by the **domain name service** (**DNS**). Generalizing the concept, an address translation transforming address A->address B is provided by a translator that can be reached in address B format (specifying a DNS service requires that the IP address for it is provided).

There have been considerable efforts to promote secure DNS, known as DNSSEC. The valiant effort to add security to the DNS must be applauded, but the fact remains that the old 'insecure' DNS continues to live and will do so for the foreseeable future. There are many products, DNS clients in this case, that have taken dependency on DNS services. A service cannot take away a supported interface, secure or not, without the risk of breaking clients. New endpoints, featuring enhanced security, can be added, and clients could be configured to use those. And while it sounds good in theory, implementation would present problems, as only the clients configured to use the secure service endpoints can be secure. This classification is transitive, as all clients on a chain of calls need to be considered secure. Practical implementation of validating such a dependency chain is not easy to accomplish. Having components secure by design without needing some special configuration would go a long way to ease this task.

Another interesting observation is the technique to layer blockchain networks on top of the global network. A network is determined by:

- Node connectivity
- A SA signing assertion honored by applications running on the network

A natural question to ask is whether SA is applicable to blockchain networks only or if the concept has applicability to global networks. The IP does not define an SA. In practice, the **Certificate Authorities** (**CAs**) have become de facto SAs on the Internet global network.

Chapter 6: Authentication and Authorization

This chapter contains some of the most important concepts in the security realm, the concepts describing authorization and authentication paradigms. And the primary observation is that authorization is the main objective. Coming from the non-digital world, the overarching goal is that service providers must authorize entities requesting a service. The simplest example would be the actions performed by a street vendor who will give a unit of the product (or service) to whoever pays for it. In this case, the payment, in whatever form, provides needed authorization. Authentication enables more elaborate authorization mechanisms:

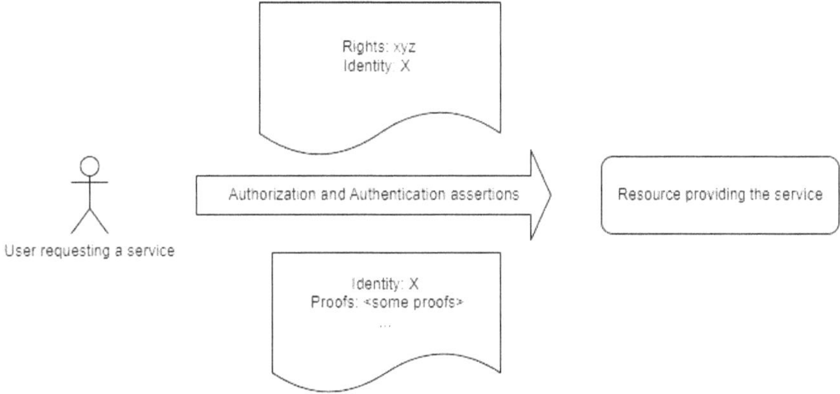

Figure 9.8: *Authorization and authentication assertion presentation*

In this chapter, we describe the main ticket presentation ceremony, called bearer and **proof-of-possession** (**PoP**). The bearer one is simple, but exposes the danger of leaking the authorization artifact to the wrong parties, who can then use it in a malicious manner. Imagine losing a hundred-dollar bill. Whoever finds it may use it in any way they find appropriate, which is not necessarily the way that matches the rightful owner's intent. The PoP technique mitigates the above issues largely at the expense of complicating the presentation ceremony by requiring a PoP-signed authenticator.

A related model is to require an identity proof to accompany the authorization proof. The details are presented in the chapter. The mechanics of presentation implement weak and strong versions, where the strong one allows for a single identity only to accompany the authorization proof. Imagine that the authorization, say a hundred-dollar bill, can only be used by a single identity, for example, a person named **John Doe**. By contrast, the weak binding will allow the bill to be used by multiple identities if the identity proof includes some known property value, for example, **Citizenship** = **X**.

To simplify the discussion, we will consider the strong binding model, though the conclusions would apply to both strong and weak binding models. Binding the authorization to the identity proof allows the PoP mechanism used for identity proof presentation to carry over to the authorization proof. To use an example, if the identity proof is a picture ID, this picture plays the role of PoP proof, which carries over to the authorization proof presentation. In simple terms, the authorization proof will not be accepted without an identity proof, and to have the identity proof accepted, the presenter's face must match the picture on the identity proof. It is not to say that the authorization proof may not require a PoP of its own. The identity proof may not have one, unless it is explicitly required. But doing so will overcomplicate the scheme. Instead of service accepting authorization bound to an identity, it has to be stated that authorization is bound to an identity that has been proven to meet certain requirements, for example, a picture ID must be used as an identity proof. And even then, the enforcement of the proof is left to the entity accepting it. Picture ID may be required, but checking that the picture matches the presenter's face is enforced by the entity accepting the identity.

Another important and interesting topic related to authentication is the concept of **two-factor authentication** (**2FA**) or, more generally, **multi factor authentication** (**MFA**). Mixed in is the issue of phishing-resistant authentication. Reader attention is drawn to the fact that MFA and phishing resistance are orthogonal. An authentication could meet MFA requirements and not be phishing-resistant, and vice versa. To add to this, phishing can lead to a persistent or temporary credential compromise. To use an example, a phished password can be used multiple times until it is changed. A phishing-generated code has a limited lifetime. Going further, the phished code may have a limited lifetime, but the artifact resulting from using the code may have a lifetime that exceeds that of the code. To avoid all this, we can consider credentials to be phish-resistant or not, regardless of their lifetime. A useful corollary expressed in the chapter was that:

Any user input is phishable.

And while this is true, there are a few details here that should be brought out. Credentials of any type presented as input are indeed phishable, but then one has to consider if physical access is required to redeem the phished credentials. As an example, consider that physical access to a device is required to use a phished gesture that enables device access. It can be said, then, that the interface recognizing the credential becomes part of it. For example, all interfaces that recognize a password as valid become part of the password definition. However, it is impossible to know this set of interfaces.

As an example, consider a password or gesture used to access a device. We cannot know if the same password or gesture can be used as authorization to access a cloud service. A viable course of action for online services is not to allow using a password as a means of identity authentication. Using MFA / 2FA terminology, authentication can be based on key possession. The recent increase in PassKeys usage presents such a use case, see detailed writeup here. The key feature, in the author's opinion, is that in the PassKeys use case, user input is NOT used at the cloud service for authentication.

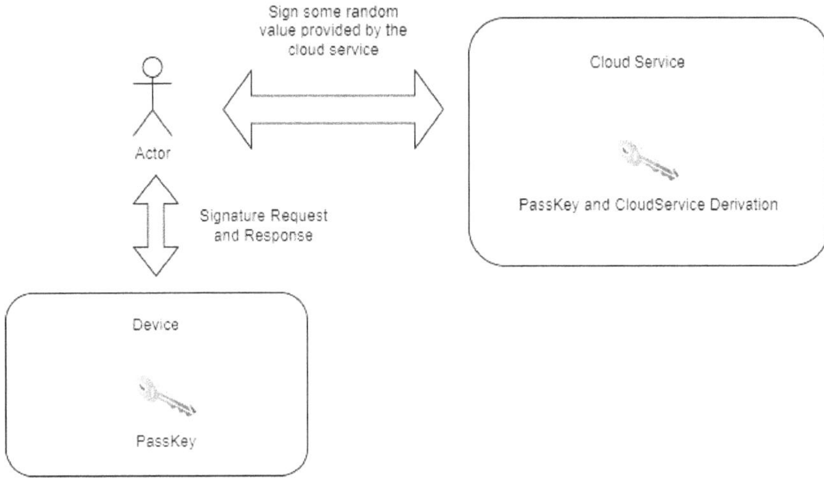

Figure 9.9: *Passkeys*

Passkeys reside on a device. The usage protocol does not send a passkey or derivative over the network. Instead, the passkey encrypts or signs some verifier-provided random value. And the passkey is never exposed to the owner, so they cannot provide it as input to the authentication user interface, real or not. This makes it phishing-resistant. While this sounds great, it is generally not possible to prove that these guidelines are followed by clients. The cloud-based services can do their part, but clients have to do it as well to have an end-to-end secure system. Software products by known vendors can fulfill this promise.

In the MFA story, using multiple factors protects against various attacks on a single factor. Using PassKeys or any form of phishing-resistant credentials protects against a single attack, phishing in this case, irrespective of the number of credentials used. The astute reader will ask if we can have credentials that are both MFA and phishing-resistant. Two of the MFA factors – knowledge and bio – are not phishing resistant. If we accept this is true, the conclusion would be that authentication cannot be multi-factor (MFA) and phishing-resistant at the same time. As stated earlier, phishing resistance implies that no user input is required, and only the possession factor has this property. It must be said that some kind of input or gesture is required to authenticate and authorize possession of the device. But this input is not seen by the cloud service. In this context, we can talk about chained multi factor authentication, where different factors are seen by different services. In our example, access to the passkey on the device is authenticated and authorized with some user input or gesture, and access to the cloud service is authenticated using the passkey on the device. Taken as a whole, the experience qualifies as a chained multi-factor. That said, it should also be stated that the cloud service, or any service for that matter, cannot assert the multi-factor property of the authentication process.

Chapter 7: Encryption

If we are to call out the most important takeaways from the chapter, these will be that:

- Encryption/decryption requires a key with associated key management. Terms **Data Encryption Key** (**DEK**) and **Key Encryption Key** (**KEK**) are introduced.
- Encryption of data at rest and in transit is introduced. There are some notable differences. For data in transit, the **Transport Level Security** (**TLS**) protocol is most often used. Some aspects of the protocol and its integration with data transmitting transports are examined in detail.
- The data encryption concept is often confused with that of data integrity. The two terms are similar, and both require a key to be used in the classic implementation. The unique part is that integrity can be asserted in public blockchains, but encryption cannot. The example illustrating this phenomenon says that the assertion **A is married to B** can be asserted to be true by multiple entities, but cannot be kept a secret.

Encrypting data at rest and in transit is shown in the following figure:

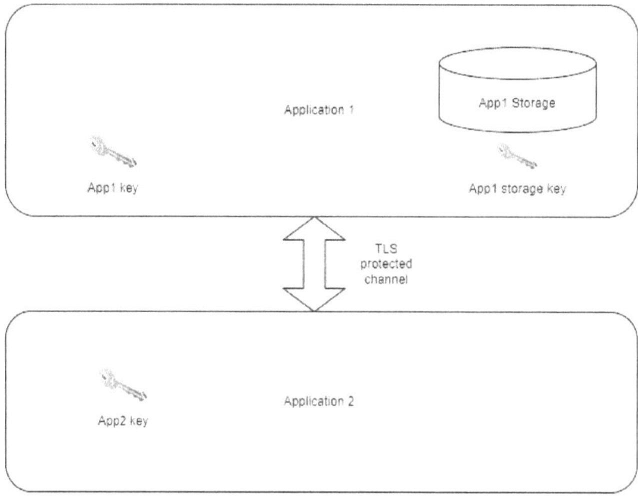

Figure 9.10: *Data encryption*

Note that the keys used to encrypt/decrypt data at rest and in transit are generally different. Requirements are different as well. To highlight the main difference, the lifetime of the data in rest is generally unlimited, and from there, the need to decrypt and serve it to authorized requestors has an unlimited lifetime as well. This unlimited lifetime brings in the need to do key rotation and data re-encryption using the new key. This is because key lifetimes are limited. This is not the case for data in transit. The session key negotiated during the handshake, according to the TLS protocol, is used during the entire data transmission process. Re-encrypting data due to key changes is not necessary. It can be said that different challenges are brought in each case. Encrypting data in transit requires protocol interoperability. Having standard TLS implementations is of great help to achieve the interoperability goal. The challenges presented when encrypting data at rest are different. The need to re-encrypt would be the biggest one. On the other side, assuming only Application 1 needs to access the encrypted data, the interoperability issues are avoided.

Chapter 8: Economic Models

Economic models are the engines behind business development. Businesses deliver value to their customers and, in return, they receive some form of compensation that we call revenue. The goal is, not surprisingly, that the cost incurred to deliver the revenue, often known as cost of goods delivered or COGS for short, is less than the revenue so the business can deliver a profit to sustain itself. Product security is part of COGS. It is required, no matter what the economic model is.

Consider the following figure:

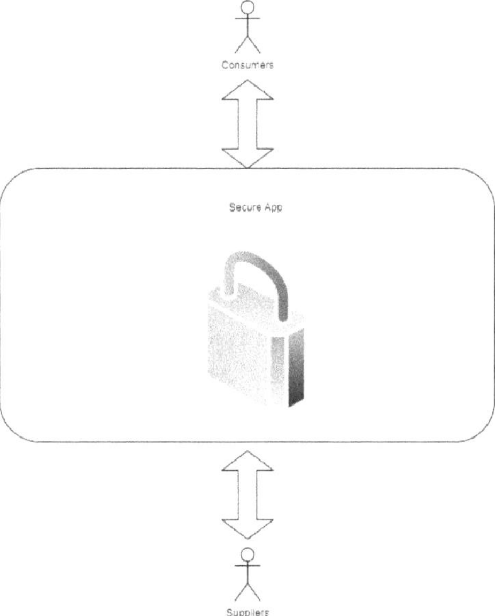

***Figure 9.11:** Application with security features*

There are multiple possible business models described in the chapter. And all of them rely on a secure application to be presented to customers. As described, there are two main assets that call for protection. This is the customer data handled by the application, as well as the intellectual property behind the vendor's product, whether it is a hardware device offered, a piece of software running on a customer-owned device, service software, or other types of software.

There are two contemporary economic models that attracted special attention. One is software implementing blockchain architectures. The compute node owners get rewards in the form of the network token (for example, bitcoin for the bitcoin network) for running the appropriate blockchain software.

Conclusion

There have been many topics discussed, which could create uncertainty as to the relative importance of each. This is natural, as there are multiple points that can be of interest to the reader depending on the context. The author would like to list some of the points that he finds to be important to most readers. These would be, in no order:

- Security metrics
- Cloud and blockchains
- Role of authentication, authorization, and data encryption
- Data integrity and confidentiality

The list can go on, though the most important thing would be to formulate the security-related assertions for the product that would resonate with customers. An example of such an assertion, presented in the Economic Models chapter, says that the *Bitcoin Network has never been hacked*. It would make sense to have an original assertion that highlights the product being offered to customers. For example, one can say that the email service offered to the customers has never been hacked. This must be true, though the precise statement would be that the **service has not reported hacks**. Whether or not a service has been hacked is unknown. It is known for its consequences of hacks, such as press reports about customer data leaks, monetary losses, and so on. Some hackers would appropriate application data through encryption with a hacker-controlled key or other methods and demand monetary rewards to give the data back. This is known as **ransomware**. Using the vocabulary here, we can call it a security breach stemming from the lack of proper authorization applied to data writes, and while encryption, as discussed in *Chapter 7, Encryption*, provides protection against unauthorized reads, it does not protect against unauthorized writes. Ransomware usually does not need to understand data content. It only needs the ability to make the data inaccessible to authorized readers and, then, give it back once the ransom is received. The proliferation of ransomware tools and schemes is a testament to the willingness and available incentives to attack the weakest point in the network. Indeed, encrypting data to protect against unauthorized reads loses its value when writes are left unprotected by this technique. We can also refer to these as protecting data integrity and confidentiality. The protection against unauthorized writes protects data integrity.

The thing to remember would be that blockchain architectures protect the integrity of the data written to a blockchain node. A node cannot, by itself, modify the blockchain data. But it does not provide confidentiality, as any blockchain node can read the blockchain data. The chapter about encryption goes into homomorphic encryption methods that, in theory, can provide needed confidentiality to blockchains. As an important concept, we need to consider what keys are being used for what purpose. The keys are described as follows:

- **End user key:** This is the public/private key pair where the public key provides an address in the blockchain data store, and the private key is used to sign transactions that modify the entry in the blockchain data store pointed to by the public key. Interestingly, transaction processing modifies two records in the blockchain database. Modifying one requires a signature, while the other does not. If we take as an example the transaction **A sends X tokens to B**, modifying A's record requires a signature with A's private key, whereas modifying B's record does not require a transaction signed by B.
- **Blockchain node key:** When transactions are propagated from node to node, there needs to be a way to establish a secure channel to the partner node. Also, in some consensus algorithms, the blockchain node key is also used to sign the blockchain record as proof that the block was generated by an authorized node.
- **Distributed Application (dApp) key:** If the transaction is to be processed by a specific application, it is addressed by a value representing it.

In this section, the author would like to re-emphasize the secure by design principle and point out the difficulty of adding security features later on. This observation was made when discussing DNS security design. Designed originally without security in mind, it has proved challenging to add that security later. A good principle to go by is that each request needs to be authenticated and authorized. To add to this is the principle of mutual authentication. Clients need to authorize services they are talking to, and vice versa.

Index

A

Application Identities,
implementing 245-247
Application Protocols,
implementing 82-84
Application Security 3
Application Security,
architecture 4
Application Security,
fundamentals
Administrator Identity 6
App Deployment Identity 6
Blockchain 8
Cloud Admin Identity 6, 7
Cloud Security 6
Modern App 4
Application Security,
optimizing 10, 11
Application Security, vulnerabilities
Authorization Logic Bugs 3
Code Injection 3
Application Structure 75
Application Structure,
configuring 76-79
Application Structure,
implementing 75, 76
Application Structure, rules 80-82
Asset 125
Asset, types
Compute 125
Storage 126, 127
Authentication 150
Authentication, mechanics
Multi Factor Authentication
(MFA) 150
Possession 152

Authorization 144
Authorization, concepts
  Bearer Token Presentation 146
  Proof-of Possession (PoP) 147
  Tickets/Token 146
Authorization, configuring 145
Authorization Distinct,
    cases 158-160
Authorization, results
  Nonrepudiation 148
  Revocation 148, 149
Azure 29
Azure Applications 100
Azure Applications,
    configuring 100, 101
Azure Applications, tenancy 101
Azure Cloud, optimizing 12
Azure, configuring 30
Azure Networking 132, 133
Azure Networking,
    optimizing 133, 134
Azure Networking,
    preventing 135, 136
Azure, resources
  Crypto Mining 57
  Depth Defense 62
  Guest Attack Vector 57
  Virtual Networks 56
  VMWare Solution 61
Azure, sections
  Authentication 168, 169
  Authorization 170
Azure Security, services
  Entra ID 14
  Managed Identities 15
Azure, services
  Azure Compute 127
  Azure Networking 132
  Azure Storage 128
Azure Storage 128
Azure Storage, concepts 130-132
Azure Storage,
    configuring 128-130
Azure Storage Encryption 198
Azure Storage Encryption,
    ways
  Data API 199
  Granularity 199

B

Blockchain 8
Blockchain, approaches
  Homomorphic Encryption 33
  Tumbler 34
Blockchain, architecture 35
Blockchain Design 234
Blockchain Design,
    optimizing 234, 235
Blockchain,
    distinguishing 163, 164
Blockchain,
    encrypting 197, 198
Blockchain Keys,
    preventing 167, 168
Blockchain, optimizing 8
Blockchain, principles 53, 54
Blockchain, sections
  Authentication 165
  Authorization 166
Business Models,
    optimizing 231, 232

C

CA, illustrating 89-92
Cell Combines Compute 122
Cell Combines Compute,
optimizing 122-124
Certificate Authority (CA) 88
Clean Room 24
Clean Room, illustrating 24, 25
Cloud Admin 20, 21
Cloud Applications 87
Cloud Hosting 69
Cloud Resources, preventing 248, 249
Cloud Security 225
Cloud Security, configuring 9, 10
Cloud Security,
optimizing 240-242
Cloud Security, takeaways 242
Cloud Service Model 233
Cloud Service Model,
optimizing 233
Code Signing 93, 94
Compute, optimizing 114-116
Compute, perspective 119, 120
Compute/Storage 26
Compute/Storage, configuring 27
Compute/Storage, ensuring 28
Confidential Applications 87, 88
Confidential Compute 21
Confidential Compute,
configuring 21-23
Confidential Compute Promise 243
Confidential Compute Promise,
configuring 243
Context Implementation,
optimizing 216
Control Plane 48
Control Plane, configuring 62, 63
Control Plane,
implementing 49-51
Control Plane, roles
Load Balancing 65
Network Segmentation 64
Route Translation 65
Crypto Mining 57-60

D

dApps 96
dApps, identity
Client 98
Service 98
dApps, illustrating 96, 97
dApps, properties 96
Data Encryption 178
Data Encryption Key (DEK) 182
Data Partitioning 102, 103
Data Partitioning, patterns
Applications 103
Organization Identifier 104
Users 103
Data Replication 121
Data Replication,
illustrating 121, 122
Data Security Posture (DSP) 191
DEK, configuring 182, 183
Delegation 161
Delegation, concepts 161, 162
Device Security 211
Device Security, terms 212
DSP, terms
Rest Considerations 195
Transit Practical 193-195

E

Economic Models 255
Economic Models, optimizing 255
Edge Computing 139, 140
Enclave 23, 24
Enclave, configuring 30, 31
Enclave, demonstrating 25, 26
Encryption 178
Encryption, configuring 179-181
Encryption, takeaways 254
Encryption, techniques
  Partitioning 186
  Re-Encryption 188

F

First Party 102
First Party, implementing 102

G

Greenfield/Brownfield 113
GSSAPI 216
Guest Attack Vector 57

H

Homomorphic Encryption 33
Hybrid Cloud 46

I

Identity Flows 104
Identity Flows, implementing 104-107

K

Key Management 199
Key Management, configuring 200-202
Kubernetes 138
Kubernetes Event-Driven Autoscaler (KEDA) 139
Kubernetes, patterns
  Edge Computing 139
  Kubernetes Event-Driven Autoscaler (KEDA) 139
Kubernetes, utilizing 138, 139

M

MFA, factor 150
MFA, sections
  Goals 150, 151
  Secret Answers (SAs) 151
Modern App 4
Modern App, configuring 4, 5
Modern App, drawback 5
Multi-Cloud 46
Multi-Cloud, analyzing 47, 48
Multi-Cloud, terms
  Control Plane 48
  Multi-Tenancy 51
  Noisy Neighbor 53
Multi Factor Authentication (MFA) 150
Multi-Tenancy 51
Multi-Tenancy, implementing 51, 52

N

Networking 117
Networking, configuring 118, 119
Noisy Neighbor 53
Non-Immutable Identifiers 85

Non-Immutable Identifiers, configuring 85-87
Non-Unique Identifiers 85

O

OAuth2 94
OAuth2, optimizing 94, 95
OpenID Connect 95
OpenID Connect, roles
  Access Tokens 95
  ID Tokens 95

P

Partitioning 186
Partitioning, architecture 187
Philosophies 31
Philosophies, configuring 32
Phish-Resistant Authentication 154
Phish-Resistant Authentication, illustrating 155
Phish-Resistant Authentication, points
  MFA Promise 156
  Mutual Authentication 156
Phish-Resistant Authentication, statements 154
Possession 152, 153
Possession, ways
  Bio 153
  Phish-Resistant Authentication 154, 155
  Symmetrical / Asymmetrical Models 157
Private Cloud 40
Private Cloud, configuring 43
Private Cloud, optimizing 40-42
Private Cloud, preventing 43-45
Proof-of Possession (PoP) 147, 148
Public Cloud 38
Public Cloud, configuring 38, 39
Public Cloud, preventing 244, 245

Q

Queues / Asynchronous Process 136
Queues / Asynchronous Process, configuring 137

S

Security Metrics 2, 3
Security Point 114
Serverless Architectures 124
Serverless Architectures, optimizing 124, 125
Stateless 116
Storage 116, 117

T

TLS, configuring 189, 190
TLS, ensuring 92, 93
TLS, illustrating 190, 191
Transport Level Security (TLS) 92

Tumbler 34
Tumbler, optimizing 34

V

Virtual Networks 56, 57
VMWare Solution 61

Z

Zero Trust Documentation 209, 210
Zero Trust Documentation, models
Advertising 221
Cloud Business 223
Device/Hardware 211
Economic 210
Software 213, 214

www.ingramcontent.com/pod-product-compliance
Lightning Source LLC
Chambersburg PA
CBHW061806210326
41599CB00034B/6899

* 9 7 8 9 3 6 5 8 9 4 6 9 1 *